The
Chinese Language

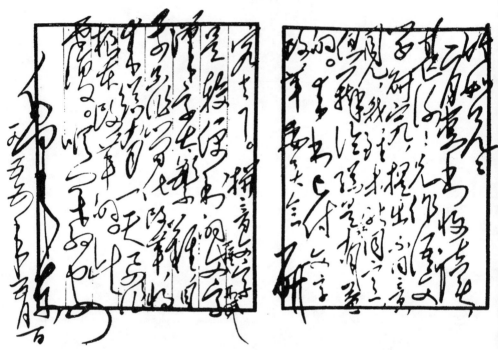

Letter written by Mao Zedong in 1955 endorsing a "basic reform" involving a transition from Chinese characters to alphabetic writing (see page 295).

The Chinese Language

FACT AND FANTASY

JOHN DEFRANCIS

Published with the support of the
Maurice J. Sullivan & Family Fund
in the University of Hawaii Foundation

University of Hawaii Press
Honolulu

First printing 1984
Paperback edition 1986

95 96 97   7 6 5 4

Library of Congress Cataloging in Publication Data

DeFrancis, John, 1911–
  The Chinese language.

  Bibliography: p.
  Includes index.
    1. Chinese language—Writing. 2. Chinese language—
Reform. 3. Chinese language—Social aspects. 4. Chinese
language—Psychological aspects. I. Title.
PL1171.D38 1984   495.1   84–8546
ISBN 0–8248–0866–5

ISBN 0–8248–1068–6 (pbk)

To

the neglected memory of

LU XUN

as an ardent advocate
of Chinese language reform

The chief commander of
China's cultural revolution,
he was not only a great man of letters
but a great thinker and revolutionary.
Lu Xun was a man of unyielding integrity,
free from all sycophancy or obsequiousness;
this quality is invaluable among colonial
and semi-colonial peoples.
Representing the great majority of the nation,
Lu Xun breached and stormed the enemy citadel;
on the cultural front he was
the bravest and most correct, the firmest,
the most loyal and the most ardent national hero,
a hero without parallel in our history.
The road he took was the very road of
China's new national culture.

Mao Zedong, 1940

The greatest masterpiece in the world is his *Story of Ah Q*
But even greater in his life was his activity for Latinization

Guo Moruo, 1936

Contents

Illustrations

Tables

Preface

This book has grown from the original essay presented in the Introduction to the present form as it became apparent that the subject matter transcends the narrow field for which it was originally intended. The nature of the Chinese language, and more particularly the nature of the Chinese writing system, as I have belatedly come to realize, also bears more broadly on such areas as linguistics, psychology, and education, especially as it applies to psycholinguistic problems in the teaching of reading.

This realization has led me to present the material in a way that may prove useful to several kinds of readers. First are the specialists in the Chinese field, who will, I believe, find in it new data and fresh insights, as well as of course much familiar material. Second are the specialists in other fields, notably linguistics, psychology, and education, whose interest in aspects of Chinese that impinge on their disciplines requires a more sharply focused treatment than is currently available. Finally, this book should prove useful to students in all these fields, as well as to the public at large, whose need for meaty fare appetizingly presented has helped influence the manner of presentation.

In the attempt to reach out to these three groups, some of the material may have been oversimplified for the specialist readers, and some may be rather heavy going for nonspecialists and students. With a bit of indulgence from the former and effort from the latter, however, I believe the book will be of interest and value to all.

In preparing this book I have had the good fortune to benefit from the aid, advice, and criticism of many colleagues and friends. I am particularly grateful to the following scholars for advice leading to the expansion of my original material to its present form: William S-Y.

Wang of the University of California at Berkeley for drawing my attention to the interest of students of linguistics and psychology in certain aspects of Chinese; David Ashworth of the University of Hawaii for noting the efficacy of the introductory material in stimulating student interest when presented in courses even at the undergraduate level; and Jonathan Spence of Yale for noting gaps in my presentation which needed to be filled to ensure comprehensive coverage of Chinese in its spoken and written forms.

I am grateful to other colleagues who were kind enough to read the manuscript in whole or in part and to discuss it with me. It was a particular pleasure to join my Chinese colleagues at the University of Hawaii in numerous luncheon meetings where we thrashed out many of the points discussed in the present work. Apart from those already named, I extend special thanks to the following scholars with whom I have had fruitful discussions: Robert Cheng, Ho Shang-hsien, Hsieh Hsin-i, Y. C. Li, Danny D. Steinberg, Laurence C. Thompson, Anatole Lyovin, and Albert J. Schütz, all of the University of Hawaii; Shirley Jenkins and Samuel Robert Ramsey of Columbia; Samuel Martin of Yale; Björn Jernudd of the East-West Center in Honolulu; Paul Kratochvíl of Cambridge University in England; Helmut Martin of Ruhr-Universität Bochum in Germany; Alexis Rygaloff and Alice Thorner of l'Ecole des Hautes Etudes en Sciences Sociales in France; Hu Tan of the PRC Central Institute for National Minorities; and Zhou Youguang of the PRC Committee on Chinese Language Reform. I am also indebted to Professor Zhou for making the seal design on the half-title page and for finding another expert calligrapher to write the characters for the cover.

Although I have benefited much from the comments and criticisms so generously offered, I have by no means always acted on them; any errors of fact or interpretation are therefore solely my responsibility.

Introduction
The Singlish Affair

> The world is of the opinion that those who know
> Chinese characters are wise and worthy, whereas
> those who do not know characters are simple and
> stupid.
>
> Zheng Qiao (1104–1162), *Tong Zhi*
> [Encyclopedic annals]

This is a report on my discovery of material exposing what has since come to be called The Singlish Affair. The discovery came about when I chanced upon a forgotten carton of wartime documents in the Tōyō Bunko Library in Japan while pursuing research on the fate of the Chinese writing system in China, Korea, Japan, and Viet Nam.[1]

The material consists of a hodgepodge of manuscript documents and notes prepared by a small secret group of scholars with the innocuous name of the Committee on English Language Planning. Attached directly to the office of General Tōjō, the supreme commander of the Japanese armed forces, the committee was headed by his close personal friend, Prof. Ōno Kanji, and included only three other members, all collaborationists from lands occupied by the Japanese—a Chinese, Lǐ Yìlián; a Korean, Kim Mun-yi; and a Vietnamese, Phi De Giua. Information is lacking on how these four scholars came to be selected for membership in the committee, a point of considerable interest, for it would be hard to imagine a less harmonious group of coworkers. The documents reveal that they were continuously involved in ethnocentric bickering on what to an outsider seem to be quite trivial points of detail.

On only one thing were they fully agreed. This was the astonishing notion that, in anticipation that first Hawaii, then Australia and New Zealand, and eventually the continental United States itself would be conquered and incorporated within the Japanese empire as part of an expanded East Asia Coprosperity Sphere, it was necessary to plan for the day when policy would be implemented for reforming the writing systems of these English-speaking countries by forcing them to abandon their traditional orthography based on the Latin alphabet and to adopt instead a system based on Chinese characters.

The precise nature of this projected new system of writing was a matter of acrimonious dispute among the scholars. To the various schemes that they proposed, and to the single scheme, whatever it might turn out to be, that they were mandated by General Tōjō to try to reach agreement on, they gave the portmanteau name of Singlish.

RATIONALE FOR SINGLISH

Although information is lacking on how this grandiose idea originated, the rationale for it was most clearly stated by the Vietnamese member of the committee, the venerable Phi De Giua, who at nearly eighty years of age was apparently the oldest, though only by a decade or so, of this group of hoary academicians. From what little additional information I have been able to glean about him he appears to have been a scholar of considerable erudition both in traditional Confucian learning and in Western, especially French, scholarship. He was an unyielding advocate of a return to the pre-French Vietnamese orthography—that is, the abandonment of the French-promoted romanization, called *Quốc Ngũ'* ("National Language")*, and the restoration of Vietnamese writing based on Chinese characters. He was also virulently anti-Western. These attitudes explain the rationalization he presented for the promotion of Singlish, a rationalization centered on two main themes.

In a position paper, Phi De Giua argued that Asian hegemony (he was writing at the height of Japanese victories in 1942 and 1943) justified imposing the superior culture of Asia on the decadent West. He invoked in support of this thesis the same argument which as a young man in his early twenties he had heard presented by Resident General Paul Bert in 1886 in justification of French control over Viet Nam. Phi De Giua recalled the following passage from a letter addressed to scholars like himself by Paul Bert in the hope of winning their collaboration:

> If, four hundred years before Christ, when our ancestors were subsisting on fruits, and when Confucius was writing the Book of History, a Chinese fleet had invaded our shores, bringing to these rude tribes an already refined civilization, advanced arts and sciences, a strongly organized social hierarchy, and an admirable moral code, Chinese

---

*English renderings of expressions given in transcription have been placed in double rather than single quotation marks to follow popular rather than technical usage.

influence would have implanted itself legitimately and would have been dominant for a period that no one can imagine. The great Oriental nations, so precocious in their development, have been arrested; the Hindu, Siamese, Annamese, and Chinese civilizations have remained what they were for two thousand years. We, on the other hand, have gone forward. . . .

Now the eternal law of history has intervened. In our turn, we arrive with our fleets, our equipment both pacific and warlike, and legitimately acquire our commanding influence. [Chailley 1887:327–328]

Now, said Phi De Giua, what Paul Bert envisaged might have happened over two thousand years ago was actually taking place: "The eternal law of history" was seeing a great Oriental nation that had gone forward arrive with its fleet, with its equipment both pacific and warlike, and legitimately acquire its commanding influence over the arrested civilizations of the West. Recalling further that Paul Bert, and even more openly another colonial administrator, Etienne Aymonier, had worked for the ascendency of the French language over Vietnamese—Aymonier (1890:10–11) had even envisaged the Vietnamese abandoning their language for French—Phi De Giua argued that the time had now arrived for the countries of Asia, under Japanese leadership, to turn the tables on the West by creating what he called an East-West Cocultural Sphere in which, continuing his sly paraphrasing of Paul Bert, he said the modern Asian disciples of Confucius would do what the sage himself should have done over two thousand years ago—namely, bring the benefits of an already refined civilization, especially its superior writing system, to the rude peoples of the West.

The second argument advanced by Phi De Giua was a so-called linguistic justification centering on the thesis that "ideographic Chinese writing" was superior to "alphabetic Western writing" and should therefore replace it. He cited the fact that the Chinese characters had functioned successfully, for more centuries than the upstart nations of the West could boast in their histories, as the basis for the writing systems of such disparate languages as "isolating,[2] monosyllabic" Chinese and Vietnamese and "agglutinative, polysyllabic" Korean and Japanese. He said the characters were just as well suited to represent the inflectional languages of the West and indeed were fully capable of serving as what he variously called "the universal script" and "the international written language."

Phi De Giua invoked the names of the German philosopher and mathematician Gottfried Wilhelm Leibniz (1646–1716) and the modern French sinologist Georges Margouliès as exponents of the superiority of Chinese characters as a universal means of intellectual communication.[3] In his extensive references to Margouliès it is apparent that Phi De Giua had succeeded, surprisingly quickly, in obtaining access to a book-length study that the French sinologue published in 1943 under the title *La langue et l'écriture chinoises.* He especially quotes the appendix to this work, in which, after a lengthy eulogy of the Chinese writing system, the author takes up *"le problème d'une langue internationale"* and finds the solution in the universal use of Chinese characters.[4] Margouliès envisioned that the semantic value of the characters would be the same in all languages, just as is the case with the arabic numerals, and that they would merely be pronounced differently and arranged in different order according to the phonological and syntactical habits of each language that they represented.[5]

CHINESE ÜBER ALLES

Lǐ Yìlián, the Chinese member of the committee, seized upon Phi De Giua's presentation to advance the view that the English-speaking countries should be made to repeat the history of Korea, Japan, and Viet Nam in first adopting the Chinese language and the Chinese writing system *in toto* as the primary system of intellectual communication. He pointed out that Chinese had been introduced into Viet Nam not long after the assertion of Chinese suzerainty in 111 B.C., into Korea about the same time, and into Japan a few centuries later. For a great many years (more than a millennium in the case of Viet Nam), classical Chinese was the only medium of written communication in all three countries. He acknowledged that these countries lacked an indigenous system of writing when they first came in contact with Chinese culture, whereas the English-speaking countries were equipped with an orthography of sorts, albeit one based on mundane letters rather than on the aesthetic characters. Nevertheless, paralleling the views expressed by Aymonier, Lǐ argued for the adoption of classical Chinese as *la langue véhiculaire* in the educational systems of the English-speaking countries. He did not specify whether English in both its spoken and written forms was to be completely eliminated, with all instruction to be given exclusively in Chinese from the first day of class in the first year of primary school (as Aymonier recommended for French in Viet Nam), or whether the use of a spoken form of English would be permitted to explain Chinese in the initial stage, which might last for one, two, or even three or more years of school before the complete transition to classical Chinese could be effected. In any case, following Aymonier, he envisaged the eventual abandonment of their native language by the subject peoples; at best only a few vestigial words of English would be absorbed into Chinese.

The non-Chinese members of the committee objected to these views as unrealistic. They felt that this extreme approach might work in Hawaii, Australia, and New Zealand with their smaller populations but argued that it was not feasible to expect that the more numerous Americans in the continental United States could be made to abandon completely both their spoken and written languages for Chinese. Lǐ Yìlián thereupon retreated to the position that in the initial stage, while tolerating the use of their own speech by the natives, all writing in English should be sternly forbidden and only writing in classical Chinese should be allowed. At first this approach would require the importation of a substantial number of Chinese scholars, as had happened in the case of Korea, Japan, and Viet Nam in their initial contacts with Chinese, but eventually, Lǐ said, an indigenous class of collaborationist scholars would emerge who would be able to express themselves in the new medium of writing. These scholars, following the path of their predecessors in Asia, could be counted upon to guard their monopoly of learning, take pride in their newly acquired knowledge, extol the merits of Chinese over their own language as a medium of communication, and develop a refined literature the appreciation of which would be restricted to those few with enough resources to acquire a command of classical Chinese.

Lǐ envisaged, for example, that Westerners would start their schooling, as in the traditional Chinese educational system, with the study of the classical Chinese rhymes contained in the Zhou dynasty (1027–221 B.C.) *Book of Poetry*. Here is the opening stanza of such a poem widely quoted in anthologies of Chinese literature, for which I provide a transcription and character-for-character translation:

野 有 死 麝	yě yǒu sǐ jūn	wilds there's dead doe
白 茅 包 之	bái máo bāo zhi	white reeds shroud it
有 女 懷 春	yǒu nǚ huái qūn	there's girl feels Spring
吉 士 誘 之	jí shì yòu zhi	fine knight tempts her

BROKEN CHINESE

The other committee members were opposed to the idea that Westerners should be made to start their study of Chinese with something
as difficult as classical poetry. They pointed out that poetry, even
more than other forms of writing, is dependent for its beauty on how
it sounds, and it is precisely with respect to pronunciation that foreigners are most seriously guilty of speaking broken Chinese. Lǐ
Yìlián conceded that it would be easier to teach Americans to write
elegant Chinese than to get them to pronounce Chinese with any
degree of accuracy. He was aware even some of the most highly
acclaimed Chinese programs in American universities had failed to
give their students a modest command of spoken Chinese. Tones
would undoubtedly be the first casualty, as they had been in Korea,
Japan, and, to a lesser extent, Viet Nam, where the indigenous language was either tonal to begin with or became tonal in the course of
its history. Lǐ Yìlián admitted that Americans, notoriously incapable
of pronouncing Chinese even approximately correctly, were sure to
massacre the poem cited here by pronouncing it with outrageous
phonetic distortions, much as if the lines were written in traditional
English orthography:

> yeah yo s-s-s june
> bye maugh baugh jer
> yo new hwigh chune
> gee sher yo jer

Warming to the subject, he said Americans would surely confound
mā ("mother"), *má* ("hemp"), *mǎ* ("horse"), and *mà* ("revile"),
pronouncing all of these words as undifferentiated *ma*. Thus if they
were to say something that they might write in their traditional
orthography as *my ma* it would be impossible to tell whether they
were saying *mǎi mā* ("bury mother"), *mǎi má* ("buy hemp"), or *mài
mǎ* ("sell horses"). These words are, of course, clearly distinguished
when written in Chinese characters or when accurately pronounced in
Chinese.

The other committee members, however, were not much concerned with the phonetic modifications that Americans would make
in pronouncing what they called Sino-English, which they said would
inevitably come into being, just as Sino-Korean, Sino-Japanese, and

Sino-Vietnamese had resulted from the phonetic modification of Chinese words as pronounced by speakers in the borrowing countries. They were perfectly aware, to give one example, that the modern Chinese word *guó* ("country"), which when it was borrowed in the first few hundred years of our era was pronounced something like *kwuk* in Chinese, became Sino-Korean *kuk*, Sino-Japanese *koku*, and Sino-Vietnamese *quốc*. Lǐ Yìlián was sure that it would undergo even greater distortion when borrowed into Sino-English. What else, he observed, could one expect of people who perpetrated such monstrosities as the GI distortion of "Chiang Kai-shek" as "Chancre Jack"?

The Korean member remarked, rather smugly, that in the inevitable process of bringing many Chinese loanwords into English he hoped it would be possible to avoid the Vietnamese, and more especially Japanese, precedent of basing the Chinese borrowings not on a more or less homogeneous variety of Chinese but on phonologically quite disparate forms belonging to different Chinese dialects during different periods of time. Thus a Chinese character meaning "to kill" was taken over into Japanese as *seti* in the "go'on" pronunciation of the Shanghai area in the third to sixth centuries and as *satu* in the "kan'on" pronunciation of Northwest China in the seventh to tenth centuries;[6] in addition to these pronunciations in Chinese loanwords it was also used to represent the stem of the purely Japanese word *korosu* for "to kill." In defense of such different pronunciations, which make it very difficult for Japanese to know what reading to assign to Chinese characters, the Japanese member, Ōno Kanji, pointed out that English was not without similar problems, citing the case of the following expressions:

4th (fourth), where the *four* is of Germanic origin.
4to (quarto), where the *quar* is of Latin origin.

While acknowledging the existence of such variant pronunciations of the same written symbol, Kim Mun-yi remarked that they were no more numerous in English than in his own language. Kim urged that every effort should be made to emulate the Korean success in avoiding excessive irregularity and complexity in phonological borrowings.

All four members agreed, in any case, on the need for the large-scale importation of Chinese loanwords into English and indicated their own preferences regarding the terms that should be brought in. Lǐ Yìlián, an avid performer on the two-stringed Chinese violin who was inordinately proud of having played *èrhú* ("second violin") in some of the leading Chinese orchestras, was eager to have his instrument replace the conventional Western violin and to import the terminology accompanying this change. He noted that the term *èrhú*, for example, would probably be taken over as *erhoo*, a phonetic-semantic borrowing whose Sino-English pronunciation was not far from the original. The committee compiled a list of ten thousand such phonetic-semantic loanwords they believed were needed to improve the English vocabulary.

CHINESE CHARACTERS AS PHONETIC SYMBOLS

Although there were varying degrees of concern over the problem of Sino-English distortion of Chinese loanwords, with the Chinese member naturally expressing the greatest worry on this score, all four members expressed even greater concern about the problem that had plagued their own countries: how to express non-Chinese terms in Chinese characters. The Chinese were the first to deal with this problem, which they did by extending the principle, already adopted in their own language, of using characters to express sounds. In the *Book of Poetry* the cries of birds were expressed by characters used solely for their phonetic value. When the Chinese were confronted with the problem of expressing foreign terms and names, as happened on a large scale with the introduction of Buddhism in the first century A.D., they did so by further extending the use of Chinese characters as phonetic symbols. The word Buddha itself came to be represented by a character which at one time had a pronunciation something like *b'ịwat* and now, after a long process of phonological change, is pronounced *fó*.

The phonetic use of Chinese characters was also applied by the Koreans, Japanese, and Vietnamese in rendering words in their own language. The earliest recorded example of this usage in Viet Nam occurred in the year 791 when two Chinese characters with the modern pronunciation *bù* and *gài* and the literal but irrelevant meanings of "cotton cloth; arrange; publish" and "to cover; roof; to build" respectively were used in their phonetic value to transcribe two Vietnamese words which are usually identified as *bô cái* ("father and mother") (DeFrancis 1977:22). In Korea and Japan this phonetic use of Chinese characters to represent indigenous words has an even longer history.

Such writing was called *Idu* ("Clerk Reading") in Korean; *Man'-yōgana* (literally "Borrowed Names of the *Man'yōshū*," one of the earliest works in which this system was used) in Japanese; and *Nôm* or *Chū'Nôm* in Vietnamese, a name which in the original Chinese form had the meaning "babbled words" but was changed by the Vietnamese to a nonpejorative character meaning "southern words" (DeFrancis 1977:27–28).

The committee members agreed that their English-speaking subjects should be permitted a similar use of Chinese characters to render English names and terms. Thus the personal name Anna was to be rendered as 安娜. This for Chinese-speaking purists would have the pronunciation *ān-nǒ*. There was some disagreement, however, over which characters should be selected to represent these names. Should the first syllable, for example, be represented by the *ān* 安 meaning "peace" or by the *àn* 暗 meaning "dark, gloomy"? Should the second syllable be the *nǒ* 娜 meaning "elegant, fascinating" or the *nà* 衲 meaning "to patch"? Lǐ Yìlián held out for the use of characters with pejorative meanings. He pointed out that the Chinese had done just this in rendering foreign names into Chinese in their early contacts with Westerners before they were forced to abandon the practice in the nineteenth century in treaties imposed upon them by the imperialist powers. Phi De Giua agreed with Lǐ and also noted with considerable glee that the surname of Paul Bert's unsuspecting successor, Paul Doumer, was given a Vietnamese rendering that sounded like the vulgar Vietnamese expression which in expurgated translation can be rendered as *đu-mẹ* "to copulate with one's mother." (DeFrancis 1977:127). Although the other committee members sympathized with this crude but subtle way of mocking the despised Westerners, they all finally agreed that from a long-range point of view it was better to adopt characters with auspicious or at least neutral meanings, as in the name Anna, which was already well established in Chinese in the form cited.

The scholars agreed, on the basis of precedents in their own countries, that one of the first uses of English expressions written in Chinese characters would undoubtedly occur in rendering English words, including personal and place-names, in an otherwise wholly classical Chinese passage. This approach was somewhat as if an American using the Latin alphabet and composing in Latin were to write "John amat Mary, sed Mary non amat John."

ENGLISH WRITTEN IN CHINESE CHARACTERS

From discussion of the isolated rendering of English words in Chinese characters the scholars passed on to consideration of the inevitable next step that would repeat the history of writing in their own countries. This was the major extension of the use of Chinese characters in their phonetic value to represent the indigenous Korean, Japanese, and Vietnamese languages in their entirety. In applying the characters to the English language, the committee prepared a sample text from which I quote the following opening passage of fourteen characters:

1	2	3	4	5	6	7	8	9	10	11	12	13	14
佛	爾	斯	國	爾	恩	得	色	文	伊	爾	斯	阿	鈎

A brief examination of this passage shows that the characters are not being used in their semantic values, for their meanings, as the following glosses show, make no sense:

1	2	3	4	5	6	7
Buddha	you	this	country	you	grace	get

8	9	10	11	12	13	14
color	writing	he	you	this	groan	hook

If we examine the characters with respect to their phonetic value, we find that they would be rendered in present-day Mandarin as follows:

1	2	3	4	5	6	7	8	9	10	11	12	13	14
fó	*ěr*	*sī*	*guó*	*ěr*	*ēn*	*dé*	*sè*	*wén*	*yī*	*ěr*	*sī*	*ā*	*gōu*

At first glance this rendering too seems to make no sense, especially since the Chinese script gives no indication of what syllables are to be read together—that is, whether the first five syllables, for example, are to be read as indicated (that is, separately), as *fó ěr-sī guó-ěr*, or as *fó-ěr sī-guó-ěr*, or as any one of the hundreds of other combinations that might be possible. However, some knowledge of how Chinese transcribes foreign sounds provides clues in the decipherment. Thus several of the characters are conventionally used to transcribe certain foreign sounds, and we also see that some of them are repeated:

爾 *ěr* (2, 5, 11) is often used for *r*
斯 *sī* (3, 12) is often used for *s*
得 *dé* (7) is often used for *d*
阿 *ā* (13) is often used for *a*

With hints such as these, we arrive at the following:

fó-ěr (for) sī-guó-ěr (sguor) ēn-dé (end)
sè-wén (sewen) yīěr-sī (yirs) ā-gōu (agou)

Not much knowledge of the contrastive phonology of Chinese and English is needed to recognize this passage as "Four score and seven years ago." The whole of Lincoln's Gettysburg Address was rendered by the committee in the same fashion, but this excerpt is enough to reveal the general procedure adopted in transcribing the sounds of English by the use of Chinese characters.

MIXED USE OF CHARACTERS

At this point in their deliberations the committee members turned their attention to the possibility of the mixed use of Chinese characters in their semantic and phonetic values. Here they were simply following the evolution of writing in Korea, Japan, and Viet Nam. It was pointed out, for example, that in the opening passage of the Gettysburg Address the numbers mentioned there could just as well be represented by Chinese numerals. The following table contrasts the alternative phonetic and semantic representations of the numbers in question:

		Phonetic
four	佛 爾	*fó-ěr* (meanings irrelevant)
score	斯 國 爾	*sī-guó-ěr* (meanings irrelevant)
seven	色 文	*sè-wén* (meanings irrelevant)

		Semantic
four	四	(pronunciation *sì* irrelevant)
score	廿	(pronunciation *niàn* irrelevant)
seven	七	(pronunciation *qī* irrelevant)

Among the documents discovered in the Singlish file are two texts from which I cite the following opening passage:

A.   1   2   3   4   5   6   7–8
     四   廿   和   七   年   斯   以前

B.   1   2   3a–3b   4   5   6   7–8
     四   廿   恩得   七   年   斯   阿鈎

It is readily apparent that we have here two different Singlish versions of the opening passage in the Gettysburg Address. In both cases the grammar is English, not Chinese. Text A makes greater use of characters as semantic units; only the sixth character is used in its phonetic value. Character 1 means "four," character 2 "score," and character 4 "seven." Character 3 occurring between the two numbers for "score" and "seven" is a conjunction meaning "and" that is never used in this position in Chinese. Character 5 means "year." Characters 7–8 form a compound meaning "ago, before." Its position at the end of the phrase happens to coincide with the position that its equivalent occupies in English. Thus, except for the sixth character, all others are used in their semantic value. If we represent characters used semantically by capitalized words and characters used phonetically by italics we can render Text A as follows:

A.   1   2   3   4   5   6   7–8
     FOUR   SCORE   AND SEVEN   YEAR   s   AGO

Text B makes greater use of characters as phonetic symbols. In addition to character 6 *sī* as *s* we have 3a–3b *ēn-dé* as "and" and 7–8 *ā-gōu* as "ago." Text B can therefore be rendered as:

B.   1   2   3a–3b   4   5   6   7–8
     FOUR   SCORE   *and* SEVEN   YEAR   s   *ago*

At this point Ōno Kanji made a strong bid for a further extension in the use of Chinese characters along lines most extensively developed by the Japanese. He pointed out that so far the committee had been considering the application of Chinese characters to English in three different ways common to the Koreans, Japanese, and Vietnamese—as purely phonetic symbols, as purely semantic symbols, and as mixed phonetic-semantic syllables. He illustrated each of these uses as follows:

1. *Purely phonetic:* representing the sounds of English words by using similarly sounding Chinese characters without regard to their meaning—for example, the use of 佛 爾 *(fó-ěr)* to represent "four." (The meanings of *fó* ["Buddha"] and *ěr* ["you"] are irrelevant.)
2. *Purely semantic:* representing the meanings of English words by using Chinese characters with the same meanings without regard to their sound—for example, the use of 四 to represent "four." (Its pronunciation of *sì* is irrelevant.)
3. *Phonetic-semantic:* representing Chinese loanwords taken into English by using characters in both their original phonetic and semantic values—for example, 二 胡 ("second violin"), which would be read as *erhoo* in Sino-English.

To these three uses of Chinese characters in Singlish, Ōno proposed a fourth in which the characters would function as rebus symbols, which means to represent English words or syllables by Chinese characters whose English meanings resemble the intended words or syllables in sound.

To illustrate the manner in which this extended use developed by the Japanese should be applied to English, Ōno drafted a memo in which he showed how the simple Chinese character 二 could also be used as a rebus symbol. The basic semantic value of this character is "two"; it also has the derived meaning "second" in some usages. Its pronunciation in Chinese is *èr,* which in Sino-English would become *er*—fairly close to the Chinese original except for the lack of tone. As a rebus symbol it would be used to symbolize English words homophonous with "two," namely "to" and "too." He further explained these four usages by presenting the following illustration of the character's use in sentences which, to focus attention on the varied uses of the character, he wrote as a mixture of Chinese and English orthography:

1. Purely phonetic: To 二 is human. (To err is human.)
2. Purely semantic: It's 二 o'clock. (It's two o'clock.)
   The 二 violin is out of tune. (The second violin is out of tune.)

3. Phonetic-semantic: The 二 hoo is out of tune. (The erhoo is out of tune.)
4. Rebus: It's 二 your advantage. (It's to your advantage.)
                           It's 二 expensive. (It's too expensive.)

In this way the character 二 would acquire several different meanings and readings in Singlish, a state of complexity that Ōno insisted would not be excessive for Singlish as a whole. Singlish would still be easier than the character-based orthography used in Japanese.

Ōno also argued that the attention of Singlish readers, like those in Japan, would be kept always on the alert by the constant need to guess just how a character is being used. In fact, he predicted that some writers would follow the Japanese lead in deliberately making their texts difficult to read and creating graphemic puns and puzzles. He illustrated this point by composing the first of the preceding sentences, first using the Chinese character in its rebus value and then in its purely phonetic value:

二 二 is human.

The committee members could not decide whether only the first three usages should be applied to English, as the majority advocated, or whether all four should be used, as the Japanese member stubbornly insisted. There were several other major points that evoked sharp disagreement among the committee members. Each advanced his own Singlish version of the Gettysburg Address incorporating his pet preferences.

VIETNAMESE VS. JAPANESE VS. KOREAN MODELS

The Vietnamese member advanced a version that was more in keeping with the way in which his forebears had adapted Chinese characters to his own language. He noted that after a stage of exclusive use of classical Chinese as the instrument of written communication, the Vietnamese began to use Chinese characters chiefly for their phonetic value to represent the words of Vietnamese, and toward this end they even coined new characters that more or less resembled traditional characters but were unintelligible to Chinese readers. So he proposed that to represent English "four," instead of simply using the character

四 ("four") they should create the new character 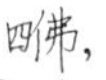, the left-hand side of which, consisting of the character 四, would give the meaning "four," and the right-hand side, consisting of 佛 (*fó*, whose meaning "Buddha" is irrelevant), would suggest the sound. In this way every syllable in English would be written with a distinctive character that would at least give some indication of the sound and might in some cases, as in the one just cited, also provide a semantic clue.

The other members of the committee objected to this approach on the grounds that since English had more than eight thousand distinct syllables, to represent each one of them by a separate character would place too much of a burden on readers and writers of such a Singlish script. They remarked, rather caustically, that Vietnamese with its approximately 4,800 distinct syllables had a notoriously difficult script based on Chinese characters that had died out because it was so cumbersome, whereas those in the other Sinitic countries had survived.

The Japanese member of the committee proposed instead that they follow the precedent initiated by his own countrymen in the evolution of their writing system. While initially the Japanese had used whole Chinese characters to represent Japanese sounds, they subsequently abbreviated the characters and eventually developed the simple kana syllabaries known as hiragana and katakana. Thus the Chinese character 加, which is now pronounced *jiā* but had the pronunciation *ka* when the Japanese took it over some fifteen hundred years ago (its meaning of "add" is irrelevant here), was abbreviated to か in hiragana and to カ in katakana. Thereafter the Japanese syllable *ka* was represented by these abbreviated forms, and no longer by the full form, and other sounds were similarly provided with simple syllabic representations. Similarly, the unstressed English syllable *an* could be represented by a reduced form of the Chinese character 恩 (*ēn*; the meaning is "grace" but this is irrelevant), for which the Japanese member suggested the abbreviated form  written with one continuous stroke of the pen. The syllable *de* could be represented by a reduced form of the character 得, for which , which could also be written with one continuous stroke of the pen, was suggested. In response to objections made by his colleagues, Ōno acknowledged that the simpler syllabic structure of Japanese made it possible to represent that language with only forty-seven signs, whereas considerably more would be needed for English, but he pointed out that the result would still be much easier than the Vietnamese proposal. As in

Japan, he said, writers of Singlish would compose in a mixture of standard characters and abbreviated syllabic signs. The phrase "four score and seven" could be rendered by replacing the whole-character approach (shown first below) with the reduced-character modification (shown in the second line) for the characters representing the sound *and:*

四	艹	恩得	七
四	艹	ℓ ⅳ	七
FOUR	SCORE	*and*	SEVEN

Ōno Kanji pointed out that, as in Japan, the more characters a writer used, the more he could display his erudition. He also noted that women were the first to write exclusively, or almost exclusively, in the simple syllabary—the well-known *Tale of Genji* is an early (eleventh century) example of such writing—and he predicted that "women and other less well educated writers" of Singlish would produce some works entirely in the simple syllabary that he was proposing for English. He did not envision that the more complex characters would ever be completely eliminated from the Singlish script, however, since the scholars could be counted upon, as always, to show their erudition by larding their compositions with as many characters as they could.

The Korean member of the committee advanced the view that a Japanese-style Singlish orthography, while simpler than the Vietnamese proposal, was nevertheless not as good as one modeled on Korean writing. He pointed out that the Koreans, like the Japanese, had gone through the stages of first using pure Chinese, then using whole Chinese characters to represent some Korean sounds, and then mixing both. They had improved upon the Japanese reduced-character syllabary, however, by producing, as long ago as the middle of the fifteenth century, a completely new set of phonetic (more properly, phonemic) symbols called hangul that took the further step of representing the basic units of sound. The common surname Kim, for example, which would be represented in Chinese by the single character 金 and in the Japanese syllabary by the two symbols キ ム having the value of *ki* for the initial and *m(u)* for the final, could be represented in the Korean alphabet by three separate symbols for *k, i,* and *m.* In Korean orthography these three letters, owing to Chinese

influence, are written not sequentially but in a square, as 김, much if we were to write Kim as KI
M.

TH	SE	TEN	YO	AR	RE	IN	RI	NO	HA	BE	WRIT
E	N	CE	U	E	AD	G	GHT	W	S	EN	TEN

TH	WA	TO⁷
IS	Y	O

In the Singlish orthography the simple hangul alphabet could be combined with characters as in the Korean writing system. Though denouncing the idea, advanced especially by Koreans of communist persuasion, that the Chinese characters should be eliminated completely from the Korean orthography, which would then be written solely in the phonetic hangul alphabet, Kim Mun-yi nevertheless seemed open to the possibility that the English speakers might be permitted to eschew characters in Singlish if they would abandon their atrocious orthography for the superior hangul script.

CHINESE CHARACTERS AS A UNIVERSAL SCRIPT

There was general support for the principle, common to both Korean and Japanese orthographies, that in the Singlish orthography the main words should be written in characters and the verb endings, conjunctions, and so forth in a phonetic script. The Chinese and Vietnamese members of the committee, however, aware that their languages as traditionally written lacked a simple system of representing sounds, were jealously opposed to the use of anything like the Korean or Japanese creations in the Singlish orthography. Instead they insisted that if the general principle of combining semantic characters with phonetic symbols was adopted for Singlish, one might just as well retain the conventional roman letters instead of using hangul or creating a whole new set of symbols on the Korean or Japanese models. They therefore argued that the opening phrase of the passage cited should be written like this:

四 卅 and 七 年s ago

To show how the Chinese characters could function as a truly universal writing system they also presented the same passage in a Sino-

French orthography. I cite the following opening phrase, to which I have appended the equivalent in conventional French:

Il y a 四 廿 七 年 s

Il y a QUATRE VINGT SEPT AN*s*

The foregoing excerpts from the Singlish file appear to represent the last stage of the committee's deliberations. It was, however, by no means the final or definitive form which the committee was struggling to achieve. There were still many points of disagreement. The Korean member, for example, argued that the word *"and"* should be written, Korean style, as AN. The Vietnamese member pressed for
                                                                    D
the creation, Vietnamese style, of new characters not already existing in Chinese to represent peculiarly American concepts. He suggested, for example, that the two existing Chinese characters 金 meaning "gold" (its pronunciation *jīn* is irrelevant) and 豆 pronounced *dòu* (its meaning "bean" is irrelevant) be combined to create the new character 鈺, which would suggest the meaning and indicate the approximate pronunciation of the American slang term *"dough"* for money or wealth. The Chinese member, though happy that the characters which were his country's great contribution to Eastern civilization would now also be bestowed upon the West, wanted assurance that the characters would neither be reduced in number, as some Japanese had proposed from time to time, nor simplified by reduction in number of strokes, as some Chinese whom he denounced as communists proposed.[8] The most nearly satisfied of the group was the Japanese member, who thought they were arriving at a form of Singlish that most closely approximated the principles developed by his ancestors in creating the script so beloved by all right-thinking Japanese. On the whole the four members felt they had cause to congratulate themselves because they were succeeding in the attempt to promote in a planned way what had happened haphazardly in Korea, Japan, and Viet Nam when these countries groped to adapt Chinese characters to their own needs.

The documents relating to The Singlish Affair throw no further light on the deliberations of the Committee on English Language Planning nor even on what eventually became of its members. Their names do not appear in any other connection. There are indications, however, that their mentor, General Tōjō, evaluated their work very highly and intended to implement their proposals as soon as his forces completed the conquest of the English-speaking populations.

In the war crimes trial of General Tōjō his role in The Singlish Affair received no mention. The four members of the committee who were his accomplices in this dastardly affair succeeded in remaining in complete obscurity, thus avoiding being brought before the bar of justice. There is reason for believing, in fact, that they are still at large and, under assumed names, are continuing to influence the writing systems of their own countries and have joined with Western accomplices to plot further advances for the Chinese characters on an international scale.

EPILOGUE

When the foregoing essay was first presented to some colleagues several years ago, I assumed they would immediately catch on to what I was doing. To my utter consternation, this assumption turned out to be unwarranted. I therefore added a note specifically stating that the Committee on English Language Planning never really existed and that the so-called Singlish Affair is a figment of the imagination—a literary device designed to make more interesting an otherwise unadorned discussion of the Chinese writing system, its adaptation in the writing systems of Korea, Japan, and Viet Nam, and some of the problems involved in its use as a universal system of writing.

Yes, the whole of the preceding essay is a joke. Actually, it is a very serious joke, one intended as entertainment, to be sure, but entertainment with a purpose. My primary purpose was to poke fun at the romantic nonsense about Chinese characters that culminates in the notion that they can function as a universal written language. What better way to point up the absurdity of this idea, I thought, than by burlesquing it?

But even specialists, contrary to all my expectations, were, with few exceptions, fooled by my elaborate joke. In retrospect it is clear that my original expectation that they would be able to penetrate my ploy was quite unreasonable. Thus it is I rather than my readers who displayed inadequate understanding. My colleagues were better able than I to appreciate that the attachment to characters can be so intense as to make quite plausible an all-out defense of character-based scripts and the desire to extend their application to users of alphabetic systems. So much nonsense has been written about Chinese characters that my parody turns out to be not as obviously implausible as I had thought it to be. There were other factors, of course, in the acceptance of my essay at face value, including the mechanical aspect of footnotes and references (all of which, incidentally, are authentic) and other features that give the essay the appearance of ordinary academic writing, in which seriousness is generally expected to be cloaked in solemnity rather than in humor.

Apart from the specialist colleagues for whom the essay was primarily intended, many others, including students at various levels, have read it in mimeographed form. Their almost unanimous reaction has been one of delight on discovering that they have undergone an entertaining but highly unorthodox educational experience. The approach has proved to be a particularly effective teaching device because students who might ordinarily be daunted by a straightforward analysis of complex problems have been led to ponder the issues so unconventionally illustrated in the introductory essay and have been stimulated to go into them more deeply.

There is indeed need for a thorough rethinking of the issues involved. Foremost among these is the nature of the Chinese language. This fundamental issue is so clouded by confusion and error that considerable effort is needed to separate fact from fantasy in order to arrive at a clear understanding about Chinese. It is to this effort that the rest of the book is devoted.

The initial aim of the present work was to ridicule certain romantic notions about Chinese as a universal script which though technically feasible in theory, as shown in The Singlish Affair, must be dismissed as impractical if one makes a hardheaded effort to analyze the ideas in detail and to test them by implementation—a procedure which will inevitably deflate the panegyrics for writing systems that deserve rather to be characterized as Rube Goldberg scripts on a par with that cartoonist's most madcap contraptions for doing simple tasks in preposterously complex ways. Another aim was to bring home the essence of the language policy practiced by *all* colonial powers, a policy that the distinguished linguist Einar Haugen (1973) has savagely but appropriately called "linguistic genocide."

The expansion from essay to book has the added purpose of presenting some basic facts about Chinese in its spoken and written forms countering the pervasive myths that have grown up around it. Some of the myths are amusing; others are anything but funny in view of the quite serious harm resulting from them. To counter the deeply entrenched mythology about Chinese requires not merely a presentation of dry facts. It also requires sharp and specific criticism of the myths and their perpetrators.

The criticism has taken the form of burlesque in The Singlish Affair and that of somewhat popularized exposition in the rest of the book. A complete popularization is impossible, however, since the complexity of the subject and the need for concrete detail require careful analysis based on extensive research. In general the academic style adopted throughout the book is based on the belief that sound scholarship is not incompatible with having fun.

In The Singlish Affair I have indulged in a number of puns and word games that in some cases are perhaps impenetrable private jokes. In the case of the names of the four members of the "committee," for example, those who know the meaning of *kanji* as "character" will perhaps recognize "Ōno Kanji" as an intended pun on "Oh, no characters!" Phi De Giua might more easily be identified if we follow the Vietnamese pronunciation and give the first syllable the sound *fee* rather than *fie,* in which case the name will sound more like the intended "fille de joie." Kim Mun-yi is the feeblest joke of all: "Kim" means "gold," and "Mun-yi" is supposed to evoke "money." The most complex is the name Lǐ Yìlián. Those who know Chinese may get the point if it is written in characters: 禮義廉 or, in simplified characters, 礼义廉. The three characters mean respectively "propriety, morality, modesty" and form part of a four-character phrase listing a number of Confucian virtues of which the fourth is 恥 (*chǐ* "a sense of shame"). The omission of the fourth character is part of a Chinese word game in which the reader is supposed to guess the last item when it is omitted (Kroll 1966)—much as if we had to tell what is lacking in the list of the three Christian virtues of "Faith, Hope, and ____." The omission of the fourth character is expressed as 無恥 or 无恥 (*wú chǐ* "lacking a sense of shame"). In short, calling someone Mr. Lǐ Yìlián seems to praise him as Mr. Propriety, Morality, and Modesty but actually insults him as Mr. Shameless.

In keeping with my description of the original essay as a serious joke, I shall conclude by taking up again the tongue-in-cheek reference in the final paragraph to the fact that the four members of the "committee" involved in the dastardly Singlish Affair had managed to avoid being brought before the bar of justice. I intend to see that justice is done by presiding, in the manner of the omnipotent Walter Mitty, as chief justice of a tribunal trying the case of those plotting further advances for the Chinese characters on an international scale. Emulating the operatic Mikado's "object all sublime . . . to let the punishment fit the crime," I hand down the following dread decree:

> Anyone who believes Chinese characters to be a superior system of writing that can function as a universal script is condemned to complete the task of rendering the whole of Lincoln's Gettysburg Address into Singlish.

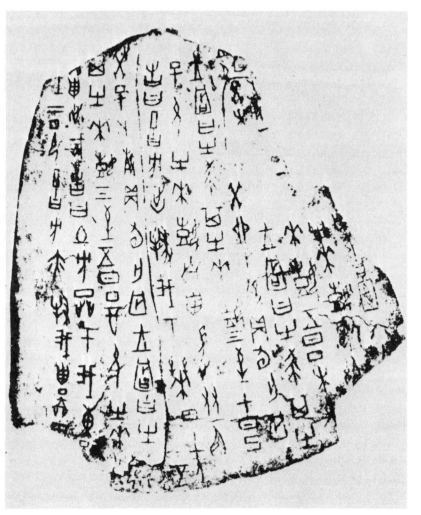

FIGURE 1. Chinese Writing: Oracle Bone Inscription
This Shang dynasty inscription incised on an animal shoulder bone asks if there will be any calamities, notes the spirits' affirmative answer, and reports later verification that calamities did indeed occur. Reprinted with permission of the publisher from Tsuen-hsuin Tsien, *Written on Bamboo and Silk* (Chicago: University of Chicago Press, 1962), p. 32.

FIGURE 2. Chinese Writing: "Radical + Phonetic" Characters
An assembly of Shang and Zhou dynasty graphs "compiled expressly to illustrate the advanced nature of the [radical + phonetic] form of characters from the earliest times of which we have examples." The asterisked characters were no longer used after the spelling reform of the Qin dynasty (221–207 B.C.). Reprinted with permission of the publisher from Barnard, "The Nature of the Ch'in 'Reform of the Script,'" in David T. Roy and Tsuen-hsuin Tsien, *Ancient China: Studies in Early Chinese Civilization* (Hong Kong: The Chinese University Press, 1979), pp. 202–203.

FIGURE 3. Chinese Writing: Calligraphy as Art

Regular, running, and cursive styles of writing displayed respectively in *(a)* a stone rubbing of a pair of commemorative scrolls written in 1953 by Shao Lizi, a prominent Guomindang supporter of the PRC; *(b)* a rubbing of a commemorative inscription written about the same time for the same commemorative purpose by Mao Zedong; and *(c)* a hanging scroll with a poem written by the seventeenth-century poet and calligrapher Fu Shan. *A* and *b* taken from Chen and Chen, *Jimei Aoyuan tike tanben; c* reprinted with permission of The Art Museum, Princeton University. The Jeannette Shambaugh Elliot Collection.

Wú Lǎo

（吴 老）

Sū Jīnsǎn
（苏金伞）

Wǒménde xiàozhǎng—Wú Lǎo	我们的校长——吴老	我們的校長—吳老
Niánjì dà	年纪大	年紀大
Shēntǐ huài	身体坏	身體壞
Jīngshén hǎo!	精神好！	精神好！
Shàngjí zhǐ ràng tā	上级只让他	上級只讓他
Měi-tiān bàngōng liǎng xiǎoshí,	每天办公两小时，	每天辦公兩小時，
Tā què cóng-zǎo-dào-wǎn,	他却从早到晚	他却從早到晚
jìhuà zhège,	计划这个，	計劃這個，
Ānpái nàge,	安排那个，	安排那個，
Bù xiǎodé xiūxi.	不晓得休息。	不曉得休息。
Yǒushíhòu lǐngdǎo kāihuì,	有时候领导开会，	有時候領導開會，
Yī kāi yī zhěngtiān,	一开一整天，	一開一整天，
Tóngzhìmen quàn tā xiē-yī-xiē,	同志们劝他歇一歇，	同志們勸他歇一歇，
Tā zǒngbù líkai zuòwèi.	他总不离开座位。	他總不離開座位。

FIGURE 4. Chinese Writing: Characters vs. Pinyin
Three versions (Pinyin, new simplified characters, and old complex characters) of part of a poem dedicated to Wu Yuzhang (1878–1966), language reformer and president of People's University. The third version is the author's addition. From *Yuwen Xiandaihua* no. 3 (1980): 349.

	a	o	e	-i	er	ai	ei	ao	ou	an	en	ang	eng	ong	i	ia	iao	ie	iu	ian	in	iang	ing	iong	u	ua	uo	uai	ui	uan	un	uang	ueng	ü	üe	üan	ün
b	八	帛				白	北	保		半	本	邦	崩		必		表	别		扁	賓		丙		不												
p	怕	坡				𠂢	培	泡	剖	判	盆	旁	朋		皮		票	丿		片	品		平		菐												
m	馬	末				買	每	毛	某	曼	門	忙	孟		米		苗	蔑	謬	免	民		明		木												
f	乏	佛					非		缶	凡	分	方	風												夫												
d	大		悳			代	得	刀	斗	旦		當	登	東	弟		弔	爹	丢	典			丁		度		多		兑	段	盾						
t	𦐇		特			台		匋	亠	覃		唐	疼	同	梯		挑	帖		天			亭		土		妥		推	彖	屯						
n	那		呢			乃	内	𡿺	耨	南	嫩	襄	能	農	尼		鳥	圼	牛	念	您	娘	寧		奴		諾			暖				女	虐		
l	拉		勒			賴	累	老	婁	闌		郎	冷	龍	力	倆	尞	列	留	連	林	良	另		彔		羅			𤔔	侖			呂	掠		
z	雜		則	子		在	賊	早	走	贊	怎	臧	曾	宗											足		左		最	鑽	夋						
c	擦		册	此		才		曹	湊	參	岑	倉	層	從											粗		錯		崔	篡	寸						
si	薩		色	死		塞		掃	叟	散	森	桑	僧	松											肅		𧴪		隋	算	巽						
zh	乍		折	之		宅	這	召	州	占	貞	章	正	中											主	爪	卓	曳	隹	專	准	庄					
ch	叉		車	赤		差		巢	丑	詹	臣	昌	成	虫											出		綽	揣	垂	川	春	床					
sh	殺		舌	尸		篩	誰	少	手	山	申	尚	生												叔	耍	朔	師	水	閂	隼	雙					
r			惹	日				擾	肉	然	人	攘	扔	容											入		若		瑞	軟	閏						
j															及	甲	交	皆	久	見	今	將	京	冂										句	欮	卷	君
q															七	掐	丂	切	求	欠	親	羌	青	睘										去	缺	全	裙
x															西	夏	小	血	休	先	心	向	星	兄										虛	穴	玄	旬
g	生		戈			改	給	高	冓	甘	根	岡	更	工											古	卦	果	乖	貴	官	丨	光					
k	卡		可			開		考	口	看	肯	康	坑	孔											苦	夸	括	快	盔	欵	困	狂					
h	哈		禾			害	黑	好	后	含	很	行	亨	厷											胡	化	火	褱	灰	奐	昏	皇					
φ	阿		咢		兒	㝵		敖	歐	安	恩	卬			一	亞	夭	也	又	炎	因	羊	雁	用	五	哇	我	外	韋	丸	文	王	翁	于	月	元	云

FIGURE 5. Chinese Writing: An Aborted Syllabary of 398 Signs
This syllabary representing the 398 basic syllables of Standard Chinese is based on the Soothill Syllabary with additions to fill in his gaps (see discussion on pages 97–99).

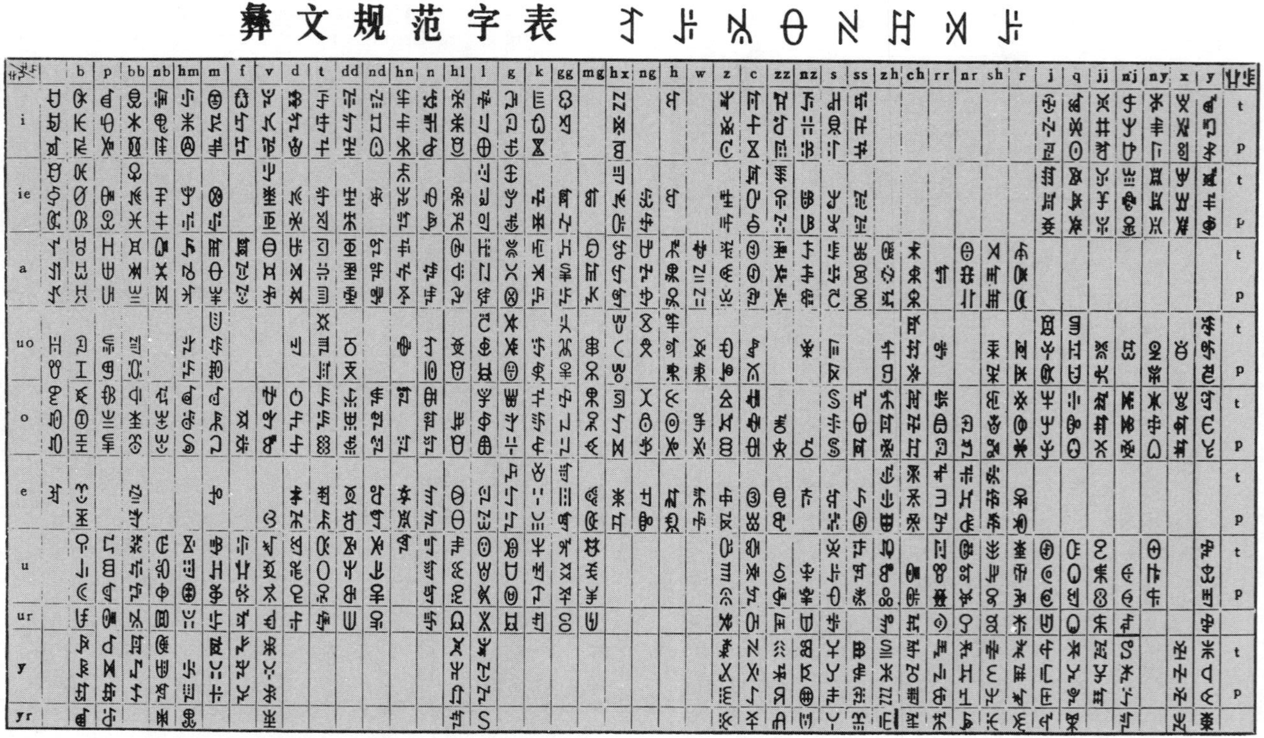

FIGURE 6. Yi Writing: A Standardized Syllabary of 819 Signs

A syllabary standardized in 1975 from the thousands of centuries-old symbols used by the Yi or Lolo nationality in Southwest China. The illustration shows the 756 most commonly used signs (see discussion on page 91).

す。安陽県の地下に眠っていた「甲骨文字」の破片が，十数万点も出て来ました。

以後今日まで約90年，学者たちが，苦労して解読しているうちに，様々なことが解って来ました。まず第一に，漢字の起源がわかったことです。殷の滅亡前百数十年，つまり3200年前までさかのぼれます。今から3000年前にはすでに，文章を記録しうる程度の漢字が出来ていた，ということが解りました。

現代中国の組織的発掘作業

今日，中国の考古学的発掘はどんどん進められています。民間考古隊と言って，例えば新しく荒地を開墾するとなると，人民公社とか，工場労働者の建設隊の中に，考古学の短期教育を受けた若い人がちゃんと入っています。何かおかしい物をみつけると，すぐ近くの専門家に連絡して，共同発掘をする全国的な組織ができています。

今年から数年にわたる最大のプロジェクトは，殷の王朝のさらに前の文化を解明することだと言われています。司馬遷によると，殷の前に「夏」の王朝があった。我々は今まで，夏の王朝などは伝説の時代だと考えていたわけですが，この数年来の発掘によって，漢字やすぐれた青銅器を持つ殷の文化が，突然発生するはずはない。必ずその前段階があるでしょう。それで，次のプロジェクトは，「夏の王朝のあとを探す」ということになっているのです。

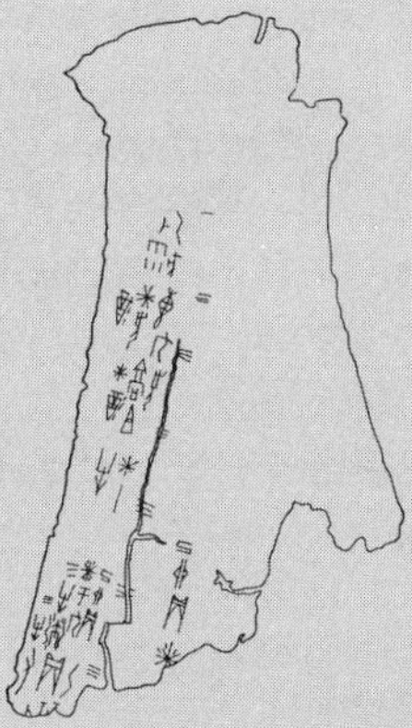

	〈呉音〉		〈漢音〉	
m	マイ	米	べい	mb
	メ	馬	ば	
n	ナム	男	だむ	nd
	ヌ	奴	ど	
ni	ニン	人	じん	ri
	ネン	然	ぜん	
濁音	ゴ	期	き	清音
	ゲ	下	か	
	ザイ	才	さい	
	ダイ	大	たい	
	ヂ	地	ち	

一貫した言語文化の継承

二番目に重要なことは，この殷代の言語が，文字においても文法においても，又言葉の発音の系統においても，現代までひと続きの筋が通っていることが明らかになったことです。途中で断絶がおこったことはありません。これが，中国語と中国文化の，ものすごく芯の固い所です。

例えば，中国語には，他動詞が前に来て，客語が後に来るという固い原則がありますが，甲骨文字でもま

FIGURE 7. Japanese Writing: Characters Plus Syllabic Kana

Kanji and hiragana intermixed in the main text. The kanji under the oracle bone are accompanied on the left by the katakana rendition of their *go'on* pronunciation and on the right by the hiragana rendition of their *kan'on* pronunciation. Reprinted from *AJALT* (Association for Japanese-Language Teaching), 1978, p. 3.

非鐵金屬類는 産出量에 있어서는 鐵鋼에 훨씬 미급하나 種類가 약 70여종에 달하며 用途도 극히 多樣하므로 近代産業에 없어서는 아니 되는 중요한 素材이다. 따라서 非鐵金屬의 消費水準은 鐵鋼의 경우와 마찬가지로 國力과 産業發展의 한 尺度가 되고 있다.

그럼에도 불구하고 1950년대 말까지 우리 나라 非鐵金屬工業은 극히 미미한 상태에 있었다. 1936년에 설립된 長項製鍊所가 유일한 國內金屬製鍊業體로서 銅과 소량의 鉛을 생산하고 있었을 뿐이며, 그나마도 낡은 施設과 鑛石 조달의 부진으로 正常操業을 하지 못했다. 이러한 狀態에서 UNKRA 資金에 의하여 낡은 施設의 一部를 改替하고 附帶施設을 增設하여 運營難을 해결코자 하였으나, 여러 가지 어려운 與件을 근본적으로 해결하지 못하여 操業狀態는 계속 不振相을 면치 못하였다.

그러나 60년대에 들어와 工業化가 적극적으로 추진되면서 非鐵金屬의 需要가 급격히 증가함에 따라 銅과 鉛을 생산하고 있는 韓國鑛業 長項製鍊所의 施設을 수차에 걸쳐 확장하는 한편, 亞鉛과 알루미늄製鍊工場을 새로이 건설하였다.

우리 나라 製鍊業界에서 核心的인 역할을 담당하고 있는 長項製鍊所는 1次5個年計劃기간 중 運營體制를 韓國鑛業製鍊公社로 國營化한 후 銅製鍊施設을 당초의 年産能力 3천톤에서 7천톤 規模로 확대하였고, 3,600톤 규모의 鉛生産施設을 추가 증설하였다. 2次5個年計劃 기간 중에도 계속되는 需要增加에 대응하여 施設擴大를 추진했으며, 73년 12월에는 長項製鍊所의 銅生産能力을 18천톤으로, 鉛生産能力을 6,500톤으로 각각 확장함으로써 非鐵金屬類의 自給化에 박차를 가하였다. 1971년 정상궤도에 오른 長項製鍊所는 다시 民營化되었다.

FIGURE 8. Korean Writing: Characters Plus Alphabetic Hangul
This excerpt from the Korean-language government publication *The Korean Economy Yesterday and Today* (Seoul, 1965), p. 62, represents one of the two contending orthographies in South Korea, the other being the more popular Hangul-only script. In North Korea all publication is in the simpler Hangul script, underlined in the first line of the excerpt.

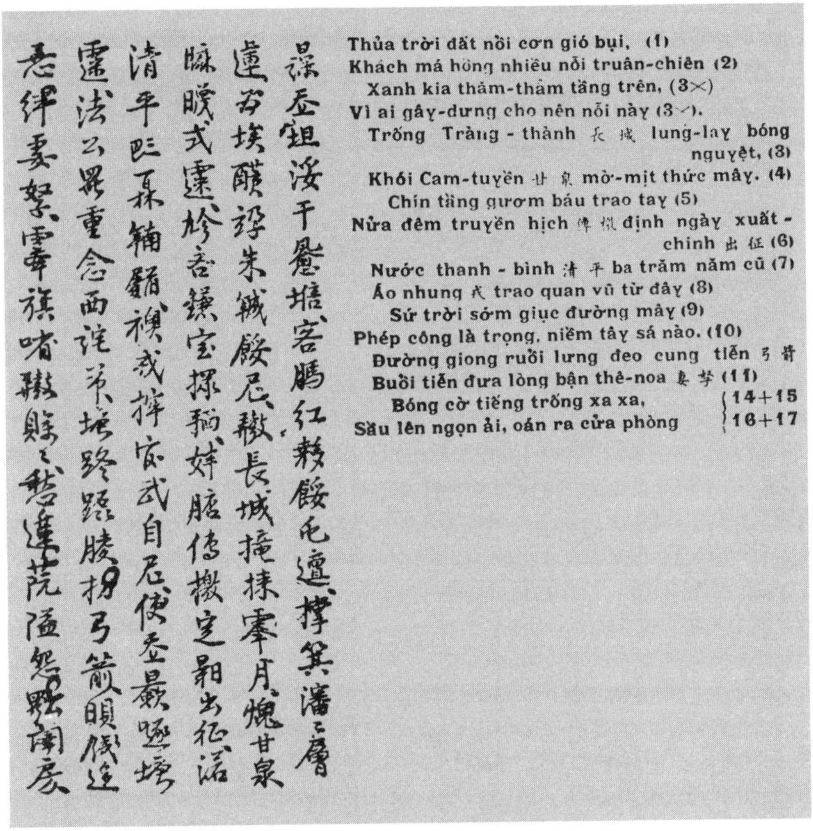

Thủa trời đất nổi cơn gió bụi, (1)
Khách má hồng nhiều nỗi truân-chiên (2)
Xanh kia thăm-thẳm tăng trên, (3✕)
Vì ai gây-dưng cho nên nỗi này (3✓).
Trông Tràng - thành 長 城 lung-lay bóng nguyệt, (3)
Khói Cam-tuyền 甘 泉 mờ-mịt thức mây. (4)
Chín tầng gươm báu trao tay (5)
Nửa đêm truyền hịch 傳 檄 định ngày xuất - chinh 出 征 (6)
Nước thanh - bình 清 平 ba trăm năm cũ (7)
Áo nhung 戎 trao quan vũ từ đây (8)
Sứ trời sớm giục đường mây (9)
Phép công là trọng, niềm tây sá nào. (10)
Đường giong ruổi lưng đeo cung tiễn 弓 箭 (11)
Buổi tiễn đưa lòng bận thê-noa 妻 孥 (11)
Bóng cờ tiếng trống xa xa,   {14+15
Sầu lên ngọn ải, oán ra cửa phòng {16+17

FIGURE 9. Vietnamese Writing: Chu Nom vs. Quoc Ngu
Quoc Ngu transliteration (right) of a Chu Nom translation (left) of an excerpt from the poem "Complaint of a Warrior's Wife," originally written in classical Chinese by the eighteenth-century Vietnamese poet Dang Tran Con. Reprinted with permission of the publisher from John DeFrancis, *Colonialism and Language Policy in Viet Nam* (The Hague: Mouton, 1977), pp. 157–158.

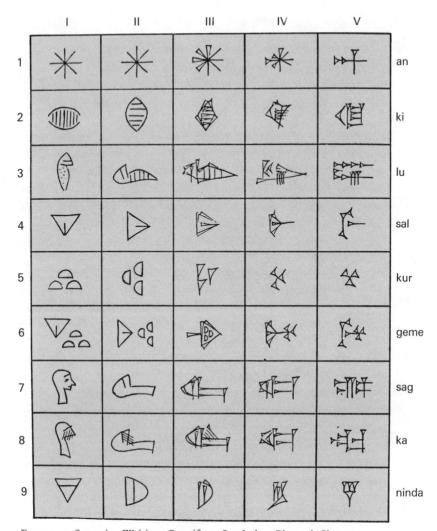

	I	II	III	IV	V	
1						an
2						ki
3						lu
4						sal
5						kur
6						geme
7						sag
8						ka
9						ninda

FIGURE 10. Sumerian Writing: Cuneiform Symbols as Phonetic Signs

The origin and development of nine representative cuneiform signs from about 3000 B.C. to about 600 B.C. The shift from pictographic to stylized forms was accompanied by a shift from semantic to phonetic values for the signs. The latter have been added on the right. The original meanings are as follows: (1) heaven, (2) earth, (3) man, (4) pudendum, (5) mountain, (6) slave girl, (7) head, (8) mouth, (9) food. Reprinted with permission from Samuel N. Kramer, *The Sumerians: Their History, Culture and Character* (Chicago: University of Chicago Press, 1963), pp. 302–304.

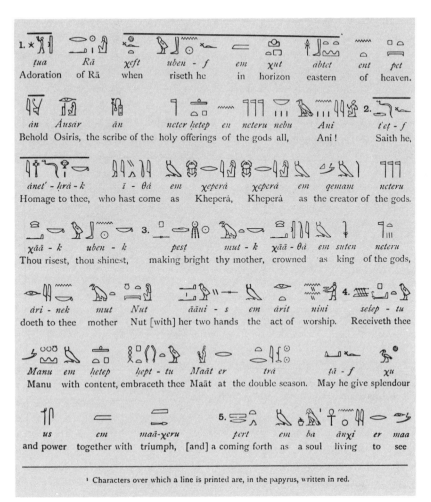

1.								
ṭua	*Rā*	*χeft*	*uben - f*	*em*	*χut*	*ābtet*	*ent*	*pet*
Adoration	of Rā	when	riseth he	in	horizon	eastern	of	heaven.

ån	*Åusår*	*ån*	*neter ḥetep*	*en*	*neteru nebu*	*Ani*	2. *t'eṭ - f*
Behold	Osiris, the scribe of the	holy offerings	of	the gods all,	Ani!	Saith he,

ảnet' - ḥrả - k	*ỉ - θả*	*em*	*χeperả*	*χeperả*	*em*	*qemam*	*neteru*
Homage to thee,	who hast come	as	Kheperả,	Kheperả	as the creator of	the gods.

χảả - k	*uben - k*	3. *pesṭ*	*mut - k*	*χảả - θả*	*em suten*	*neteru*
Thou risest,	thou shinest,	making bright	thy mother,	crowned	as king	of the gods,

ảri - nek	*mut*	*Nut*	*ảảui - s*	*em*	*ảrit*	*nini*	4. *seśep - tu*
doeth to thee	mother	Nut	[with] her two hands	the	act of	worship.	Receiveth thee

Manu	*em*	*ḥetep*	*ḥept - tu*	*Maāt er*	*trả*	*ṭả - f*	*χu*
Manu	with content,	embraceth thee	Maāt	at the double season.	May he give splendour

us	*em*	*maả-χeru*	5. *ṭert*	*em*	*ba*	*ảnχi*	*er*	*maa*
and power	together with	triumph,	[and] a coming forth	as	a soul	living	to	see

¹ Characters over which a line is printed are, in the papyrus, written in red.

FIGURE II. Egyptian Writing: Hieroglyphic Symbols as Phonetic Signs
Hieroglyphic text, interlinear transliteration, and word-for-word translation of the opening lines of a popular funeral book of about 1500 B.C. Reprinted with permission of the publisher from E. A. Wallis Budge, *The Egyptian Book of the Dead* (London: Routledge & Kegan Paul, 1969), p. 1.

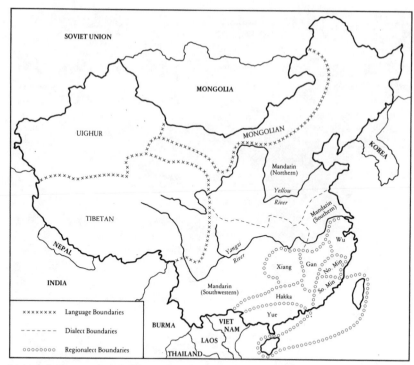

Linguistic Geography of China
See discussion in Chapter 3, especially pages 64–66 and Table 2 on page 67.

Part I

RETHINKING
"THE CHINESE LANGUAGE"

I think that the scholars who have almost let themselves be drawn into forgetting that Chinese is a spoken language have so exaggerated the influence of
Chinese writing that they have, so to say, put the
writing in place of the language.

                                    Wilhelm von Humboldt

1.

*On Defining
"Chinese" and "Language"*

The idea that Chinese characters constitute *"la langue internationale par excellence"* derives part of its support from a sort of Exotic East Syndrome characterized by the belief that in the Orient things strange and mysterious replace the mundane truths applicable to the West. It is also due in part to the equally superficial tendency to bandy terms about without a precise understanding of what they mean. In thinking about the Chinese language we must avoid this confusion by clearly specifying what we have in mind.

Take the word "language." Linguists—not polyglots but scholars concerned with linguistics, the science of language—generally use the term in the restricted meaning of speech. In their view language must be clearly distinguished from writing. Speech is primary, writing secondary. The two are related, but by no means identical, and the areas where they coincide or differ need to be carefully noted.

The attempt by linguists to reserve the term "language" as a designation solely for speech is part of their persistent but largely unsuccessful battle against the confusion resulting from the popular use of the term to encompass diverse forms of human communication without distinguishing the properties specific to each. But perhaps the confusion is better avoided not by trying to monopolize the term, which seems hopeless, but by carefully noting its range of meanings and stressing the distinctions among them. This is what has been attempted in the present work, the title of which, from the purely linguistic point of view, leaves something to be desired. Apart from its being a concession to popular usage, the title is justified because of the care taken throughout the book to distinguish between the spoken and written aspects of the Chinese language.

Failure to make this distinction is a major source of confusion—as

illustrated by the case of the textbook writer who after remarking that
the largest Chinese dictionaries contain about fourteen thousand [*sic*]
characters goes on to say that "two thousand are sufficient for the
speech of a well-educated man" (Barrett 1934:viii). This comment
evokes a picture of our "well-educated man" parading about like a
comic strip figure with character-filled balloons coming out of his
mouth. More typically misleading is the frequent dinner-table situation in which Chinese guests, when asked about their language,
blandly assume that it is an inquiry about Chinese writing (which
may indeed have been the case) or simply do not recognize the distinction and thus regale their listeners by dragging out the shopworn
example of how the character for "woman" and the character for
"child" are charmingly combined to form the character for "good."
Incongruities and muddleheadedness of the kind just noted irritate
scholars who realize that it would take much time and many pages to
dispel the misinformation so glibly imparted in a sentence or two.

Confusion in the use of the term "language" to mean both speech
and writing is sometimes avoided by those aware of the difference
between the two by referring to the former as "spoken language" and
the latter as "written language." Where the context makes the exact
meaning clear, the word "language" alone can be used to refer to one
or the other concept or to both.

But even if we are careful to specify that the language we are talking about is spoken language it may sometimes be necessary to
explain what sort of oral communication we have in mind. The
speech of educated Chinese, like that of educated Americans, differs
from that of their uneducated counterparts, and all these speakers
make use of different styles of speech in different situations. Slang,
colloquialisms, regionalisms, polite usage, and formal style exist in
Chinese, as they do in English. Some forms of language are considered incorrect. Such an attitude toward language usage is *prescriptive*
—an approach adopted, with varying degrees of flexibility, by authorities such as language teachers and compilers of dictionaries. It
contrasts with the nonjudgmental *descriptive* linguistic approach that
merely analyzes who speaks how in what situations. Statements about
spoken Chinese must either specify the kind of speech in question or
generalize in a way that cuts across the various kinds of speech.

Even the term "Chinese" requires clarification. It is used to refer
both to a people and to their language in both its spoken and written
forms. In its application to people the term "Chinese" refers to the

segment of the population of China that is called "Han Chinese" after the name of the great Han dynasty of 206 B.C. to A.D. 220. According to the 1982 census results, the Han Chinese comprise some 93 percent of the population, which is now said to total slightly more than a billion people. The remaining 7 percent consist of fifty-five ethnic minorities such as the Mongols, Tibetans, and Uighurs (SSBC 1982:20). In its application to language the term "Chinese," or more specifically "spoken Chinese," refers to the speech of the Han Chinese. The ethnic minorities speak non-Chinese languages, except for the approximately six-and-a-half million Chinese-speaking Moslems of the Hui nationality.

But the "Chinese" spoken by close to a billion Han Chinese is an abstraction that covers a number of mutually unintelligible forms of speech. Some two-thirds to three-quarters of the Chinese-speaking population speak what is loosely called Mandarin in English or *Pǔtōnghuà* ("Common Speech") in Chinese. Within this category there are differences roughly of the magnitude of the differences among the British, American, and Australian varieties of English. The remaining quarter to a third of the Chinese-speaking population are divided into several groups, such as the Cantonese, Hakka, and Min, with forms of speech so distinctive that they are mutually unintelligible. A native of Peking and a native of Canton, for example, cannot understand a word of what the other says in his own form of speech. According to the eminent Chinese linguist Y. R. Chao (1976:24, 87, 97, 105), these forms of speech are as far apart as Dutch and English or French and Spanish or French and Italian. As a result, just as a statement true for Dutch may not be true for English, one true for Cantonese may not apply to the other forms of "Chinese." To speak of *the* Chinese language is to suggest a uniformity which is far from being the case.

There is also a temporal factor to be taken into account. Chinese in both its spoken and written forms has undergone great changes over the years, as have all other languages as well. If Confucius could undergo a resurrection he would be quite unable to carry on a conversation with one of his descendants today. Nor would the two be able to communicate in writing unless the present-day descendant of the sage had received a more than average education comparable to that of a modern European who has learned to read Latin. Classical written Chinese differs so much from the written language of today that intensive training is needed to master both. Failure to distinguish what period we are talking about and ignoring the changes that have taken place over time are other common sources of confusion and misunderstanding.

One example of this confusion is the belief that Chinese is the oldest language in the world. This myth derives much of its currency from the confusion of speech and writing. As far as the latter is concerned, Chinese writing is not the oldest in the world in the sense of its being the first to be created. Sumerian writing is older by about a millennium and a half (Gelb 1963:63). Chinese writing is the oldest only in the sense that among the scripts in use today, Chinese characters have the longest history of continuous use. As far as Chinese speech is concerned, since it has exhibited the tendency of all speech to change with the passage of time, there is considerable question as to whether it is even proper to talk about age. The spoken Chinese of today is not the spoken Chinese of two thousand years ago, just as the spoken English of today is not the same as whatever ancestral form spoken about the time of Christ we trace English to. In a sense all languages spoken today are equally young and equally old. Again we must be careful not to confuse speech and writing.

All the forms of speech and writing that have been mentioned here are included in what is popularly called "Chinese." Such generalized usage is justified only when we are careful to define just how the term is being used and to separate its various aspects without thoughtlessly taking a fact about one aspect and applying it to another.

Authors who are clear in their own minds about the range of meanings involved in these terms are usually careful in their use of specific terminology. Careful readers of such authors are likely to obtain a clear understanding of what is being said. But confused and careless writers, and careless readers of such writers (and of careful authors as well), can create a cloud of misunderstanding. This has indeed happened to Chinese on a scale that appears to exceed that for any other form of human communication.

To separate fact from fantasy in this miasma of misunderstanding there is need for a careful consideration of "Chinese" or "Chinese language" in its various forms—what it is and what it is not. Since the greatest confusion and misunderstanding involve the Chinese characters, these need especially careful attention. A good starting point in considering all these matters is "spoken Chinese."

2.

A Sketch of Spoken Chinese

Although the term "spoken Chinese" has a more restricted range than the broad expression "Chinese," it too suffers from a lack of precision in view of the wide varieties of speech that are usually subsumed under this name. "Spoken Chinese" includes the speech that can be heard throughout the area stretching from Manchuria in the northeast to Guangdong in the southeast to Yunnan in the southwest to Gansu in the northwest. The varieties of speech in this huge area are legion—ranging from forms with minor differences to others that are mutually unintelligible. Indeed, even among people whose speech is considered to be the same there are individual differences that lead linguists to assert that in fact no two persons speak exactly alike, since each person has his own idiolect which distinguishes him in certain points of detail from everyone else.

In a situation of such diversity there is obviously great danger that a statement true about one kind of spoken Chinese may be completely false with respect to another variety. Generalizations about spoken Chinese can be exceedingly misleading when carelessly advanced without qualification. In any case generalization itself is impossible without some understanding of the diversities among which general features are to be sought. It would appear, therefore, that spoken Chinese can best be described by starting with a restricted form of speech before proceeding to the more and more diverse forms in order to build up an approximate picture of the complex whole.

In selecting what kind of speech to describe it is best to choose a form that somehow stands out as of special importance. This criterion naturally suggests the speech of educated speakers in the capital city of Peking (Běijīng). This form of spoken Chinese had about the same role in China as the speech of educated Parisians in France. It is more or less the basis of the Common Speech that under various names has been promoted as the national standard in China.

In case of need we could narrow our model to the idiolect or individual speech of a specific person. Such a procedure would have the advantage of enabling us to derive our information by observing the speech of a specific individual and checking our conclusions by testing them against what that speaker actually says. Much of the danger of making inaccurate generalizations could thereby be avoided since we could check whether they are true of So-and-So speaking in such-and-such a situation. In any case it is well to remember that speech is not a vague disembodied entity but a series of tangible sounds emitted from the mouth of an actual person.

THE SYLLABLE

In observing the sounds of our typical speaker we note that, as in all forms of Chinese speech, the syllable plays a crucial role. It consists of phonemes or basic units of sound that determine differences in meaning—for example, the sounds represented by the letters *b* and *p* in English "bat" and "pat." There are two kinds of phonemes in Chinese: *segmental* phonemes, which may be thought of as sequential sounds, and *suprasegmental* phonemes or tones, which in a sense are added to the syllable as a whole. The Chinese syllable made up of those phonemes is moderately complex—more so than Japanese, less so than English. Japanese has only 113 different syllables (Jorden 1963:xxi). Chinese has 1,277 tonal syllables; if tones are disregarded, as is frequently done by Chinese as well as Westerners, the number of what may be called "segmental syllables" or "basic syllables" is variously estimated at 398 to 418, depending on just what form of speech is taken as the basis and whether exclamations and the like are counted.[1] English has more than 8,000 different syllables (Jespersen 1928:15). An English syllable can contain a maximum of seven phonemes, as in the word "splints." The Chinese syllable has a maximum of four segmental phonemes and one suprasegmental phoneme, as in the case of *jiàn* ("see") and *huài* ("bad").

CONSONANTS

The segmental phonemes can be divided into two types: consonants and vowels. There are twenty-one initial consonant phonemes, eighteen of which are represented by single letters and three by two letters: *zh, ch, sh*. There is a final consonant represented by *n*, which is also an initial, and another by *ng*, which occurs only in final position. Pekingese also has a distinctive final *r* sound which has a somewhat uncertain status in the national standard (Barnes 1977). Despite the way in which they are spelled, all Chinese consonants are single consonants. There are no consonant clusters in Chinese, so that the single English syllable "splints" would have to be represented by four syllables: *sī-pŭ-lĭn-cĭ*. The initial consonants have the following very rough approximations in English:

Chinese	English	Chinese	English
b	*p* in "spy"	*j*	*tch* in "itching"
p	*p* in "pie"	*q*	*ch-h* in "each house"
m	*m* in "my"	*x*	between *s* in "she" and *s* in
f	*f* in "fie"		"see"
d	*t* in "sty"	*zh*	*ch* in "chew," but unaspirated
t	*t* in "tie"	*ch*	*ch* in "chew"
n	*n* in "nigh"	*sh*	*sh* in "shoe"
l	*l* in "lie"	*r*	*r* in "rue"
g	*k* in "sky"	*z*	*t's* in "it's Al"
k	*k* in "kite"	*c*	*t's* in "it's Hal"
h	*h* in "hut," but rougher	*s*	*s* in "Sal"

Although the letters in the left-hand column occur both in English and in the transcription of Chinese, in many cases they are pronounced differently in the two languages. A distinctive feature of the Chinese consonants is the opposition of aspirated (with a puff of air) versus unaspirated (without a puff of air) in the pairs *b-p, d-t, g-k, j-q, zh-ch,* and *z-c*. In English the opposition is one of voiced versus voiceless—that is, whether or not pronounced with a vibration of the vocal cords that can be felt by holding one's Adam's apple while articulating the sounds. The difference in pronunciation between, for example, the *p* in "spy" and the *p* in "pie" does not make for a difference in meaning in English. It does in Chinese, however, so the two *p* sounds are differentiated by the spellings *b* and *p*.

The group *j, q, x* consists of palatals pronounced with the tip of the tongue pressing against the lower teeth and the blade of the tongue pressing against the palate. The group *zh, ch, sh, r,* consists of retroflexes made with the tip of the tongue curled back and pressing against the roof of the mouth.

VOWELS

The vowels comprise simple vowels and complex vowels—that is, diphthongs and triphthongs. There are six simple vowels. The simple Chinese vowels have the following very rough approximations:

Chinese	English
a	*a* in "father," but closer to *e* in "yet" in words of the type *yan* and *yuan*
e	*e* in "yet" after *i* and *u*
	u in "up" when final (except after *i* and *u*) and before *n* and *ng*
	e in "they" before *i*
i	*i* in "it" after *z, c, s* and before *n* and *ng*
	e in "error" after *zh, ch, sh, r*
	i in "Mimi" elsewhere
o	*o* in "low" before *u*
	o in "worn" after *u*
	wo in "worn" after *b, p, m, f*
	oo in "wood" before *ng*
u	*u* in "lute" except before *n*
	oo in "wood" before *n*
ü	German *ü* in *über* or French *u* in *tu* (that is, English *i* in "Mimi" pronounced with the lip-rounding of *u* in "lute")

The phoneme *ü* is so written only in the syllables *nü* and *lü* to distinguish them from *nu* and *lu*. Otherwise it is written as *u* without danger of confusion because the two phonetic values of this letter are determined by the preceding consonant; the *ü* value occurs only after the semiconsonant *y* and the palatal initials *j, q, x,* and the *u* value occurs elsewhere.

The complex vowels, as we shall see, consist of a simple vowel nucleus and an on-glide vowel or an off-glide vowel or both. There are three on-glide vowels: *i, u, ü*. When these vowels occur initially they function as semiconsonants and are then written respectively as *y, w, yu,* as in *ye, wa, yue*. There are two off-glides, *i* and *o/u,* as in *hai, hao, hou.*

If we let a capital V stand for the vowel nucleus and a small v stand for an on-glide or off-glide, the vowel in a Chinese syllable can be represented by the following formula: (v)V(v). This formula indicates that the vowel in a syllable must include a simple vowel nucleus and may also contain an on-glide or an off-glide or both, giving the following four vowel types:

    V: *a, e, i, o, u, ü*
  vV: *ia, ie, iu, ua, ui, uo, ue* (pronounced *üe*)

Vv: *ai, ao, ei, ou*
vVv: *iao, uai*

If we let C stand for consonants and boldface **V** for vowels, whether simple or complex, the Chinese syllable can be represented by the following formula: (C)**V**(C). This formula indicates that the syllable must contain a vowel and may also contain an initial consonant or a final consonant or both, giving the following four syllable types:

V : *a, ya* (=*ia*), *ai, yao* (=*iao*)
CV : *la, lia, lai, liao*
VC: *an, yan* (=*ian*)
CVC: *lan, lian*

TONES

One of the well-known features of Chinese is its suprasegmental phonemes: the tones. Chinese is not unique, however, in being a tonal language. So are some of the languages of Southeast Asia, Africa, and those of the Latin American Indians, and there are a few words in Swedish distinguished only by tonal differences.

The variety of Chinese being described here has four tones. These are not fixed notes on a scale but relative sounds or contours that vary according to the normal voice range of individual speakers. They can be represented in the following chart:

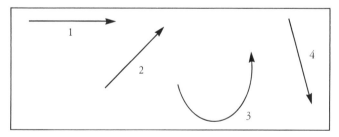

Tone 1 is high level, tone 2 high rising, tone 3 low dipping, tone 4 high falling. The tone symbols imitate these contours. They are written over the nuclear vowel in a syllable, as in *jiā, méi, hǎo, huài*. Some syllables are distinguished by absence of tone; they are said to be atonic or to have a neutral tone. The word *wénzi* ("mosquito") differs in pronunciation from *wénzì* ("writing") in having a neutral tone on the second syllable.

Suprasegmental phonemes or tones, which give Chinese speech its distinctive musical or singsong quality, must be distinguished from intonation. The latter also exists in tonal languages. It is superimposed on the basic phonological elements—that is, on the consonants, vowels, and tones. Tones perform like consonants and vowels in distinguishing meaning in Chinese, as indicated by *mā, mǎ, mǐ, bǐ* meaning respectively "mother," "horse," "rice," "pen." One reason why tone signs are frequently omitted in transcription of Chinese expressions, especially when these are embedded in a text in English or some other Western language, is the typographical difficulty of representing the tones in Western publications. This technical problem can be easily overcome, however; in fact, even a small portable typewriter can be inexpensively modified to allow for tone representation by arranging for two dead keys with two tone marks each. Another reason for omission of the tone signs is simple disregard of their significance—a far more important factor.

MORPHEMES AND WORDS

Apart from the phonological features described above, the Chinese syllable is distinctive in that, in most cases, it constitutes a morpheme, the smallest unit of meaning. Because most syllables have meaning they are often considered to be words. Exactly what constitutes a word is a much debated matter in every language, however, particularly so in the case of Chinese. In English we usually think of the expression "teacher" as a single word made up of two morphemes: a free form *teach* and a bound form *er* ("one who does something"). But in Chinese the equivalent term *jiàoyuán,* though similarly made up of the free form *jiào* ("teach") and a bound form *yuán* ("one who does something"), is often described as a compound made up of two words. On the basis chiefly of such an approach, in which every syllable is defined as a word, Chinese is commonly described as monosyllabic. This approach is rejected by many scholars who consider that it has been unduly influenced by the character-based writing system.

To be sure, Chinese does have many words of one syllable, such as *wǒ* ("I"), *hǎo* ("good"), *lái* ("come"). It also has many expressions, whatever they might be called, made up by combining morphemes of varying degrees of freedom either in the manner of the just-cited *jiàoyuán* ("teacher"), which combines a free morpheme with a mere suffix (one of a small but productive group of word-formative elements), or by combining two or more syllables that are clearly free words, as in the case of *tiělù* ("railroad"), which is made up by combining *tiě* ("iron") and *lù* ("road") in exactly the same manner as the English equivalent. There are also expressions of more than one syllable in which the individual syllables have no meaning of their own. An example of this is the expression *shānhú* ("coral").

The classification of words, which means identification of parts of speech, is another matter of disagreement. Nevertheless, although the terms used are subject to different interpretations, there is general agreement on referring to some things in Chinese as nouns, verbs, and other familiar names for parts of speech. There are two main word groups that can be labeled as nominal expressions and verbal expressions. As in the case of Chinese parts of speech generally, these expressions are often defined in terms of their positional relationship to each other. Roughly speaking, nouns are things that follow measure words and measure words are things that follow numbers. Verbs are things that come after negation markers.

One of the characteristics of Chinese nouns is that they are mass nouns comparable to the English mass noun "rice." The English noun needs to be quantified by measure words to produce such phrases as "a grain of rice," "three pounds of rice," "three bowls of rice," and so on. In Chinese, not only *mǐ* ("rice") but also *rén* ("person") are mass nouns. Both require measure words: *sānjīn mǐ* ("three pounds [of] rice") and *sānge rén* ("three persons"—or, to render it in the manner dear to the hearts of aficionados of Pidgin English, "three piecee person"). Just as foreign students of English have to memorize phrases like "a flock of sheep," "a herd of cattle," "a crowd of people," so students of Chinese must memorize that *zhāng* is the appropriate measure word for flat objects like paper and tables whereas *tiáo* is the measure word for long narrow things like snakes and roads.

Another feature of nouns in Chinese is that they do not undergo change to distinguish singular and plural. In this respect they are like the English word "deer." Out of context the sentence "He saw the deer" is ambiguous. Did he see one deer or several? Many students in Chinese language classes needlessly fret about the overall lack of the singular-plural distinction. But as in the case of English "deer," either the context will remove the ambiguity or if necessary number can be indicated by such devices as using a quantifying expression, as in *sānge rén,* which is unmistakably a "three-person" matter.

There is a large group of nouns called portmanteau expressions that are formed by combining syllables of other words, somewhat in the manner of "Cal Tech" for "California Institute of Technology." *Běidà* is short for *Běijīng Dàxué* ("Peking University"), *Wěngǎihuì* for *Wénzì Gǎigé Wěiyuánhuì* (literally "Writing Reform Committee"). Reduced forms of this sort represent a marked tendency toward abbreviation that is influenced by a writing system which even in its contemporary form in its turn has been influenced by the terse style of classical Chinese.

Verbal expressions, which can be identified by their ability to follow negative markers, comprise several subcategories. Apart from the familiar transitive and intransitive verbs, there is a group, called coverbs, which are akin to prepositions, and another group, usually referred to as stative verbs, which are less technically called adjectives. In contrast to English adjectives, but like those in Russian, they incorporate the idea which we represent by words like "am," "is," "are," as illustrated by *Wǒ hǎo* ("I am-fine").

Although linguists frown on the practice of describing a language by noting features of another language that it does not have, for speakers of English it may be useful to note that Chinese can get along quite happily without our obligatory indication of tense. *Tāmen zài zhèr* could be either "They are here" or "They were here." The verbal expression *zài* ("to be at a place") does not need to indicate tense because time will be clear either from the context or from the presence of a nominal expression referring to time, such as *jīntian* ("today") and *zuótian* ("yesterday").

Chinese is characterized by having *aspect* rather than tense. This technical term refers to the way a speaker looks at an event or state. It is a prominent feature of Russian verbs and can be illustrated in English by a contrast such as "They eat Chinese food" and "They are eating Chinese food." In Chinese the one-word sentence *Hǎo* ("Good") contrasts with *Hǎole* ("It has become good"). The aspect marker *le* in *Hǎole* is one of a category of particles that are few in number but important in function. Among other things they indicate whether or not a verbal action is continuous or has ever been experienced. Students of Chinese find this one of the most difficult features of the language.

Chinese contrasts with other languages, notably Japanese, in the way it increases its stock of words by borrowing from foreign sources. Japanese even more than English borrows foreign words by imitating the original pronunciation as closely as the borrowing language permits, as in the case of English "chauffeur" from the French with the same spelling but slightly different pronunciation. As Mao Zedong noted in a conversation with Nikita Khrushchev,[2] the Chinese prefer to borrow by translating—that is, by the technique of translation loans rather than phonetic loans. The translation loan *diànhuà* ("electric talk"), for example, has now replaced the earlier phonetic loan *tiĕ-lĕ-fēng* for "telephone." With few exceptions, phonetic imitation of foreign words is limited to proper names, such as *Ní-kè-sēn* for "Nixon."

PHRASES AND SENTENCES

In Chinese the relationship of parts of speech to each other is characterized by the general feature that modifying elements precede the elements they modify. Adjectives come before nouns and adverbs before verbs. The equivalents of our relative clauses occur before nouns as modifying elements, as in German. Example: *Zhèibĕn wŏ-zuótian-zài-zhèr-mǎi-de shū* ("this I-here-yesterday-bought book"—that is, "this book that I bought here yesterday"). Here the modifying phrase is connected with the modified noun *shū* ("book") by the subordinating particle *de*.

Chinese is frequently said to be an SVO language—that is, one in which the sentence order is subject-verb-object. Many linguists prefer to describe Chinese sentences as of the topic-comment type. The topic, the main thing that is being talked about, is mentioned at the beginning of the sentence and then a sentence, which may even be of the SVO type, says something about it, as in *Zhèiwèi xiānsheng nǐ jiànguo tā méiyŏu?* ("This gentleman have you ever seen him?"). This topic-comment construction often gives the impression of considerable looseness in the Chinese sentence. On the other hand, Chinese has the reputation of having fixed word order, in contrast to highly inflected languages like Latin and Russian, where noun endings that indicate subject and object permit the reversal SVO to OVS to have exactly the same meaning—in contrast to English, where "John loves Mary" is quite different in meaning from "Mary loves John." This fixed word order is more often found in formal speech or written Chinese than in informal speech, which permits a surprising amount of flexibility if stress, juncture, and intonation are taken into account (DeFrancis 1967b).

Features such as these are important in Chinese, as in all languages, but apart from treatment in technical studies they tend to be slighted in general works, such as in textbooks for teaching the language.[3] The ambiguity in writing of *Tāmen bù qù, wǒ yě bù qù* disappears if we note that differences in intonation and juncture distinguish the two meanings "They're not going, (and) I'm not going either" and "(If) they don't go, I won't go either." As this sentence shows, Chinese tends to avoid the use of sentence or phrase connectors. Expressions equivalent to "and" or "if . . . then" exist in Chinese, but they are used much less frequently than in English. Chinese sentences in most styles of the language tend to be short and seemingly loosely connected.

In contrast to English, which is a sentence-oriented language, what might be considered omissions or deletions are much more common in Chinese, which is context-oriented. Thus the answer to the English question "Do students like him?" must be something like "Yes, students like him," whereas the Chinese equivalent *Xuésheng xǐhuan tā ma?* can be answered simply with *Xǐhuan* ("like"), with deletion of both the subject *xuésheng* ("students") and the object *tā* ("him"). Such terseness presents difficulties for foreign students of the language who lack the native speaker's intuitive grasp of what might be called contextual rules as well as of such neglected features as stress, juncture, and intonation.

Such things, and much more, must be taken into account for a fully detailed description of spoken Chinese. Here I have merely presented an outline. A really thorough presentation such as that contained in Y. R. Chao's monumental *Grammar of Spoken Chinese* (1968a) requires more than eight hundred pages to describe a language which is every bit as sophisticated an instrument of oral communication as the better-known languages of the world.

OVERVIEW

The picture of great complexity that emerges from a full-scale analysis of spoken Chinese contrasts with the widespread myth that it is impoverished because it lacks such features common to European languages as their complex phonologies and systems of conjugation and declension. This view has been noted by Karlgren (1926:16) in his comment that the distinctive structural features of Chinese

> give modern Chinese a stamp of excessive simplicity, one is tempted to say *primitiveness*. It is therefore not surprising that in the nineteenth century, when attention was directed for the first time to linguistic

families and their characteristics, Chinese was taken as the type of the primitive, underdeveloped languages—those which had not yet attained the same wealth of inflections, derivatives, and polysyllabic words as the European languages.

Subsequently this nineteenth-century view was replaced in some minds by the notion that Chinese actually represents a higher stage of linguistic development because it dispenses with unnecessary features such as conjugations and declensions that were retained in varying degrees by European languages. Neither view has much to commend it. Instead of adopting a sort of master-race theory of superior and inferior languages it is more accurate to say that all languages have the capacity for expressing whatever thoughts its speakers want to express and that they simply possess different strategies for doing so.

The mastery of these strategies is a necessary part of learning a language—indeed it is the very essence of language learning. The ease or difficulty in achieving this mastery is a subjective matter that basically has nothing to do with the nature of the language itself. Chinese has the reputation of being a hard and unfathomable language. The French reflect this in saying *"C'est du chinois"* where we say "It's Greek to me." This reputation is only partially deserved since it generally stems from a confused approach to the subject.

There is a difference, in the first place, in the amount of difficulty experienced by native speakers and by foreign learners of the language. Chinese have no more difficulty in learning to speak than do others born into one of the thousands of other linguistic environments around the world. For native speakers, all languages seem to be equally easy. Children throughout the world share the marvelous capacity of facile language learning.

It is the foreign learner, especially the foreign adult learner, who may have difficulties in mastering Chinese. Leaving aside the variable of individual differences in ability, there is also the problem of the specific differences between Chinese and whatever the learner's native language happens to be. A speaker of French or German, for example, will have no problem with the Chinese vowel sound represented by the letter *ü,* which does present a problem for speakers of English.

As far as English speakers are concerned, in regard to pronunciation they will have no great difficulties with the segmental phonemes of Chinese, none of which is likely to be as hard to master as the

French *r*. Tones are more of a problem, but not so great as is generally thought. Learning Chinese vocabulary requires more work than learning French vocabulary because the former is completely unrelated to English, whereas, thanks especially to the Norman conquest of England in the eleventh century, as well as an earlier ancestral affinity, there are many vocabulary items which are similar in the two languages. Chinese grammar is probably easier than French grammar with its complex verb conjugations, agreement of nouns and adjectives, and other features that are largely lacking in Chinese. Chinese is probably easier than French also with respect to the manner in which each language represents its sounds. French spelling presents puzzles as to how things are actually pronounced, as in the case of *chef* ("chef, chief"), where the *f* is pronounced, and *clef* ("key"), where it is not. Chinese spelling based on the official Pinyin system, which I shall use throughout this book, is much more regular and hence a more reliable guide to pronunciation.

This important plus for the Chinese transcription system is frequently overlooked by those who approach it with the ethnocentric idea that it should conform to their notions of the value of certain letters. This attitude, apart from being a display of arrogant or at least thoughtless provincialism, is also nonsensical because the presentation of a particular sound in a way that would please speakers of English might well cause problems for speakers of French or German or other languages. The specific solutions arrived at by the Chinese in representing the sounds of their language are all solidly based on both theoretical and practical considerations and add up to a system that does an excellent job of representing Chinese speech. The task of learning to speak Chinese is greatly facilitated by the excellence of the Pinyin system.

Overall, for a native speaker of English, learning to speak Chinese is not much more difficult than learning to speak French. It is in the traditional writing system that the greatest difficulty is encountered. The blanket designation of "Chinese" as a hard language is a myth generated by the failure to distinguish between speech and writing. Perhaps we can put things in perspective by suggesting, to make a rough guesstimate, that learning to speak Chinese is about 5 percent more difficult than learning to speak French, whereas learning to read Chinese is about five times as hard as learning to read French.

3.

Idiolects, Dialects, Regionalects, and Languages

In round figures there are about a billion people who are considered to be speakers of Chinese. Each person within this huge linguistic community has his own idiolect or particular way of speaking that distinguishes him in certain details from every other speaker. Strictly speaking, therefore, there are about a billion idiolects in China.

It is not too difficult a matter to isolate and describe a specific idiolect. In effect just this was done in the course of developing the official norm that is basically represented by the speech of educated natives of Peking. In the 1920s Y. R. Chao, a phonetician and all-around linguist of note, as a member of a group of scholars concerned with language standardization made some phonograph recordings of his own speech as a help in fixing the norm. As he himself was only semifacetiously fond of saying, he was for a while the only speaker of the Chinese national language.

Once we get beyond what might be called the Chao Idiolect, which was more or less the basis of the sketch of spoken Chinese presented in the preceding chapter, or any other specific idiolect, a problem arises: How do we categorize the huge number of Chinese idiolects? Upon examination the differences among these idiolects turn out to extend over an enormously wide range. Some differences are so minor that they are barely perceptible. Others are more readily apparent but still do not depart very far from the norm. Still others are of such a degree as to raise the question whether the different forms of speech should even be grouped together.

There is no easy way to measure the degree of difference among the Chinese idiolects. A rough and ready yardstick might be to differentiate between "minor" differences defined as those not large enough to impair intelligibility and "major" differences defined as those so great that people cannot understand each other. On this basis the billion idiolects of spoken Chinese must be divided into a number of groups. Within each group there are minor differences but between groups there are major differences of such magnitude that they produce mutual unintelligibility.

"DIALECTS" OR "LANGUAGES"?

There is considerable controversy over what to call these different varieties of spoken Chinese, a matter that forms part of the global problem of the relationship between dialect and language (Haugen 1966). In English the varieties of spoken Chinese are usually referred to as "dialects." Many linguists, however, prefer to apply the term dialect only to mutually intelligible forms of speech and to designate mutually unintelligible forms as "languages." In their view, as expressed by the American descriptive linguist Leonard Bloomfield (1933:44), Chinese is not a single language but a family of languages made up of a variety of mutually unintelligible languages.

The criterion of intelligibility as the dividing line between "dialect" and "language" is not as clear-cut as might appear at first thought. In a situation of geographic proximity it often happens that there is a continuum of speech with only minor differences between neighboring speakers but major differences between those at the extremities. If we represent the continuum by the letters of the alphabet *ABCDEFGHIJKLMNOPQRSTUVWXYZ*, there is mutual intelligibility between A and B, between B and C, . . . between M and N, . . . between X and Y, and between Y and Z, yet A and Z cannot communicate with each other. This is the situation, for example, between Paris and Rome and between Peking and Shanghai.

Yet this frequently cited analogy can be quite misleading. It suggests a steady progession of differences and some sort of numerical equivalence among the groups represented by the letters A to Z. In actual fact, at some points in the progression the differences tend to be greater than at others. And the number of speakers who can be placed at the two extremes of A and Z on the basis of their ability to converse with members of one or the other group far exceeds those in the intermediate groups. The number of people who can converse with speakers from Peking may be over 700 million. The number of speakers who can converse with speakers from Shanghai is about 85 million. Neither group can converse with the other, and the speakers who can serve as linguistic intermediaries between the two represent a relatively insignificant number.

The fact that we cannot draw a hairline separating the forms of speech spoken in Shanghai and Peking does not invalidate the need to emphasize their mutual unintelligibility and, if possible, to find a label that would draw attention to their distinctiveness. From this point of view the term "dialect" is unsatisfactory. Both in popular usage and in general linguistic application the term designates kinds of speech in which the differences are relatively minor in the specific sense that they are not great enough to impair intelligibility. The term is therefore appropriate when applied in such expressions as Peking dialect, Nanking dialect, Sichuan dialect, and others of the innumerable mutually intelligible subdivisions of Mandarin. But to add "Shanghai dialect" to the foregoing list would give the totally false impression that it differs from the Peking dialect no more than do the others in the list. To lump together all these forms of speech as more or less equivalent "dialects" is to perpetuate one of the most pervasive and pernicious myths about Chinese. It is to avoid this fantasy that scholars such as Bloomfield have insisted on referring to the kinds of speech spoken in Shanghai and Canton as languages rather than dialects.

In an attempt to find some analogy that would explain the Chinese situation to Western readers, Paul Kratochvíl (1968:15–16) has qualified his use of the term "dialects":

> We should perhaps be closer to a proportional depiction of the internal composition of Chinese and of the mutual relationship between Chinese dialects if we compared Chinese to a group of related languages. If, for example, a great number of historical events had not taken place in Europe and if speakers of Portuguese, Spanish, French, and Italian coexisted at the moment in a single political unit, if they had been using Latin as their common written form of communication up to the twentieth century, and if they considered, say, French as spoken in Paris as the most proper means of oral communication, they could be, although with a rather large pinch of salt, compared to the speakers of four large dialectal areas in China.

The rather large pinch of salt required to accept this well-conceived analogy between the European "languages" and Chinese "dialects" becomes a veritable shaker-full if we are required to accept the designation of "dialects" in the usually accepted meaning of the term as a label for the situation in China. Nevertheless, however justified Bloomfield's terminology might be from a strictly linguistic point of view, it involves some danger because in the popular mind (and often in actual fact) much more than merely linguistic differences separate entities comprising different languages. All too often differences in language when reinforced by religious, economic, political, and other differences lead to deep-seated animosity and demands for political separation. The One-Language, One-Nation concept is one of the major attributes of the modern nation-state.

These facts help to explain why even those Chinese whose linguistic sophistication might lead them to follow Bloomfield's approach almost invariably choose the word "dialects" when writing in English, though Y. R. Chao goes so far as to speak of "dialects (or languages, if you like)" and to refer to them as "practically different languages" (1976:97, 105). We are thus confronted by a terminological dilemma. To call Chinese a single language composed of dialects with varying degrees of difference is to mislead by minimizing disparities that according to Chao are as great as those between English and Dutch. To call Chinese a family of languages is to suggest extralinguistic differences that in fact do not exist and to overlook the unique linguistic situation that exists in China.

Crucial to a resolution of this dilemma is a clear understanding that the Chinese linguistic situation is unique in the world. History has no precedent for a situation in which a single if occasionally disrupted political entity has so long held together huge solid blocs of people with mutually unintelligible forms of speech in which a linguistic difference has not been compounded by profound extralinguistic differences. The 50 million or so Cantonese comprise one such bloc. Yet the linguistic difference that separates a Cantonese speaker from his compatriot in Peking is not exacerbated, as it is in Canada, by religious differences that further separate French Catholics from English Protestants. It is not aggravated, as it is in Belgium, by economic differences that further separate French-speaking Walloons from Netherlandic-speaking Flemings. It is not reinforced, as in the case of Spanish and French, by a political boundary that separates the two languages. It is not marked by an accumulation of differences, by a complex of extralinguistic forces, that in the cases just cited have contributed to the desire for political as well as linguistic separation. Although centrifugal forces have existed, and still exist, among the Chinese, their linguistic differences have never possessed the disruptive power they have had in many other areas of the world. In fact, the Chinese situation provides support for the contention made by Geertz in his study of primordial sentiments and civil politics (1963) that linguistic diversity does not inevitably lead to a primordial conflict over language of such intensity as to threaten the very foundations of the state.

OFFICIAL CHINESE CLASSIFICATION

The problem of nomenclature for this unique situation exists more in English than it does in Chinese. The official Chinese designation for the major forms of speech is *fāngyán*. Some scholars writing in Chinese make a distinction between *fāngyán* ("regional speech") as a designation for major regional forms of speech that are mutually unintelligible and *dìfang-huà* ("local speech") as a designation for lesser local varieties whose differences are not great enough to impair intelligibility. Others make the same distinction by prefixing *fāngyán* with *dìqū* ("region") and *dìdiǎn* ("locality"); that is they use *dìqū fāngyán* ("regional speech") for a major regional speech such as Putonghua and *dìdiǎn fāngyán* ("local speech") for its minor variations as spoken in Peking, Nanking, Xi'an, and other localities. This fundamental distinction is lost when all such distinctive Chinese terms are equally rendered as "dialect," as is usually done by both Chinese and Western writers on the subject. Not all writers are as careful as Bodman (1967:8) to note this term's wide range of meanings by pointing out that "Chinese usage commonly has 'dialect' in a loose as well as in a more precise sense. Loosely used, it refers to regional speech which should properly be called 'language,' such as Mandarin, Wu, Hakka, etc. Stricter usage refers to Mandarin dialects, the Peking dialect, etc."

A possible solution to our problem is to adopt English terms that would closely parallel the distinction that exists in Chinese. Since *fāngyán* is literally "regional speech," we could either adopt this designation or coin an abbreviation such as "regionalect" for the mutually unintelligible varieties of Chinese. The term "dialect" can then be reserved for its usual function of designating mutually intelligible subvarieties of the regionalects. But far more important than the particular terminology adopted is a firm understanding of the factual basis for grouping the idiolects of Chinese into distinct categories distinguished by the criterion of intelligibility.

At the Technical Conference on the Standardization of Modern Chinese that was held in Peking in 1955, it was officially decided that Chinese should be considered as comprising eight *fāngyán* with a

total of 541 million people. Since the number of speakers is now estimated to have increased to about a billion people, if we use the same
linguistic divisions (with other commonly used designations added in
parentheses) and the same proportion of speakers for each of the
regional forms of speech, the present situation can be summarized as
in Table 1.

Table 1   Chinese Regionalects

Linguistic Division	Speakers
Northern (Putonghua, Mandarin)	715 million (71.5%)
Jiangsu-Zhejiang (Wu)	85 million (8.5%)
Cantonese (Yue)	50 million (5.0%)
Hunan (Xiang)	48 million (4.8%)
Hakka	37 million (3.7%)
Southern Min	28 million (2.8%)
Jiangxi (Gan)	24 million (2.4%)
Northern Min	13 million (1.3%)

There is a good deal of guesswork applied to the various regionalects. Even the number of such regional forms of speech and their
specific designations are the subject of disagreement among specialists in the field. Such disagreement does not, however, seriously
affect the general picture of the linguistic situation of China.

PUTONGHUA

It is clear that among the eight regionalects the one designated as
"Northern" is by far the most important numerically. This term can
be considered as more or less equivalent to the more commonly used
expression Putonghua ("Common Speech"). The latter term, however, actually comprises a dual aspect in that it includes a narrow and
wide meaning. In its narrow sense the term refers to the official norm
that in its essentially Pekingese form is being promoted as Modern
Standard Chinese. In its wider meaning the term stands in contrast to
other regionalects as an all-inclusive designation that embraces the
various local varieties of Mandarin referred to by such terms as Peking
dialect, Nanking dialect, Sichuan dialect, and so on.

The 700 million or so people belonging to the Putonghua linguistic community comprise by far the largest group of people in the
world who speak the same language. The English-speaking community, even if one includes people in India and other countries who
have learned English as a second language, is probably less than half
as large.

Native speakers of Putonghua occur as a solid bloc in the huge area that extends from Manchuria through north and central China to the southwestern provinces of Sichuan and Yunnan and the northwestern provinces of Gansu and Ningxia. They are also to be found scattered throughout other parts of China. Some 2 to 3 million more or less native speakers of what they still call *Guóyŭ* ("National Language"), a rose by another name for Putonghua ("Common Speech"), migrated to Taiwan after Japan's expulsion from the island in 1945 and the defeat of the Guomindang government in the Chinese civil war that ended in 1949. In the same period smaller numbers of speakers of Mandarin migrated to the United States and other countries in the wake of earlier migrants who came chiefly from the southeastern coastal areas. In addition to all these native Putonghua speakers there are indeterminate millions of regionalect speakers, not to mention speakers of other languages such as those of the national minorities in China, who have also acquired command of the standard language.

Within the Putonghua speech community there are some relatively minor differences—minor compared to those among the regionalects —which like those in the English-speaking community are not great enough to cause any serious problem of communication. Nevertheless they are not insignificant. In the case of Mandarin as spoken in Taiwan, perhaps the most prominent difference, apart from what may be considered as inevitable sociolinguistic changes in a divided language, is in the pronunciation of the series of retroflex initials. The native speakers of Mandarin who took over Taiwan after 1945 comprised only 2 or 3 million people as against the 5 or 6 million inhabitants already there. Most of the latter are native speakers of what is variously called Taiwanese or Fukienese or Min, spoken in the adjacent mainland province of Fujian (or Fukien), from which their ancestors migrated some three centuries ago. Guoyu was imposed on this non-Mandarin majority as the only language of education. In the process some changes took place under the influence of the local forms of speech. The merger of the initials *zh*, *ch*, *sh*, with *z*, *c*, *s* is the most prominent of these changes. The same development seems to be under way in Mainland China, but at a slower pace.

Differences of this sort are noted by linguists through the device of isoglosses: lines on maps that show boundaries in the use of specific features—words, pronunciations, and so on. Bundles of isoglosses are used to delimit boundaries between dialects or other linguistic groups. Although detailed work along these lines has not been done in China, there is general agreement on identifying Northern Mandarin, Southern Mandarin, and Southwestern Mandarin. The latter group includes part of Hubei, Hunan, and Sichuan. Southern Mandarin includes part of Jiangsu, Jiangxi, Anhui, and Hubei. Northern Mandarin accounts for the rest. Because the boundaries of these areas are not clearly defined, dialect differences are frequently treated in unsystematic or sporadic fashion. Often a few scattered examples are used to illustrate a situation which would doubtless appear quite complex if treated in detail.

An important distinction within Mandarin is that between "sharp" and "round" sounds (Chao 1976:101)—as in the case of the word for "west," which in the Nanking dialect sounds a little like English *she,* and that for "sparse," which is a little like English *he.* In the attempts that have been made to create phonetic systems of writing, the question as to whether or not to take account of this distinction has been a frequent subject of debate. When the problem arose in the mid-fifties of adopting a standard Pinyin transcription, the decision was made to abandon the earlier attempts to show the distinction and instead to follow the undifferentiated Peking pronunciation *xī* for both "west" and "sparse" (DeFrancis 1967a:145).

Forrest (1948:205–208) mentions a number of other differences within Mandarin. A general feature of the Yangzi River region is the confusion of initial *l* and *n*. The merger of final *n* and *ng* also occurs in Southern Mandarin but is not confined to that area, being found even in Hubei. Tonal differences are widespread. In Hankou, words in the Peking high level tone have a rising inflection. Corresponding to Pekingese *shù* ("tree") one hears *fŭ* in the city of Xi'an, and in place of *shuǐ* ("water") one hears *fèi.* Here initial *f* corresponds to Pekingese *sh* and the tones are reversed. Apart from the widespread differences in pronunciation there are also differences in vocabulary. Northern Mandarin *shòu* ("to receive") is commonly used in a sort of passive construction. Southern Mandarin prefers the passive form *bèi* ("to suffer"). This usage is felt to be somewhat bookish by speakers of Northern Mandarin, but it has nevertheless been chosen to be the official Putonghua usage in this construction.

OTHER REGIONALECTS

The preceding examples of differences on the dialect level within the single regionalect of Putonghua, however extensive they may appear to be, are as nothing compared to the differences that separate other regionalects from Putonghua and also from each other. The extent of these differences is often minimized for various reasons, including the tendency to make comparisons between regionalects on the basis chiefly of the speech of educated speakers. Paul Kratochvíl (1968:18) makes the important point that there is considerable "vertical differentiation" among speakers within the regionalects (or "dialects" in his terminology):

> There are today great differences, particularly in vocabulary, but also on other levels, between various language forms within each dialectal area in China, connected with the social position and mainly the educational background of individual speakers. These differences range from forms used only by uneducated speakers up to rather strange local variants of language forms used only in the sophisticated milieu of literary discussions among intellectuals. If differences between Chinese dialects were to be described in detail, it would have to be done for each of the socially and educationally conditioned variants separately.

Differences in Chinese speech are most pronounced at the lower social level. Paul Serruys, a Western linguist with extensive experience as a missionary among peasants, stresses this point in the following passage (1962:114–115):

> Examining the Standard Language as opposed to dialectal speech, the difference is much more than a difference in pronunciation. . . . The masses of the people do not know any characters, nor any kind of Standard Language, since such a language requires a certain amount of reading and some contact with wider circles of culture than the immediate local unit of the village or the country area where the ordinary illiterate spends his life. From this viewpoint, it is clear that in the vast regions where so-called Mandarin dialects are spoken the differences of the speech which exist among the masses are considerably more marked, not only in sound, but in vocabulary and structure, than is usually admitted. In the dialects that do not belong in the wide groups of Mandarin dialects, the case is even more severe. To learn the Standard Language is for a great number of illiterates not merely to acquire a new set of phonetic habits, but also to learn a new language, and this in the degree as the vocabulary and grammar of their dialect are different from the modern standard norms. It is true that every Chinese might be acquainted with a certain amount of bureaucratic terminology, in so far as these terms touch his practical life, for example, taxes,

police. We may expect he will adopt docilely and quickly the slogan language of Communist organizations to the extent such as is necessary for his own good. But these elements represent only a thin layer of his linguistic equipment. When his language is seen in the deeper levels, his family, his tools, his work in the fields, daily life and in the village, differences in vocabulary become very striking, to the point of mutual unintelligibility from region to region.

These comments by Serruys reveal the need to abandon the widespread myth that regional forms of speech are largely identical except for pronunciation. Kratochvíl's stress on the need to make separate descriptions for "each of the socially and educationally conditioned variants" also reveals a new measure of complexity in a subject which, if not slighted by offhand comments that minimize the differences, would require a vast amount of detailed discussion to do it full justice. The subject is marked by a voluminous technical literature, some of which has been ably summarized by Egerod (1967). Here it must suffice to take a few miscellaneous examples as illustrations.

The Wu regionalect with its approximately 85 million speakers is a distant second to Putonghua. It is spoken in Zhejiang and Jiangsu, which includes the city of Shanghai, China's largest. One of its outstanding characteristics, said to have been derived from earlier historical forms now lost in Putonghua, is the retention of voiced initials. Whereas Peking has only an aspirated-unaspirated contrast, Shanghai adds a voiced contrast. Hence it has one set of initials that can be represented by *b, p, p'*, in which *b* is voiced, *p* unvoiced and unaspirated, and *p'* unvoiced and aspirated. In contrast to the twenty-one initial consonants of Putonghua, Wu boasts twenty-seven in the Suzhou dialect and thirty-five in that of Yongkang. Its dialects have six to eight tones compared to only four in Putonghua. In some dialects near Shanghai singular personal pronouns have two forms approaching nominative and accusative in usage, in contrast to the invariant forms in Common Speech.

The Yue regionalect, also called Cantonese from the main city in which it is spoken, is marked by a richer inventory of final consonants. In addition to the two in Putonghua, it has the finals *p, t, k, m*. The number of tones varies between six and nine depending on the dialect and analytical approach. In contrast to the modifier-modified order typical of Putonghua, there are many examples in Yue dialects of the order modified-modifier. Some words known from classical Chinese which no longer exist in Putonghua are to be found in Cantonese. There is a prefix *a* used with relationship terms and terms of address that does not exist in Standard Chinese. Expressions meaning "more" and "less" used to qualify the extent of an action are placed after the verb in Cantonese, before the verb in Pekingese. Moreover, Y. R. Chao (1976:99) notes that the best-known divergence of Yue, and Wu also, from Mandarin is their use of the word order direct object–indirect object in place of Standard Chinese indirect object–direct object—that is, "give water me" instead of "give me water."

As the foregoing notes suggest, the greatest differences among the regionalects are in the area of phonology, the least in the area of grammar. Vocabulary differences fall in between these extremes. This frequently made summary of the differences is misleading, however, since its comparative ranking obscures the fact that all the areas are marked by substantial differences—almost total at the phonological level, enormous at the lexical level, and still quite extensive at the grammatical level. In an interesting study comparing the Taiwanese form of the Min regionalect and Mandarin, Robert Cheng (1981) finds that 30 percent of the vocabulary as a whole is different (apart from the overall difference in pronunciation), a figure that rises to 50 percent in the case of function words (adverbs, prepositions, demonstratives, measures, question words, conjunctions, particles). With respect to grammar, Serruys considers claims of uniformity to be true "only if one considers the Chinese language on a very broad historical and comparative scale." Presenting some examples of grammatical differences, he concludes: "A close look at the grammars of the non-Mandarin dialects, however, will show that in reality their distance from the standard language is very wide" (1962:138–141). According to a recent estimate (Xu 1982:15), the differences among the regionalects taken as a whole amount, very roughly, to 20 percent in grammar, 40 percent in vocabulary, and 80 percent in pronunciation.[1]

A more extensive analysis than that intended here would have to pile up a great many details along the lines presented above. This could be done for the regionalects already discussed and also for the other regionalects—namely Xiang, spoken only in Hunan; Hakka, spoken side by side with other regionalects chiefly in Guangdong and Guangxi; Gan, spoken chiefly in Jiangxi; Southern Min, spoken in southern Fujian (for example in Amoy), Taiwan, Hainan Island, and other areas; and Northern Min, spoken in northeastern Fujian. A detailed inventory of the special features of each regionalect would show them to be so much more extensive than the differences noted within Putonghua that it would make plain, if it is not already obvious, that these forms of speech must be placed in a different category from the dialects of Putonghua.

As in the case of Putonghua, each of the seven other regionalects can be further subdivided into various dialects, each with its own distinctive features. Some of these dialects show such a degree of difference that they are sometimes treated as regionalects rather than as true dialects. The analogy presented earlier of varieties of speech stretching over a continuum that defies clear-cut divisions applies with special force to the linguistic situation in the southeast coastal area.

Apart from disagreement among specialists concerning the precise number of regionalects and their classification, there has also been a lack of agreement regarding their history. Bodman (1967) pays tribute to Karlgren's seminal contribution to this linguistic research but notes the new points of view that have received more general acceptance. Karlgren in making his reconstruction of seventh-century Ancient Chinese proceeded on the misconception that his primary sources, such as the dictionary *Qie Yun,* represented a homogeneous dialect, which he identified as that of the capital city of Chang'an in Shaanxi, and was the prototype from which most forms of contemporary Chinese are descended. An opinion more generally held today is that Karlgren's reconstruction is a somewhat artificial "overall system" based on many dialects. Disparities existed then as they do today, and though the various forms currently in existence share a common ancestor, this archetype is not to be found in a single dialect as recent as the seventh century.

NON-CHINESE LANGUAGES

To round out the picture of "Chinese"—that is, of the eight regionalects each with its own multitude of dialects—it may be useful to place these diverse forms of speech in their wider linguistic context. The conglomerate known as "Chinese" is one of a more distantly related group of languages known collectively as Sino-Tibetan. Apart from Tibetan this group includes a host of closely related languages in the Himalayan region, as well possibly as some other languages in Southern China and Southeast Asia, including Burmese and the Tai

family. The precise relationship of the languages that exist in this linguistically complex area is, however, by no means settled. There is
considerable disagreement among specialists regarding the problem
of classification, a subject that is under constant reexamination. In
China itself, besides the languages belonging to the large Sino-Tibetan family, there are others belonging to other language families.
Chief among these are Mongolian and Uighur, which belong to the
geographically widespread Altaic family of languages. The non-Chinese languages are spoken by fifty-four national minorities with a
total population of some 50 or 60 million.

Apart from its already noted membership in the Sino-Tibetan family of languages, Chinese does not appear to have any affinity with
any other language. This point needs to be stressed to counteract the
myth of the supposed affinity of Chinese with the languages of the
neighboring countries of Korea, Japan, and Viet Nam. The fact of
the matter is that, so far as we know, it has no genetic connection
whatsoever with these three languages. This statement relates to the
original state of Korean, Japanese, and Vietnamese when they first
came in contact with Chinese some 1,500 to 2,000 years ago. Over
the centuries, however, these languages did borrow huge amounts of
vocabulary from Chinese.

In their origins Korean and Japanese are generally believed to be
distantly related to the large group of Altaic languages that include
Mongolian, Manchu, and the Turkic languages of central and western
Asia. These are all agglutinative languages marked by the piling up
of suffixes to root words. They are nontonal languages whose SOV
(subject-object-verb) order contrasts with the SVO order of Chinese.
As for Vietnamese, most specialists think it belongs to still another
completely different language family that includes Khmer (Cambo-
dian). Its tonal feature is believed to be indigenous in origin and to
have been reinforced later by extensive borrowing of Chinese lexical
items. In short, these three languages are basically no more related to
Chinese than is English.

When Korea, Japan, and Viet Nam first came in contact with
China, they had no writing, whereas China had a highly developed
system of writing that was already some two thousand years old.
China also had sophisticated schools of philosophy, a centralized state
with a literate bureaucracy, an appealing religion with a vast body of
dogma, a rich literature especially strong in historiography. Small
wonder that China's neighbors drew heavily on the treasures of this

literate culture. They began by borrowing the writing system itself. They progressed from writing in Chinese to adapting the characters to their own languages. They engaged in large-scale borrowing of concepts and the words to express them. As already noted in "The Singlish Affair," the character 國 was borrowed to express the concept "country, nation, state," and its pronunciation was adapted to the local way of speaking. This procedure is similar to the English borrowing of French words with pronunciation modified to suit the English tongue.

Such borrowings, however important from a cultural point of view, do not basically alter the nature of the borrowing languages. English remains a Germanic language despite its extensive borrowing from French. Korean, Japanese, and Vietnamese retain their original essence despite their extensive borrowing from Chinese. Speakers of these four languages can no more understand each other's speech than can an Englishman and a Frenchman carry on a conversation unless one has learned the other's language. Nor can Asians read each other's writing any more than can an Englishman and a Frenchman merely because they have some written words like "nation" in common. The popular notion that Korean, Japanese, and Vietnamese are offshoots of Chinese is one of those myths that, as usual, owes much of its currency to confusing speech with writing and misunderstanding the nature of the writing systems based on Chinese characters.

The nonrelationship of Chinese to these languages, the relationship it does have with some other languages, and its division into regionalects and dialects are summarized in Table 2. Think of "Sino-Tibetan" as being on the same level as Indo-European, which includes the major languages of India and Europe, "Chinese" as being on the level of the Germanic or Romance groups within the Indo-European family, the "regionalects" as being on the level of English, Dutch, and German within the Germanic group or French, Spanish, and Italian within the Romance group, and the "dialects" as being on the level of the British, American, and Australian dialects of English or the Neapolitan, Roman, and Tuscan dialects of Italian. It must be remembered that if these parallels are to be seasoned with a large pinch of salt, we must pour a whole shaker-full over the uncritical practice of designating as "dialects" such divergent forms of speech as those of Peking, Shanghai, and Canton. At the very least it is necessary to emulate those who if they use the term at all are careful to explain its nuances of meaning.

Table 2 "Chinese" in Its Linguistic Context

Unrelated Language Families	Related Languages or Language Families	Mutually Unintelligible Regionalects	Mutually Intelligible Dialects

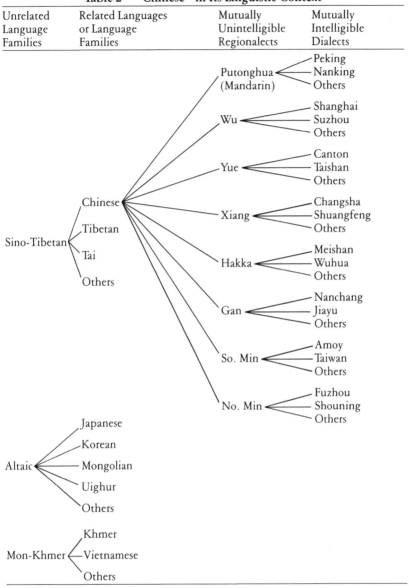

For the geographic distribution of the linguistic units located in China, see map on page 34.

Part II

RETHINKING
CHINESE CHARACTERS

One must deplore the general tendency . . . (alas, too prominently figuring in Sinological research on this continent) of insisting that the Chinese in the development of their writing, as in the evolution of many other of their cultural complexes, followed some mysterious esoteric principles that set them apart from the rest of the human race.

Peter H. Boodberg

4.
What's in a Name?

The marks on paper that are usually recognized as peculiar to the writing systems developed in China, Korea, Japan, and Viet Nam have been given a variety of names, some neutral and noncommittal, others explicit but more controversial. Designations such as graphs, characters, signs, or symbols apply equally well to all kinds of writings. More specialized is the term "Chinese characters." This label is not as unambiguous as might appear at first glance. In Japan, Chinese characters are called kanji (from Chinese *Hànzì,* literally "Chinese characters"), but the two terms are not completely synonymous since a few characters have been created in Japan that are different from those used in China. Moreover, and more important, the Japanese writing system is not confined to Chinese characters but includes also the indigenous phonetic symbols called kana. Korean writing has also used a mixture of Chinese characters and purely phonetic symbols. As for Vietnamese, the indigenous Nom characters look like Chinese characters but were never used outside of Viet Nam and are unintelligible to readers of Chinese without special study. Apart from the possible need at times to be more specific by taking these differences into account, the term "Chinese characters" is usually clear enough to serve as an overall designation for the basic symbols used in all four countries.

A recently coined synonym for "Chinese characters" is "sinographs" (Rogers 1979:283). Its chief virtue lies in using one word in place of two. Both terms, of course, emphasize the Chinese origins of the symbols. Other aspects of the characters are emphasized in other designations. A popular view of the nature of Chinese writing is reflected in the widespread use of the designations "pictographs" and "pictograms." These terms are meant to indicate that the basic units of writing are pictures divorced from sound. Their meaning is supposed to be readily discernible even when the symbols are conventionalized or stylized in form. Specialists, however, apply the designation only to the earliest characters in China.

Other widely used terms are "ideographs" and "ideograms." Some people, specialists included, use these terms only out of habit, without attaching any special significance to them, more or less as popular equivalents for "Chinese characters." For some specialists, however, and for the public at large, the terms have a specific meaning in designating written signs that represent ideas, abstract as well as concrete, without regard to sound (Creel 1936:98–99; Margouliès 1957:82). The same sign is considered to evoke the same idea in the minds of different viewers, though they might well verbalize it in different ways, as in the case of English speakers responding to a particular ideograph by thinking "habitation, residence, dwelling, house, home" or some other related term while French speakers think "habitation, résidence, maison, demeure."

Some scholars are opposed to this view of Chinese characters as representing concepts and insist instead that they represent specific words. They have therefore advanced the designation "logograph"— that is, a graph that represents a word (from the Greek *logos:* "word"). Synonymous with the logographic concept (DuPonceau 1838:110; Boodberg 1937:332) is the expression "lexigraphic" referring to words in the lexicon or vocabulary (DuPonceau 1838:xiv). The key point of disagreement leading to these terms is whether a character conveys meaning directly or through the intermediary of the word.

A modification of the logographic concept has been suggested by some students of writing who argue that Chinese characters represent morphemes rather than words and hence should be called "morphemic" (Kratochvíl 1968:157) or "morphographic" (Robert Cheng 1980:personal communication). Here much of the disagreement centers on a controversial question: What constitutes a word? For some, a word in Chinese is a syllable in speech and a character in writing. For others, syllable and character represent at most not a word but rather a morpheme, the smallest unit of meaning. By this definition a word may in fact include more than one syllable and be represented by more than one character. This is a secondary point of disagreement, however, and supporters of "logographic," "lexigraphic," "morphemic," and "morphographic" are united in opposition to the "ideographic" interpretation.

Still other designations are advanced by students of the subject who contend that most Chinese characters, actually 90 percent according to the frequently cited estimate by Karlgren (1923:4), contain phonetic elements that should also be taken into account along with the semantic elements that are universally recognized as a distinctive feature of Chinese characters. Such terms as "phonetic compounds" (Karlgren 1923:16), "phonograms" (Karlgren 1936: 161), "phonetic complexes" (Wieger 1965:10), "phonetic indicators" (Gelb 1963:118), and "phonic indicators" (Yau 1983:198) stress the phonetic aspect in this large group of characters.

The belief that both the semantic and phonetic aspects should be taken into account in the naming of Chinese characters has led to terms like "phonosemantic" (Pelliot 1936:163; Cohen 1958:52) and "ideophonographic" (Bunakov 1940; Cohen 1958:45). A similar approach has led Krykov to designate one class of characters as "phonoideograms" (1980:25–26). Chinese writing has been classified as "logo-syllabic" by Gelb (1963:10) and as "word-syllabic" by Bloomfield (1933:285–286) and Gelb (1973:818–819), though these authors appear to apply their terms to the characters as a whole and not to the component elements.

The terms suggested by Pelliot, Bunakov, Cohen, and Krykov tie in a semantic element with a phonetic element without specifying the nature of either, though Cohen adds a bit more detail to the phonetic aspect by further references to "syllabograms," "syllabo-phonograms," and "syllabic phonograms" (1958:49, 53, 55). The terms advanced by Gelb and Bloomfield are the most precise, particularly if their scope is refined, since they relate Chinese characters both to words and to syllables.

As the foregoing confusion of names amply demonstrates, there are wide differences of opinion when it comes to describing Chinese characters. A long hard look at these characters is needed if we are to make our way through this terminological maze and reach clear conclusions about the nature of Chinese writing.

5.

From Pictographs to What?

Chinese characters constitute a system of writing so obviously different in appearance from Western scripts as to arouse wonderment about their precise nature and, as it were, their *modus operandi*. Everyone knows, at least in a general way, that Chinese characters originated as pictographs, that for several millennia they have been used to record the history and culture of a great civilization, and that they have come down today in forms which though highly stylized are clearly related to their origins. But just how are the Chinese characters constructed? How does the writing system work?

STRUCTURE OF CHINESE CHARACTERS

Chinese characters are constructed from basic units called "strokes" —that is, marks made with a single continuous motion of the pen. There are three general categories of strokes: dots, lines, and hooks. These can be illustrated as follows:

dots: ╱ ╲
lines: ─ │ └
hooks: ╱ ╵ 乙

The strokes included in these three categories can be more specifically described in terms of their contour, their initial or terminal characteristics, the direction in which they are written, and other features. All strokes can be considered as going from some central starting point toward any direction from northeast to southwest as follows:

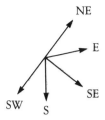

The descriptive names that might be given to some of the strokes could include an indication of the direction in which they are written —for example, southwest dot (ʼ), northeast hook (╱). Depending on the degree of refinement desired, from one to several dozen basic strokes might be identified, although Chinese roughly distinguish only some half dozen. These strokes are the building units of Chinese characters but in themselves have no particular significance, any more than do the three strokes in the letter *R* or the four strokes in the letter *E*.

Characters are said to contain such-and-such a number of strokes. In fact, they are sometimes arranged in dictionaries according to their number of strokes. The simplest character contains only one stroke; it represents the word *yī* ("one"). The most complex character contains sixty-four strokes; it is a rare dictionary item defined as *tiè* ("verbose"). These two characters are:

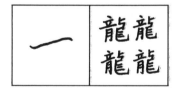

Some of the traditional complex characters were simplified by government decree in the 1950s by reducing the number of strokes, as in the case of nine-stroke 馬 reduced to three-stroke 马 for *mǎ* ("horse").

Learners first practice basic strokes and then combine them to form characters. Apart from writing each stroke correctly, students must learn to write them in the proper sequence, bearing in mind such general rules as "top before bottom" and "left before right." Textbooks show the sequence of strokes by building up characters in various ways. The examples below show the sequence of strokes and also the direction in which each stroke in a character is written.

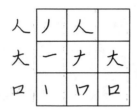 

Students must also learn to vary the size of the strokes so that the total effect will be one of pleasing balance among the elements. This balance is conditioned by the requirement that all characters, regardless of their simplicity or complexity, should be written so that they take up the same amount of square space—as in the case of the one-stroke character for "one" and the sixty-four-stroke character for "verbose" cited above. Paper ruled into squares of an inch or so on each side is used for practice by beginning students of writing.

Teachers usually start their students off with characters that are simple because they are made up of only a few strokes and interesting because they are easily related to their pictographic origins. In the following examples the top character is the early pictographic version of the second millennium B.C. and the bottom character is the later traditional form, now some two thousand years old:

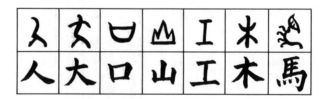

The pronunciation and meaning of these characters are as follows:

1. *rén* ("man, person"). The pictographic form represents a walking man.

2. *dà* ("big, large"). The pictographic form is a stick drawing of a man with outstretched arms.

3. *kǒu* ("mouth"). The pictographic form is already as stylized as the modern version.

4. *shān* ("mountain"). The pictographic form clearly represents mountain peaks.

5. *gōng* ("work, labor"). The pictographic form represents a carpenter's square.

6. *mù* ("tree"). The pictographic form is an already stylized drawing of a tree.

7. *mǎ* ("horse"). The pictographic form represents a horse in

upright position. The traditional form, as noted above, has recently been further simplified.

Simple characters such as these occur as independent characters and also as component elements in compound or multielement characters. In writing the components of compound characters the same rules of sequence apply as in the case of basic strokes—for example, "top before bottom" and "left before right." These two rules account for almost 90 percent of the characters in current use. About 64 percent of the characters in the 1971 edition of *Xinhua Zidian* have a left-right structure and 23 percent a top-bottom structure (Chen 1982:55). Here are some examples of multielement characters:

The third character is made up of two reduplications of the same element 木. The previously cited complex character of sixty-four strokes is made up of four reduplications of the sixteen-stroke character 龍. Independent characters when used as partial components in compound characters sometimes occur in different positions in these more complex graphs. Thus in the fifth and sixth characters the component elements 口 and 木 appear in reverse order vertically. The component element 山 occurs to the left of 工 in the first character and above it in the fourth. Such shifts in position make for quite different characters: the fifth character is *xìng* ("apricot"); the sixth is *dāi* ("foolish").

When the same element occurs in different positions the basically identical strokes are modified in some way, as in length or thickness of stroke, though the latter goes by the board when beautiful brush-written characters are replaced by those written with an ordinary ballpoint pen. The modifications are made so that the relative proportions of the individual strokes enable the whole character to fit into the required square space. This extremely diverse modification of the basically identical strokes and their possible location in quite diverse positions within the imaginary square constitutes one of the main reasons why simple mechanical composition of characters from basic strokes, as might be envisaged by adapting them to typewriters, has proved to be impossible. The attempts made in this direction, apart from being impractical, have resulted in distorted shapes that are aesthetically unacceptable.

Aesthetics plays an exceedingly important role in Chinese writing, more so than in any other system of writing. Calligraphy has been elevated to an artform. In scrolls displayed as wall hangings, the characters are often executed in such a way that they resemble graphic designs rather than easily recognizable symbols (see Figure 3). The calligraphic style is one of a wide variety of styles, somewhat analogous to the type fonts and individual writing in alphabetic scripts, that are conditioned by the instrument used in writing, the degree of deliberateness in executing the strokes, and individual idiosyncrasies of different writers. Some of these variations can be seen in Figure 3 and in the following presentation of the character for *mǎ* ("horse") in four different ways: (1) the "regular" style (the Chinese equivalent of our block letters), written with a ball-point pen; (2) the same, written with a brush; (3) the "running" style, written with a brush; and (4) the "cursive" style, written with a brush:

As can be seen from these examples, the running and cursive styles, and even the more deliberate regular style, involve a telescoping or distortion of the original strokes or components of characters, as in the case of the four dots, already the stylized representation of the four legs of a horse, which are merged into a single straight line in some styles of writing and in the new simplified form. Such changes complicate the task of analyzing the structure of Chinese characters from the point of view of their origin and subsequent evolution.

PRINCIPLES OF FORMATION

That Chinese characters originated from pictographs is a matter of unanimous agreement. In this respect Chinese writing is not in the least distinctive. It is the general if not quite unanimous opinion among specialists on this subject that all writing originated in the drawing of pictures (Gelb 1963), though one scholar traces some Sumerian cuneiform symbols to tokens of various shapes and markings used for accounting purposes from the ninth millennium B.C. on (Schmandt-Besserat 1978).

The earliest Chinese writing known to us consists of inscriptions incised on bones and shells for purposes of divination in the Shang dynasty (ca. 1500–1028 B.C.). At that time Chinese civilization had already reached a high level of sophistication. Chinese writing had also evolved into a complex system far removed from the various forms of picture writing that Gelb insists on classifying not as true writing but as "forerunners of writing." In fact, one student of the subject emphasizes that "every important principle of the formation of modern Chinese characters was already in use, to a greater or less degree, in the Chinese of the oracle bones, more than three thousand years ago" (Creel 1937:160).

The principles governing the formation of Chinese characters have particular significance in the case of compound characters—those which are not simple pictographs but complex graphs composed, as we have seen, of recurrent partials. This is by far the largest category of Chinese characters. A clear understanding of the principles of formation is therefore crucial to an understanding of the Chinese system of writing.

In Chinese tradition there are said to be six such principles. Four of the six (1, 2, 3, and 5) are based on the composition of the characters; two (4 and 6) are based on their use (Wieger 1965:10–11). Principle 6 involves a tiny group of "derived characters" about which there is so much disagreement (Chao 1948:63) that I am simply omitting it from this brief discussion. Although the names of these principles have been variously translated, I shall rely on my own designations in explaining them.

First is the "pictographic principle." This can be illustrated by the well-known examples of a circle with a dot or horizontal line inside for "sun" and a crescent with one or two lines for "moon" (Karlgren 1940:nos. 404 and 306). The Shang forms ⊝ and ☽, as is readily apparent, had already evolved from simple pictures into stylized figures. The meaning of these figures when seen in isolation might be guessed at but could be known with assurance only by being learned. This is certainly true of the even more stylized forms 日 and 月 in use today. Other examples of pictographic characters are the seven simple characters we discussed in the preceding section.

Second is the "simple indicative principle." This can be illustrated by the Shang characters for "one, two, three" (Karlgren 1940:nos. 394, 564, 648) and for "above, below" (Karlgren 1940:nos. 726 and 35). These are presented below together with their modern equivalents:

	1	2	3	"above"	"below"
Shang:	一	二	三	二	二
Modern:	一	二	三	上	下

As is apparent, especially from the Shang characters for "two" and "above," these "simple indicators" despite their simplicity are nevertheless quite conventionalized diagrams indicative of the ideas represented.

Third is the "compound indicative principle." The characters in this group are all compound or multielement graphs whose meaning is derived by combining the meanings of their constituent parts. A stock example of this principle is the combining of 日 ("sun") and 月 ("moon") to form the complex character 明 as indicative of the word *míng* ("bright").[1] Here too the relationship between form and meaning is purely conventional and must be learned.

Fourth is the "phonetic loan principle." This is akin to the rebus device of representing a word by the picture of an object whose name resembles the word in sound, as in the case of our children's game in which the picture of a human eye is used to represent the pronoun "I." A stock example in Chinese is the use of the Shang character 來, a pictograph for a kind of wheat *(Triticum aestivum)* that was anciently called *ləg*, to represent the homophonous word *ləg* ("to come"), a concept which is hard to represent by a picture or a diagram. This character has come down in the stylized form 來 (now simplified to 来) and with the modern pronunciation *lái*.

Fifth is the "semantic-phonetic principle." This is an extension of the previous principle in which the different homophonous words represented by the same character are differentiated by adding semantic elements to the common underlying phonetic element. The characters that result from this combination are generally referred to as "phonetic compounds." What I have designated as the "phonetic element" is usually called simply the "phonetic" and refers to a syllable of sound. My "semantic element" is variously designated as key, classifier, determinative, signific, or radical; the last term, unfortunately, is the most common but also the most misleading, since the semantic element is not the basic root but a later accretion to the really basic phonetic. This point is underscored by the observation that in the early stages of Chinese writing "characters were borrowed without adding radicals, or sometimes by adding radicals that did not ultimately become standard" (Elman 1982:498).

Chao (1948:61–62) distinguishes three categories of characters based on the semantic-phonetic principle. In one category, a loan character is enlarged by the addition of a semantic element to give some idea of the category of concepts to which a meaning belongs. Thus in the case of the word 然 (*rán:* "to burn"), which acquired the additional meaning of "thus, so," in order to distinguish the two meanings the original character was reserved for the new meaning, and a new character 燃 was created by adding the element 火 ("fire") to reinforce the original meaning of "to burn."

In another category, the enlarged character results from an extension of meaning of the original word represented by the character. Sometimes the enlargement represents the derived meaning, as in the case of 方 (*fāng:* "square, in a general sense") enlarged to 坊 (*fāng:* "square, marketplace") by the addition of a semantic element 土 meaning "earth." Sometimes the enlargement represents the original meaning and the simpler character the derived meaning, as in the case of 文 *(wén),* whose original meaning of "line, streak" came to be represented by 紋 (with an added "silk" element), while its extended meaning of "writing, literature, culture" was represented by the original character.

A third category consists of "pure phonetic compounds" in which the semantic element is added to a phonetic element that was never a phonetic loan or semantic extension in the first place. Rather, it was specifically used for its sound to combine with the semantic element —such as *táng* ("sugar"), whose written form 糖 consists of the semantic element 米 ("cereal foods") on the left and the purely phonetic element 唐 *(táng)* on the right.

The evolution of the three categories of characters based on the semantic-phonetic principle can be made clearer if the examples just cited are summarized as follows:

		Original Character	Semantic Addition	New Character
1.	*rán*	burn → thus 然	fire 火	burn 燃
2.	*fāng*	square 方	earth 土	market-place 坊
	wén	line → writing 文	silk 糸	line 紋
3.	*táng*	*táng* 唐	cereal 米	sugar 糖

In many cases the same element, though it may be primarily one or the other, has both a semantic and a phonetic function, as is true of 黄 (*huáng* "yellow") in 癀 (*huáng* "jaundice"), where it is joined with the semantic element 疒 ("sickness"), and in 磺 (*huáng* "sulfur"), where it is joined with the semantic element 石 ("stone"). In the case of 蝗 (*huáng* "locust") the phonetic element chosen to combine with the semantic element 虫 ("insect") is 皇 (*huáng* "emperor"). Was this phonetic chosen rather than the homophonous character for "yellow" simply for its sound or because of some idea of the locust as an imperial member of the insect world? In the case of the rendition for the *huáng* meaning "sturgeon" we have two variants, one written with the "yellow" phonetic and the other with the "emperor" phonetic, both combined with the semantic element for "fish":

> 魚 "fish"
> 鳇 "fish" + *huáng* "yellow" = *huáng* "sturgeon"
> 鳇 "fish" + *huáng* "emperor" = *huáng* "sturgeon"

While etymological research might succeed in clarifying the basis for some of the variation, in many cases, as one specialist in Chinese paleography concludes, "it is simply a matter of the whim of the writer" (Barnard 1978:203).

Scribal whim goes far to explain a diversity bordering on chaos in the forms of the Chinese characters as they evolved in the Shang dynasty and during the long years of political and administrative disunity in the Zhou dynasty (ca. 1028–221 B.C.). The situation was aggravated by the fact that characters were created by writers living in different historical periods, which inevitably meant changes in sounds over the years, and speaking different dialects, which inevitably affected their choice of phonetic elements in the creation of new characters.

APPLICATION OF THE PRINCIPLES

With the establishment of the unified empire of Qin in 221 B.C., an attempt was made to reform the system of writing by standardizing the characters. One aspect of the reform involved a further simplification in the form of the characters. The pictographic forms of the Shang dynasty, which had already undergone some stylistic simplification in the "great seal script" of the Zhou period, were now further simplified in the "small seal script" of Qin. This script in turn gave way to the "scribal script" and then to the "regular script," which in the Han dynasty (206 B.C.–A.D. 220) became the form that has been in general use ever since, until the recent simplification. The accompanying table shows the evolution of these styles for the two characters for *lái* ("come") and *mǎ* ("horse"):

| | Shang | Great Seal | Small Seal | Scribal | Regular | Simplified |

The Qin reform, as detailed by Barnard, also involved the elimination of many older characters, some of which had already become obsolete, others of which were replaced with an existing or newly created character. In the process many characters that were once in use became undecipherable and must now be placed in the category of what have been called "descendentless" graphs (Barnard 1978).

One of the key questions concerning the Qin reform, and indeed concerning the whole evolution of Chinese characters, involves a determination of what principles, among those enumerated above, were adopted at various stages in the creation or modification of the characters. One approach to this question might be to note, if we can, the actual number of characters that were created on the basis of one or another principle.

Data based on a second-century dictionary by Xu Shen, a twelfth-century work by Zheng Qiao (1104–1162), and the great Kang Xi dictionary of 1716 are available for the four principles dealing with the composition of characters (Morohashi 1960:1453··32). Similar data are available for the approximately one-fourth of Shang characters that have been deciphered to date (Cheng Te-k'un 1980:34).[2] This information is summarized in Table 3.

One of the striking things about this table is the increase in the number of characters in the Chinese lexicon. From the approximately 1,000 deciphered characters (out of a total of 4,500) on the Shang oracle bones, the number increased to almost 10,000 in the Han dynasty despite the Qin reform that eliminated so many characters.

Table 3   Structural Classification of Characters

Principle	Oracle Bones (Shang dynasty)	Xu Shen (2nd century)	Zheng Qiao (12th century)	Kang Xi (18th century)
Pictographic	227 (23%)	364 (4%)	608 (3%)	
Simple indicative	20 (2%)	125 (1%)	107 (1%)	±1,500 (3%)
Compound indicative	396 (41%)	1,167 (13%)	740 (3%)	
Semantic-phonetic	334 (34%)	7,697 (82%)	21,810 (93%)	47,141 (97%)
Total	977	9,353	23,265	48,641

The number soared to 23,000 in the twelfth century and to almost 49,000 in the eighteenth. These figures, of course, include many variant and obsolete forms.

Equally striking is the high proportion of semantic-phonetic compounds relative to the three other categories. It would also seem that the pictographic principle, although important at the beginning stages of the Chinese script, was soon relegated to a position of insignificance. The same can be said of the two "indicative" principles. The number of characters formed on the basis of the first three principles, all of which can be considered primarily semantic in nature, remained virtually stagnant from Xu Shen through Zheng Qiao to Kang Xi (1,656, 1,455, ±1,500). Virtually all new characters were based on the semantic-phonetic principle. One wonders how much earlier than Xu Shen had the semantic approach shot its bolt. The importance of the phonetic approach is attested as early as Shang by the cautious estimate of one scholar that "radical + phonetic" combinations comprised 20 percent of the characters inscribed on bones and shells (Zhou Youguang 1979:315) and by the later figure of 34 percent cited above. To this must be added the substantial number of characters in the preliminary stage of phonetic loans, such as the character for "wheat" used for the homophonous word "come." It is quite plausible, as Kennedy contends (1964:241), that "at some period shortly after or coincident with the oracle bone period Chinese writing became an organized system of syllabic writing." All this means that the conveying of meaning through the medium of characters without regard to sound gradually came to play a distinctly minor role in the Chinese writing system as it evolved, like all other writing systems, from pictographic origins to a complex fusion of semantic and phonetic aspects. It also means that the common parlor game of characterizing Chinese writing by regaling the uninitiated with pictographic examples such as "sun plus moon equals bright" is a bad case of the tail wagging the dog.

DISAGREEMENT OVER THE PRINCIPLES

The importance of the phonetic element in Chinese characters has frequently been overlooked despite the fact that many scholars, both Chinese and Westerners, have drawn attention to its crucial role in Chinese writing. According to a recent survey of Chinese phonological study in late imperial China, "it had been recognized generally by the seventeenth century that the phonetic element of each character was the decisive element in establishing its meaning" (Elman 1982: 497). Particularly perceptive are the views credited to the phonologist Chiang Yung (1681–1762), who is known as Jiang Yong in Pinyin:

> Arguing that in antiquity the number of written characters, i.e. ideographs and pictographs, was limited, whereas the number of spoken words, i.e. sounds referring to things, objects, concepts, etc. was unlimited, Chiang theorized that all characters had had sounds attached to them but many sounds had not yet had characters devised for them. Chiang saw this situation as the fundamental linguistic, dare one say transformative, dynamic whereby, through a system of borrowed characters, oral discourse generated a phonetically derived written language. Chiang's recognition of the priority of the spoken language explained why so few characters were pictographs and ideographs. [Elman 1982:498]

To be sure, not all scholars are in agreement with this line of thought. The interpretation of some of the data presented above and the application of the principles governing character formation to the analysis of specific characters have been the subject of considerable dispute among specialists in Chinese. A good illustration of this disagreement is a celebrated exchange between two leading Chinese specialists, Professors Creel and Boodberg, in a series of articles published between 1936 and 1940. These two represent two extremes in the approach to Chinese characters. Creel emphasizes the semantic aspect, Boodberg the phonetic. Both have made important contributions to scholarship—Creel primarily through his work on Shang and Zhou society, Boodberg through his work on Chinese historical phonology.

Creel (1936) initiated the war of words with an article entitled "On the Nature of Chinese Ideography" in which he set out to demolish the opinion expressed by Karlgren (1923:4), a pioneer in the modern attempts at the historical reconstruction of Chinese phonology, that "nine-tenths of Chinese characters consist of one 'signific' and one 'phonetic'." In Creel's opinion, based on an analysis of several samples of written materials spanning more than two millennia, the figure was only half that claimed by Karlgren. Creel also took exception to the basis on which Xu Shen and others assigned characters to one or another principle of formation. In his view a great many characters that were classified on a phonetic basis should really have been assigned to one of the three semantic categories. In support of this view he presented alternative explanations for a number of specific characters.

Professor Boodberg, who has a penchant for esoteric phraseology, countered Creel in an article (1937) entitled "Some Proleptical Remarks on the Evolution of Archaic Chinese" in which he presented phonological explanations for characters that Creel had explained on semantic grounds. He also illustrated the need for reconsidering the semantic classification of characters by contending that in the case of Zheng Qiao's 740 "compound indicative" characters, for example, "the majority have to be immediately reclassified as phonetic compounds." Creel (1938) came back with a sharply worded article, "On the Ideographic Element in Ancient Chinese," in which he reiterated his position against that advanced by Boodberg and elaborated on his analysis of a number of Chinese characters. This response so infuriated Boodberg that in an article (1940) entitled " 'Ideography' or Iconolatry?" he tore into Creel's approach, especially as expressed in the latter's textbook *Literary Chinese by the Inductive Method*. Boodberg denounced Creel's "charades" and "sur-realistic phantasies of the ideographs" and expressed his perturbation at "the rise of a methodology which produces, not in comparatively innocuous special articles, but in textbooks through which a new generation of sinologists is expected to be trained, puerilities," such as the explanations of characters presented in Creel's book. Paul Pelliot, the editor of the learned journal *T'oung Pao* in which most of this acrimonious exchange took place, had earlier (1936) chided Creel for minimizing the phonetic aspect of Chinese characters. Now he brought the running battle to a close as far as his journal was concerned with the rather lame excuse that in bringing up comparisons with Sumerian the authors had extended the discussion beyond the scope of the journal.·

A gentler but no less clear rejection of Creel's views is contained in a recent article by Noel Barnard (1978). The author disagrees with Creel's attempt "to view the phonetic aspect of the script as being a highly overrated feature." Pointing out that controlled archeological excavations have brought forth a great deal of new evidence on early Chinese writing, he stresses the important role of "radical + phonetic combinations" in pre-Qin characters. On this point Barnard also takes exception to the opinion expressed by Karlgren that such combinations were restricted in use in early Zhou (about 600 B.C.) and that the majority were created in late Zhou, Qin, and Han when elucidating "radicals" were added to the borrowed characters. In explanation of the disappearance no later than Qin of many radical + phonetic combinations, Barnard also states that "it becomes increasingly evident that phonological considerations had much to do with the discarding of these graphs." The Qin reformers, he says, "were definitely interested in preserving as much as possible complete characters, or particular elements of characters, that presented at the time—I believe it correct to assume—a clear indication of the current pronunciations." To this statement he adds that "the substitution of *modern character replacements* for archaic multielement graphs has been demonstrated to have been largely effected upon a phonetic basis—the old phonetic element being no longer representative of the current pronunciation."

A NEW CHARACTERIZATION

What Barnard in careful detail has shown to be true of the pre-Qin period in regard to the importance of the radical + phonetic combinations appears to apply with perhaps even greater force to the later stages of Chinese writing. This is now the prevailing opinion among most specialists in the field. We can therefore now attempt to reply to the question posed earlier: from pictographs to what?

Of the many specific names that have been proposed for Chinese characters, it is apparent that some, such as "pictographic," are completely inappropriate. The same is true of "ideographic," as will be shown in greater detail later. It also seems that none adequately describes a situation in which an overwhelming majority of the characters contain both a semantic element suggesting a broad category of meaning and a phonetic element suggesting a specific syllable of sound. "Logographic," "lexigraphic," "morphemic," and "morphographic" are good as far as they go, but they do not go far enough. Such terms as "phonosemantic" and "ideophonographic" suggest the two key aspects in question, but they are not sufficiently precise. Gelb's "logo-syllabic" and his and Bloomfield's "word-syllabic" come closest to meeting the requirements, but the "logo" and "word" part of the names needs to be amended to account for the fact that characters should more properly be considered as representing not words but morphemes. I think we should therefore answer the question posed at the beginning of this section by saying that Chinese characters have evolved from pictographic symbols to a morphosyllabic (or possibly syllabomorphemic) system of writing.[3] As to what to call the individual Chinese characters themselves, it follows from this suggested nomenclature that something like "morphosyllabogram" or "morphosyllabograph" would be appropriate, but since these are undesirable jawbreakers, I suggest that we quite simply call them "Chinese characters."

The name "morphosyllabic" is, I believe, an improvement over "logographic," "lexigraphic," "morphemic," and "morphographic" because none of these terms tells us how we get from graph to meaning. This is accomplished, as the next two chapters will show, chiefly by means of the syllabic sound represented by the phonetic element.

simple languages (e.g., Hawaiian and Maori) to sixty or more for the phonologically most complex languages (e.g., some Caucasian languages such as Abkhazian), with most languages falling in the thirty-to-fifty range (Stubbs 1980:48). In the alphabets, roughly speaking, one symbol, which may be a single element such as *t* or *h* or a digraph such as *th*, ideally represents one sound (or one set of morphophonemically related sounds). Departures from this ideal, as in the case of notoriously deficient or clumsy systems such as those used to represent English and Arabic, do not invalidate their inclusion in the broad category of alphabetic systems of writing.

In syllabic systems, such as the two varieties of Japanese kana, a whole syllable is represented by a single grapheme, as illustrated by the use of the single symbol 力 for what we represent with the two Latin letters *ka*. The systems in this category contain an inventory of symbols called a syllabary to represent the individual syllables of speech. The number of different syllables varies much more widely than do phonemes among the languages of the world, as indicated by the fact that Japanese has only 113 whereas English has more than 8,000. Japanese with its simple syllabic structure can manage to get by, with only minor tinkering, with an inventory of only 47 symbols. In the case of several languages with more complex syllabic structures —namely Sumerian, a language of unknown affiliation, Accadian, a Semitic language, and Hittite, an Indo-European language—considerably more cuneiform symbols were needed for writing systems that were basically syllabic despite significant departures from the rough ideal of one syllable–one symbol. Frequently more than one symbol was used to represent one and the same sound. For example, the "chiefly monosyllabic" Sumerian language had twenty-three symbols pronounced *du* that scribes could choose from to represent that syllable (Chiera 1938:63). At times, however, the same cuneiform symbol was used for several sounds, as in the case of the single sign for the syllables *tag, tak, taq* (Gelb 1963:69). Despite such underdifferentiation, the overall inventory of syllabic signs was quite large. Accadian apparently had between 285 (Driver 1976:138) and 350 (Ober 1965: 10). Hittite had about 350 (Gordon Fairbanks 1981:personal communication). More systematic syllabaries created in modern times are similarly characterized by a large inventory of symbols (Gelb 1963: 206–208). One of the best known, still in use, was created in the nineteenth century for the Vai language spoken in Liberia. The majority of syllables in this language are of the consonant plus vowel type, but even with this simple syllabic structure a syllabary of more than two hundred signs was needed (Scribner and Cole 1981:32).

The most striking example of the large number of symbols needed for syllabic representation is the writing of the Yi people, called Lolos by Westerners, a minority nationality with a population of more than 4.8 million scattered throughout the provinces of Yunnan, Guizhou, Sichuan, and Guangxi in Southwest China. The Yi language, which belongs to the Tibeto-Burman group of the Sino-Tibetan family, has an unusually simple—for a Sino-Tibetan language—syllabic structure. According to Ma and Dai (1982), this structure can be represented by (C)V, in which (C) stands for a nonobligatory initial consonant (of which there are forty-three) and V stands for a vowel (of which there are ten) together with its tone (of which there are four). For centuries the language has been written with thousands of unstandardized syllabic symbols that some Qing dynasty sources have likened to tadpoles. In 1975 a standardized syllabary based on the principle of one syllable–one sign was officially adopted. The syllabary consists of 819 signs—756 commonly used ones (Figure 6) plus 63 used to transcribe loanwords, chiefly from Chinese—made up of from one to eight strokes.[1] This appears to be by far the largest standardized syllabic script ever created.

CLASSIFYING CHINESE CHARACTERS

Coming now to Chinese, if we ask whether it had an alphabet, the answer is obviously no. The Chinese characters are not based on any inventory of symbols comparable to the alphabetic scripts used to represent English, Russian, Arabic, and other languages.

Does Chinese then have a syllabary? At first glance the answer to this question too seems to be in the negative. A closer scrutiny suggests a possible positive answer, however, or perhaps a "yes, but" answer. Although the Chinese case is different from the syllabic scripts used for Sumerian and Japanese, Chinese can be seen to have some significant points of similarity with them.

The Japanese syllabaries are distinctive in several ways. They evolved from a miscellaneous assortment of full and reduced Chinese characters used phonetically to a fixed system of simple syllabic signs. They provide a fixed inventory of syllabic signs from which to draw for phonetic representation of spoken words. They arrange the symbols in a fixed order that can serve such functions as dictionary listing.

The cuneiform syllabaries, on the other hand, appear to have evolved more or less haphazardly. The syllabaries that have come to light are of very late date, the seventh century B.C., some 1,500 years after the disappearance of Sumer as a political entity, and they were developed not by the Sumerians but by their conquerors, who compiled "bilingual syllabaries or dictionaries which were translated into their own language, Accadian" (Kramer 1961:5, 9, 21). The more systematic arrangement of the cuneiform symbols was largely the creation of Western scholars.

This matter of arranging things in some sort of order is a good starting point for our consideration of the situation in Chinese. For something like a millennium and a half, it would appear, the Chinese had no special way of grouping their characters. This raises the rather intriguing question of how hapless student scribes went about looking up a character among the 4,500 of the Shang dynasty and the 6,000 to 7,000 (Barnard 1978:212) of Zhou. One wonders also just how the Qin reformers filed characters as they undertook the herculean task of culling over the chaotic assortment of graphs in the process of deciding which to discard and which to retain or revise.[2]

The arrangement of characters into some sort of order was not accomplished until about A.D. 120. At that time Xu Shen compiled an etymological dictionary in which he arranged 9,353 characters under 540 semantic keys, best called "significs" but most often, as already noted, quite misleadingly called "radicals." The characters were ordered on the same principle but with considerable differences in detail in the seventeenth-century dictionary *Zihui* and the great Kang Xi dictionary of 1716. Instead of Xu Shen's classification under 540 semantic categories, the later dictionary reclassified the characters under 214 significs. This system, the sociolinguistic aspects of which are discussed in a stimulating article by T'sou (1981), has been the standard way of arranging characters ever since. However, with the introduction of simplified forms for some of the traditional characters after 1956 in the PRC, the classification has again been reconsidered, with no clear decision as yet as to whether to increase or decrease the number of categories. Recent publications have variously classified characters under 186, 189, 191, 225, 226, and 250 radicals, in addition to the traditional 214.[3] The disparate number of categories of course entails different sequencing and numbering of the radicals (much as if we changed the order of our alphabet), thus adding to the woes of those who need to work with both forms of characters and to use reference tools with different serial arrangements of the radicals and the characters subsumed under them.

These disparate figures underscore the subjective and indeed arbitrary nature of the semantic classifications that have been imposed on the Chinese characters. Xu Shen's 540 significs, Kang Xi's 214, and the more recent 186 to 250 are in no sense a systematic or in any area complete taxonomy of concepts. Each is a haphazard hodgepodge of concepts ranging from the specific to the general: mankind, ten, knife, mountain, step with the left foot, water, fire, tongue, insect, cowry, mineral, door, wind, high, ghost, bird, dragon, and so on. These radical systems constitute a procrustean bed into which all Chinese characters have been forced by dictionary-makers. And forced indeed they were at times, as puzzled students are aware as they attempt to guess what component of a character has been chosen as its radical and hence where the character is likely to be found in a dictionary. The deficiencies of semantic classification can be illustrated by the fact that a popular student dictionary (Mathews 1945) contains a "List of Characters Having Obscure Radicals" that includes one-twelfth of its 7,773 graphs.

Apart from the obvious difference of opinion in the dictionaries as to what constitutes a signific and how many of them there are, equally striking is the fact that the arrangement by radicals, especially the one in preponderant use since the compilation of the Kang Xi dictionary, was so late in coming into being. This arrangement was imposed upon the full-blown and in a sense final graphemic lexicon of Chinese, for very little has been added to the almost fifty thousand characters of the eighteenth-century dictionary. Most striking of all is the fact that the Chinese chose a semantic basis rather than a phonetic one for their system of classification.

ATTEMPTS AT PHONETIC CLASSIFICATION

As in the case of Sumerian, it remained for Western scholars to attempt the task of imposing a phonological classification on the disorderly conglomeration of Chinese characters, a task that essentially involves searching out whether these are based on some sort of underlying Chinese syllabary.

There is something of a mystery about what appears to be the first attempt along these lines. Marshman (1814:33) reports his excitement on seeing an otherwise unidentified "manuscript Latin-Chinese

Dictionary which classed the characters according to their names." He calls the names "primitives" and notes that "all the characters of the dictionary, about nine thousand, were formed from *eight hundred and sixty-two characters, by the addition of only one element*" (Marshman's emphasis). From his illustrations of the primitives it is apparent that Marshman is dealing with a classification based on categories of phonetic elements. Thus he notes that the primitive 利 *(lì)* forms part of sixteen characters of which "eleven of the names are the same syllable with that of the primitive; and all, except one, have the same initial." But such is Marshman's fixation on the role of semantics in character formation that he thinks the primitives "communicate a general idea" and thus completely misses the significance of what is right under his nose. This oversight leads him to far-fetched etymologies based on the meaning of "profitable" or "advantageous" for what the list of characters clearly shows is simply the phonetic use of *lì* (1814:52, 63).

The first to publish a conscious attempt at phonetic classification of characters was a Catholic missionary, J. M. Callery, who in 1841 published his *Systema phoneticum scripturae sinicae* in which he identifies a syllabary of 1,040 characters. In the 1880s a Protestant missionary, W. E. Soothill, classified some 4,300 characters on the basis of 895 phonetics.[4] In 1915 another Catholic missionary came up with "858 phonetic prolific elements" as a result of what he emphasized were researches "circumscribed in the *practical* domain" (Wieger 1965). Less practical but more scientific are the various publications of the Swedish sinologist Bernhard Karlgren, whose path-breaking doctoral dissertation on the reconstruction of the seventh-century Chinese phonetic system was followed by a dictionary of "some six thousand of the most common characters" (Karlgren 1940:11), most of them "phonetic compounds" classified under 1,260 phonetics (Karlgren 1923).

Besides these attempts at phonetic classification by Westerners, there has been one recent attempt by a Chinese scholar. Zhou Youguang, a member of the Committee on Chinese Language Reform who has done much valuable work on Chinese characters, presents a study, unfortunately limited only to simplified characters, in which he identifies a set of 1,348 phonetic elements (1978b:172–177).

The disparity in number of phonetics identified by these scholars reflects the differences of opinion in trying to impose order on the essentially disorderly mass of Chinese characters. It underscores the fact that there was no fixed syllabary upon which the Chinese could draw in creating characters. Instead, the characters as a whole formed a sort of grab bag to be dipped into at will by individual creators of new characters who lived in widely different historical epochs and had widely different dialect backgrounds. As Robert Cheng concludes in his illuminating case study of the character-creation process for Taiwanese (1978:307), "Throughout the history of written Chinese, millions of characters must have been invented and used by individuals for morphemes in everyday speech." However, the fact that the attempts at orderly classification, despite their differences, were able to place most characters in from 858 to 1,260 phonetic categories (or 1,348 counting Zhou's estimate) indicates that the selection of phonetic elements in the creation of characters was not completely a matter of chance.

There are interesting points of similarity between the various syllabaries and the two sets of significs created by Chinese lexicographers —that is, those of the Xu Shen and Kang Xi dictionaries. In both cases the creation of the classification schemes occurred very late: within the last three centuries of the 35-century-long history of Chinese writing, if we leave aside Xu Shen's first halting effort. In both cases the results are subjective and marked by sharp differences of opinion among their creators in identifying and counting the semantic and phonetic elements. Both are gravely imperfect schemes.

The imperfection of the schemes is evidenced by the forced and sometimes seemingly arbitrary allocation of characters under one or another key. In the case of the radical classification, placing the character 王 (*wáng* "king") under the radical 玉 (*yù* "jade") seems quite arbitrary since there does not appear to be any semantic connection between the two, as there is supposed to be between a radical and the characters subsumed under it. The character 玉 (*yù* "jade") is written as 王—that is without the dot—when it occurs as the radical component of a character, and in this form it is identical with 王 (*wáng* "king"), the origin of which is obscure. Apparently the character for "king" is placed under the "jade" radical because of their identity in shape, not because of any semantic relationship. Again, it is no help at all to know that the radical in 孔 (*kǒng* "hole") is no. 39 "child," the radical in 實 (*shí* "true") is no. 40 "roof," the radical in 理 (*lǐ* "principle") is no. 96 "jade," the radical in 紅 (*hóng* "red") is no. 120 "silk," and so on for countless other characters, including many that like those just cited are of very high frequency. Fertile imaginations, to be sure, can often come up with fanciful explanations in cases like these. Whodunit buffs, for example, by exercising their little grey cells can doubtless offer a solution to the mystery of how the character 刷 (*shuā* "brush") acquired its meaning from the combination of radical 18 刂 (*dāo* "knife") and the two additional components 尸 (*shī* "corpse") and 巾 (*jīn* "shroud"). While such explanations may be useful as mnemonics they essentially belong to the category of folk etymology, a favorite pastime of students of Chinese.

In the case of the phonetic classification, Soothill (1942:nos. 71, 72) considers 王 (*wáng* "king") and 匡 (*kuāng* "basket; to aid") as two separate phonetics, whereas Karlgren (1940:no. 739) places them both under the phonetic 王 *(wáng)* because in his reconstruction of their seventh-century pronunciation they differed only in having slightly different initials (**giwang* versus **k'įwang*).

Although the radical and phonetic schemes have much in common in their many imperfections, there is one major difference between the two—namely, that the radical system has acquired an official status and is generally accepted, whereas none of the phonetic schemes has won much recognition. The main reason for this difference is that the dictionary classification of characters by their significs makes it imperative to pay attention to these elements. The phonetic elements, on the other hand, are more easily ignored, a situation further aided by the common idea that the characters have little to do with sounds anyway.

This is a highly unsatisfactory state of affairs. A closer look at the attempts to discover a Chinese syllabary shows that the phonetic elements have a great deal to do with the sounds of Chinese characters. In undertaking this scrutiny it is necessary at the outset to be more specific about a matter that is too often handled in an offhand manner. I refer to the frequently made assertion, which seems to have originated with Karlgren (1923:4), that 90 percent of the characters are phonetic compounds—that is, they are of the "radical + phonetic" type. (Actually, as estimated in Table 3, this figure may be as high as 97 percent.) Karlgren's estimate, as noted earlier, was challenged by Creel. But the disagreement about the proportion of characters that contain a phonetic element misses the main point. It is not enough to know exactly what the figure is. We must also deal with the implication that because a character contains a graphic element labeled a "phonetic," this necessarily helps in deducing the pronunciation of the character. This is not always true, any more than a spelling in English infallibly indicates a particular pronunciation, as indicated by the case of "bow" in "bowknot" and "bowsprit." As we have seen, each of the various Chinese syllabaries mentioned earlier presents a subjective analysis of the phonological grouping of characters, and what may have appeared obvious to one compiler may not be so evident to a user of a compilation. Thus we must try to ascertain on a somewhat more objective basis what proportion of characters contain a *useful* phonetic element—that is, one which gives information of real help to the ordinary reader in guessing the pronunciation of the character of which it forms part.

In making this attempt I shall rely on the material presented by Soothill, even though his work is inferior in scholarship to some of the other studies, especially to the scientific productions of Karlgren. Karlgren's material, however, is cumbersome to work with. Soothill's is the easiest of all in this respect. The present purpose will be well enough served if we make use of Soothill's material since it is likely, if anything, to understate the situation being described. In any event the essential picture would not, I believe, be altered by a more refined analysis based on Karlgren. This belief can be checked by anyone interested in challenging or refining my analysis.

THE SOOTHILL SYLLABARY

We can begin this analysis by noting that of the 1,277 tonal syllables in Chinese, only 558 occur in what I shall refer to as the "Soothill syllabary." These 558 syllables are represented by 895 characters. In most cases a syllable is represented by only one character, but there are many cases among the 558 in which the same syllable is written in more ways than one—as many as twelve in the case of the syllable *yi*, which is variously written as follows:

忘 異 睪 易 乙 執 邑 弋 義 亦 乂 曳

This unstandardized representation of Chinese on the syllabic level parallels the equally unstandardized representation of English on the phonemic level, where "its forty-odd sounds are spelt in more than 600 different ways" (Zachrisson 1931:4)—single letters or combinations of letters, as in the case of the sound *s* represented by *s* in "seed," by *c* in "cede," by *sc* in "scent," by *ss* in "less," and by *ps* in "psalm."

Overall the Soothill syllabary presents a one-to-one correspondence for most syllables, a several-to-one correspondence for some syllables, and no representation for as many as 719 syllables. The majority of the nonrepresented syllables are ones whose segmental phonemes or basic phonemes are represented but not their tones, as in the case of the syllables *mā* and *mǎ,* whose segmental phonemes *ma* are represented by the character 馬 *(mǎ).* Of the 398 basic syllables of Chinese, 312 are represented in Soothill's work and 86 are not.

From the disparity between 719 unrepresented tonal syllables and 86 unrepresented basic syllables, which are equivalent to only some 258 tonal syllables (since there are on the average about three tonal syllables per basic syllable), it is apparent that tones are the primary casualty in representation of Chinese by syllabic signs, as they are in representation of Chinese by Western phonemic transcription that indiscriminately writes *yi* for *yī, yí, yǐ, yì.* The Chinese also, it appears, consider tone representation to be the most dispensable part of their phonetic system of writing, except that instead of writing no tone they use a character with a specific built-in tone as a phonetic in characters that are sometimes pronounced with different tones, as in the case of the third-tone phonetic 馬 *(mǎ* "horse") used in the first-tone character 媽 *(mā* "mother"), in the fourth-tone character 罵 *(mà* "revile"), and in the neutral-tone character 嗎 *(ma* "question particle"). (Some attempt is made, however, to use an appropriately toned phonetic when one is available, as indicated by the fact that all characters pronounced with the second-tone syllable *má* are represented not by the third-tone phonetic *mǎ* "horse" but by the second-tone phonetic 麻 *má* "hemp.")

The omission of eighty-six basic syllables in the Soothill syllabary is due largely to the fact that most of these syllables, such as *gei, seng,* and *nin,* are attached to only one character, or to a very limited number of characters, so that the problem of phonetic elements for the characters representing these syllables is of little concern. Soothill's aim was not to produce a scientifically constructed syllabary but to identify, among the hodgepodge of characters used by the Chinese as phonetic elements, the more productive and hence more useful elements as an aid in the study of Chinese characters. Nor have the Chinese themselves shown any interest in producing such a systematic, standardized syllabary. This would actually be easy enough to do. One procedure might be to select 1,277 characters to represent the equal number of tonal syllables on a one-to-one basis. Another approach might be to select 398 characters as basic syllables which with four added tone marks are all that would be needed for accurate and relatively simple syllabic representation of Chinese. A table of such characters, Soothill's plus additions to fill in his gaps, is presented in Figure 5 as a sort of might-have-been standardized syllabary of Chinese that can be said to have been aborted by the Chinese failure to open up the path that eventually led the Japanese to the creation of their simple kana syllabaries.

Instead of developing a fixed syllabary of this sort, the Chinese left creators of characters, who might be professional scribes or just ordinary scribblers, free to make use of any existing character to represent all or part of the pronunciation of a new character. In view of this haphazard use of phonetic elements, it is not surprising that Soothill's list of phonetics fails to account for the pronunciation of certain characters and gives only partial hints of the pronunciation of many others.

Examination of the Soothill syllabary reveals two further points of note. The first is that, apart from serving as phonetic elements in other characters of which they form part, most of the 895 phonetics occur as independent characters with individual meanings. Moreover, these 895 phonetic elements occur not just in some other characters but, as will be shown below, in almost all other characters.

In view of all this, I think there is much justification in labeling the 895 phonetics as the Soothill syllabary and looking upon it as a sort of Chinese syllabary, albeit a very poor one, since virtually all Chinese characters consist either wholly or in part of these phonetic elements. There are, however, at least two reasons why there might be objections to this characterization. The first is the appallingly large number of units contained in the syllabary. We normally expect a syllabary to be within reason numerically, like the well-known kana syllabaries of only forty-seven signs in Japanese. In point of fact, however, such an expectation is unreasonable. Ideally, in phonetic representation, except for morphophonemic spellings, there should be one-to-one correspondence between sound and symbol. Since in every language there are far more syllables than phonemes, syllabic representation must inevitably require more symbols than phonemic representation. Moreover, the more phonologically complex a language, the more symbols will be needed for syllabic representation. In contrast to the mere 113 syllables of Japanese, Chinese may at one time have had as many as 3,877 different syllables (Kennedy 1964:113–114). It is apparent that the 850 to 1,260 signs of the reconstructed syllabaries, excessive though they appear to be, were actually too few in number, so that underdifferentiation, a feature common to *all* systems of writing, was particularly pronounced in the case of Chinese.

The problem of underdifferentiation in Chinese is compounded by the fact that syllabaries are less amenable than alphabets to manipulation to compensate for the lack of one-to-one correspondence. Although the twenty-six letters of the English alphabet are not enough to provide one-to-one correspondence for the thirty-two "simple primary phonemes" of English identified by Bloomfield (1933:91) or the "forty-odd sounds" referred to by Zachrisson (1931: 4), we can represent the phoneme /ŋ/ by making use of two letters *n* and *g* to form the digraph *ng*, thus enabling us to distinguish "sing" from "sin." Chinese lacks this flexibility. To be sure, it has syllabic symbols in which the finals /n/ and /ŋ/ are distinguished, but these form fixed parts of whole syllables, such as

貧 平 *pín, píng*
笨 蹦 *bèn, bèng*

In choosing specific characters to differentiate two syllables ending in *n* and *ng*, it may be possible to make the differentiation in the finals, but at the cost of being unable to differentiate the initials or the vowels or the tones because these are fixed parts of the whole syllable represented by the syllabic sign and the choice available to us may not be sufficient to distinguish all the phonemes of the syllable. The way in which this limitation works in actual practice can be illustrated by the example of the recent change of the complex character 燈 (*dēng* "lamp") to the simplified form 灯. The phonetic element in the complex character is 登 (*dēng*), exactly the same in pronunciation as that of the complex character itself. The phonetic element in the simplified character is 丁 *(dīng)*. This element was obviously chosen for its simplicity, but while it correctly represents the initial *d*, the final *ng*, and the high level tone, it fails to represent correctly the vowel *e*.

If we bear in mind the foregoing remarks and recall the Vai syllabary of 200-odd signs, the cuneiform syllabaries of 280 to 350 signs, and especially the Yi Syllabary of 819 signs, it might not be too difficult to accept the idea of a Chinese syllabary of 850 or more signs were it not for an even more important objection—namely, that unlike the Japanese kana syllabaries, the Chinese syllabary is extremely complex and only partially reliable. The Chinese did not follow the

Japanese procedure of simplifying their syllabic signs to only a few strokes. Nor did they adopt the procedure of limiting their syllabary to a fixed number of signs to be used in representing the totality of their language. Instead their complex syllabic signs were applied to only 90 percent or so of their characters, and then not always consistently.

FIT BETWEEN PHONETIC AND CHARACTER

A major reason why the Chinese syllabary is only partially reliable in representing the pronunciation of Chinese characters is that historical changes in the form of the characters and the way they have been pronounced have tended to distort what may once have been a closer fit between sound and symbol. To understand this crucial matter of fit, we need to think of each character in the phonetic-compound category in terms of two symbols and two sounds. One symbol is the phonetic element; the other is the whole character of which the phonetic element is part. One sound is the pronunciation of the phonetic element; the other is the pronunciation of the whole character. Each of these two sounds or pronunciations is invariably a syllable, such as *mǎ, fǎn, lǔ.* Sometimes the syllable that constitutes the pronunciation of the phonetic element corresponds 100 percent, even to tone, to the syllable that represents the pronunciation of the whole character. Sometimes the pronunciation of the phonetic element correctly indicates the pronunciation of the whole character except for tone. Sometimes only part of the pronunciation of the phonetic element corresponds to some part of the pronunciation of the whole character, such as the initial or the final. Sometimes the pronunciation of the phonetic element has no point of correspondence with the actual pronunciation of the whole character.

These remarks can be illustrated by looking into Soothill's dictionary, in which the Chinese characters are arranged by their phonetic components. The pronunciations given for these components, and for the characters of which they form part, are those of present-day Mandarin. To be technical, we should cite the Ancient Chinese pronunciations as well, but since our aim is chiefly to check the utility of the phonetics for the average linguistically unsophisticated reader, the current ones will do.

Among the 895 phonetic elements identified by Soothill, we find phonetic 74: 皇 *(huáng)*. As an independent character, it has the meaning "emperor." As a phonetic element, which it is in seven other characters, its meaning becomes irrelevant and only its pronunciation *huáng* counts. This pronunciation indicates with 100 percent accuracy, even to tone, the pronunciation of all seven characters of which phonetic 74 is part. Phonetic 72 匡 (*kuāng* "to aid") enters into two other characters:

筐 *kuāng* "basket" (with radical 118 "bamboo")
眶 *kuàng* "eye socket" (with radical 109 "eye")

In the first case the character is pronounced identically, even as to tone, as the phonetic. In the second case the pronunciation is the same except for tone. Phonetic 71 王 (*wáng* "king") is the phonetic element in seven characters:

汪 *wāng* "watery" (with radical 85 "water")
往 *wǎng* "toward" (with radical 60 "step with the left foot")
枉 *wǎng* "oppression" (with radical 75 "tree")
旺 *wàng* "bright" (with radical 72 "sun")
弄 *nòng* "toy with" (with radical 55 "hands folded")
聖 *shèng* "sacred" (with radical 128 "ear")
玉 *yù* "jade" (radical 96 "jade")

In four cases the phonetic *wáng* correctly indicates the pronunciation for the segmental phonemes but not for the tones, one being first tone, two third tone, and one fourth tone. In two cases, namely *nòng* and *shèng*, the two characters and their phonetic *wáng* have only the final *ng* in common. The seventh character is none other than *yù* "jade." Here, obviously, the pronunciation of the "phonetic element" has no point of correspondence whatsoever with the pronunciation of the whole character. (As a further complication, phonetic 71, it should be noted, is also the phonetic of phonetic 72 and phonetic 74.)

The syllabic nature of the phonetic elements will perhaps become clearer if we note in the following table the three degrees of possible correspondence between phonetic element and full character as illustrated by characters formed with phonetic 74 皇 *huáng* ("emperor"), phonetic 255 馬 (*mǎ* "horse"), and phonetic 391 堯 (*yáo* "lofty").

Complete identity

皇 *huáng*

惶 *huáng* "afraid" (with radical 61 "heart")

煌 *huáng* "brilliant" (with radical 86 "fire")

蝗 *huáng* "locust" (with radical 142 "insect")

隍 *huáng* "moat" (with radical 170 "mound")

鰉 *huáng* "sturgeon" (with radical 195 "fish")

遑 *huáng* "hasten" (with radical 162 "run")

凰 *huáng* "female phoenix" (with radical 16 "bench")

Identity except for tone in some cases

馬 *mǎ*

瑪 *mǎ* "agate" (with radical 96 "jade")

碼 *mǎ* "weights" (with radical 112 "stone")

螞 *mǎ* "ant" (with radical 142 "insect")

鎷 *mǎ* "masurium" (with radical 167 "metal")

媽 *mā* "mother" (with radical 38 "female")

榪 *mà* "clamp" (with radical 75 "tree")

禡 *mà* "sacrifice" (with radical 113 "omen")

罵 *mà* "scold" (with radical 30 "mouth")

嗎 *ma* "question particle" (with radical 30 "mouth")

Partial similarity in segmental phonemes

堯 *yáo* (*y* changes to *i* after a consonant)

僥 *jiǎo* "lucky" (with radical 9 "man")

澆 *jiāo* "sprinkle" (with radical 85 "water")

磽 *qiāo* "stony soil" (with radical 112 "stone")

翹 *qiáo* "tail feather" (with radical 124 "feather")

曉 *xiǎo* "dawn" (with radical 72 "sun")

驍 *xiāo* "fine horse" (with radical 187 "horse")

撓 *náo* "scratch" (with radical 64 "hand")

橈 *náo* "oar" (with radical 75 "tree")

譊 *náo* "dispute" (with radical 149 "word")

鐃 *náo* "hand-bells" (with radical 167 "metal")

嬈 *ráo* "graceful" (with radical 38 "female")

繞 ráo "wind around" (with radical 120 "silk")

蕘 ráo "rushes" (with radical 140 "grass")

蟯 ráo "tapeworm" (with radical 142 "insect")

饒 ráo "abundant" (with radical 184 "food")

燒 shāo "burn" (with radical 86 "fire")

The phonetic elements such as those just described are present in the characters belonging to the phonetic-compound category in combination with semantic elements, the significs or so-called radicals. Since there are 214 radicals and 895 phonetics in Soothill's syllabary, there are almost 200,000 possible combinations of the two. In actual fact only a fraction of this number actually occurs, so that if we imagine a matrix with numbers 1 to 214 on one side and 1 to 895 on the other, there would be many empty squares. More important, however, is the fact that all but a small percentage of Chinese characters can be fitted into this matrix.

It may be informative to note some examples in which a few radicals combine with a few phonetics to produce a number of combinations that are phonetically related through their common phonetics and semantically differentiated by their different significs. Table 4 (adapted from Gabelentz 1881:50–51) presents characters formed by combining four radicals (those numbered 9, 64, 75, 85 and meaning "man," "hand," "tree," "water" respectively) and four phonetics (Soothill's nos. 264 áo "ramble," 282 cān "reflect on," 391 yáo "lofty," 597 fǔ "begin").

As one can see from reading across the rows, the meanings of the radicals give a broad hint of the meanings of the compound characters. As reading down the columns shows, the meanings of the phonetics, on the other hand, do not. It is only their sounds that count. But it is also apparent from Table 4, and from the previous references to phonetics 71, 72, and 74, that the phonetics are only partly reliable as guides to the pronunciation of the full characters, and one may wonder about the basis for placing some of the characters together. On this question there are indeed differences of opinion.

With respect to Soothill's phonetics 71 and 72, it has already been noted that Karlgren lumps these together under one phonetic because earlier in their history they closely resembled each other in sound. Karlgren's historical reconstructions, though challenged in certain important details on methodological grounds (Serruys 1960;

Kratochvíl 1977), suggest the additional help that a knowledge of phonology, especially historical phonology, is able to provide in relating the pronunciation of the phonetic to that of the full character. Still further help can be derived from a knowledge of more than one Chinese dialect since the relationship between phonetic elements and full characters is different for different dialects because of their differing phonological histories. Individual readers of Chinese will therefore differ greatly in their pronunciation-guessing ability, which will of course be much greater for native speakers than for struggling foreign students of the language. Generally speaking, throughout the discussion the points of correspondence that have been mentioned are limited to those that might be noted by the average reader on the basis of the present-day pronunciation of Chinese. This oversimplified approach doubtless compounds my underestimation of the phonetic component in Chinese writing.

All this should be noted with particular care by nonspecialists in Chinese. The references to Chinese historical phonology should receive special attention because it is widely believed that the great achievements of nineteenth-century linguistics with respect to comparative and historical phonology of Indo-European languages are uniquely due to the existence of alphabetic scripts, and that such work is impossible in character-based systems of writing. But it is precisely because the phonetic element exists in Chinese characters that scholars like Karlgren have been able to do historical reconstruction that results in our knowledge of how Ancient Chinese was pronounced in the seventh century.

EFFECTIVENESS OF PHONETIC ELEMENTS

While insisting on the importance of the phonetic component in Chinese characters, we must also, as the previous discussion makes plain, guard against the tendency to accept without question broad statements to the effect that nine-tenths of Chinese characters contain a phonetic element. It should now be clear that we must note how effective these elements really are in suggesting the pronunciation of the characters of which they form part. Moreover, we must not forget that the 895 phonetics identified by Soothill have an independent existence. This means that we must look for more concrete data regarding the phonetic clues to be found in the course of reading Chinese.

Table 4 Combinations of Radicals and Phonetics

Radical	Phonetic 264 (áo)	Phonetic 282 (cān)	Phonetic 391 (yáo)	Phonetic 597 (fǔ)
9 亻	傲 (áo: "proud")	傪 (cān: "good")	僥 (jiǎo: "lucky")	俌 (fǔ: "help")
64 扌	摮 (áo: "shake")	摻 (shān: "seize")	摲 (nǎo: "scratch")	捕 (bǔ: "catch")
75 木	槝 (áo: "barge")	槮 (shēn: "beam")	橈 (náo: "oar")	楠 (fǔ: "trellis")
85 氵	滶 (áo: "stream")	滲 (shèn: "leak")	澆 (jiāo: "sprinkle")	浦 (pǔ: "creek")

Table 5 Occurrence of Phonetics in Chinese Characters

1 Rank Order by Frequency	2 Independent Phonetics	3 Phonetic Compounds	4 Compounds with Useful Phonetics	5 Col. 4 / Col. 3	6 Col. 2 + 4 / Col. 1
1–100	52	48	5 + 5 + 8 =18	10 + 10 + 17 =37%	70%
1,001–1,100	22	78	17 + 12 + 13 =42	22 + 15 + 17 =54%	64%
2,001–2,100	7	93	15 + 16 + 43 =74	16 + 17 + 46 =79%	81%
3,001–3,100	7	87	29 + 20 + 16 =65⁵	33 + 23 + 18 =74%⁵	72%
4,001–4,100	3	88	31 + 14 + 12 =57⁵	35 + 16 + 14 =65%⁵	60%
Total 500	91	394	97 + 67 + 92 =256	25 + 17 + 24 =66%	69%

We note, first of all, that some phonetics not only occur independently but also occur quite frequently by themselves. This is important because a frequently occurring character obviously has a greater bearing on the reading process than one which occurs only once, say, in a million characters of running text. Moreover, we must note whether the phonetic element in a specific phonetic compound is useful or not in enabling us to guess the pronunciation of the whole character. Phonetics that are completely identical to that of the whole character, or identical except for tone, are clearly useful in our guessing game. More marginal are those in which there is correspondence only in some of the segmental phonemes.

With these considerations in mind, let us examine a cross section of 500 characters out of the 4,719 different characters that were found to occur in a frequency count made by Chen Heqin (1928) of 900,000 characters of running text. The results of this examination are presented in Table 5.

The first column in Table 5, in which the characters in Chen's list have been ranked by frequency (the most frequent being ranked 1 and the rarest 4,719), shows the rank order by frequency of five samplings of one hundred characters each that were chosen for examination. Column 2 notes that of the one hundred most frequently occurring characters in Chinese, fifty-two are independent characters which are to be found among Soothill's 895 phonetics. It also notes that there are twenty-two such independent phonetics among the characters having the rank order 1,001–1,100, seven among those having the rank order 2,001–2,100, and so on. Column 3 tells us how many of the remaining characters in the sample of one hundred can be classified as phonetic compounds—that is, contain one of Soothill's 895 phonetics: forty-eight in 1–100, seventy-eight in 1,001–1,100, ninety-three in 2,001–2,100, and so on.[6] Column 4 tells us how many, and column 5 tells us what proportion, of the phonetic compounds have phonetic elements that suggest the pronunciation of the characters of which they form part. The first figure refers to the number of characters with complete identity, including tone, between phonetic element and full character; the second figure refers to the number identical except for tone; the third figure refers to the number where only some of the segmental phonemes correspond (at least half of these—enough, in my judgment, to be of use in our pronunciation-guessing game); and the last figure refers to the total of the preceding three. In the first hundred characters, for example, five

(10 percent) of the forty-eight phonetic compounds have completely identical phonetics, five (10 percent) have phonetics identical except for tones, and eight (17 percent) have phonetics with only partial correspondence in the segmental phonemes—making a total of eighteen (37 percent) with useful phonetics.[7] Column 6 shows the total percentage of independent phonetics and compounds with useful phonetics.

From Table 5 we can see that in our total sample of 500 characters, 91 (18 percent) are independent phonetics and 394 (79 percent) are phonetic compounds, leaving only 15 (a mere 3 percent) with no phonetic aspect at all. High-frequency characters include fewer phonetic compounds than do rare characters. Conversely, the characters of highest frequency, such as the first hundred, are strikingly represented by phonetics functioning as independent characters. The fact that decreasing rank order of frequency is marked by a decreasing number of independent phonetics (52–22–7–7–3) but by a greater number of phonetic compounds (48–78–93–87–88), especially compounds with useful phonetics (18–42–74–65–57), means that the two opposite trends cancel each other out and make for a consistently high proportion (60 to 81 percent) of characters with a useful phonetic aspect.

Note also that the hundred most frequently occurring characters alone comprise an astonishing 47 percent of the total of 900,000 characters of running text counted by Chen Heqin,[8] and that the 1,100 most frequently occurring characters comprise approximately 90 percent. If a reader of Chinese knew only a hundred characters, almost every other character in a piece of writing would be familiar to him. With a knowledge of 1,100 characters, only every tenth character would be unfamiliar, and in two-thirds of the remaining 90 percent of the characters there would be a useful phonetic clue to help the reader recall the pronunciation of the character. Indeed, this two-thirds figure of useful phonetic clues also applies to the 10 percent of the characters with a lower rank frequency than 1,100. Thus a reader with a knowledge of the phonetic component in Chinese writing has two chances out of three of guessing correctly the pronunciation of any given character he is likely to encounter in reading.

Success in guessing the pronunciation of a character depends on the type of character. As the preceding paragraphs indicate, the characters in Chen Heqin's list can be placed in three phonetically determined groups: (1) those in the Chinese syllabary—that is, Soothill's

895, which are, by definition, 100 percent phonetic; (2) phonetic compounds, 100 percent of which nominally contain phonetics, though these may vary in their actual usefulness; (3) nonphonetic characters—that is, those other than Karlgren's 90 percent in the "radical + phonetic" category. For purposes of comparison it is useful to note the distribution of these three groups in the Soothill dictionary, the Chen Heqin list, and the Kang Xi dictionary. This distribution is indicated in Table 6.

Table 6   Distribution of Phonetically Determined Characters

Type of Character	Soothill	Chen Heqin	Kang Xi
Syllabary	895 (21%)	660 (14%)[9]	895 (2%)
Phonetic compound	3,405 (79%)	3,917 (83%)	43,777 (90%)[10]
Nonphonetic	0 (0%)	142 (3%)	3,969 (8%)
Total	4,300 (100%)	4,719 (100%)	48,641 (100%)

Although the figures for the Soothill and Kang Xi dictionaries are of some interest, the most significant figures in Table 6 are those based on Chen Heqin's count, since this number reflects characters used in real life, not those embalmed in dictionaries. The fact that only about 660, or three-quarters of Soothill's syllabary, appear in Chen's list of characters particularly speaks to this point.

There is no way, short of examining every one of the estimated 3,917 phonetic compounds on Chen's list, to determine how many of the 895 phonetics besides the 660 independent ones actually occur as part of the compounds. But let us assume that all of them do and hence must be memorized. A knowledge of these 895 will, obviously, include the 660 that occur as independent phonetics. But in addition they provide the basis for guessing the pronunciation of other characters in Chen's list. According to the figures provided in Table 5, we can do so with complete accuracy for 25 percent of the characters, with accuracy except for tones for another 17 percent, and with somewhat less but still sufficient accuracy for still another 24 percent—in all, 66 percent of the 3,917 phonetic compounds, namely 2,585. A knowledge of the syllabary will thus provide a key to the pronunciation of two-thirds of the 4,719 characters in Chen's list. My guess is that the proportion might be a little less for Soothill's dictionary and a little more for Kang Xi. This is a far cry from a good phonetic system, but it is certainly a farther cry from no phonetic system at all.

This discussion has been based on the old complex characters, since these are the forms used in Soothill's and Chen Heqin's works. I have

not studied what difference, if any, exists between the complex characters and the simplified forms now used in China. With respect to
the latter, we have only the figures provided in the thoughtful study
by Zhou Youguang (1978b) of the characters contained in the 1971
edition of the *Xinhua Zidian*. The comparability of our materials is
difficult to determine. Without attempting a detailed comparison,
we may briefly note that Zhou provides figures which can be tabu-
lated as follows:

1,348 (17%)	phonetic elements
6,542 (81%)	phonetic compounds
185 (2%)	"isolated" (nonphonetic) characters
8,075 (100%)	

Zhou considers that 3,117 (48 percent) of the 6,542 phonetic compounds contain useful phonetic elements, which he defines as phonetics identical except for tones—that is, excluding those with only
partial correspondence in the segmental phonemes. If we add this
figure to the 17 percent comprised by the phonetics themselves, this
means that a total of about 65 percent of the characters in the dictionary are phonetically identifiable on the basis of what we might call
the "Zhou syllabary." If the criterion of usefulness is extended to
include phonetics with only partial correspondence in the segmental
phonemes, the overall figure would be even higher, a fact that is to
be explained, in part at least, by Zhou Youguang's use of a larger syllabary, which obviously makes for greater correspondence between
phonetic element and phonetic compound. In any case his study
shows that the phonetic aspect remains important in simplified characters despite the fact, as shown by Sally Ng (1976), that no special
use was made of the phonetic principle in the process of simplifying
the characters.

It might be useful to check my claim of 66 percent utility, as I
defined it, against a small sample text. An examination of Lu Xun's
famous story "Diary of a Madman" shows that of the first hundred
characters in the diary, fifty-eight are independent phonetic characters. The remaining forty-two are all phonetic compounds, of which
fourteen (33 percent) contain phonetic elements that give some useful hints regarding the pronunciation of the characters of which they
form part.[11] This means that no less than 72 percent of the characters
in this small sample have a significant phonetic aspect.

CHINESE AS A SYLLABIC SCRIPT

It should be apparent that there is much justification for considering the Chinese script to be basically—that is, more than anything else—a phonetic system of writing. The question then arises as to where to place Chinese among other phonetic schemes. Since a Chinese character is not made up of letters representing phonemes, it certainly cannot be classified with orthographies such as Spanish and German, which are rather efficiently phonemic, or even with English, which is less efficiently phonemic—take, for example, the Chinese-style "phonetic elements" that are inconsistent in the sounds they represent, like the *ough* of "though," "thought," "through," "tough," "bough." The Chinese phonetic elements represent not phonemes but syllables. This makes them closer to the kana, Vai, Yi, cuneiform, and hieroglyphic systems. We should therefore classify the Chinese phonetic elements together with all these systems as constituting a single broad family of syllabic scripts.

The Chinese syllabary is of the same order of size as the 819-unit Yi syllabary, but the latter has two points of superiority in that the symbols are simple in structure and there is a one-to-one correspondence between sound and symbol. The kana syllabaries have more or less the same advantages plus the added advantage of being much smaller in size. Comparatively speaking, the Japanese syllabaries are quite simple and efficient. Their forty-seven symbols do a reasonably good job of representing the sound system of Japanese with its mere 113 different syllables. In contrast, the Chinese syllabary, which must cope with a far more complex syllabic system (3,877 syllables in earlier Chinese and 1,277 in current standard Chinese if tones are included, 398 if tones are excluded), is not only appallingly large but also quite unstandardized and hence extremely inefficient—all this of course due to the fact that it has not been manipulated and refined like the Japanese syllabaries but throughout its history right down to today has evolved in a more or less haphazard manner. This extreme inefficiency should not, however, blind us to the essential fact that the Chinese syllabary does provide useful phonetic clues in the overwhelming majority of Chinese characters. Moreover, the fact that the Chinese syllabary is an extremely bad one, whereas the Japanese syllabaries are fairly good, should not lead us to conclude that we must not classify the Chinese system of writing together with the Japanese kana systems as syllabic, any more than the badness of English spelling, compared to the excellence of Spanish, invalidates classifying our orthography together with Spanish as phonemic or, more accurately, morphophonemic.

The Japanese syllabaries are relatively efficient because there is something approaching a one-to-one correspondence between spoken syllable and its written representation. Finnish even more than Spanish is an example of phonemic writing whose well-known efficiency stems from a similar correspondence between spoken phoneme and graphic representation. Chinese and English are inefficient because what may at one time have been a close correspondence between sound and symbol has now broken down. In the case of English, as already noted, "its forty-odd sounds are spelt in more than 600 different ways" (Zachrisson 1931:4). Here are some examples of the vagaries of English spelling:

Same Sound *(o)*, Different Spellings	Same Spelling *(o)*, Different Sounds
so *(o)*	so
sow *(ow)*	to
sew *(ew)*	on
oh *(oh)*	honey
owe *(owe)*	horse
dough *(ough)*	woman
doe *(oe)*	women
beau *(eau)*	borough
soak *(oa)*	
soul *(ou)*	

The situation in English is the exact parallel of that in Chinese, except that the vagaries are on the phonemic level whereas in Chinese they are on the syllabic level:

Same Sound *(lì)*, Different Spellings	Same Spelling (立), Different Sounds
粒 (立)	粒 *(lì)*
俐 (利)	拉 *(lā)*
儷 (麗)	泣 *(qì)*
溧 (栗)	位 *(wèi)*
瀝 (歷)	
礪 (厲)	

The poor correspondence between sound and symbol in both English and Chinese is not surprising if we keep the matter in historical perspective. As Gelb (1979:1041) observes:

> While the connections between language and writing are close, there has never been a one-to-one correspondence between the elements of language and the signs of writing. The "fit" (i.e., the correspondence) between language and writing is generally stronger in the earlier days and weaker in its later stages. This is because a writing system when first introduced generally reproduces rather faithfully the underlying phonemic structure (structure of sounds). In the course of time, writing, more conservative than language, generally fails to keep up with the continuous changes of language and, as time progresses, diverges more and more from its linguistic counterpart. A good example is the old Latin writing, with its relatively good "fit" between graphemes (the written letters or group of letters that represent one phoneme or individual sound) and phonemes as compared with present-day French or English writing, with their tremendous divergences between graphemes and phonemes. In some cases, recent spelling reforms have helped to remedy the existing discrepancies between writing and language. The best "fit" between phonemes and graphemes has been achieved in the Korean writing in the 16th century [*sic*] and in the Finnish and Czech writings of modern times.

It is because of the widespread discrepancies noted above that Kōno (1969:85) places English in the category of logographic scripts along with Chinese while Zachrisson (1931:5) goes so far as to contend that "English shares with Chinese the doubtful honor of being made up chiefly of ideographs, pictures of words which must be seen and remembered." Both views are wrong, Zachrisson's ridiculously so, since even sight words like "the" and "one" that are often taught to children without regard to "phonics" are by no stretch of the imagination pictures totally devoid of phonetic clues, as witness *th* in "the" and *n* in "one."

If we compare the Chinese and Japanese writing systems as a whole, the Japanese system being the mixture of sinographs or kanji and syllabic kana in general use, it appears that the latter has an edge in at least two respects. In the first place, the simpler phonological structure of Japanese has resulted in the falling together of many "phonetic elements" which were pronounced differently in the original Chinese. These elements therefore have greater predictive value in indicating the pronunciation of characters of which they form part. Secondly, and more important, in a running text Japanese has a distict advantage over Chinese in that the mixture of purely phonetic kana and partially phonetic sinographs, which occur in the ratio of 5 to 3 in current publications (Liu 1969:50), makes for a higher proportion of phonetic writing overall. Moreover, the concurrent use of purely phonetic symbols in such functions as case markers and verb endings makes it easier for readers to segment a text—that is, to determine what goes with what.

This Japanese advantage is shared by Korean, which has the added advantage of having borrowed Chinese characters with even less phonetic irregularity than in the case of kanji. As a result the phonetic element in sinographs used in Korean writing appears to be more useful than is the case in Japanese. It is of interest to note that an attempt has been made, somewhat along the lines of Soothill's work, to assemble a sort of Sino-Korean syllabary. Basing his work on a Korean dictionary of 2,200 sinographs, which is close to the number in general use today, Allocco (1972) has devised a study aid in the form of a syllabary of some four hundred characters on the basis of which it is possible to predict with 100 percent accuracy the pronunciation of half the characters in the dictionary.

There is one other element that bears on this question of the inferiority of the Chinese system of writing relative to the Japanese, not to mention the Korean. The kana syllabaries were created more than a thousand years ago. But after the beginning of Japan's modern era in 1868, and even as recently as after World War II, they underwent a process of simplification and standardization that marks the culmination of what Miller describes as "a long process of gradual reduction in graphic redundancy." In a sense, he continues (1967:125–126),

> the present-day *kana* syllabaries were not so much invented as they were left standing as the end products of centuries of slow and gradual attrition, which chipped away the grander outlines of a once prolix and redundant graphic system, so that by the modern period there was left only a bare (and very efficient) skeleton of the original.

The Chinese writing system, on the other hand, is more inefficient precisely because *there has been no parallel development of simplification and standardization in the case of its syllabary.* The exact situation in Chinese can be seen most clearly if we note the implications of

Barnard's discussion of the Qin writing reform of the third century B.C. that was cited earlier. The procedure adopted by the Qin reformers of standardizing the characters by selecting phonetic elements that most closely resembled the then current pronunciations must be viewed in its full significance as a veritable spelling reform.[12] As Chao Yuen Ren notes (1976:92), however, "the so-called phonetic compounds represented sounds fairly closely when they were made, but often are no longer appropriate for modern pronunciations."

The fact that there has not been another spelling reform since the third century B.C. goes far to explain why the phonetic elements do such a poor job of representing present-day pronunciation. English and French spelling are only a few hundred years out of date, Chinese more than two millennia. If English spelling remains unchanged for another millennium and a half, in the year 3500 (at which time it will approximate the age of present-day Chinese spelling) will future scholars wonder how to explain the ability of a system so seemingly divorced from speech to function as a means of conveying thought?

7.
How Do Chinese Characters
Convey Meaning?

The question posed in the title is part of the specifically Chinese aspect of the universal problem of reading, a subject that has engendered a vast literature, some of it highly polemical, stemming from conflicting theories in the fields of psychology and pedagogy. Most of the literature deals with English and other Western languages. There is a small and little-known body of material dealing with Chinese that has been produced mainly by scholars in the field (see Tzeng et al. 1977; Tzeng, Hung, and Garro 1978; Tzeng and Hung 1980; Treiman, Baron, and Luk 1981). Better known and more influential are the frequent references by psycholinguists and other specialists to the Chinese writing system in relation to reading. These scholars have taken up the ideographic concept promoted by Creel, Margouliès, and others and claim that Chinese characters show how readers can grasp meaning from written symbols without what they call "decoding to sound" (Smith 1973:74). Is this really the case?

APPROACHING THE PROBLEM

In approaching this question it is desirable to distinguish—as reading specialists should always do but often don't—between deciphering something new and recalling something learned, between learning to read and using a highly developed skill, between careful scrutiny of a difficult word or phrase and rapid reading of easy or familiar material, and between various other aspects of the wider problem. Let us start, then, by speculating about a quite specific question: How might a literate Chinese derive meaning from a single isolated unknown character? As a typical character we can take one belonging to the vast majority of graphs that consist of two parts: a semantic element and a phonetic element. Can it be that they are there for a reason, that the reader makes use of both? How might a native speaker of Chinese go about doing so?

At times the semantic elements—that is, the significs or radicals—do indeed provide a significant clue to the meaning of a character, as in the case of the mouth radical 口 in identifying the meaning of the character 喃 *(nán)* as "to babble." Sometimes the signific is of no help at all, if not actually misleading, as in the case of 罵, one of the ways of writing *mà* ("to revile"). The bottom part of this character is the useful phonetic 馬 *(mǎ)*, but the top part is the hardly illuminating radical 皿 ("net"). Sometimes use of one radical or another can have a special significance, as in the case of removing an ethnic slur from the name of the Zhuang minority in southwest China, which used to be written with the dog radical but after 1949 was first written with the human radical and was later changed to a completely different character with the respectable meaning "sturdy":

> 獞 *Zhuàng* (with the dog radical)
> 僮 *Zhuàng* (with the human radical)
> 壯 *Zhuàng* ("sturdy")

Although the radicals give some information in many cases, for the most part they provide little more than a very vague hint. The reader must use this hint to reach the specific idea that the word or morpheme represented by the whole character is meant to convey. The hint provided by the radical reminds one of the guessing game that asks "Is it animal, vegetable, or mineral?" After receiving an answer the questioner goes on to ask additional questions, each narrowing the range of possibilities until the solution to the puzzle is reached. I suggest as a hypothesis that readers of Chinese go through some such procedure in making use of the phonetic and semantic elements in their character-guessing game.

A SINGLISH APPROACH

The procedure to follow in using the two elements can perhaps best be conveyed if we look at the problem from a Singlish point of view. Let us start by noting the two Chinese radicals 氵, which stands for the word meaning "water," and 亻, which stands for the word meaning "man." Next we create composite Singlish characters by combining the semantic elements for "water" and "man" on the left with some other element on the right:

1a. ⟩X   2a. ⼦X

In these Singlish characters the letter X could be replaced by any squiggles we want. The two-stroke letter X has been chosen because it is easy to remember. It is meant to play the role of the so-called Chinese phonetic, which in actual Chinese characters consists of a series of strokes that represent nothing individually (they are *not* letters) but taken together have a certain phonetic value, more specifically a syllabic value. Let us say, since we are dealing with Singlish characters, that X has the pronunciation *rane* (rhymes with *Dane*). Now we create two more Singlish characters:

1b. ⟩ rane   2b. ⼦ rane

The Singlish characters 1b and 2b exist only in our minds. They are the radicals we recall from 1a and 2a plus the sound we think of in recollecting what the "phonetic" symbol X stands for. Putting it a little differently, more nearly as Chinese readers would view the matter, we think of the Singlish character 1a as having the radical "water," the phonetic X, the pronunciation *rane* for the phonetic X, and a pronunciation for the whole character that we guess also to be *rane* because of the hint provided by the phonetic X. Similarly, character 2a has the radical "man," the phonetic X, the pronunciation *rane* for the phonetic X, and a guessed pronunciation *rane* for the whole character.

We now ask: Do readers, in deciphering characters 1a and 2a on first encounter, and in identifying them later once what they stand for has been learned, go directly from the symbol to the meaning? Or do readers go through the intermediary stage, represented by 1b and 2b, in which the characters are considered in connection with their pronunciation?

In what we might call the direct approach, readers must employ some such procedure as thinking of 1a versus 2a as "the X having to do with water" versus "the X having to do with man." This strategy will not get them very far in deciphering these unknown characters. They must use some additional means, such as consulting a dictio-

nary, after which on encountering the characters again they are supposed to recall the meanings directly by using only the total configuration of 1a and 2a consisting of the common element X and the
differentiating radicals for water and man.

In the indirect approach, in which readers use their knowledge of
the pronunciation of the characters, as in 1b and 2b, they employ a
version of Twenty Questions in trying to arrive at the meaning of the
two homophonous words pronounced *rane*. In so doing they seek further clues by asking, in the manner of our guessing game, "Is the
rane animal, vegetable, or mineral?" The radical of the first character
suggests the answer "mineral." The radical of the second character
suggests the answer "animal." They then guess that "mineral rane
= rain" and "animal rane = reign." Readers might also start by
evoking from the radicals the words (*not* directly the concepts)
"water" and "man" and then going on to guess that "water rane =
rain" and "man rane = reign." It is also possible that the semantic
and phonetic clues are in fact operated on not sequentially but simultaneously.

For a variety of reasons, the solution to these Singlish character
puzzles, and to others involving real Chinese characters, may not be
as easy as it has been made out to be in these examples. Perhaps the
written word is not part of the readers' vocabulary. Perhaps the
readers are poor guessers. Perhaps the phonetic and semantic clues
are so inadequate that even good guessers would fail, as might be the
case, to take our Singlish examples, if the phonetic X were pronounced *Dane* whereas the whole character is pronounced *rane*, so
that only the final *ane* of the phonetic X is a valid clue. In these cases
our "indirect readers," like the "direct readers," must seek help elsewhere, perhaps from the context or by consulting a dictionary, after
which they memorize that "water Dane = water rane = rain" and
"man Dane = man rane = reign." But unlike the direct readers,
our indirect readers, once they have learned the pronunciation of a
character, will make use of their knowledge of its pronunciation when
they again encounter the character.

The difference between the two approaches can be made clearer,
perhaps, if we use our Singlish characters in sentences such as the following:

1a. The ⟩X lasted forty days. ("The X-having-to-do-with-water
lasted forty days.")

2a. The 亻X lasted forty days. ("The X-having-to-do-with-man lasted forty days.")

1b. The 氵rane lasted forty days. ("The rane-having-to-do-with-water lasted forty days.")

2b. The 亻rane lasted forty days. ("The rane-having-to-do-with-man lasted forty days.")

The approach embodied in sentences 1a and 2a, which make no use of phonetic clues, is clearly insufficient. On the other hand, the approach embodied in sentences 1b and 2b, which do use the phonetic clue, easily enables readers to disambiguate the sentences and to understand them as representing the following:

1. The rain lasted forty days.
2. The reign lasted forty days.

The discussion of the decipherment process and disambiguating technique in terms of two made-up Singlish characters can now be illustrated with concrete examples by citing two authentic Chinese characters with forms a little like our imaginary ones:

1. 汀   2. 仃

The common phonetic element on the right of both characters (phonetic 2 in the Chinese syllabary) has the pronunciation *dīng*. The second character, which has the man radical and means "alone," is pronounced *dīng*. In this case the phonetic element represents the four phonemes (initial *d*, vowel *i*, final consonant *ng*, and high level tone) with 100 percent accuracy. The first character, which has the water radical and means "sandspit," is pronounced *tīng*. In this case the phonetic element represents the four phonemes with 75 percent accuracy—actually more if we take into account that *t* is the aspirated equivalent of unaspirated *d*.

In attaching meaning to the two real characters, Chinese readers, like our "indirect readers" of the Singlish characters, will probably go through a mental process involving both the radical and the phonetic —in one approach starting with the semantic element, in another with the phonetic. In the first approach, that starting with the semantic element, they begin by deriving from the radicals the words (*not* directly the concepts) for "water" and "man." Then they think of the pronunciation *dīng* for the phonetic. Finally they combine the semantic and phonetic elements by thinking of the second character as "man *dīng* = alone" and the first as "water *dīng* = water *tīng* = sandspit." In the second approach, that starting with the phonetic element, they think: "The *dīng*-having-to-do-with-man means alone, the *dīng*-having-to-do-with-water is actually pronounced *tīng* and means sandspit."

A WIDER VIEW OF DISAMBIGUATION

In Chinese, as both the preceding pair of real Chinese characters and the pair of made-up Singlish characters indicate, completely or largely homophonous syllables written with a common phonetic can be distinguished in meaning by different radicals. In English, as indicated by the words "rain," "reign," and "rein," homophonous words are sometimes distinguished in meaning by different spellings. The disambiguating procedure in English is largely the result of historical changes in pronunciation, as in the well-known case of "knight" versus "night." In Chinese, on the other hand, the disambiguating technique appears to have been created deliberately. Take, for example, the character 來 *(lái)* cited in the discussion of the phonetic-loan principle in Chapter 5.

The character 來 *(lái)*, it will be recalled, was originally a pictograph meaning "wheat" and was later used as a rebus symbol to represent the sound of the homophonous syllable meaning "come." Subsequently the original use was abandoned. But the new function as a syllabic symbol received a further extension. Apart from its independent use in the meaning "come," it also came to be used as the phonetic element in the radical + phonetic compound 徠 *(lái:* "come")—that is, with the addition of radical 60 彳 ("step with the left foot"). The rebus use of the character 來 received still another extension when the graph entered into the radical + phonetic compound 萊 *(lái:* "thistle")—that is, with the addition of radical 140 艹 ("grass"). Here the character 來 has lost both its original meaning of "wheat" and its secondary meaning of "come" and is further used purely in its syllabic value to indicate the pronunciation of still another homophonous but semantically unrelated word. We have here an evolutionary development in writing that can be outlined as follows:

1. 來 (*lái:* "wheat")
2. 来 (*lái:* "come")
3. 徠 (*lái:* "come")
4. 萊 (*lái:* "thistle")

The Chinese procedure of adding different radicals to a common phonetic is similar to the procedure adopted in both Mesopotamia and Egypt of using "determinatives" to suggest the semantic category of homophonous words (Gordon 1968:20–21). Such a disambiguating technique in which many complex significs are joined with even more numerous and perhaps even more complex phonetics undoubtedly provides better visual clues than do the few simple letters of our alphabet—though at the cost, of course, of considerably greater effort in mastering the more complex writing system in the first place.

In noting the disambiguating function of the Chinese determinatives, the miscalled "semantic elements" or "radicals," it should be observed that the function is not always carried out by a truly semantic contribution from the semantic element. As noted in the previous chapter dealing with the radical classification of characters, the meaning of the radical often gives no clue to the meaning of a character, and indeed the radical can often be downright misleading—as in the case of 理 (*lǐ* "principle") being distinguished from its completely homophonous phonetic element 里 (*lǐ* "mile") by the addition of the jade radical. In cases like this the disambiguating function of the radical is purely graphic, somewhat as if in English we distinguished "reign" from "rain" by writing the former as "Rain"—that is, using capitalization not in its usual semantic function of indicating proper nouns but merely as a means of visually setting off one otherwise identically written homonym from another.

The semantic elements represented by the radicals were not always added because they were needed as disambiguating elements. Unnecessary elements are a common feature in writing systems, most of which, as Edgerton reminds us, were created by people without linguistic sophistication. "The habitual employment of absolutely useless signs," he adds, "is a conspicuous characteristic of Egyptian orthography" (1940:481–485). It is likely that radicals were required in Chinese only to the extent to which the written style departed from actual speech, but eventually they were mechanically generalized for all characters. A similar point of view is expressed by Boodberg (1957:115):

> Egyptian and cuneiform, where the use of semantic determinatives remained optional and the determinatives themselves detachable from the graphs they determined, moved on apace toward phonetization. In Chinese, the determinatives, semantic or phonetic, were welded securely to their graphs so as to form one single graphic body; diagrammatic structure became thus the dominant type of character building. This may have been caused by a more pronounced homonymy of the Chinese vocabulary, but it must have also been influenced by an aesthetic imperative in the Chinese which prompted them, apparently quite early in the development of the script, to enforce the principle of EQUIDIMENSIONALISM . . . of the graphs.

The presence of semantic elements such as the radicals does not mean that these constitute the chief feature of the Chinese writing system. Quite the contrary, Chinese writing has always evidenced a connection with speech that goes beyond the presence of phonetic elements in characters. Apart from the direct connection between spoken sound and its written representation, there are in Chinese, as in all languages, other ties between spoken word and written symbol. Language is, after all, a great deal more than just its lexicon, whether spoken or written. In contrast to the primitive picture writing of the North American Indians, which never gets beyond the stage of loosely related drawings of considerably less than definite interpretation, Shang writing has all the earmarks of a fully developed graphic system whose characteristics have been determined by a spoken language. The characters are used in a fixed order which resembles the syntactical patterns of later Chinese and are employed in various functions such as noun, pronoun, verb, adverb, adjective, preposition, demonstrative, numeral, and conjunction (Chen Mengjia 1956: 85–134). Such linguistic elements are completely lacking in Amerindian protowriting.

All this attests to the fact that in the case of Chinese also, to borrow one scholar's description of Egyptian, "the main (though not the only) feature of the script is phonetic" (Gordon 1968:24). The main feature, the phonetic, is represented by syllabic graphs, as in the case of 來 *(lái)*. The secondary feature, the semantic, is represented by the added radicals.

TWO COUNTERARGUMENTS

Apart from the discredited contention by Creel and others that what is generally considered to be a phonetic element in the large category of "radical + phonetic" characters should in most cases really be interpreted as having a semantic function, a recent study by Yau Shun-chiu (1983) presents a novel argument for the primacy of the semantic aspect over the phonetic aspect. On the basis of his observations in sign languages and oral languages, he concludes "that there is a universal natural order in the arrangement of linguistic elements in human communication systems, and that this order is governed by cognito-perceptive constraints proper to our species." Reporting on "an investigation into the temporal arrangement of the components of archaic Chinese ideograms" in the first millennium and a half of their development, he speaks of

> the growing practice of adding an extra grapheme to a semantic category base to form a new character. . . . The function of the additional grapheme can be analyzed on two different levels, phonetic and graphic. On the phonetic level it can only suggest an approximate pronunciation of the character to which it is attached. . . . I label these additional graphemes *phonic indicators*. On the graphic level, the same grapheme will function as what I call a *graphic differentiator* in that it distinguishes visually the character to which it is attached from the rest of the set of characters under the same semantic category.

The views advanced by Yau are intriguing, but his supporting evidence, while perhaps explaining the evolution of some characters, particularly the relatively small number of genuinely pictographic origin, does not appear to be sufficient to negate the more commonly held opinion that what actually happened in the creation of most "radical + phonetic" combinations was the addition of the former to the latter and not the other way around.

My own specific desciption of Chinese writing as primarily syllabic has evoked from Paul Kratochvíl, the author of an important work on Chinese language and writing (1968), the following comment:

> The Chinese writing system was never syllabic, except perhaps for a brief period during which the *same* character represented two different morphemes (the *lái* episode). This clearly did not last long, the radi-

cal + phonetic system developed, and since then it has been a *mor-phemic* script. [1981: personal communication]

It is arguable, however, that the addition of semantic elements, the radicals, to the initial syllabic elements, the phonetics, does not invalidate labeling Chinese as syllabic writing. Nevertheless, out of regard for the fact that the characters have never, to be sure, been based on a fixed and well-defined syllabary, it would seem that the Chinese writing system throughout its history might better be described as morphosyllabic rather than merely morphemic.

AMPLIFICATION OF THE TERM "MORPHOSYLLABIC"

More precisely, the term morphosyllabic is intended to suggest that each character is pronounced as a single syllable and represents a single morpheme. Moreover, for the overwhelming majority of characters, those in the radical + phonetic category, it is meant to suggest that the radical represents a morpheme that may provide a clue to the meaning of the whole character whereas the phonetic represents a syllable that may suggest the pronunciation of the character. In general, the syllabic value of the phonetic is of such overriding importance that the Chinese writing system should be considered to be basically a phonetic system of writing of the syllabic type. Moreover, the essence of its being of the syllabic type is not merely that each character is pronounced as a syllable, which is not a particularly illuminating characterization of the writing system, but that the pronunciation of the characters is obtained through the intermediary of component syllabic symbols—that is, the phonetic elements or phonetics.

The term "morphosyllabic" is therefore more informative than "logographic," "lexigraphic," "morphemic," or "morphographic." These terms merely say that Chinese characters represent words or morphemes, without telling us just how they do so. The term morphosyllabic is meant to suggest that they do so via the intermediary of some element representing a syllable. They therefore stand in contrast to the English logographs "9" and "&," which convey no indication of how the symbols are vocalized. Of course, Chinese has many graphs of the "9" and "&" type that provide no useful phonetic information, but the majority of characters do provide some information of this kind.

To be sure, the Chinese writing system is not wholly one thing or another. (But neither is any other writing system, given, for example, the existence of some nonalphabetic and indeed nonphonetic symbols such as numerals in English.) As Gelb remarks, "There are no pure systems of writing just as there are no pure races in anthropology and no pure languages in linguistics" (1963:199). The term morphosyllabic suggested for Chinese simply accounts for more of the facts than any other name, and that is the best that can be expected in a situation where no label is 100 percent satisfactory.

ASCENDENCY OF PHONETIC ELEMENTS

It may be objected that since all characters have a semantic element (which may or may not be useful) and almost all have a phonetic element (which also may or may not be useful), why is the phonetic aspect considered more important than the semantic—so much so that it forms the chief basis for characterizing the writing system? The answer to this is twofold. In the first place, contrary to the common impression of Chinese as an ideographic or semantic system of writing, semantic predictability, a function chiefly of the well-known radical system, is far inferior to phonetic predictability, a function chiefly of the less well-known system of phonetic elements. In the second place, readers can derive more meaning from phonetic clues that are directly tied to morphemes, poor though the phonetic representation may be, than they can from semantic clues that at best are only loosely related to such generally imprecise concepts as those of the radicals. Indeed, so long as writing actually reflects speech and not some sort of perhaps never spoken style such as classical Chinese, semantic clues are not needed and can even be ignored when they lead off in a different direction from that suggested by phonetic clues.

A good example of the ascendency of the phonetic aspect in Chinese writing is the following little test that I have tried out repeatedly, always with success, on readers of Chinese:

我又一个个个两个地地

There is great semantic distortion in this sentence, as indicated by the following meanings of the characters: "I again one unit unit unit two unit earth earth." There is also phonetic distortion, as indicated by the transcription of the individual characters: *wǒ yòu yī ge ge ge liǎng ge dì dì.* After an initial double take, readers invariably see through the semantic misdirection, correct the phonetic distortion to *wǒ yǒu yīge gēge liǎngge dìdi,* and decipher the intended message as "I have one older brother and two younger brothers."

We can also illustrate this point by examining the nineteen characters at the beginning of Lu Xun's story "Diary of a Madman." A semantic approach based on presenting only the meanings of the radicals of these characters yields the following:

1   2   3   4   5   6   7   8   9

man big sun to-divine, double-standing-man woman white moon legs.

10   11   12   13   14   15   16   17   18   19

spear one   see   also,   self sun one ten evening shield.

A phonetic approach, in which the characters are simply transcribed on the basis of their phonetic elements as defined by Soothill, yields the following:

1   2   3   4   5   6   7   8   9

jīn tiān miǎn pǔ, gèn nǚ sháo yuè guāng.

10 11   12   13 14 15 16 17   18   19

wǒ bù jiàn yě, jǐ shì yī shí duō wǔ.

When these two approaches to identifying the nineteen characters were submitted to several native readers of Chinese, the semantic approach appeared as almost total gibberish and made possible the very shaky identification of only one or two characters. Success would probably not be any greater if we were to take into account any other semantic clues that a character might have since, as Kennedy has reckoned (1964:452), "the odds *against* the meaning of a character being equal to the sum of the meanings of its parts are about fifty to one."

When the phonetic approach was applied in our little test, there was unanimous agreement on the identification of seven of the characters and partial agreement on another two: *jīntian* ("today"), *yuèguāng* ("moonlight"), *wǒ bù jiàn* ("I not see"), and *shí duō* ("ten-odd"). If we combine these meanings with *X*'s for the undeciphered characters, we get the following: "Today *X X, X X X* moonlight. I not see *X, X X X* ten-odd *X.*" This is not enough to make

sense of the whole passage, to be sure, but it clearly provides an excellent point of departure for the additional steps needed to decipher
the text.[1]

But what about the characters which lack a phonetic element or
have phonetic elements whose pronunciation is not useful in determining the pronunciation of the whole character? Here, of course,
there is no phonetic crutch to rely on. Such characters must be
learned by brute force, as it were, mainly by memorizing the total
configuration or by handling the graphic components with some sort
of mnemonic approach. This strategy applies, for the most part, to
the characters that constitute the Chinese syllabary, as well as to those
additional characters (none in Soothill's dictionary, some 3–10 percent in Kang Xi) that lack a phonetic element. The Kang Xi 3–10
percent cannot be considered a serious problem, as most of the characters are obscure variants or archaisms of the "yclept" type in
English. The main burden is learning the 895 phonetics, or that portion of them that may be considered really useful, since in some cases
it may be more practical to memorize a whole character and its pronunciation than to make use of its obscure and seldom used phonetic. As to the so-called phonetic compounds with phonetics that
are not useful, these too must be learned as purely graphic structures,
and insofar as this category includes some commonly used characters
this task does indeed add considerably to the burden of memorization.

But to recognize that there are too many characters without clear
phonetic clues is not at all to say that the Chinese writing system lacks
a phonetic basis or that it conveys meaning without regard to sound.
Rather, we must consider Chinese writing as an orthography in which
the relation of sign to meaning is mediated primarily through a
sound system based on a defective inventory of syllabic signs and
quite secondarily through a semantic system based on an even more
defective inventory of significs or radicals.

Just how superior the phonetic element is appears with even
greater clarity in a study, summarized in Table 7, which shows that
the purely semantic characters comprise only a tiny minority of all
Chinese characters and that in the major category of radical plus phonetic characters the phonetic element is far superior in predicting pronunciation than is the semantic element in predicting meaning, all of
which means that, since speakers of Chinese can derive meaning from
sound, the phonetic element, abysmally bad though it is in Chinese

Table 7   Semantic Versus Phonetic Aspects of Chinese Characters

Class of Characters	Percent of Characters	
I. Purely Semantic Characters		
A. pictographic	1.3	
B. simple indicative	.4	
C. compound indicative	1.3	
	3.0	3.0
II. Radical plus Phonetic Characters		
A. Semantic Aspect[2]		
1. identity in meaning between radical and compound	1.0	
2. clear but imprecise relationship between radical and compound	22.3	
3. less clear and even less precise relationship	27.1	
4. no or obscure relationship	46.6	
	97.0	
B. Phonetic Aspect		
1. complete identity between phonetic and compound	24.2	
2. identity except possibly for tones	16.5	
3. useful similarity in segmental phonemes	23.3	
4. no useful similarity in segmental phonemes	33.0	
	97.0	97.0
		100.0

as compared to other systems of writing, emerges as by far the more powerful factor in determining the meaning of characters in the course of reading Chinese.

The fact that such an imperfect phonetic system as the Chinese, which is incomparably more deficient than the frequently caricatured English orthography, can function as well as it does is due to the redundancy in writing that enables native readers of character-based scripts to manage with a system of clues far less efficient than those provided by better schemes such as Spanish or German or even English. English orthography, bad as it is, presents no great problem even when subjected to further distortion. Victorian readers of the operas of Gilbert and Sullivan had no trouble identifying the naughty word used by the crew of *H.M.S. Pinafore* when they sang that their captain "hardly ever swears a big, big D——." Th nglsh lngg, s ths xmpl shws, cn b wrttn lmst wtht vwls. It——also possi— to guess —— pronun— and —eaning —— unknown or —effective or eve— missing —— —hen —eading wha— is —itten, as you —— do-ing —— now.

As the preceding sentences show, even a highly deficient phonetic notation that represents only bits and pieces of the language enables readers to guess the full pronunciation and meaning of what they are reading. Ability to do so will of course vary widely depending on the endowments and training of the reader. Skilled native speakers and readers of a language will naturally enjoy a huge advantage in this elaborate guessing game in comparison to unskilled native readers and struggling foreign students, whose limited knowledge of vocabulary, structures, content, and other aspects of written matter means that for them redundancy may be minimal or even nonexistent. Such readers will find it difficult indeed to cope with defects in the written message.

Guessing the pronunciation and meaning of characters when reading has been honed to a fine skill among users of character-based scripts. This is necessarily so because the Chinese writing system, although conveying meaning in a way that is basically the same in principle as other phonetic schemes, does so in a uniquely inefficient manner. The failure to discern that Chinese characters are an extremely bad example of phonetic writing, but phonetic writing all the same, has led to a mistaken view of the Chinese writing system that can only be labeled as the Ideographic Myth.

Part III

DEMYTHIFYING
CHINESE CHARACTERS

A myth . . . provides a technique for handling the
unknown, for naming the unknown without offer-
ing a solution. Science, on the other hand, proceeds
to name an unknown in order to solve it.

Albert Cook, *Myth and Language*

8.
The Ideographic Myth

The concept of ideographic writing is a most seductive notion. There is great appeal in the concept of written symbols conveying their message directly to our minds, thus bypassing the restrictive intermediary of speech. And it seems so plausible. Surely ideas immediately pop into our minds when we see a road sign, a death's head label on a bottle of medicine, a number on a clock. Aren't Chinese characters a sophisticated system of symbols that similarly convey meaning without regard to sound? Aren't they an ideographic system of writing?

The answer to these questions is no. Chinese characters are a phonetic, not an ideographic, system of writing, as I have attempted to show in the preceding pages. Here I would go further: There never has been, and never can be, such a thing as an ideographic system of writing. How then did this concept originate, and why has it received such currency among specialists and the public at large?

ORIGIN OF THE MYTH

The concept of Chinese writings as a means of conveying ideas without regard to speech took hold as part of the chinoiserie fad among Western intellectuals that was stimulated by the generally highly laudatory writings of Catholic missionaries from the sixteenth to the eighteenth centuries. The first Western account of the fascinatingly different Chinese writing was the comment made by the Portuguese Dominican Friar Gaspar da Cruz in 1569:

> The Chinas [Chinese] have no fixed letters in their writing, for all that they write is by characters, and they compose words of these, whereby they have a great multitude of characters, signifying each thing by a

character in such sort that one only character signifies "Heaven,"
another "earth," and another "man," and so forth with everything
else. [Boxer 1953:161–162]

Cruz's remarks about Chinese were given wider currency when they
were repeated by Juan Gonzales de Mendoza in a book that went
through thirty editions in the principal European languages before
the end of the century.

A more authoritative description of Chinese writing was advanced
by the renowned Jesuit missionary Matteo Ricci (1552–1610). His
original manuscript, written in Italian, was not published until 1942,
but it was used by a fellow missionary, Nicola Trigault, as the basis for
a "liberal version" in Latin that was published in 1615 and went
through ten editions in various European languages in the next few
decades (Ricci 1942:CLXXVI–CLXXVII). From this Latin version of
Ricci's observations, European readers learned that the Chinese have
a system of writing "similar to the hieroglyphic signs of the Egyptians" and that they "do not express their concepts by writing, like
most of the world, with a few alphabetic signs, but they paint as
many symbols as there are words." Readers also learned that "each
word has its own hieroglyphic character," that "there are no fewer
symbols than words," and that "the great number of characters is in
accord with the great number of things," though thanks to combining them the characters "do not exceed seventy to eighty thousand"
(Trigault 1615:25–29, 144).

The popularity among European scholars of these early works on
things Chinese is matched by the huge eighteenth-century collection
of missionary reports and essays entitled *Mémoires concernant l'histoire, les sciences, les arts, les moeurs, les usages, &c des Chinois, par
les missionaires de Pekin*. Here the discussion of Chinese characters
was introduced in an article signed "Ko, Jéf." He was one of a number of Chinese converts who spent some time in France and provided
information to the missionaries. In his discussion of the characters the
author presented the view that

they are composed of symbols and images, and that these symbols and
images, not having any sound, can be read in all languages, and form
a sort of intellectual painting, a metaphysical and ideal algebra, which
conveys thoughts by analogy, by relation, by convention, and so on.
[*Mémoires* 1776:24]

This view was taken up and expanded on by the well-known Father J. J. M. Amiot in a longer article in which he described characters as

> images and symbols which speak to the mind through the eyes—images for palpable things, symbols for mental ones. Images and symbols which are not tied to any sound and can be read in all languages. . . . I would be quite inclined to define Chinese characters as the pictorial algebra of the sciences and the arts. In truth, a well-turned sentence is as much stripped of all intermediaries as is the most rigorously bare algebraic demonstration. [*Mémoires* 1776:282–285]

It is a curious fact, however, that while the notion that Chinese writing conveys ideas without regard to sound was widely held, no special name appears to have been coined for it. Westerners had made the acquaintance of Chinese in the sixteenth century. Friar Gaspar da Cruz, as noted above, referred to the Chinese symbols as "characters," and the Jesuit missionary Alessandro Valignani, who visited Macao in 1577, referred to Chinese characters as "that innumerable multitude of exceedingly intricate ciphers which pass for writing" among the Chinese (Bartoli 1663:147). It seems that for the next 250 years and more Chinese writing was referred to simply by such noncommittal terms as "characters" and "symbols."

It was not acquaintance with Chinese but decipherment of Egyptian hieroglyphic writing following Napoleon's conquests in North Africa that led to the coining of several expressions related to the ideographic idea. According to the *Oxford English Dictionary*, the English term "ideographic" was first used in 1822 to describe Egyptian writing. The French term *"idéographique"* was first used in the same year (Robert 1977:957). This was the very year that the French scholar Champollion announced his success in deciphering the Egyptian script. It turns out that the English term represents a direct transliteration of the French expression coined by Champollion in a celebrated letter announcing his discovery (Champollion 1822; Anonymous 1822).

Decipherment of this script had long been impeded by the notion that it was symbolic of ideas, particularly mystical or spiritual ones. It was not just the discovery of the famous Rosetta Stone, with its bilingual text in three scripts (Hieroglyphic Egyptian, Demotic Egyptian, and Greek) that made this possible. As Gordon (1968:24) stresses: "The decipherment of Hieroglyphic Egyptian required the replacement of the deep-seated notion of symbolism by the correct view that the main (though not the only) feature of the script is phonetic."

Champollion's success in deciphering the Egyptian script was due to his recognition of its phonetic aspect. He believed that what he called "the alphabet of the phonetic hieroglyphs" existed in Egypt "at a far distant time," that it was first "a necessary part" of the hieroglyphic script, and that later it was also used to transcribe "the proper names of peoples, countries, cities, rulers, and individual foreigners who had to be commemorated in historic texts or monumental incriptions" (1822:41–42). These insights won by Champollion are supported by the succinct description of the Egyptian system of writing made by a recent authority: "The system of hieroglyphic writing has two basic features: first, representable objects are protrayed as pictures (ideograms), and second, the picture signs are given the phonetic value of the word for the represented objects (phonograms). At the same time, these signs are also written to designate homonyms, similar-sounding words" (Brunner 1974:854). The same authority also stresses that "hieroglyphs were from the very beginning phonetic symbols. . . . Egyptian writing was a complete script; that is, it could unequivocally fix any word, including all derivatives and all grammatical forms" (Brunner 1974:853–855).

Champollion, however, overemphasized the use of "phonetic hieroglyphs" in transcribing foreign names (in his account this seems to be their only use), and he also obscured the significance of his own discovery by calling the Egyptian symbols "ideograms" and the writing "ideographic." Moreover, referring to the use of the symbols to write words foreign to the language, he added (1822:4): "The Chinese, who also use an ideographic script, have exactly the same provision, created for the same reason." It is ironic that the scholar who demonstrated the falsity of the old belief in Egyptian as symbolic and nonphonetic should have helped to popularize terms that powerfully reinforced the popular misconception of both the Egyptian and Chinese systems of writing.[1]

THE ESSENCE OF WRITING

This misconception involves the precise nature of writing—not just Egyptian or Chinese writing but all forms of writing. The problem is not so complex as we make it out when we let ourselves get bogged down in consideration of detailed differences among the great varieties of writing. It becomes quite simple if we limit consideration of the written forms, be they signs or symbols or characters or pictures or whatnot, to the principles involved in the two basic aspects of *form* and *function*.

As to form, there is nearly unanimous agreement that writing started with pictures. As to function, there is less agreement. Did an Indian or Egyptian or Chinese picture of the sun convey an idea directly, or did it evoke a spoken word and through this intermediary convey the meaning?

Gelb insists on viewing the question in terms of two stages in the development of writing. In the first stage, in which he places what he calls "forerunners of writing" (1963:59), the symbols are clearly pictographic in form, though he prefers to call them "descriptive" or "representational." Just how did they function in conveying meaning? Gelb is not very clear, except in a negative sense of how they did *not* function in systems such as those of the North American Indians. In these systems the symbols did not represent specific sounds. Indeed, Indian pictographs were not even formalized or conventionalized and never transcended a sort of ad hoc quality in that they most often dealt with specific situations, were aimed at specific persons, and lacked generality or continuity in time. A typical example of Indian pictography, one in which it comprises more than the usual isolated symbol or two, is a message passed on by an Indian agent from a Cheyenne father to his son informing him of the transmission of $35. Another is a come-up-and-see-me-some-time invitation from an Ojibwa girl to her lover (Gelb 1963:31–32). Both require elaborate interpretation to be understood by anyone but the immediate persons involved. For the latter the symbols apparently comprised a sort of prearranged code. As noted by Mallery, the author of the most exhaustive studies available of the pictographs of American Indians, "comparatively few of their picture signs have become merely conventional. . . . By far the larger part of them are merely mnemonic records" (1886:15–16). The meager information contained in the Amerindian pictographic symbols stands in contrast to the great amount of knowlege about the economic, social, religious, and other aspects of Sumerian, Egyptian, and Shang societies that can be obtained by reading their voluminous written records.

In the second stage, the pictographic form may be carried over from the first but the wholly new principle of using them to represent sounds makes its appearance, at first haltingly, then increasingly, until it eventually becomes the dominant feature. At this point, "full systems of writing" come into being (Gelb 1963:60).

One must insist on this clear dividing line between the two stages of writing. If we look only at the surface similarity in the depiction of objects in various forms of writing, we shall overlook the significance of the use of a particular picture or sign as a purely phonetic symbol. To lump together the writing of the American Indians and the early Chinese and Egyptians because of some similarity in graphic forms is to fall victim to the kind of befuddled thinking that is indicated by calling all of them pictographic or ideographic.

This point is of such overriding importance that we must pursue it a bit further by viewing Chinese writing in terms of the two-stage approach. Suppose we illustrate the matter by taking up once again the character for "wheat." We can summarize its form and function in the two stages as follows:

Stage 1: Protowriting
   Form: Pictograph of wheat: 來
   Function: To represent the idea "wheat"
Stage 2: Real Writing
   Form: Pictograph of wheat: 來 or 來
   Function: 1. To represent the word /əg² ("wheat")
            2. To represent the word /əg ("come")

Stage 1, the era of protowriting akin to that of the American Indians, is assumed but not attested. We have no record of such a stage, although some evidence of pre-Shang writing is beginning to emerge (Aylmer 1981:6; Cheung 1983), but since elsewhere attempts at writing started with the drawing of pictures, we assume the same for Chinese. Whether the pictures were vocalized—that is, represented concepts that were expressed orally in one definite way—is a matter of disagreement. In any case there would be no indication of their having a specific phonetic value.

By the time we come to Shang writing we are already well into stage 2: real writing. It is not a completely new stage, however, as there are overlaps in certain areas. The chief overlap is in the form of the symbols. These are identical in the two stages, or perhaps those in the second stage are somewhat more stylized, a matter of no particular importance. There may be overlap also for the first function, that of representing, either directly or indirectly, the concept "wheat."

The second function is, however, completely new in that it introduces the rebus use of the pictograph meaning "wheat" to represent another word with the same sound but with a totally different meaning. The rebus idea can be illustrated in English by the use of the four following pictographs depicting a human eye, a tin can, a seascape, and a female sheep or ewe:

Taken together these pictographs make no sense as meaning-symbols but do make sense as sound-symbols: eye can sea ewe. The rebus idea seems obvious to us since we use it in children's games, but it actually constitutes a stupendous invention, an act of intellectual creation of the highest order—a quantum leap forward beyond the stage of vague and imprecise pictures to a higher stage that leads into the ability to represent all the subtleties and precision expressible in spoken language. Writing is now directly, clearly, firmly related to language: to speech. If there was ever any question whether a symbol had a sound attached to it, this now receives a positive answer. In the earliest form known to us, the character for "wheat" was borrowed to represent the word "come" precisely because both were pronounced in the same way.

In human history it seems that the idea of using a pictograph in the new function of representing sound may have occurred only three times: once in Mesopotamia, perhaps by the Sumerians, once in China, apparently by the Chinese themselves, and once in Central America, by the Mayas. (Conceivably it was invented only once, but there is no evidence that the Chinese or the Mayas acquired the idea from elsewhere.) The idea that was independently conceived by these three peoples was taken over, as were at times even the symbols themselves, though often in a highly modified form, by others who made adaptations to fit a host of totally different languages. One of the major adaptations, generally attributed to the Greeks, was the narrowing of sound representation from syllabic representation to phonemic representation (Gelb 1963; Trager 1974), after an earlier stage of mixed pictographic and syllabic writing (Chadwick 1967).

The precise form in which the words in these languages are represented is a matter of quite secondary importance. With regard to the principle, it matters little whether the symbol is an elaborately detailed picture, a slightly stylized drawing, or a drastically abbreviated symbol of essentially abstract form. What is crucial is to recognize that the diverse forms perform the same function in representing sound. To see that writing has the form of pictures and to conclude that it is pictographic is correct in only one sense—that of the form, but not the function, of the symbols. We can put it this way:

QUESTION: When is a pictograph not a pictograph?
ANSWER: When it represents a sound.

The use of the pictograph for "wheat" to represent the homophonous word *ləg* ("come") transformed the function of the symbol from pictographic depiction of an object to syllabic representation of a sound. This change in function has been the essential development marking the emergence of all true systems of writing, including Chinese.

SINOLOGICAL CONTRIBUTION TO THE MYTH

The fact that some Chinese pictographs have not undergone a change in form parallel to the change in function has tended to obscure the significance of the change that did take place. As a result, the phonetic aspect of Chinese writing is minimized by many people, even specialists in the field. Creel in the United States and Margouliès in France are leading exponents of a view that has been taken over, in even more simplistic form, by the public at large. Both scholars are aware that there is a phonetic aspect in Chinese writing. Yet their attention is so narrowly focused on the nonphonetic aspect that their otherwise useful contributions to learning (especially Creel's informative and readable *The Birth of China*) are unfortunately diminished. Their discussions of Chinese writing are confused and contradictory— at one time seeming to say one thing, at another something else, but coming down ultimately to a conclusion that is completely untenable.

Creel (1936:91–93) says:

That Chinese writing was pictographic in origin does not admit of question. On the other hand, Chinese is not, and was not three thousand years ago, a pictographic language in the sense that it consisted of writing by means of pictures all or most of which would be readily understood by the uninstructed. . . . The Chinese early abandoned the method of writing by means of readily recognizable pictures and diagrams. . . . It was in part because the Chinese gave up pictoral [*sic*] writing that they were able to develop a practicable pictographic and ideographic script, with comparatively little help from the phonetic principle. To draw elaborate pictures of whole animals, for instance (as is done on some of the Shang bones), is too slow a process. The course taken in many parts of the world was to conventionalize the picture, reduce it to a simple and easily executed form, and then use it to represent homophonous words or parts of words. The course the Chinese have chosen has also been to conventionalize and reduce, but they then use the evolved element for the most part not phonetically, but to stand for the original object or to enter with other such elements into combinations of ideographic rather than phonetic value. This parting of the ways is of the most profound importance.

The last two sentences are the crux of Creel's thesis. Where Boodberg and others, as noted earlier, see phonetic elements, Creel sees elements that are conventionalized or reduced forms used "to stand for the original object or to enter with other such elements into combinations of ideographic rather than phonetic value." This emphasis on ideographic symbols that are merely conventionalized forms of pictographs leads Creel into the fanciful explanations of Chinese characters that were so sharply condemned by Boodberg.

Boodberg's refutation contained in learned journals known only to specialists could do little to counter the impact of Creel's views expressed in his popular *The Birth of China*. Here Creel says: "We have specialized on the representation of sounds; the Chinese have specialized on making their writing so suggestive to the eye that it immediately calls up ideas and vivid pictures, without any interposition of sounds" (1937:159).

If we take this statement at face value without qualifying it with "What the author really meant to say was . . ."—a practice that runs the risk of misinterpreting what the author meant—the statement is absurdly false, as can be attested by any reader of this book who has not studied Chinese. Simply look at the characters sprinkled throughout the work and note how many or how few immediately call up ideas and vivid pictures without any interposition of sounds.

The qualification that we hesitate to read into Creel's statement is suggested by the author himself, but in the same specialized journal

mentioned earlier and quoted to the effect that Chinese is not "a pictographic language in the sense that it consisted of writing by means
of pictures all or most of which would be readily understood by the
uninstructed." But if the ability to grasp an idea "immediately" or
"readily" from symbols that are "a practical pictographic and ideographic script" though not "pictoral writing" is limited to those who
presumably must be classified as "the instructed," this makes the
otherwise absurd statement inanely true. For it is equally true that
the instructed can immediately grasp an idea whether it is expressed
in Chinese characters, in Egyptian hieroglyphs, in Japanese kana, or
even in our less than perfect English orthography. All literates are
conditioned, like Pavlov's dogs, to respond to certain culture-bound
stimuli. The written word "chicken" evokes in my mind precisely the
same picture—or pictures—as the written character 鷄 (or 鸡), except
perhaps that in the first case I may salivate in anticipation of Ken-
tucky fried chicken and in the second of chicken cooked in soy sauce.

Apart from the error of thinking that Chinese characters are
unique in evoking mental images, where Creel and others from Friar
Gaspar da Cruz right on down go astray in their characterization of
Chinese writing is to succumb to the hypnotic appeal of the relatively
few characters that are demonstratably of pictographic origin and to
extrapolate from these to the majority if not the entirety of the Chinese written lexicon. The error of exaggerating the pictographic and
hence semantic aspect of Chinese characters and minimizing if not
totally neglecting the phonetic aspect tends to fix itself very early in
the minds of many people, both students of Chinese and the public
at large, because their first impression of the characters is likely to be
gained by being introduced to the Chinese writing system via some of
the simplest and most interesting pictographs, such as those presented at the beginning of Chapter 5. Unless a determined effort is
made to correct this initial impression, it is likely to remain as an article of faith not easily shaken by subsequent exposure to different
kinds of graphs. This may also explain the oversight even of specialists who are aware of the phonetic aspect in Chinese characters,
including such able scholars as Li and Thompson (1982:77), who
refer to Chinese writing as "semantically, rather than phonologically
grounded" and consider that a character "does not convey phonological information except in certain composite logographs where the
pronunciation of the composite is similar to one of its component

logographs." It takes a profoundly mesmerized observer to overlook as exceptions the two-thirds of all characters that convey useful phonological information through their component phonetic.

MYTH VS. REALITY

A limited number of pictographic or semantic characters, like the limited number of what Bolinger (1946) calls "visual morphemes" and Edgerton (1941) "ideograms in English writing," or even the extensive but still limited systems such as mathematical or chemical notation, cannot be considered indicative of full systems of non-phonetic writing that can function like ordinary orthographies to express nearly everything we can express in spoken language. The fact is that such a full system of nonphonetic writing has never existed. The system of Chinese characters, the Sumerian, Accadian, and Hittite cuneiform systems, and the Egyptian hieroglyphic system were none of them complete systems of semantic writing. For Sumerian and Accadian, Civil (1973:26) provides figures summarized in Table 8 showing the relative importance of phonetic versus semantic elements in various texts. With respect to Egyptian, Edgerton says that "of the total number of signs in any normal hieroglyphic or hieratic text, the overwhelming majority will not be ideographic at all but phonetic" (1940:475). The same is true of Chinese, as was shown in great detail in Chapter 5.

Table 8   Semantic Versus Phonetic Aspects of Cuneiform Symbols

Symbols	Sumerian	Accadian
Syllabograms	36.4–54.3%	85.6–95.7%
Logograms	60.3–42.8%	6.5–3.5%
Classifiers	3.1–2.9%	7.6–0.7%

Nonphonetic symbols occur in every writing system. But using the existence of these symbols, however numerous, to conclude that whole systems not based on sound have existed, or even that such systems are possible, are unwarranted assumptions that lead inevitably to the complete obfuscation regarding the nature of writing that is expressed in the Ideographic Myth.

This myth, it is apparent, exists in two aspects. Both must be rejected. The first is that the Chinese characters constitute an existing system of ideographic writing. This has been shown to be factually untrue. The second aspect is the validity of the ideographic concept itself. I believe it to be completely untenable because there is no evidence that people have the capacity to master the enormous number of symbols that would be needed in a written system that attempts to convey thought without regard to sound, which means divorced from spoken language. A few, yes, as in any writing system, including English with its numerals and other "visual morphemes." Even quite a few, given the large number of Chinese syllabic signs and graphs without good phonetic clues. But while it is possible for a writing system to have many individual "ideographs" or "ideograms," it is not possible to have a whole writing system based on the ideographic principle. Alphabetic writing requires mastery of several dozen symbols that are needed for phonemic representation. Syllabic writing requires mastery of what may be several hundred or several thousand symbols that are needed for syllabic representation. Ideographic writing, however, requires mastery of the tens of thousands or hundreds of thousands of symbols that would be needed for ideographic representation of words or concepts without regard to sound. A bit of common sense should suggest that unless we supplement our brains with computer implants, ordinary mortals are incapable of such memory feats. The theory of an ideographic script must remain in the realm of popular mythology until some True Believers demonstrate its reality by accomplishing the task, say, of putting *Hamlet* or at least Lincoln's Gettysburg Address into English written in symbols without regard to sound.

OBJECTIONS TO THE TERM "IDEOGRAPHIC"

We need to go further and throw out the term itself. Boodberg proposed doing so years ago when he sharply criticized students of early Chinese inscriptions for neglecting the phonological aspect of Chinese writing and for "insisting that the Chinese in the development of their writing . . . followed some mysterious esoteric principles that set them apart from the rest of the human race." Boodberg added (1937:329–332):

> Most students in the field have chosen to concentrate their efforts on the exotically fascinating questions of "graphic semantics" and the

study of the living tissues of the *word* has almost completely been neglected in favor of the graphic integument encasing it. . . . The term "ideograph" is, we believe, responsible for most of the misunderstanding of the writing. The sooner it is abandoned the better. We would suggest the revival of the old term "logograph." Signs used in writing, however ambiguous, stylized, or symbolic, represent *words*.

The last sentence should be given the utmost emphasis: Chinese characters represent words (or better, morphemes), not ideas, and they represent them phonetically, for the most part, as do all real writing systems despite their diverse techniques and differing effectiveness in accomplishing the task.

Boodberg's objections to describing Chinese writing as ideographic were anticipated by a century in a remarkable book by Peter S. DuPonceau. The author, a leading scholar who was president of the American Philosophical Society, was one of the outstanding general linguists of the first half of the nineteenth century in the United States. Although his work has been briefly noted by Edgerton (1944) and by Chao (1940), it has not received the attention it deserves among Chinese specialists. I must confess to having failed to check his views until quite recently, a failure which has put me in the position of reinventing the wheel. For DuPonceau, with an insight that is truly astonishing in view of the limited sources available to him, presents cogently reasoned arguments against the notion of Chinese as an ideographic script and against the whole concept of ideographic writing. His presentation, though faulty in some points (as noted by Chao 1940), constitutes what is probably the most extensive refutation yet written of the Ideographic Myth.

DuPonceau (1838:106–107) summarizes the background of the ideographic concept by noting the general opinion that Chinese writing

is an ocular method of communicating ideas, entirely independent of speech, and which, without the intervention of words, conveys ideas through the sense of vision directly to the mind. Hence it is called *ideographic,* in contradistinction from the *phonographic* or alphabetical system of writing. This is the idea which is entertained of it in China, and may justly be ascribed to the vanity of the Chinese literati. The Catholic at first, and afterwards the Protestant missionaries, have received it from them without much examination; and the love of wonder, natural to our species, has not a little contributed to propagate that opinion, which has taken such possession of the public mind, that it has become one of those axioms which no one will venture to contradict.

But DuPonceau does venture to contradict, and in no uncertain terms. In a succinct statement which might well serve as a credo for all students of Chinese to memorize, he concludes (1838:xxxi):

1. That the Chinese system of writing is not, as has been supposed, *ideographic;* that its characters do not represent *ideas,* but *words,* and therefore I have called it *lexigraphic.*
2. That ideographic writing is a creature of the imagination, and cannot exist, but for very limited purposes, which do not entitle it to the name of writing.
3. That among men endowed with the gift of speech, all writing must be a direct representation of the spoken language, and cannot present ideas to the mind abstracted from it.
4. That all writing, as far as we know, represents language in some of its elements, which are words, syllables, and simple sounds.

The conclusions obtained so long ago by DuPonceau are matched by the equally insightful observations of his contemporary, the French sinologist J. M. Callery. In the introducton to his syllabary of 1,040 phonetic signs Callery states (1841:i):

If the works of the illustrious Champollion had not already proved conclusively that the Egyptian hieroglyphics, previously regarded as symbolic signs, are, for the most part, nothing but *phonetic* signs, that is to say, signs destined to represent the different sounds of the language, I would perhaps not dare to raise my feeble voice to say before the scholarly world that the Chinese characters are also, for the most part, nothing but phonetic characters intimately tied to the sounds of the language, and not symbolic or ideographic signs, as has generally been believed up to now; however, since the barrier of prejudice has been overcome, and in almost all the sciences the eminently rational procedure of observation has been adopted, I am hazarding to put under the eyes of the public the result of my researches on the phonetic system of Chinese writing.

It is a pity that "the eminently rational procedure of observation" adopted by DuPonceau and Callery has been so much neglected by modern scholars. It is disheartening to see how pervasive is the idea that the Chinese in the development of their writing have followed, in Boodberg's words, "some mysterious esoteric principles that have set them apart from the rest of the human race." It is particularly disheartening to see levelheaded scholars suddenly taking leave of their critical faculties when confronted by Chinese characters. One reason for the pervasiveness and tenacity of the myth, I am now convinced, stems from the use of the word "ideographic." The term itself is responsible for a good deal of the misunderstanding and should be replaced, since its repetitious use, as in the big lie technique and in subliminal advertising, insidiously influences our thinking.

Boodberg has suggested that it be replaced by the term "logographic," others by "morphemic." These terms have been widely adopted in academic circles, but many scholars apparently see no real difference between them and "ideographic." In his discussion of Sumerian writing, Civil (1973:21) quotes a French writer who uses the term *"idéographique";* Civil follows it immediately with the bracketed explanation "[i.e., logographic]." A college textbook on linguistics (Geogheghn et al. 1979:131–1) equates the two terms in the following statement: "In *logographic writing systems* each character that is used represents either a concrete or abstract concept or idea. (For this reason, they are also called ideographic.)" Kolers, who believes that "there are two major writing systems in the world today, the semantic and the phonetic" (1970:113), makes no distinction between the two concepts underlying the two terms in his confused references to Chinese writing as a system that is "not phonetic" and contains "logographic compounds" that are "derived from pictures" and are "intuitively appealing" (1969:353, 357, 360). These typical examples show that the term "logographic" is simply being taken as a fancier equivalent for "ideographic" and is not fulfilling the expectation of Boodberg and other sinologists that it would help avoid misconceptions regarding the basic nature of Chinese writing. Both terms are inadequate and misleading because they fail to indicate that the process of getting from graph to word / morpheme involves the phonetic aspect of the latter and because this failure leaves the way open to the idea that we get from graph to word / morpheme by means of some nonphonetic, in a word, "ideographic," approach. Only the adoption of some such term as "morphosyllabic," which calls attention to the phonetic aspect, can contribute to dispelling the widespread misunderstanding of the nature of Chinese writing.

The term "ideographic" has been used not only by those who espouse its basic meaning but also by others who do not necessarily accept the concept but use the term out of mere force of habit as an established popular designation for Chinese characters. I find, to my chagrin, that in my previous publications I have been guilty of precisely this concession to popular usage without being aware of the damage it can cause. As a repentant sinner I pledge to swear off this hallucinogen. I hope others will join in consigning the term to the Museum of Mythological Memorabilia along with unicorn horns and phoenix feathers.

9.

The Universality Myth

The Universality Myth is the logical extension of the Ideographic Myth. It is based on a threefold belief that:

1. Chinese characters enable a speaker from Peking and another from Canton to communicate in writing even though they cannot understand each other's speech. The Dominican Friar Gaspar da Cruz in his treatise of 1569 was the first to advance the view that "in China there are many differences in language, for which reason many of them do not understand each other's speech, yet they understand each other's writing" (Boxer 1953:73, 161–162). This view has been expressed countless times in the past four centuries. Most recently we find the psychologist Frank Smith stating that in Chinese "the written words are symbols for ideas, but not for specific sounds or even specific words. Thus speakers of different Mandarin and Cantonese spoken languages can still write to each other" (1979:60).

2. Chinese characters make it possible to read today's newspapers as well as poems written a thousand years ago and philosophical essays written long before Christ. As Margouliès expresses it: "Everything that has been written in Chinese can be read with equal facility today, completely disregarding the tremendous changes that the sounds of the language have undergone in a period of almost three millennia" (1957:102).

3. Chinese characters can function as a universal means of communication among people speaking totally unrelated languages. Extending his comment about the inability of Chinese to understand each other, Friar Gaspar da Cruz added: "Nor do the Cauchinschinas [modern southern Vietnamese] nor the Japões [Japanese] [under-

stand] the Chinas [Chinese] when they speak, yet they all understand each other in writing" (Boxer 1953:162). A recent restatement of this frequently expressed view is the conclusion reached by Margouliès (1957:269) in his presentation of Chinese characters as a universal script:

> This brief examination appears to have exhausted the theoretical diffi-culties that might be envisaged. It shows that languages with quite different structures, whether invariant or inflectional, can perfectly well employ one and the same ideographic writing while still main-taining their personality intact and without needing to have any char-acters specific to them other than a few everyday terms, minimal in number—those of Annamese barely reach a few dozen.

All three characteristics are suggested by the Reverend Joshua Marsh-man in a panegyric summarized by his description of Chinese charac-ters as having "permanent perspicuity" (1814:558).

UNIVERSALITY: CHARACTERS VS. ALPHABETS

The statements quoted above, like the Ideographic Myth, are either absurdly false or inanely true. They are absurdly false if they are based on the notion that Chinese characters immediately call up ideas, a notion that was shown to be absurdly false for those not instructed in Chinese. For those so instructed, the statements are inanely true. But there is more to the fatuousness than this. Implicit-ly or explicitly, the statements are meant to contrast Chinese charac-ters with the familiar alphabetic scripts of the West. Chinese charac-ters, it is believed, can do all these things, whereas alphabetic scripts cannot.

The fact of the matter is that alphabetic scripts also (1) enable speakers of different dialects or languages to communicate in writing even though they cannot understand each other's speech; (2) enable Western readers to read today's newspapers as well as literature writ-ten centuries and even millennia ago; (3) can function as a universal means of communication among people speaking totally unrelated languages. Alphabetic scripts can do all these things, and they can do them more easily and more efficiently than can Chinese characters.

The trouble with all the claims of universality is that they seldom specify the conditions that would give concrete reality to the high-sounding generalities. Lest my own counterstatements suffer from the same defect, I propose to deal with the Universality Myth by examining how specific individuals might go about learning to engage in communication of the types mentioned. Let us start by imagining two pairs of individuals:

Wang Lin is from Peking and Kwok Wah is from Canton. They cannot understand each other's speech, as the two forms are as far apart as French from Spanish or French from Italian or Dutch from English (Chao 1976:24, 87, 97, 105). Nor can they communicate in writing, since both are illiterate.

Jean Blanc is from Paris and José Mantoyo is from Madrid. They cannot understand each other's speech. They also cannot communicate in writing since both are illiterate.

QUESTION: What does it take for Wang Lin and Kwok Wah on the one hand, and Jean Blanc and José Mantoyo on the other, to be able to communicate with each other in writing?

ANSWER: To achieve literacy in a form of writing common to each group of individuals, they will have to complete all the tasks summarized in the table below.

Tasks in Achieving Literacy

A. Tasks for Mandarin-speaking illiterates learning to read and write Standard Chinese:
1. Learning the basic structure of characters
2. Learning three thousand characters
3. Learning the differences between spoken Mandarin and written Standard Chinese
4. Practice in reading and writing

B. Tasks for Cantonese-speaking illiterates learning to read and write Standard Chinese:
1. Learning the basic structure of characters
2. Learning written Standard Chinese grammar different from Cantonese
3. Learning written Standard Chinese vocabulary different from Cantonese
4. Learning three thousand characters
5. Practice in reading and writing

C. Tasks for French-speaking illiterates learning to read French:
1. Learning the French alphabet
2. Learning the basic technique for relating letter combinations to words and phrases
3. Learning the difference between spoken and written styles
4. Practice in reading and writing

D. Tasks for Spanish-speaking illiterates learning to read French:
   1. Learning the French alphabet
   2. Learning the basic technique for relating letter combinations to words and phrases
   3. Learning French grammar
   4. Learning French vocabulary (at least the three thousand words of "Français fondemental")
   5. Practice in reading and writing

In the case of the Chinese illiterates, what they are learning is the modern vernacular written style. This written Standard Chinese includes a variety of substyles that differ in varying degrees from actual speech. The differences include many vocabulary items and structural patterns carried over from literary or classical Chinese. The gap between speech and writing is even greater for the speaker of Cantonese because what he has to learn to read is not, as widely believed, a form of writing that is equally accessible to speakers of all forms of spoken Chinese. Modern written Chinese is actually based on one specific variety of spoken Chinese, namely Mandarin or Putonghua, and therefore favors speakers of this form of spoken Chinese and disfavors speakers of other varieties. Even if we suppose that he pronounces the characters in his own fashion and is spared the considerable task of learning how they are pronounced in Mandarin, a Cantonese speaker must still learn many additional things that are different from his way of speaking. These include, in addition to the classical borrowings already noted, several points of grammar (different grammatical particles, for example, and the order indirect object–direct object in Mandarin versus direct–indirect in Cantonese) and a not inconsiderable number of vocabulary items (for instance, the personal pronouns).

In the case of the European illiterates, the written form they are learning is the modern written style. As in the case of Chinese, but to a much smaller degree, there is a gap that native speakers must bridge between the spoken and written styles. A native speaker of Spanish, even if we suppose he makes no attempt to speak French, must still learn some things that are more difficult for him than for his French counterpart. The alphabet may present a little more of a problem for him, since the French speaker will find it easier to make the connection between phonemes or words and their graphemic representation. A more important problem for the Spanish speaker is learning French grammar; the differences between French grammar and his own are greater than those between Cantonese and Mandarin. An equally important problem, perhaps, is the matter of vocabulary; here too the differences are greater than those between the two forms of Chinese.

If it is objected that the way the Spanish illiterate is presented as learning to read and write French is artificial, the answer is that for purposes of comparison an attempt has been made to parallel the Chinese situation. Of course, if Spanish/Cantonese illiterates seeking to read and write standard French/Chinese first learn to understand spoken French/Mandarin and to speak it, or if they first learn to read in their own form of speech (there is a literature in Cantonese too), the situation would be altered in certain details, but the final conclusion would, I believe, remain the same. In any case for a valid comparison we must assume roughly comparable conditions, the famous "All things—and persons—being equal."

There are two main aspects to the foregoing comparison. One is identification of the specific tasks confronting each of the four learners. The second is estimating how long it takes to perform each task. The main points of comparison involve vocabulary, syntax, and mastery of the writing system. It appears that it will take the Cantonese illiterate considerably less time to learn the lexical and syntactical features of Mandarin that are new to him than it will for the speaker of Spanish to do the same in the case of French. But when we come to the writing system, the advantage enjoyed by the Chinese with respect to vocabulary and grammar is greatly outweighed by the much greater difficulty of the characters compared to the alphabetic script.

My Chinese colleagues estimate on the basis of their own experience and direct contact with the Chinese educational system that it takes seven to eight years for a Mandarin speaker to learn to read and write three thousand characters and another year or two for a speaker of Cantonese to reach the same level in Standard Chinese. Wu Yuzhang, a leading language reformer in China, says it takes pupils six years to master three thousand characters (Serruys 1962:73). In Hong Kong, primary school children learn five or six hundred characters for each of the six years of schooling (Leong 1973:387). My colleagues in French and Spanish estimate it would take the two imagined European illiterates less than half the time to reach a comparable level of proficiency in French.

There is, to be sure, room for disagreement on the details of the crude picture sketched above. Nevertheless, the overall picture is clear. It seems incontestable that both Europeans will find it easier to learn to read and write French than it will be for either Cantonese or Mandarin speakers to learn to read and write Chinese. If we could add up the combined number of hours needed for the two members of each group to accomplish the same thing, the total would be enormously greater in the case of Chinese written in characters than in the case of French written in an alphabetic script. Even more significant, it would also be enormously greater for Chinese written in characters than for Chinese written in Pinyin. That is to say, it would be much easier for illiterates from Peking and those from Canton, even if the latter remain incapable of speaking Mandarin, to acquire the ability to communicate with each other by learning to read and write Standard Chinese written in Pinyin rather than in characters. Where, then, is the vaunted marvel of tongue-tied Chinese o'er-leaping barriers in speech by communicating with each other by means of those magical Chinese characters?

What about the ability of present-day Chinese to read things written in earlier times? Apart from learning the characters in their current meanings, Chinese must also learn the frequently different meanings of characters in earlier usage and the definitely different syntactical structures of classical versus contemporary written Chinese. This ability involves considerable training in tasks notorious for their difficulty—tasks that involve mastering differences at least as great as those between current English and the language of Chaucer. Without going into great detail, it should be readily apparent that an illiterate Chinese, regardless of whether he speaks Cantonese or Mandarin, will have a much greater task in learning to read classical Chinese than will an illiterate European, regardless of whether he speaks Spanish or French, in learning to read Latin. In the case of those already literate in current Chinese or French, it is doubtful that Chinese readers would enjoy any advantage over Europeans in respect to the amount of additional effort required to read classical Chinese in contrast to Latin.

NONUNIVERSALITY OF CLASSICAL CHINESE

The claim advanced by Margouliès and others that the universality of Chinese characters is also attested by their use in Japan, Korea, and Viet Nam turns out on examination to be equally spurious. In discoursing on this theme Margouliès makes no attempt to show just how the universality is manifested in the use of characters in these three countries. It is apparent, however, that he has in mind the two quite different ways in which characters were taken over by China's neighbors (1957:266–268).

The first way involves the outright adoption of classical Chinese. In a reference to the borrowing of Chinese writing by the Japanese, Koreans, and Vietnamese, Margouliès (1957:266) states that "a Chinese text could be read and understood by these peoples provided only that they were acquainted with the order of the Chinese words in the sentence, that is, only part of the syntax of the language, without, on the other hand, their knowing Chinese phonetically or being able to pronounce aloud the text which they understood." Thus, according to Margouliès, the Japanese, say, could read a text in classical Chinese without knowing how to pronounce the characters as long as they knew the order in which the words were arranged in Chinese in contrast to their own language.

But this knowledge is not so easily acquired as blithe references to the problem might suggest. The four Asian languages in question differ enormously in their grammatical structures—as might be expected considering that they do not even belong to the same language family. To help cope with the different grammatical structures of Chinese and Japanese, the Japanese have devised a system to indicate how to convert Chinese word order into Japanese word order. The system is somewhat analogous to one that might be devised as a trot for students of Latin. Take, for example, the opening passage of Caesar's *Gallic Wars:*

> *Gallia est omnis divisa in partes tres.*
>   2   3   1   4   5   7   6

This is easily read as

> all Gaul is divided into three parts.
> 1   2   3   4   5   6   7

As in the case of a Japanese reading Chinese, our readers of Latin can manage to decipher the text without knowing how to pronounce it.

This matter of pronunciation cannot, however be glossed over in such a cavalier fashion, especially since phonological clues, as in *divisa* = divided, appear to provide English-speaking students with an aid that is commonly supposed not to exist in the case of Chinese characters. Margouliès repeatedly compares Chinese characters with numerals; the latter can be read by Westerners of different linguistic backgrounds, each reader "pronouncing them in his own way, but all understanding them in an identical way" (1957:121). This frequently made analogy of the universality of Chinese characters is actually quite misleading. It is true that the numerals 1, 2, 3 and their Chinese equivalents 一 二 三 can be read as "one, two, three" in English, as *"un, deux, trois"* in French, or as *"yī, èr, sān"* in Chinese. This does not mean, however, that all Chinese characters are actually read in such completely different ways.

Suppose an Asian reading a Chinese text encounters the expression 先 生, modern *xiānsheng* ("teacher, Mr."), the earlier pronunciation of which Karlgren (1940:nos. 478, 812) transcribes as **tsiənseng*. If the expression is read aloud or subvocally, it will be pronounced by a Japanese as *sensei,* by a Korean as *sŏnsaeng,* and by a Vietnamese as *tiên-sinh.* It is obvious that all these expressions are attempts to approximate the Chinese pronunciation. Hence it is not only the meanings of Chinese characters that are involved in reading Chinese. So also, to some extent, are their pronunciations, which foreign readers attempt to reproduce as best they can, given their different phonological habits that have resulted in the well-known Sino-Japanese, Sino-Korean, and Sino-Vietnamese readings of the characters.

That Japanese, Koreans, and Vietnamese when reading Chinese pronounce the characters "in their own way" therefore really means that they mispronounce them in their own way. This amounts to little more than the extension into reading of the obvious fact that most people in attempting to speak a foreign language do so with an accent that frequently betrays their native speech.

NONUNIVERSALITY OF CHARACTERS

This matter of reading characters with a foreign accent applies with even greater force to the second way that Margouliès has in mind in speaking of their adoption by China's neighbors. In a somewhat opaque comment that texts written with the "automatically universal" characters are not compiled "in a single language," Margouliès seems to be referring to the use of Chinese characters to write Japanese, Korean, and Vietnamese. In each case, he says elsewhere

(1957:266–268), the characters are rearranged to fit the grammatical patterns of the borrowers. This presentation is in line with the popular notion that Asian borrowers of Chinese characters are able to communicate with each other although they cannot understand each other's speech.

While it is true that Asians cannot understand each other's speech, the precise nature of this inability needs to be clarified. The frequently cited example of the numerals being mutually intelligible despite different pronunciations is misleading, because terms such as 先 生 used in common are not as unrelated in pronunciation as "one, two, three" in English and *"yī, èr, sān"* in Chinese. A good part of the lexicon of Japan, Korea, and Viet Nam has been borrowed from Chinese. Thus the term 先 生 for "teacher, Mr." is not merely a Chinese term that might be "mispronounced" in reading a Chinese text; it is a perfectly good phonetic loanword borrowed into Japanese, Korean, and Vietnamese with the native but related pronunciations noted earlier (though not with exactly the same usage).

The phonological influence of Chinese on the three neighboring languages goes further than this simple example might suggest. In these languages, as in Chinese, the characters 先 and 生 appear with the indicated pronunciations in other expressions that the Japanese, Koreans, and Vietnamese have borrowed from Chinese. They also appear as phonetic elements (respectively nos. 39 and 41 in the Soothill syllabary) in compound characters, where they function, as in Chinese itself, as the syllabic equivalents of the phonemic letters used in Western alphabets. The result of all this is that in Japanese, for example, some 60 to 70 percent of the total vocabulary, according to a prominent Japanese linguist, consists of what he calls "Chinese character words," which he says "are those introduced directly or indirectly from China since the introduction of Chinese culture in ancient times, or are words contrived in Japan through imitation" (Kindaichi 1978:40).

The Asian adoption of Chinese characters should therefore be equated with the way speakers of English have borrowed French words, such as "nation," which they took over by approximating its pronunciation [nasyɔ̃] as [neyšən]. The parallel is *not* with speakers of various languages throughout the world seeing the numerals and pronouncing them differently in different languages. Such an analogy would imply that speakers of English might pronounce the French loanword *chauffeur* as "driver."

The foregoing paragraphs are not intended to minimize the difficulty of oral communication among the four Sinitic countries. They are intended merely to clarify the specific nature of this difficulty. The same need for clarification arises in the case of the frequently made assertion that the borrowers of Chinese characters merely have to rearrange them to suit their own grammatical patterns. The problem is not as simple as that. In the case of Japanese and Korean, in addition to knowing how to arrange Chinese characters in Japanese and Korean word order, it is also necessary to be thoroughly acquainted with the use of the indigenous kana syllabaries or hangul alphabet in such functions as indicating case and inflectional endings and other indigenous items. By way of illustration, it would be criminally irresponsible to advise someone that because a Chinese-character expression can be rendered as DRINKABLE, it is therefore safe for him to take some Japanese medicine whose label might be rendered as DRINKABLEnai, airily disregarding the kana suffix *nai* ("not").

A very rough analogy here might be to the situation in English in which some texts, especially those in certain academic spheres such as the sciences, have a high proportion of words of Latin origin. Overall the English lexicon is about 50 percent of Germanic origin and 50 percent of Latin origin (Potter 1966:36). Function words tend to be derived from Germanic, content words from Latin, so that highly specialized texts may well have a proportion of 30 to 40 percent Germanic for function words and 60 to 70 percent Latin for content words. In Korean publications it is estimated that some 50 to 60 percent of the text is written in Chinese characters; the rest is written in hangul (Liu 1969:67; Suh 1974:37). Characters tend to be used for content words, most of which are of Chinese origin; hangul tends to be used for function words and other words of Korean origin.

The situation is somewhat similar in Japanese, where, as noted above, some 60 to 70 percent of the total vocabulary is based on Sino-Japanese elements. There is also in Japanese an added complication in the unprecedented variety of meanings and pronunciations, some purely native (e.g., *korosu,* cited p. 7) and some Sino-Japanese (e.g., *sensei*), that came to be attached to the borrowed characters. As a result, the characters were not merely arranged in Japanese word order and combined with kana indicating such things as inflections and case; they were traditionally supplemented by furigana symbols which were written alongside the characters to indicate what reading and hence what meaning they were supposed to have in a particular context. This auxiliary system of phonetic annotation further distinguished as uniquely Japanese a character-based system of writing of such complexity as to lead one authority on Japanese to write: "One hesitates for an epithet to describe a system of writing which is so complex that it needs the aid of another system to explain it. There is no doubt that it provides for some a fascinating field of study, but as a practical instrument it is surely without inferiors" (Sansom 1928:4).

It should be obvious from this comment and from the preceding discussion that the use of Chinese characters by four Asian countries involves much more than a mere reshuffling of common lexical items. It should also be obvious that Chinese characters used by Asians speaking different languages are no more universal than are Latin letters used by Europeans who also speak different languages.

As long as a command of Latin remained part of the intellectual equipment of educated Westerners, they were able to turn at will from their current newspapers to the classics of Latin literature, and they were able to communicate with each other in writing (as classically educated Catholic priests still can) despite their inability to understand each other's speech. As to the parallel situation in written Chinese, DuPonceau remarked long ago that "there is certainly nothing in it to excite our wonder" (1838:86).

Nor is there anything to excite our wonder in the ability of Chinese, Japanese, and Koreans to look at their common graphs and determine in general terms what a piece of writing in each of these languages is about. French and English scholars ignorant of each other's speech can also look at a text in each other's language and determine whether it is about economics or chemistry or linguistics or any other discipline using a good deal of common Latinate vocabulary. But to *read* each other's writings, the Asians would have as much, if not more, to do than the Europeans in learning how their common items and additional noncommon items, such as the kana or hangul symbols, are grammatically related to each other in a running text.

THE MYTH DEMOLISHED

To sum it all up, 愛 (or the simplified form 爱) is no more universal than *amat*. In fact, the latter is easier to learn and therefore has the greater claim to universality.

Almost a century and a half ago DuPonceau devoted a major portion of his remarkable book to demolishing the Universality Myth in its various forms. To the central myth that Chinese characters have special properties not possessed by alphabetic scripts he replied that "Asiatics are not more assisted by the form of Chinese characters than Europeans are by the appearance of the groups formed by the letters of our alphabet" (1838:81).

To the arguments in favor of the all-encompassing concept of "permanent perspicuity" of Chinese characters advanced by Marshman he expostulated: "I am almost ashamed to have to answer such arguments, and yet they are urged by men to whose opinions, on other subjects, I would submit with respect. Such is the force of prejudice, which even in enlightened minds is so difficult to be conquered" 1838:85).

The force of prejudice is indeed powerful when it leads to such widespread disregard of the substantial differences among Asian writing systems and indifference to what it costs in time and effort to accomplish the wondrous things attributed to Chinese characters. It simply will not do to take knowledge of the characters as a given in making comparisons of writing systems—"It goes without saying"— or to dismiss acquiring command of the characters as a trifle, a mere bagatelle, that does not need to be taken into consideration. Wittingly or unwittingly, those who adopt such an approach are like used-car salesmen who entice prospective customers into buying expensive cars by neglecting to draw their attention to the fine print in the purchase contract that will bind them for years in working off the indebtedness. *Caveat emptor!* Would you buy a used car—or idea —from such a person?

10.

The Emulatability Myth

The caveat sounded at the end of the preceding chapter is no tongue-in-cheek turn of phrase intended merely to amuse. It is a sober warning of the consequences, some of them quite serious, resulting from the fact that just as the Ideographic Myth leads logically to the Universality Myth, so does the latter lead to the Emulatability Myth—the idea that Chinese characters provide a model to be followed in one way or another in writing without regard to sound.

THE CHIMERA OF A "UNIVERSAL LANGUAGE"

The reports of missionaries from the sixteenth century onward firmly established the idea that Chinese characters already served as a common written language among the peoples of the East and therefore could be further extended as a universal language for Europe and the rest of the world. Writing in 1681, the French scholar De Vienne Plancy expressed surprise that Chinese characters had not been adopted throughout the world "for intercourse among Nations, since they immediately signify ideas" (Knowlson 1975:25). From the seventeenth century right down to the present scholars have debated just how to utilize the universal quality attributed to Chinese characters.

Much of this discussion, however, reveals itself as quite unfocused for the simple reason that it is based on only the vaguest of notions as to exactly how the Chinese characters functioned as the basis of the writing systems of the four countries in which they were used. The discussion evinces no significant support for the idea of adopting classical Chinese itself, as the Japanese, Koreans, and Vietnamese had done in their initial borrowings from China. Nor does there seem to have been much support for the policy of directly adapting Chinese characters to write other languages along the lines already pursued by these three neighbors of China. The French scholars Margouliès and Etiemble, as noted earlier, seem to suggest both these possibilities, but their expositions are marked by high-blown rhetoric with disdain for nitty-gritty details. As The Singlish Affair makes plain, Chinese characters can indeed be extended beyond their present use to replace alphabetic writing in the case of English, French, Russian, Hindi, Arabic and all other languages, but at such an astronomical cost that this venture can only be envisaged by those so blinded by their view of Chinese characters and so lacking in responsibility that they feel no need to look below the surface and confront reality. Small wonder that the idea of directly emulating the Asian use of Chinese characters has received little serious consideration in the four centuries that the subject of Chinese as a universal script has been under discussion.

Much more attention has been devoted to the idea of developing a new "Universal Language" and "Universal Writing" based on "Real Characters" or "Universal Characters" that would adapt what were generally considered to be the underlying principles of Chinese writing—namely, that the characters represented meaning without regard to sound and that a single character was ascribed to a single thing, whether concrete or abstract. The supposed one-to-one correspondence between thing and symbol was seized upon for two reasons. The first was the tendency, against which linguists still have to inveigh, to overemphasize the role of vocabulary compared to grammar and other linguistic aspects in the working of language. The second was the need to find a means of labeling and classifying the vast amount of new scientific and technological knowledge that was coming into being. The concept of a universal set of written symbols dovetailed neatly with the concept of a universal taxonomy of nature (Slaughter 1982).

The supposed Chinese precedent inspired some of the best minds of Europe to take up the problem of developing a universal language in both its theoretical and practical aspects. Numerous schemes were created, touted by their creators as *the* solution to the universal language problem, but invariably rejected by others as their inadequacies became apparent (Knowlson 1975; Slaughter 1982).

One of the basic reasons for the failure of the proposed schemes is the now obvious impossibility of classifying all things known in tables so devised that each item would be assigned its own universal character. These attempts to invent a universal language based on a universal nomenclature were inevitably incomplete, impossibly clumsy, and wholly impractical (Knowlson 1975; Slaughter 1982). Even more fundamental, such attempts are doomed to failure at the outset because, as pointed out in the earlier discussion refuting the notion of Chinese as an ideographic script, any system of writing not based on actual speech would require feats of memory that are humanly quite impossible.

A *reductio ad absurdum* of the whole concept of a universal language that represents the universe of things on a one-to-one basis is the satiric fantasy by Jonathan Swift (1667–1745) in which Gulliver encounters in his travels a School of Languages. There professors are engaged in "a Scheme for abolishing all Words whatsover" on the grounds that "in Reality all Things imaginable are but Nouns" and "since Words are only Names for *Things,* it would be more convenient for all Men to carry about them such *Things* as were necessary to express the particular Business they are to discourse on." Gulliver adds:

> I have often beheld two of those Sages almost sinking under the Weight of their Packs . . . who when they met in the Streets would lay down their Loads, open their Sacks, and hold Conversation for an Hour together; then put up their Implements, help each other to resume their Burthens, and take their Leave. . . . Another great Advantage proposed by this Invention was that it would serve as an universal Language to be understood in all civilized Nations . . . and thus, Embassadors would be qualified to treat with foreign Princes or Ministers of State, to whose Tongues they were utter Strangers. [Swift 1977:181–183]

Leibniz is perhaps the best known of the early scientists who looked to Chinese as a possible model for a universal language, and his early interest in Chinese is still invoked despite the fact, as noted in The Singlish Affair, that he subsequently expressed his disillusionment in Chinese as a model. In spite of the disillusionment of scholars like Leibniz and the failure of innumberable schemes for a universal language, belief in the will-o'-the-wisp of a system of writing divorced from speech continues to be held and even defended by reference to Chinese as an ideographic system that transcends the barrier of differences in language. The views expressed by Margouliès perhaps point to the idea of adapting the supposed principles underlying Chinese characters to create a universal language rather than using them directly in the manner of the Chinese, Japanese, Koreans, and Vietnamese. In a more recent expression of the emulatability thesis we find the well-known anthropologist Margaret Mead calling on scholars in various fields to put aside their parochial differences and unite in seeking to create

> a written form of communication independent of any languages of the world, but dependent upon the concepts essential to high-level philosophical, political, and scientific communication. We have, of course, many such partial artificial languages now in the Arabic numeral system, in chemistry and physics, in engineering diagrams. But the most complete model we have of a written language that is independent of particular languages is the classical Chinese system of writing through which two educated men, who cannot understand a word the other speaks, may nevertheless communicate fully with each other by writing. [Mead and Modley 1968:62]

Kolers (1969) presents some good arguments against the possibility of a full system of writing along the lines envisaged by Mead and Modley, but then he proceeds to weaken his refutation by his confused handling of Chinese as a special case. He repeats the clichés about Chinese characters as a nonphonetic system akin to our numerical system and then goes on to note that the inability of the proposed schemes to present such features as "tense, aspect, mood, and the like" places a limit on their use, "barring the special learning that characterizes a logographic system such as the Chinese"—whatever that means.

CHINESE INFLUENCE ON READING THEORY

It is not enough, however, to note shortcomings in the aspect of the Emulatability Myth that seeks to create a universal language while still advancing the notion of "the special learning that characterizes a logographic system such as Chinese." Pursuit of the will-o'-the-wisp of a universal language has the result merely of wasting countless hours of time. Much more serious is the result of the thesis, which underlies Kolers' reference to "special learning," that "there are two major systems of writing in the world today, the semantic and the phonetic" (Kolers 1970:113). This belief in the semantic nature of Chinese writing leads Kolers to argue that all research into reading— that is, how we read and how children should be taught to read—

should be based on the alleged existence of two completely disparate systems of ideographic and phonetic writing. Kolers' assumption that readers of the Chinese "semantic" script go directly from print to meaning leads to the conclusion, as Gough points out (1972:335), that "if they can do it, so can we." And on this conclusion of emulatability is based a pedagogical approach to reading that affects millions of little victims of the Ideographic Myth.

There is an enormous literature on the teaching of reading. For present purposes, at the risk of oversimpifying the complexities involved in this literature, we can say that there are two main schools of thought on the subject: one arguing for the use of phonics in teaching reading, another arguing against the use of phonics and for an approach in which readers go directly from writing to meaning. Adherents of the second approach constantly buttress their argument by reference to the "ideographic" or "semantic" nature of Chinese writing. So widespread is this aspect of the Emulatability Myth, and so serious are its consequences, that the whole question merits a thorough and long-overdue airing.

We can begin by observing that the line of reasoning espoused by adherents of the emulatability approach can be summarized as "Since A is true, therefore B is true." Since readers of "semantic Chinese" read without regard to sound, therefore readers of "alphabetic English" can read without regard to sound. But what happens to this line of argument if it turns out that A is false? Does this mean that B is also false? Not necessarily. Proposition B may still be correct, but the proof of its correctness must be sought elsewhere than by citing the false proposition A. The least we can say is that confidence in the truth of B is seriously undermined when it is advanced on the basis of something so patently false. Perhaps it should also be added that specialists in reading, although responsible for the application of the Ideographic Myth to the teaching of reading, can be excused to some extent because they have been misled by specialists in Chinese.

The view espoused by Creel and others that the phonetic aspect is of little importance and that we can immediately grasp ideas expressed in Chinese characters is part of the romantic notion of reading ideas directly from "ideographs" without going through a phonetic intermediary. This notion is at the heart of the thesis expounded at wearisome length by Margouliès that Chinese characters can function as a universal script. Unlike less informed exponents of this thesis, Margouliès is fully aware that the overwhelming majority of Chinese characters contain a phonetic element as part of their makeup (1957:80–82). Nevertheless, the special property of characters— namely "the direct understanding of the sign without passing through the intermediary of the oral language"—is in his opinion "in no way modified by the presence of the phonetic." He hammers away at this theme: "Although the majority of characters contain an element indicating the pronunciation, the meaning element prevails over the sound element in the idea that one derives from the character."

Margouliès makes a distinction between the role of the phonetic element in character-based writing and in alphabetic systems (1957: 85–86). In the former it is superfluous since the reader can go directly from character to meaning. In the latter it is essential since the reader, lacking the semantic clues contained in characters, is forced to go through an intermediary stage in which "letters indicate groups of sounds which one pronounces, aloud or mentally, and these sounds, in turn, evoke the words to which they correspond."

Note that crucially different situations are involved in the assertion by Margouliès that "the meaning element prevails over the sound element" and in the commonly held view that Chinese characters "are symbols for ideas, but not for specific sounds or even specific words" (Smith 1979:60). If Chinese characters do indeed lack a phonetic basis, as Smith indicates, readers must, willy-nilly, derive meaning directly, without reading from sound, for the simple reason that there is no sound to read from. But if the characters actually have "sound elements," even if allegedly secondary to "meaning elements," this leaves open the question whether readers make use of the phonetic information available to them.

Whether or not Chinese characters have a phonetic basis can be answered, as we have seen, by examining the characters themselves. Whether or not readers make use of the phonetic information available to them is an entirely separate question that cannot be answered merely by looking at the characters. It can only be answered, if at all, by the kind of experimental research that has been so extensively done for English. The reading process in any language, as this research has shown, is an enormously complex matter involving a host of problems for which there are no simple answers. The inconclusiveness of the research and the polemical nature of the reading controversy, the frequent result of making big generalizations on the basis of little experiments and meager evidence, suggest that simple answers will not be forthcoming for Chinese either. This has already been attested by what little research and experimentation has been carried out to date for Chinese.

THEORIES OF THE READING PROCESS

The overall literature, experimental and otherwise, related to reading suggests that there are three different theories of the reading process in character-based versus alphabetic systems of writing:

1. In both systems meaning is derived directly from symbols without an intermediary phonetic stage (Smith 1973).
2. Only in character-based writing is meaning derived directly from symbols without an intermediary phonetic stage (Margouliès 1957).
3. In neither system is meaning derived directly from symbols without an intermediary phonetic stage (Tzeng et al. 1977–1983).

With respect to alphabetic scripts, after a review of the extensive research into reading, Conrad (1972:236) concludes: "At present we have to accept silent speech in reading as a near universal in cultures where alphabets are used." As to cultures with nonalphabetic scripts, Tzeng and his associates (1977:627) conclude that "phonetic code is the preferred form of representation in reading behavior across languages and across writing systems." This basic idea is repeated in later studies, and Tzeng himself, going further, would now omit the word "preferred" and assert that phonetic code is *the* form of representation in reading behavior (Tzeng 1981:personal communication). Or, as Tzeng and Wang (1983:242) also put it in reference to writing in general, "We prefer to think that recoding the visually presented script into a phonological format is an automatic and inevitable process." However, Tzeng and Hung (1980:226) stress the enormous complexity of the reading process, point out the danger of reaching generalized conclusions on the basis of limited experimentation dealing with only part of the process, and caution that "we are still only on the edge of understanding the total process of reading."

The difficulty of assessing the significance of reading research is well illustrated in the work of Treiman, Baron, and Luk (1981). In an amplification of conclusions reached in this work, Treiman states:

We and others have distinguished between (a) use of speech recoding to identify individual words and (b) use of speech recoding to facilitate memory and comprehension. The two processes could well be independent. The fact that some speech recoding occurs in the reading of Chinese sentences (Tzeng et al.) suggests that speech recoding occurs either in (a) or (b). Those authors suggest that in fact it occurs in (b) only. We showed that the total extent of speech recoding is greater in English than in Chinese. Our interpretation is that speech recoding occurs in both (a) and (b) in English but only (or primarily) in (b) in Chinese. That is, Chinese generally derive meaning without sound but do use sound in reading for other purposes. This conclusion is consistent with that of Tzeng et al. [1981:personal communication]

That reading involves two recoding processes which "could well be independent" is a hypothesis that is by no means proved or universally accepted. That English makes greater use than does Chinese of speech recoding is exactly what is to be expected if one hypothesizes a basically similar reading strategy and attributes the difference to the fact that English orthography, bad as it is, nevertheless provides more useful phonetic clues than does the even more weakly phonetic system of Chinese.

However limited, controversial, and inconclusive research on Chinese reading is, insofar as it attempts to shed light on the reading process by scientific experimentation it is a step in the right direction and deserves more serious consideration than do the subjective views expounded by Margouliès. For the latter merely looks at Chinese writing and concludes that direct reading takes place without the use of any phonetic intermediary. This is an unscientific procedure that is widely practiced but must be condemned as wholly unacceptable.

There is, however, another aspect of Margouliès' thesis which perhaps reduces the question of direct versus indirect reading to a position of secondary importance. Those who believe that meaning is derived directly from written symbols frequently draw a parallel between Chinese characters and arabic numerals. Margouliès says: "The fact is that the West also has its ideograms: these are the arabic numerals. To convince oneself of this, it suffices to ascertain that the numerals evoke directly into the mind the idea of the number that each one of them represents." The numerals, says Margouliès (1957: 82), function as universal symbols which transcend the limitation that would follow from the fact that their spoken form differs from language to language.

Leaving aside the question whether we do indeed grasp the meaning of the numerals directly without a phonetic intermediary, we should still note a little point that is glossed over in the simplistic equating of numerals and characters—namely, that there are ten of the former and thousands of the latter. If it should indeed turn out that we read numerals directly, this cannot be taken as proof that we can do the same with several thousand characters. Quantitative changes lead eventually to qualitative changes—recall what even the very small change in temperature from 33° to 32° will do to water. Surely the task of coping with thousands of symbols, especially without regard to how they sound, is qualitatively different from that of identifying the ten numerals. William S-Y. Wang is undoubtedly justified in saying (1980:200) that "To suggest that learning Chinese characters is like remembering so many arbitrary telephone numbers, as Halle did (1969:18), is to compliment the Chinese for memory feats of which few mortals are capable!"

The error in equating Chinese characters with arabic numerals has reinforced the error in viewing the characters as semantic and non-phonetic. But if we look at Chinese not as a complete system of ideographic writing but as basically a variant of phonetic writing, we might hazard the guess that the reading process too is not uniquely different. According to Goodman's theory, "reading is a sampling, predicting, comfirming process during which the reader makes use of three types of information—or cue systems—*simultaneously*. These three systems are graphophonic, syntactic, and semantic" (Allen and Watson 1976:75, emphasis added). Research studies carried out by Goodman and his associates among American schoolchildren indicate that weak readers, and all readers faced with unfamiliar items, tend to rely heavily on graphophonic clues, but skilled readers are able to make greater use of the syntactic and semantic cue systems.

In Chinese also, it may be hypothesized, skilled readers are able to make use of the wide variety of clues contained in a succession of characters. According to their ability they will be able to pick and choose which clues they will utilize and which they will ignore. These clues include: (1) the graphic structure of the characters; (2) the information provided by the phonetic if there is a useful one; (3) the hint that might be provided by a radical; (4) punctuation and other typographical information; (5) the immediate environment of each character and the larger grammatical patterns in which it occurs; (6) knowledge of the subject matter.

There are probably other aids in getting meaning from a text, but this is enough to show that the reading process in Chinese is a highly complex act which the skilled reader performs with impressive virtuosity. He certainly does not read Chinese letter by letter, since there are no letters to read, and not necessarily syllable by syllable or word by word, though he could do so if called upon or if he encounters difficulty and must slow down for a careful look at a troublesome passage. Otherwise he can skim over the material, noting the pronunciation of one character and the structure of another, seizing on a fraction of a character for its sound or its meaning, ignoring several characters because he deduces the meaning from the context, extrapolating on the basis of what he already knows of the subject matter —in short, employing a combination of strategies and skillfully using various clues and the redundancy in writing to make sense of what he reads. In general, however, and this is the main point, it seems hardly reasonable to assume that readers of Chinese will—or indeed can— totally ignore whatever aid is provided by the imperfect but by no means useless system of phonetic elements.

This view of a reading process in which Chinese readers will, when necessary, make use of the phonetic clues available to them stands in opposition to the concept of Chinese characters as a unique system of writing that either lacks a phonetic basis or has phonetic information that is not needed. In promoting this ideographic concept sinologists like Margouliès and Creel have lent authoritative support to much confused thinking about the nature of the script. This is bad enough when confined to students of Chinese whose attention is thereby distracted from pursuing more meaningful lines of research. It is far more serious when the ideographic concept is taken up by a wider audience that includes poets of the Imagist school and scholars in various fields, particularly specialists in the fields of psycholinguistics and reading.[1]

Students of reading, according to Smith (1973:51), are at odds over two main questions: Is identification of individual letters a necessary preliminary to word identification? And is identification of words a prerequisite for comprehension? Those who answer these questions in the negative have seized upon the concept of "ideographic" Chinese characters in their eagerness to win points in their arguments. In so doing they compound Margouliès' error. While denying their utility, the sinologist at least recognized the existence of phonetic elements. Some psycholinguists have been misled into overlooking or suppressing the phonetic aspect. As a result they further misrepresent the characters and by misusing them have added to the confusion.

CHINESE CHARACTERS, GEOMETRIC FIGURES, AND REBUSES

Take the frequently cited article by Paul Rozin and his students (Rozin, Poritsky, and Sotsky:1971). The authors sought to get around what they said was the difficulty experienced by some children with the "phonetic mapping" of alphabetic writing by teaching eight black children with reading problems thirty Chinese characters which they described as "a simplified version of the Chinese logographic system, with interpretation in English." In assessing the results of this endeavor, the authors concluded that "the children's success with the Chinese material" was to be explained in part on cognitive grounds: "Chinese orthography maps directly onto meaning, whereas in English orthography the relation of sign to meaning is mediated through the sound system." The authors interpret the results obtained from their tiny sample as showing "the superiority of the Chinese" and conclude, in the words of the title of their article, that "American children with reading problems can easily learn to read English represented by Chinese characters." In point of fact, this outrageously mistitled article has virtually nothing to do with Chinese or with English or even, perhaps, with reading.

In this approach to the reading problem the characters, instead of being presented as symbols with a phonetic aspect, whose utility to readers we can debate, are stripped of their phonetic significance. They become pure designs comparable to simple or compound compositions made up of shapes like circles, squares, and stars. Apart from the need to motivate the eight subjects with something exotic, such arbitrary figures would have done just as well, but their use would have made more obvious the shallowness of the research design and its irrelevance to Chinese and perhaps also to the study of reading.

This matter of misrepresenting and misusing Chinese characters is of such importance that it merits a bit more analysis. Perhaps the difference in usage of the characters in Chinese and English can be made clearer in the following presentation:

1. Chinese characters used to represent Chinese:

Character	Pronunciation	Meaning
皇	huáng	emperor
蝗	huáng	locust
見	jiàn	see

2. Chinese characters used in the manner of Rozin et al. to represent English:

Character	(Pronunciation?)	Meaning
皇	(emperor?)	emperor
蝗	(locust?)	locust
見	(see?)	see

3. Geometric characters which could be used to represent English:

Character	(Pronunciation?)	Meaning
⊠	(emperor?)	emperor
✳⊠	(locust?)	locust
⊟	(see?)	see

Type 2 is the same in principle as type 3. It is *not* the same in principle as type 1, however, since the common pronunciation *huáng* that exists when rebus-derived Chinese characters are used to represent Chinese is suppressed when they are used to represent English. If the approach embodied in type 3 is extended in the same way that Rozin et al. used the characters to write English, we can reach the following conclusion:

American children with reading problems can easily learn to read English represented by geometric characters. Proof:

 "Emperor sees locusts."

This may or may not be a valid conclusion, as it should be tested not with the fakery of three or thirty symbols but with a genuine effort involving the thousands, actually hundreds of thousands, of such geometric figures that would be needed to write English without regard to sound, something that would soon show itself to be a preposterous impossibility. In any case, however, it has nothing to do with Chinese.

The investigation does not appear to have much to do with English either, because the authors ignored, among other things, such grammatical features as number and tense. The character 车, for example, is rendered as "car," with no explanation why the rendering "cars" would not do equally well and no indication how "English represented by Chinese characters" would express what is a compulsory distinction in English. To ignore such distinctions with the excuse of simplifying things means we are no longer dealing with English but with a pseudolanguage. More than aesthetics is involved in rejecting as non-English the sentence presented by Rozin et al.: "Good brother doesn't (not) give man red car."

If it were not for the attention-getting property of Chinese characters, it is likely that this article would have received little attention. Several years earlier, and quite without fanfare, Richard W. Woodcock and his associates at the Institute of Mental Retardation in Nashville, Tennessee, had done much more extensive experimental work and had even produced teaching materials based on an approach to reading using symbols described as "pictorial, geometric, or even completely abstract." In describing his experiment Woodcock (1968:4–11) said that children

> would first learn to read using a vocabulary of rebuses and later proceed through a transition program in which traditional orthography words would be gradually substituted for the rebus vocabulary. . . .
> The results of the study demonstrate that learning to "read" rebuses is markedly easier than learning to read traditional orthography. Furthermore, the differences become even more disparate as the complexity of the vocabulary and sentences increase.

The seven volumes of materials produced by Woodcock and his associates go further than mere experimentation and actually present a whole series of books for introducing children to reading. The first volume is limited to presenting, in isolation and in sentences, several dozen graphic symbols of varying degrees of abstraction. The letter *s* is introduced in the second volume as a plural suffix to graphic symbols. Thereafter, while introducing additional rebus symbols to a

total of 150, a gradual transition is made to regular English orthography (Woodcock, Clark, and Davies 1967–1969).

In sum, Woodcock and his associates, in experiments and in actual
teaching involving more children and more symbols, had shown even
earlier that children who have difficulty in learning to read via ordinary English orthography, and indeed even mental retardates, can
learn a limited number of nonphonetic graphic symbols, can order
them in systematic patterns, can attach meaning to the symbols and
to the order in which they are arranged, and can use them not to
"read English" represented by such symbols but to make the transition to reading ordinary English. That their modestly presented work
has gone largely unnoticed, in contrast to the wide publicity and frequent citing received by an eye-catching article on reading English
represented by Chinese characters, suggests a certain superficiality in
some of the scholarship dealing with systems of writing and problems
of reading.[2]

INAPPLICABILITY OF CHINESE

Rozin and his associates conclude, on what basis is not entirely clear,
that a syllabic rather than phonemic approach might be more suitable for introducing reading. When asked the first of the two questions raised above—Is identification of individual letters a necessary
preliminary to word identification?—they would therefore answer in
the negative. This controversy over letter or phoneme versus syllable
or morpheme or word approach to reading does not arise in the case
of the traditional Chinese script, however, so the matter will be left to
be fought out by the two opposing camps concerned with alphabetic
scripts.

The second of the two questions raised above—Is identification of
words a prerequisite for comprehension?—is answered by the psycho-
linguist Frank Smith as follows: "In some languages the relation
between written and spoken forms is far more tenuous than in
English. In Chinese, for example, the written language is largely
ideographic and can be read quite independently of the reader's spoken language" (1973:73). In support of this view Smith enthusiasti-
cally reproduced the article by Rozin, Poritsky, and Sotsky in his work
and prefaced it with the following conclusion: "The implications of
the paper for the reading process are obvious: Readers do not use

(and do not need to use) the alphabetic principle or decoding to sound in order to learn or identify words" (1973:105).

Since there is no such thing as an ideographic writing system that conveys meaning without regard to sound, citing Chinese characters as an example of the concept is to misuse them as an argument in opposition to reading phonetically and, by implication at least, in favor of the superiority of Chinese characters and their ability to function as a universal means of communication. Moreover, there is little justification in making sweeping generalizations or reaching broad conclusions on the basis of what may or may not be true about a few Chinese characters and even fewer children in quite special learning situations. Anyone seriously interested in coping with reading problems can hardly share the satisfaction expressed by Rozin, Poritsky, and Sotsky with their "quite successful" gimmick of teaching eight children 30 characters, the final test in which showed that "the comprehension score was 22.5 correct answers out of 48 questions." More important, the authors themselves noted that "some of the children began to get a little bored with the Chinese as they ran into some difficulty" after learning 18 characters. If they encountered "some difficulty" with a mere 18 characters, how much difficulty and boredom are many learners likely to experience when they have to cope with 1,800 or more?

A fundamental error made by psycholinguists who uphold this type of investigation is the belief that since we can recognize many objects in the physical world around us we can equally well memorize the meanings of thousands of Chinese characters or the meanings of English words approached as ideographs. Thus Smith (1973:75) states that

> we can both recognize and recall many thousands of words in our spoken vocabulary, and recognize many thousands of different faces and animals and plants and objects in our visual world. Why should this fantastic memorizing capacity suddenly run out in the case of reading? It is surely no more difficult for a person to remember that 家 or the printed word *house* is called "house" than that ⌂ (or an actual house) is called "house." Unfortunately, we tend to believe that the alphabetic form *house* is read in an exclusive manner, simply because it is composed of letters.

This is an astonishing statement. How can the cognitive impact of little two-dimensional black-on-white symbols be compared with that of three-dimensional, multicolored, multitextured, and otherwise differentiated objects in our visual world? Smith has apparently not bothered to acquaint himself with the well-known difficulty of mastering Chinese characters. A modicum of inquiry would have revealed to him the sad but incontrovertible truth that this "fantastic memorizing capacity" does in fact run out for most Chinese, Japanese, and Koreans, not to mention Western students, when they are confronted with what actual experience has clearly shown to be the much more difficult task of recognizing and remembering many thousands of different characters.

Smith and like-minded psycholinguists have set up a straw man when they seem to postulate that all readers, even highly skilled ones, read *everything* phonetically, letter by letter; they then attempt to knock it down with the thesis, which they seek to support by invoking the example of "ideographic" Chinese, that we read *nothing* phonetically. The Chinese reality that their theory needs to confront is one of a highly imperfect system of syllabic writing in which we must suppose, lacking conclusive evidence to the contrary, that Chinese readers—like, it may be suspected, readers of alphabetic scripts— make use in varying degrees of some but not necessarily all of the phonetic clues contained in the graphic symbols.

In their eagerness to invoke the aid of the ideographic concept, psycholinguistic proponents of the Emulatability Myth have become gullible victims of an inadvertent con game in which they have been sold a bill of goods about the nonphonetic or insignificantly phonetic nature of Chinese writing. This mistake has led them at best into errors of judgment and distortion of fact and at worst into academic hucksterism. They thereby do a disservice to the very cause they are seeking to promote by raising a question whether all their assertions, including the potentially persuasive claim of the superiority of the word or syllable approach over the letter approach to reading, are as poorly thought out and supported as those based on the Ideographic Myth.

11.

The Monosyllabic Myth

"In this language there is neither an alphabet nor any definite number of letters, but there are as many characters as there are words or expressions." So said the sixteenth-century Catholic missionary Michele Ruggieri, one of the first Westerners to undertake what he called the "semi-martyrdom" of studying Chinese (quoted in Bernard 1933:149). Ruggieri's views were similar to those of his superior, Father Matteo Ricci, as paraphrased by Father Nicola Trigault, who also transmitted the opinion that in Chinese "word, syllable, and written symbol are the same" and that the words "are all monosyllabic; not even one disyllabic or polysyllabic word can be found" (Trigault 1615:25–26).[1]

Even these early observations reveal one of the main reasons for the confusion leading to the Monosyllabic Myth—namely, the failure to distinguish between speech and writing. It is the despair of linguists, who insist on keeping the two apart, that they have so little success in achieving their aim and hence must do incessant battle against the practice of using an observation about writing to reach a conclusion about speech. Thus we have the case of the previously cited textbook writer who after noting that dictionaries contain many thousands of characters adds that "two thousand are enough for the ordinary speech of a well-educated man" (Barrett 1934:viii). Another scholar, rejecting the notion of meaningless syllables in Chinese, apprises us that "for those who know enough characters . . . they are not entirely meaningless" (Yang Lien Sheng 1949:463). To think otherwise, it seems, is to reveal oneself as an ignoramus who does not know enough characters. Let us start this discussion of monosyllabism, in any case, by making some observations about Chinese speech and

writing in which we shall try to maintain the distinction between
the two.

MONOSYLLABISM DERIVED FROM WRITING

In alphabetic writing systems such as English the separation of
graphic units by white space, a relatively late development in the history of writing (Gelb 1963:19), is a popular means of defining a word
despite the somewhat haphazard way in which many of the demarca-
tions came about. In Chinese the fact that the characters in a running
text are normally set off from each other by the same amount of space
between adjacent characters regardless of how closely they may be
tied together in meaning is also an important factor in defining characters as words.

It is individual characters that form the basis for dictionary entries.
Each character is provided with a dictionary listing which gives its
pronunciation, consisting always of a single syllable, and its meaning,
which may be single or multiple. The conventional dictionary pronunciation of a character does not always correspond with the sound
in speech that the syllable is supposed to represent. Dictionaries are
notorious for providing mainly *reading* pronunciation of characters, a
notable exception being the excellent *Concise Dictionary of Spoken
Chinese* by Chao and Yang (1962), which despite its title is primarily
an analysis of characters in terms of their function in representing
speech.

A more serious objection to the handling of characters in ordinary
dictionaries involves semantics. Each character is presented as an
independent unit and is defined as having at least one meaning. The
assumption that each character represents an independent meaningful syllable leads to the conclusion that each character represents a
monosyllabic word.

MONOSYLLABISM SURMISED FROM SPEECH

The notion of monosyllabism derived from the writing system is further reinforced by the generally held view of Chinese speech. The syllable in Chinese is often considered phonologically distinct in that it
is more rigidly determined than is the case in many other languages,
such as English. Chinese syllables, with some exceptions that can be
disregarded here, are invariant in the sense that they do not undergo

the kind of internal change exhibited by English man-men, his-him, love-loved. In itself this is not a particularly distinctive or particularly significant feature. It has, however, helped to create a situation in which "the syllable is accorded a special status in Chinese . . . as a psychological unit" (Arlotto 1968:521). The syllable is held to be the type of unit between phoneme and sentence that in English is called a "word" (Chao 1968a:136). Since the syllable is represented by a character, the latter too is held to represent a word. The equating of syllable with character, the notion that both represent a word, and the fact that each individual character, and hence each individual syllable attached to it, has individual meaning, all combine to characterize both speech and writing as "monosyllabic."

In sinological circles there has been considerable dispute over the use of the term "monosyllabic" in defining Chinese speech and writing and in explaining the evolution of both. Some specialists, particularly in writing for an audience of fellow specialists, hedge their use of the term by qualifications that give it a quite technical meaning. The well-known linguist Li Fang-Kuei, for example, in discussing the Sino-Tibetan family of languages to which Chinese belongs, makes the following cautious statement (1973:2):

> One of the characteristics of this family is the tendency toward monosyllabism. By monosyllabism we do not mean that all the words in these languages consist of single syllables, but that a single syllable is an important phonological unit and often is a morphemic unit, the structure of which is rigidly determined by the phonological rules of the language, and serves as the basis for the formation of words, phrases, and sentences.

What Li describes as a mere "tendency" is popularly conceived as a fully accomplished development. His restrained comment that the single syllable "often is a morphemic unit" and his specific disclaimer that by "monosyllabism" he does not mean that all the words in Chinese and related languages consist of single syllables go unnoticed in the popular view that the syllable *always* has meaning and is not a mere morpheme but a full-fledged word. The popular misconception of the Chinese speaking entirely in words of one syllable is reinforced by some specialists who exaggerate the features noted by Li either because they lack his understanding or because in the interest of popularization they oversimplify to the point of error.

POLYSYLLABIC BUTTERFLIES

The popular notion of Chinese as a monosyllabic language and its designation as such by certain specialists has been sharply attacked by George A. Kennedy in several works which have become classics of sinological scholarship. In an article entitled "The Butterfly Case" Kennedy (1964:274–322) discusses typical dictionary procedures as illustrated by the handling of the characters referring to the insect in question. One entry presents the character 蝴 with the pronunciation *hú* and the definition "the butterfly." Another entry presents the character 蝶 with the pronunciation *dié* and the definition "the butterfly." The first entry also presents both characters as the combination 蝴蝶 with the pronunciation *húdié* and the definition "the butterfly." The second entry also presents both characters as the combination 蝴 蝶 with the pronunciation *húdié* and the definition "the butterfly" (Mathews 1945:nos. 2174, 6321). This leads Kennedy to ask in exasperation: "What, for Heaven's sake, is the word for 'butterfly'?" According to the authoritative Chao and Yang dictionary (1962:192) the word, in current transcription, is *hùdiǎr.* It thus appears that:

1. *hú* ("butterfly") does not exist in current spoken Chinese.
2. *dié* ("butterfly") does not exist in current spoken Chinese.
3. *húdié* ("butterfly") does not exist in current colloquial Chinese. (Both syllables are *reading* pronunciations.)

The pronunciation *húdié* is used, to be sure, in formal speech and has even been decreed as the official standard pronunciation. This is a further indication of the influence of bookish language on the spoken style.

THE MYTH OF FORCED POLYSYLLABISM

Did the terms *hú* and *dié* ever exist as words in spoken Chinese? Karlgren, a leading specialist who calls Chinese monosyllabic, contends in his various writings that terms like *hùdiǎr,* which he designates as synonym-compounds, came into being because in the course of time sound simplification took place and resulted in such an increase in monosyllabic homophones as to require the creation of disyllabic compounds where one syllable (or character) would have served in an earlier stage (Karlgren 1929, 1949). Kennedy rejects the whole concept of the forced creation of synonym-compounds (1964:104–118, 274–322). He points out that we have no record of the Chinese ever having even as many as four thousand distinct syllables, a number which if representing only words of one syllable would have been quite inadequate to represent the scores of thousands of expressions that the Chinese with their highly sophisticated culture must have needed to express themselves. The Chinese, Kennedy concludes, were therefore never able to form all their sentences solely with words of one syllable.

Kennedy also notes that the earliest record we have of many terms, going back to the eras of greatest phonological complexity, is as two-syllable expressions. A famous fourth-century B.C. story tells of how the philosopher Zhuangzi woke one day wondering whether it was really himself who had dreamed of being a butterfly or whether it was a butterfly that was now dreaming of being a philosopher. The term occurs seven times in the story, always with the two characters, never with only one. Kennedy notes further that one standard dictionary has 373 characters under the "insect" radical. "Of these graphs," he says, "186 are given dictionary meaning, while 187 . . . are listed as undefinable except in association with other graphs." For this section of the dictionary, he says (1964:297): "The majority of Chinese graphs stand for syllables with no independent meaning, these being no more than part of words or phrases."

In another article Kennedy pushes the origin of some disyllabic terms back to the earliest days of Chinese writing. He points out that many creatures, such as the horse, the ox, the sheep, the bird, were each represented by a single pictograph. But there were no pictographs for the butterfly, the cicada, the bat, the spider, the cricket, and many other insects. It is hardly coincidental that the first group comprised words of one syllable and the latter words of two syllables. The latter could equally well have been depicted with a single pictograph, but instead, since the tradition was apparently already established that a single character should not represent more than one syllable, they were written phonetically with two "radical + phonetic" compounds in which neither character had independent existence. Chinese writing, says Kennedy, had in fact already become "an organized system of syllabic writing" (1964:238–241). To this Zhou Youguang adds the interesting observation that many such disyllabic words can be readily identified visually by the fact that they are represented by a sequence of two characters each containing the same radical but having a different phonetic (1979:252)—that is, they have the structure AX AY, in which A represents the common radical and X and Y the different phonetics.

The analysis advanced by Kennedy refutes not so much the concept of synonym-compounds as the arguments advanced by Karlgren and others to explain the origin of the expressions subsumed under this label. In citing the fact that the Chinese term for "butterfly" first appears in a written text as a disyllabic expression, Kennedy demonstrates that if either syllable in such expressions occurs alone in subsequent literature, most of which has been written in a classical style divorced from actual speech, this obviously contradicts Karlgren's thesis and reveals a process of written monosyllabic abbreviation of earlier disyllabic terms. Similarly, in the case of *kànjian* ("see"), a term that Karlgren advances as an example of synonym-compounds that the Chinese were forced to create because sound simplification made for monosyllabic ambiguity, Kennedy notes the independent existence of monosyllabic *jiàn* ("see") from around 500 B.C. all the way down to the present and the independent existence of monosyllabic *kàn* ("look at") from about A.D. 900 to today. He notes further that *kànjian* is not a mere combining of two syllables with similar meanings but belongs to a special class of "resultative-compound" verbs that has existed in Chinese for more than two thousand years. In short, Kennedy contends that to claim phonetic impoverishment as the reason for compounding in Chinese does not conform to historical reality.

ORIGIN OF SYNONYM-COMPOUNDS

The facts indicate that some of the terms referred to as synonym-compounds originated from inner workings of Chinese that have nothing to do with sound simplification. The origin of many other terms, however, is lost in the dim recesses of the ancient past, though assiduous scholarly research may sometimes succeed in tracing the provenance of a specific term, such as *pútao* ("grape"). The usual dictionary handling of this term, similar to that for "butterfly," presents a two-character expression meaning "grape" under both the character 葡 (*pú*) defined as "grape" and the character 萄 (*tao*) also defined as "grape." In fact, however, the two syllables are inseparable and meaningless in themselves. They actually constitute a phonetic loan derived from an Iranian word *badag(a)* that entered into Chinese when the grapevine was brought back from Ferghana in Central Asia by the Chinese general Zhang Qian in 126 B.C. (Chmielewski 1958). This precise dating of the origin of a disyllabic expression in Chinese further illustrates how misleading is the dictionary procedure that gives independent meanings for each of the characters used to write the two syllables in such terms and, moreover, how unfounded is the view that such disyllabic expressions were forced upon the Chinese by phonetic impoverishment.

It is noteworthy that many early disyllabic morphemes, such as the words for "butterfly" and "cricket," are nouns. The same is true of the polysyllabic morphemes that are recent borrowings from other languages, chiefly European. The fact that most of these polysyllabic words are nouns, which are much more easily borrowed than verbs and other parts of speech, may account for the view held by many specialists that the early polysyllabic morphemes were probably all loanwords borrowed from other languages. Kratochvíl (1968:65) says that most of these terms "are of non-Chinese origin. . . . [They] came into Chinese so long ago that the origin of many of them is either unknown or hypothetical." While the foreign origin of such terms seems quite plausible, more conclusive proof is needed for what at present must be taken as assumption.

PUTTING THE LEXICON BEFORE THE LANGUAGE

Whether of foreign origin or native creation, these polysyllabic morphemes are generally written with characters whose pronunciations have no meaning or independent existence of their own in the spoken language. A frequent approach to such characters, however, is to force a semantic interpretation on them. Kennedy notes the case of a commentator who in annotating an ancient poem with the line "Chirp go the crickets" gravely tells us that crickets feed on plants, the crics eating the stems while the kets eat the leaves. This sort of approach leads Kennedy to the following comment: "A Chinese lexicon is strictly speaking not a dictionary of words at all, but at best a Collection of Syllabic Symbols, Ancient and Modern. And the major problems conjured up for themselves by western scholars are the result of putting the lexicon before the language" (1964:116–117; DeFrancis 1950:170).

As an example of the inverted approach Kennedy notes the perennial argument that even a small dictionary contains no less than thirty-eight words pronounced *ĭ* (or *yĭ*) and that the resultant ambiguity made necessary various expedients, such as Karlgren's synonym-compounds, so that people could make themselves understood in speech. In point of fact, with at most three or four possible exceptions, all these "thirty-eight words pronounced *yĭ*" are either fixed parts of polysyllabic expressions with no life of their own or obsolete terms that may or may not once have had an independent existence. As Kennedy tartly remarks, the hypothetical situation of the speaker saying *"yĭ"* and the hearer looking blank is purely a Western fabrication. That *yĭ* is ambiguous in speech is a figment of fertile imaginations that prefer gazing at entries stored in dictionaries rather than listening to utterances spoken in real life.

The popular practice of citing dictionaries to show how Chinese were forced to struggle with their problem of monosyllabism in speech usually follows a repetitious line. Consideration is confined to a few syllables that are represented by many characters in the dictionary. *Yĭ* is one of the favorites, and the problem of ambiguity in semantically overloaded syllables is made to appear even more horrendous by disregarding the four tonal distinctions, thereby potentially quadrupling the ambiguity of *yĭ*. Other favorite syllables are *li, zhi,* and *shi.*

Characteristically, none of these worrywarts think to mention syllables like *wŏ* ("I") and *niŭ* ("ox"), which are unique in speech and are uniquely represented by a single character, or to note that of the 1,277 syllables of Mandarin, 261 or 20 percent have no homophones (Chao 1968a:185) and are thus presumably completely intelligible in isolation. Chen Heqin's list of 4,719 characters averages out to 3.7 per syllable, only a tenth of the nightmarish thirty-eight "words" pronounced *yĭ*.

DEGREES OF SYLLABIC FREEDOM

Syllables like *wŏ* that are intelligible even in isolation are at the opposite extreme from syllables like *hú*, allegedly "butterfly" but actually a mere phonetic element devoid of meaning and tightly bound as part of the two-syllable expression *húdiǎr.* Between these two extremes are meaningful syllables that are semibound in the sense that they always occur bound but have a certain flexibility in joining with other syllables. There are thus three types of Chinese syllables:

1. F: free, meaningful
2. SB: semibound, meaningful
3. CB: completely bound, meaningless

These three categories are roughly comparable in English to the free form *teach*, the semibound form *er* in "teacher" and "preacher," and the completely bound forms *cor* and *al* in "coral." The first two categories are morphemes, the third is not, as is the case also with their counterparts in Chinese.

How many characters of these types are there in Chinese? Thanks to the Chao and Yang dictionary mentioned earlier, we can reply to this question, the answer to which obviously bears on the question of monosyllabism in Chinese. This dictionary enables us to classify characters, and hence the syllables attached to them, into our three categories. It labels characters only on the basis of the two categories of free and bound (our semibound) together with a category L for literary. Some characters are placed in more than one category, notably F and B. Characters in our completely bound (CB) category receive no classification label in the dictionary but are readily identifiable since they are noted as forming part of a unique fixed combination of two characters.

A random sample of two hundred characters reveals the following distribution:[2]

> 44% free (includes 7% literary)
> 45% semibound
> 11% completely bound
> 100%

Zhou Youguang, using a different corpus of characters than the approximately 4,800 of the Chao and Yang dictionary, and also perhaps having a different opinion as to whether a specific character is free or bound, says that "44 percent free is too much!" In his opinion, only 2,000 or so, or about 30 percent, of the 6,800 "modern standard characters" needed to write contemporary Chinese are free words (Zhou 1982:personal communication).

Although there are no figures for English that would enable us to make a precise comparison, it would appear that Chinese has a higher proportion of free and semibound monosyllabic morphemes than does English and a lower proportion of completely bound syllables.

As to the graphemic representation of English, leaving aside the indeterminate but hardly insignificant number of English words whose spellings give only partial indication of the pronunciation, there are in English far fewer written symbols that are completely nonphonetic and may therefore be called logographic. These include the numerals and other visual morphemes, which number well under 1 percent, actually only a few hundred compared to the "well over a million words" which according to Pei (1952:96) are contained in the most comprehensive dictionaries of modern English. This contrasts with the third or so of single Chinese characters that are either completely nonphonetic or so obscurely phonetic that they should be considered as falling in that category. The numerical disparity between Chinese and English should not, however, cause us to overlook some significant parallels between the two. These parallels are illustrated in Table 9.

Table 9   Some Chinese and English Graphemic Parallels

Symbol	Degree of Freedom	Kind of Symbol	Sound	Word	Meaning
C1 九	F	logographic	*jiǔ*	*jiǔ*	nine
C2 玖	F	phonetic	*jiǔ*	*jiǔ*	nine[3]
C3 教	F	phonetic	*jiào*	} *jiàoyuán*	teacher
C4 員	SB	logographic	*yuán*		
C5 珊	CB	phonetic	*shān*	} *shānhú*	coral
C6 瑚	CB	phonetic	*hú*		
E1 9	F	logographic	nine	nine	nine
E2 nine	F	phonetic	nine	nine	nine
E3 teach	F	phonetic	teach	} teacher	teacher
E4 er	SB	phonetic	er		
E5 cor	CB	phonetic	cor	} coral	coral
E6 al	CB	phonetic	al		

In a footnote to their dictionary Chao and Yang (1962:vi) state: "Chinese morphemes are for the most part monosyllabic. The nonsyllabic but meaningful suffix 兒 and disyllabic names of many plants and animals in which the separate syllables have no independent meanings of their own are among the very few exceptions." I am not sure I agree that 11 percent of the characters (and syllables) in the completely bound (CB) category are to be dismissed as "very few exceptions." In any case the previously cited figures of 30 or 44 percent represent the maximum picture of monosyllabism for single characters. If we take as the basis of calculation not single characters but dictionary entries, it transpires that less than 5 percent of the more than 200,000 entries in the *Modern Chinese-English Technical and General Dictionary* (McGraw-Hill 1963) consist of only one syllable. The figure would probably be much less than 1 percent if, as may well be the case, the total Chinese lexicon is about the same size as the million words of English. This turns out to be a strange sort of monosyllabism that has such a small proportion of its words as free monosyllables.

A MATTER OF DEFINITION

It is clear that a good deal of the controversy over this term is a question of definition. The view that it refers to a language and writing system consisting of words of one syllable is based on dismissing the 11 percent without meaning and viewing the remaining 89 percent as words, rather than half as real (free) words and half as bound morphemes. Those who, following Kennedy, believe that this is too cavalier an approach think it should be rejected as fostering the Monosyllabic Myth. There may be objection on other grounds as well. Arlotto prefers calling spoken Chinese "syllabically oriented" to contrast with "morpheme-oriented" or "word-oriented" languages since, he says, "monosyllabic" would be meaningful for typological comparisons "only if it could be contrasted with other languages that might be called disyllabic, trisyllabic, or polysyllabic in the same sense" (1968:522). I prefer the term "morphosyllabic." Although it lacks the sex appeal of "monosyllabic," it at least accounts for nine-tenths of the facts about Chinese syllables and characters. It also has the virtue, which "ideographic" and "monosyllabic" both lack, of helping to avoid misconceptions about the nature of Chinese language and writing.

HARMFUL ASPECTS OF "MONOSYLLABIC"

As in the case of the Ideographic Myth, the Monosyllabic Myth has fostered a kind of cliché thinking about Chinese. Because of its application to both speech and writing it has helped to obscure the difference between the two. Moreover, it has distracted scholarly attention from pursuing certain meaningful lines of research, such as a closer examination of the possible relationship between speech and writing as revealed in China's voluminous literature.

But the worst aspect of the myth is when it is taken up in a distorted version by the public at large, as for example by the illustrious and authoritative *Oxford English Dictionary,* in which "monosyllabic" is glossed as a philological term "used as the distinctive epithet of those languages (e.g., Chinese) which have a vocabulary wholly of monosyllables." I suppose that specialists wedded to the term "monosyllabic" can argue that they are not responsible if their scholarly use of the term is misunderstood outside the field (or even within the field, for that matter). Yet it seems highly unfortunate that a field which is marked by the Confucian concept of "rectification of names" should pay so little attention to the impact of the name on others.

For the impact of the term "monosyllabic" on the general public has been generally bad. The notion of speaking wholly in words of one syllable, or of reading and writing in the same fashion, in many minds carries with it a connotation of inadequacy and backwardness or at best of childish simplicity. Early in the last century a leading British literary critic was so incensed at what he conceived to be the Chinese addiction to monosyllabism and refusal to form compound words that he gave vent to the following diatribe:

> There is no instance, we believe, on the face of the earth, of a language so imperfect and inartificial [*sic*]; and it is difficult to perceive how any race of people could be so stupid, or so destitute of invention, as to leave it in such a state of poverty. . . . By what particular infatuation they have been withheld from so obvious an improvement—by what bar they have been obstructed from compounding their words, as well as their written characters, we are utterly unable to comprehend, and no writer, we think, has attempted to explain. [Quoted in Kennedy 1964:105–106]

The learned critic's inability to comprehend, which was due in no small measure to received notions about Chinese monosyllabism, for the same reason continues to characterize the general attitude toward Chinese. This is unfortunate because, apart from denigrating a language and a script of enormous complexity and sophistication, it reveals our failure to get across to the public at large the idea that the real world of Chinese speech and writing is much more fascinating than the mythological world of Chinese monosyllabism.

12.

The Indispensability Myth

The belief that Chinese characters are indispensable exists on several levels that range from the most shallow mindlessness to the most serious thoughtfulness. As usual, much of the mythology is based on a confusion of terms and on mixing up speech and writing. In its most general form the Indispensability Myth holds that Chinese cannot be written in an alphabetic script. This seemingly straightforward statement turns out on closer examination to involve a great deal of ambiguity centering on the meaning of the two terms "Chinese" and "cannot." As I have stressed repeatedly in the previous chapters, the term "Chinese" covers a wide range of meanings. The indispensability thesis needs to be tested against each of them.

CAN SPOKEN CHINESE BE ALPHABETIZED?

One of the meanings of "Chinese" is that it represents an abbreviation of "Chinese speech." We can narrow the definition considerably by limiting discussion initially to the speech of one specific speaker of Chinese, in other words to one of the billion idiolects of Chinese. Our question then becomes: Can the Chinese represented by this idiolect be written phonetically—for example, can it be Pinyinized? One way to answer this question is to consider it theoretically. The answer must then be unequivocally in the affirmative. Such an answer is based on the simple observation that scientific linguists have repeatedly demonstrated in actual practice the validity of their thesis that the speech of any individual can be written in an alphabetic script. The overall approach in such an undertaking is the same for all forms of speech in that it involves direct observation and analysis. The specific solutions vary according to the linguistic details (phonemic, morphemic, lexical, syntactical, and so forth) for each form of speech. Any student of linguistics with a modicum of competence can create an alphabetic system of writing for any form of speech in the world. To deny this elementary truth in general or in specific application to Chinese is to reject science and embrace mythology.

There can be no question, then, that it is theoretically possible to create a billion alphabetic systems for Chinese, one for each of the billion idiolects. This is obviously an impractical procedure. We must somehow group the idiolects in order to reduce the number of alphabetic systems that need to be created. Can we group the billion idiolects all together and create a single system? If not, how many groups need to be delineated?

The answers to these questions are partly theoretical and partly practical. A rough theoretical formulation is that the speech of any group of people, however diverse their specific ways of talking, can be written with a single alphabetic system so long as the forms of speech are mutually intelligible. This is precisely the situation that exists in English. Our orthography serves as a common form of writing for such diverse dialects of English as those spoken in the United States, England, Australia, and elsewhere. Because of the diverse forms of speech that it represents it can truthfully be called an interdialectical romanization of English. That this orthography does its job with something less than optimum efficiency is due to a variety of factors that relate in part to deficiencies inherent in the spelling system and in part to distance of some of the dialects from the sounds represented by the common orthography.

A practical approach to the problem of grouping speakers for the purpose of creating a common alphabetic system is simply to see if the system works. If a system does not work for some speakers, there are several possible solutions. One is to require that speakers outside a certain group learn the speech of that group to the extent necessary to use its orthography. Another is to adopt a single orthography devised in such a way that it can represent the speech of each and every group of speakers even though they remain unfamiliar with each others' speech. A third is to create separate orthographies for different groups of speakers. All three solutions have been attempted for the billion idiolects of Chinese.

The first approach is that represented by the attempts to use Guoyeu Romatzyh ("National Language Romanization") and the Putonghua Pinyin as the sole system of alphabetic writing for all the speakers of Chinese idiolects. For those whose native speech is one form or other of Guoyu or Putonghua, learning what is in effect an interdialectical romanization of Standard Chinese represents no more of a problem than that confronting speakers in various English-speaking countries. But for regionalect speakers such as the Cantonese, learning to read and write Guoyeu Romatzyh or Putonghua Pinyin requires that they first learn Standard Chinese, a task more or less akin to an English speaker having to learn Dutch for purposes of literacy. Small wonder, then, that this attempted solution has not had much success. But given time, say a few centuries, it might possibly succeed since it is a theoretically feasible means of dispensing with Chinese characters.

There have been two attempts at the second approach. One was the *"Romanisation Interdialectique"* created by some French Jesuit missionaries. This scheme had as its underlying theory the idea that historical phonology could be used to devise a single romanization which could be read in various ways by speakers of different regionalects. Thus what they said were three Pekingese homophonous words *lî* (meaning "force," "a kind of hat," and "chestnut") could be written respectively as *lyk, lyp,* and *lyt* to reflect the pronunciation in Cantonese. The northerner would pronounce these all as *lî*, and the southerner would pronounce them in accordance with the finals indicated (Lamasse and Jasmin 1931). This scheme was criticized by a fellow missionary who was a specialist in dialectology (Grootaers 1946). A more recent attempt along roughly similar lines is Y. R. Chao's "General Chinese" proposal (1976:106–143) for 2,082 romanized syllables that could be pronounced in any "dialect" and would have such a low degree of homophony that one could write text either in literary or colloquial Chinese. These schemes give the impression of being largely intellectual exercises on a par with seeking a common orthography for Dutch and English. They do not offer practical solutions.

The third solution was adopted in the Latinization movement of the thirties and forties, and by Protestant missionaries and Chinese reformers earlier, to create as many separate schemes of romanization as there are instances of mutually unintelligible forms of speech. The basis for this approach was largely the practical one of creating as simple a system as possible for a given group of speakers in order to facilitate their acquisition of literacy. There was never an overall attempt to determine the exact number of schemes that should be created or to relate the schemes to each other as part of an integrated plan of writing reform. The more or less ad hoc empirical approach is therefore all the more impressive with respect to the results that were actually achieved. Publication in various alphabetic schemes in the century from the initiation of missionary work to the cessation of Latinization activities in the 1940s is significant both for its quantity and for its quality since it includes such diverse items as the Bible, Lewis Carroll's *Through the Looking-glass,* Tolstoi's "The Prisoner of the Caucasus," Pushkin's poems, Lu Xun's "Diary of a Madman" and "Story of Ah Q," the Soviet Constitution, communist land laws, miscellaneous biographies of Westerners, newpapers and journals, and much additional literature. All this provides practical proof of the theoretical truth that the alleged impossibility of using an alphabetic script in place of Chinese characters to represent spoken Chinese is a bit of unmitigated nonsense. It also provides support for the theoretical assumption that there is in fact no significant limit to the subject matter that can be written in Pinyinized versions of the various regionalects.

CAN DICTIONARY CHARACTERS BE ALPHABETIZED?

The preceding discussion of the Indispensability Myth has been based on a definition of "Chinese" that is limited to its spoken manifestation. Strictly speaking, this is the only acceptable definition of the term. Yet this limitation is very often ignored—sometimes deliberately, sometimes out of sheer ignorance in muddling speech and writing. A popular formulation of the Indispensability Myth holds that because homonyms are so numerous in "Chinese," characters must be used to avoid the unsupportable ambiguity that would result from writing alphabetically. This view has been advanced in a typically exaggerated form by writers who even go so far as to suppress inherent tonal distinctions in order to come up with "ninety words in the *Mathews Chinese-English Dictionary* pronounced *li*" (Seybolt and Chiang 1978:23). Such suppression of phonemic tonal distinctions in Chinese is methodologically on a par with suppressing the phonemic vowel distinctions in English *pap, pep, pip, pop,* and *pup* and then complaining that alphabetic English is ambiguous because there are five words whose pronunciation is indicated by the spelling *pp.*

There has been a significant shift with respect to the idea that "Chinese" cannot be written in a alphabetic script. The concept

"Chinese" has gone beyond our interpretation of the term as spoken Chinese, an interpretation which enabled us to discuss the indispensability idea by totally disregarding Chinese characters and their use in written Chinese. Now we are asked to consider quite a different question based on some quite different and not entirely clear definitions of "Chinese." The term is variously used to refer to such concepts as Chinese characters, Chinese characters in a dictionary, written Chinese, the Chinese language written in characters, perhaps even spoken Chinese written in characters. Our new question is: Can "Chinese" as thus loosely defined be written in an alphabetic script? One possible answer to this question is that it should never have been asked in the first place. "Chinese," we might insist, must mean spoken Chinese. Whether it has been traditionally written in Chinese characters, cuneiform symbols, hieroglyphics, or anything else is totally irrelevant to the question whether Chinese (that is, current spoken Chinese) can be written in an alphabetic script.

However much we might like to adopt this entirely justifiable stand, the need to confront the Indispensability Myth in its various forms requires further discussion of the issues. Actually the answer to the new question, or rather to the new series of questions, is quite simple. It is based on the eminently practical approach of asking another, quite simple question: Can the "Chinese" you have in mind be understood if spoken aloud? If the answer is yes, then this Chinese can be Pinyinized. If the answer is no, then it cannot. We can test this approach, which consists of what might be called the Speakability Test, by applying it to various kinds of Chinese.

Those who think of "Chinese" in terms of Chinese characters often invoke such imaginary problems as the ninety words pronounced *li* (without tone indication) or the more modest thirty-eight words pronounced *yī* (with tone indication). Most of these "words," as pointed out in the earlier chapter on the Monosyllabic Myth, exist only in dictionaries. To apply our basic question is in error on two counts. The first is that it is methodologically incorrect to pick out of a dictionary —in any language—a bunch of homophonous expressions and then parade them in isolation to show how ambiguous they are. Such a procedure could also be applied to English to show that it cannot be written alphabetically. See how ambiguous "can" is! On hearing it one cannot tell which of the half dozen or so homophonous words is intended—actually as many as ten or more if we include the slang terms for prison, buttocks, toilet, and the like as well as the standard terms for metal container, to be able to, and so forth. Imagine the embarrassment of having one's buttocks confused with a tin can! To avoid such an eventuality the reasoning used in the case of Chinese would logically lead one to argue that English cannot be written with a mere alphabet but must be provided with a pictographic or ideographic Singlish script that, as in the case of the previously noted seven Chinese words written with 皇 *(huáng)* and the nine written with 馬 *(mǎ)*, would disambiguate the homonyms in isolation by the addition of a radical, resulting in the following ten "radical + phonetic" Singlish characters in which the "phonetic element" can be written either alphabetically (as on the left, with the letters *can*), or entirely, as in Chinese, syllabically (as on the right, with a picture of a can used as a rebus):

ㄌCAN 加阝 "to be able to" (with radical 19 "strength")

CAN 囙 "prison" (with radical 31 "enclosure")

厂CAN 庌 "toilet" (with radical 53 "shelter")

扌CAN 扫 "to discharge from employment" (with radical 64 "hand")

止CAN 止阝 "to put a stop to" (with radical 77 "stop")

氵CAN 氵阝 "depth charge" (with radical 85 "water")

月CAN 月阝 "buttocks" (with radical 130 "flesh")

舟CAN 舟阝 "destroyer" (with radical 137 "boat")

金CAN 釕 "metal container" (with radical 167 "metal")

音CAN 韶 "to record on disk or tape" (with radical 180 "sound")

The second error in this approach stems from the fact that many entries in Chinese dictionaries, in general contrast to those in English, are not even words. Most of those thirty-eight entries pronounced *yì* are not real words. *Yì* is simply a transcription for thirty-eight characters, and characters in Chinese dictionaries are at best morphemes and at worst might mean nothing at all—as in the case of the two characters 珊 瑚 in *shānhú* ("coral") if we follow Chao and Yang (1962:140) in refusing to give separate meanings to each of the characters. To cite *yì* as a problem in Chinese is therefore even more nonsensical than tearing one's hair over the problem of "can" in English.

The Indispensability Myth presents itself as at best fatuously true in the case of "Chinese" defined as Chinese characters in a dictionary. If one insists on distinguishing the meaning of characters in isolation, these can only be written as distinctive graphic symbols and cannot be written in an alphabetic script. The significance of this conclusion is considerably reduced, however, by the fact that what is fatuously true of Chinese is also fatuously true of English, something that tends to be obscured by the insidious Exotic East Syndrome.

CAN WRITTEN CHINESE BE ALPHABETIZED?

Taking up next the somewhat broader and more legitimate question whether "Chinese" defined as written Chinese or as the Chinese language written in characters can be written alphabetically, here too we can apply our simple Speakability Test to discover whether such "Chinese" is intelligible if read aloud. Much of Chinese writing incorporates many elements alien to speech—at times to such an extent as to make it incomprehensible when read orally. For more reasons than one this might be called unspeakable writing. In the case of such unspeakable Chinese, the Chinese characters are indeed indispensable. Only if written Chinese really conforms to the definition of spoken Chinese written in characters is it possible for the characters to be replaced by alphabetic writing.

What is involved here is the problem of writing style. Only that style which is close to speech can be written alphabetically. But in no language does the style of writing conform exactly to the style of speaking. Speaking styles change more rapidly than do writing styles. The latter tend to become formalized and fossilized. It requires a bold innovator to write in the language of ordinary people and a genius to turn it into a new literary style.

In the case of Chinese the problem consists simply of avoiding classicisms and writing in such a way as to be understandable when read aloud. But this seemingly simple task has turned out to be almost impossible to achieve because there is a basic contradiction between writing in characters and writing in a style close to actual speech. In the first place, the various styles of writing, especially the classical, have had so much greater prestige than the truly colloquial that it has proved impossible for most writers to avoid the pressure to adorn their writing with classical or literary turns of phrase and to adopt a truly popular style of writing. A good example of this pressure is reported by a young Chinese colleague of mine who as a student in

Taiwan was nearly flunked out of a course when he tried to emulate the simple Baihua ("Plain Speech") style of Hu Shi, an early proponent of writing in a style close to speech, but succeeded in getting high grades by writing his compositions in a style with more classical adornments as favored by his instructor.

Moreover, given the nature of the morphosyllabic writing system, there is also the pressure to use a one-character classical abbreviation that is intelligible to the eye instead of the two-character expression that would have to be written to be intelligible to the ear. To give a rough analogy with English, why bother to write the six letters of "Christ" and the five letters of "cross" when the single letter "X" will do in "Xmas" and "Xing," especially if these forms have greater prestige? As a result of these contradictions, the style in which Chinese has been written since the beginning of the Baihua movement after World War I is such that there is considerable question as to how much of it is capable of being Pinyinized without changes that would bring it closer to actual speech. Materials in classical Chinese are of course totally incapable of being Pinyinized.

That characters are indeed indispensable for classical Chinese is playfully illustrated by Y. R. Chao, who presents passages written in characters which when transcribed alphabetically make no sense to the ear. In the following example he presents twenty-four different characters in a passage totaling forty characters (counting four indicated by the reduplication sign) and accompanies them with a translation which makes sense, of a sort, although the sounds, represented by our added transcription, do not:

西溪犀 ₁ 喜嬉戲. *Xī Xī xī, xǐ xī xì.*
嵫熙夕 ₂ 携犀戲. *Xī Xī xì xì xī xī xì.*
嵫熙細 ₂ 習洗犀. *Xī Xī xì xì xí xǐ xī.*
犀吸溪 ₁ 戲襲熙. *Xī xī xī, xì xí Xī.*
嵫熙嘻 ₂ 希息戲. *Xī Xī xì xī xì xí xì.*
惜犀嘶 ₂ 喜襲熙. *Xī xī xī xì xǐ xí Xī.*

West Creek rhinoceros enjoys romping and playing.

Xi (surname) Xi (given name) every evening takes rhinoceros to play.

Xi Xi meticulously practices washing rhinoceros.

Rhinoceros sucks creek, playfully attacks Xi.
Xi Xi laughing hopes to stop playing.
Too bad rhinoceros neighing enjoys attacking Xi.

That this sort of game has much relevance to the indispensability problem is brought into question by Chao's own citing (1976:120–121) of the somewhat parallel problem presented by a French passage which makes no sense when written phonemically as *si si sā si si si si sā si sipre* . . . but does make sense, of a sort, if written conventionally as *si six cents six scies scient six cents six cyprès* . . .: "if six hundred six saws saw six hundred six cypresses. . . ." This probably tells us more about the divorce of classical Chinese from anything approaching normal speech than it does about the real-world problem of whether Chinese can be written alphabetically. The divorce came about quite early in the history of Chinese writing, if indeed there ever was any close correspondence between the two, a subject that specialists are not agreed upon. Kennedy (1964:115) believes that "the bulk of Chinese literature is written in language that was already obsolete at the time for both writer and reader." Li and Thompson (1982:84) in their well-documented study of the gulf between spoken and written Chinese also doubt that early written Chinese represented the spoken language of the time, and they further state that "practically all contemporary Chinese writing involves a mixture of the classical style and spoken Mandarin. The mixture is reflected at both the lexical and structural level." Playing games with artificial writing of long-obsolete language can be highly misleading if the activity is not clearly recognized as a game having virtually no bearing on current problems of writing Chinese.

Insofar as writers do succeed in writing in a style close to actual speech, their work is adaptable to alphabetic writing. As far as already existing writing is concerned, the Speakability Test can determine whether a specific publication can be readily transformed from a character version to a Pinyin version. If it cannot be transcribed character by character, the possibility exists of "translating" it into a form close enough to speech to be written alphabetically. In some cases this task might involve only minor changes—as in the case of Lu Xun's "Diary of a Madman," in which the original character version employing the classical abbreviation 已 (*yǐ:* "already") could be changed to the spoken form *yǐjing* if *yǐ* alone is not sufficiently clear.

In other cases more drastic changes requiring something closer to genuine translation might be required, as is certainly the case with all the literature in the purely classical style of writing.

This raises the delicate question of tampering with the original style in which something is written. For those able to read the original, this course is doubtless to be preferred. For those unable to do so, the choice may well be between reading a modified or translated version in Pinyin and not reading it at all. There are doubtless many purists who would insist on the original regardless of whether or not the hoi polloi are capable of handling it. Wu Yuzhang, however, looks to translation into Pinyin as a means of passing the cultural heritage of China on to the broad masses of people, who will thus for the first time have access to some of the vast literature of the past (1978:126).

The problem in Chinese is somewhat analogous to that in English regarding such classics as the Bible and Shakespeare's plays. Modern versions of the Bible are frowned upon by some people who feel that they debase the sacred book. There will doubtless be many battles in China over how, and how much of, the vast literature written in Chinese characters is to be made available to readers who cannot cope with the original. In any case it is ridiculous to claim, as do some opponents of change, that all of China's past literature will then have to be translated into Pinyin.

One aspect of the problem is that the Speakability Test is not quite so simple as has been presented thus far. Whether a particular piece of writing is intelligible if read aloud, and hence is capable of being Pinyinized, depends in large part on the intended audience. Many quite literate readers of English would be completely unable to cope with a technical discussion of quantum mechanics, radiation therapy, or a host of other subjects. In Chinese, the speakability-readability problem is capable of various solutions depending on the audience for which the Pinyinized material is intended. A dilemma exists in the fact that the work of Pinyinization must be undertaken by people who are already literate—which means literate in characters—and Chinese literati, even of the newer generation, have displayed even less capacity than their Western counterparts to write in a style capable of ready comprehension by ordinary people. The contention that materials written in Chinese characters *cannot* be written alphabetically therefore has a certain sad validity because to date most Chinese scholars cannot accept the notion that the written style should be determined by its capacity for Pinyinization. They cannot bear the thought of the cultural upheaval involved in the transition from character-based to alphabet-based writing.

CANNOT = SHOULD NOT

With these attitudes the notion that Chinese *cannot* be written alphabetically has now shifted ground to "should not." It is this interpretation of "cannot" that forms the basis for much of the contention that Chinese characters are indispensable. The shift in emphasis is not always apparent to unwary readers who fail to note that the approach is often based on unwillingness to place speech before writing and to consider the needs of people who might be unable to master the character-based system of writing.

Bernhard Karlgren has made outstanding contributions to the study of Chinese historical phonology, but in his popular writings he bears a heavy responsibility for misleading his many readers by presenting scientific-sounding but basically shallow arguments for such ideas as the Monosyllabic Myth, for which he was taken to task by Kennedy (1964:109–118), and for the Indispensability Myth, which turns out to be based largely on the "cannot = should not" equation. In one of his most popular works Karlgren (1929:39–41) extolled the virtues of classical Chinese as an indispensable medium that enables the Chinese to transcend time and space:

> Not only are the Chinese able, thanks to this excellent medium, to keep in contact with each other in spite of all the various dialects . . . [but] they are also capable of communicating intimately with the Chinese of past ages in a way that we can hardly realize. . . . In the peculiar relation between the spoken and the written language in China, and above all in the nature of the latter as being a language that can be understood by the eye but not the ear alone, we have the explanation of the strange fact that the peculiar Chinese script is *indispensable*. . . . The Chinese script is so wonderfully well adapted to the linguistic conditions of China that it is indispensable; the day the Chinese discard it they will surrender the very foundation of their culture.

Karlgren's elitist defense not only of characters, but of the classical style as well, has the musty odor of a defense of Latin against such a break with the European cultural past as upstart writing in Italian and French and English. It was shared by many Chinese in the 1920s but gave way, as the Baihua style overcame the classical, to the view that it was just the characters themselves that were indispensable, that they were indeed "the very foundation of their culture."

This view of the indispensability of Chinese characters has a grain of truth in a ton of chaff. What is most wrong with it is the failure to examine just what is involved when both opponents and supporters speak of discarding or abandoning the characters. No one has ever suggested that the vast literature written in characters actually be destroyed. It is expected to remain, like texts written in Latin, for those interested in reading the material in the original. Those capable of doing so have never been more than a small fraction of the population. Those who might like to do so in the future will probably be an even smaller fraction. "Discarding" Chinese characters simply means that education will be oriented mainly toward the vast majority, as in the West, who need to read and write in a simpler script. The "discarded" literature, like early Western literature written by Chaucer, Virgil, and Aristophanes, will remain available to those who want to make the effort to read it in the original. At worst, the Chinese people will be in the position of Western scholars who learn to read Chinese, which most of them do when they are already adults. If future Chinese students fail to learn characters it will only be because they prefer to read about their past in a simpler script and to leave it to specialists to cope with the earlier texts. The suggestion that in the future all Chinese will become illiterate in Chinese characters is as silly as the implication that all Chinese now spend their days avidly reading Tang poetry and Confucian classics.

The widely held notion that characters are the very foundation of Chinese culture reflects the apparently universal attachment that people have for the way in which a language, especially their own, is written. Contrary to the maxim that familiarity breeds contempt, in the case of writing familiarity breeds such an intense emotional attachment that people adopt a defensive attitude toward their system of writing regardless of its imperfections. To some extent this stance is due to the reluctance of those already literate to give up their favored position or to take on the chore of learning a new system whatever its possible advantages to society as a whole. It is also due to the feeling, doubtless held by illiterates as well as literates, that the writing system is the very essence of their culture. This feeling is reinforced by the fact that Chinese characters not only have a utilitarian function but also serve, in scrolls and other displays of calligraphy, as a medium of artistic expression. The role of characters in this and other spheres of Chinese life has made their psychological impact unique and uniquely strong among the writing systems of the world (Gernet 1963). Attachment to the characters has led many Chinese, as well as foreigners like Karlgren, to contend that Chinese cannot be written other than in characters for fear of causing a break with China's cultural past and indeed even splitting the country.

POLITICAL UNITY AND CULTURAL CONTINUITY

These fears are by no means mindless worries on a par with belief in the myth that Chinese *cannot* be written alphabetically for technical reasons such as the alleged homonyms. They are thoughtful concerns about real dangers that need to be faced in all their complexity, without the oversimplification represented by Karlgren's approach. Before 1949 there was indeed widespread debate about these matters in which the passionate belief of people like Lu Xun that the preservation of China required a change to alphabetic writing was countered by the equally passionate fear that such a step would mean the demise of the country.

Those opposed to characters contended that only the privileged few were able to master them sufficiently to be able to read the literature of the past. Characters were indispensable only for reading this literature. But this literature was inaccessible to the masses in its present form and could only be made accessible by translation into alphabetic writing.

The role of writing in preserving Chinese unity engendered even more heat than the question of their function in preserving China's literary heritage. While it was easy to show that only a minority of scholars could commune with the past via the characters, it was less easy to assess their relationship to Chinese unity. One widely held opinion was that both in the past and in the present the characters were a major if not the main factor in preserving the unity of China. This view was rejected by Qu Qiubai with the argument that in reality it was political unity that prevented linguistic disunity and that only the gentry were united by their knowledge of the characters (DeFrancis 1950: 221–236). In support of this argument it may be noted that the political separation between Mainland China and Taiwan has indeed brought about a sort of linguistic disunity in that the simplified characters adopted in the former and the traditional characters retained in the latter have made it difficult if not impossible to read materials published on both sides of the Taiwan Strait without special training.

The differences of opinion regarding the indispensability of the characters continue today. There has, however, been an important shift in emphasis in discussions of the subject. The previous rhetoric about getting rid of characters, which lent itself to the caricature that characters would be outlawed overnight, has been replaced by the idea that they should be retained but should be supplemented by Pinyin. If Chinese characters do have a unifying role, this function, therefore, will be preserved.

As to the role of characters in Chinese culture, language reformers assert that

> Writing is not equivalent to culture, it is only a means of conveying culture. We value the traditional culture, and we therefore also value the Chinese characters that convey traditional culture. But we value even more highly the creation of a modern culture of the present and the future, the creation of a Chinese Pinyin orthography suited to conveying modern culture. . . . The two kinds of writing will coexist and will both be used, each having its own place, each being used to its utmost advantage. (Association 1981:284–285)

Such views, because they appear to underrate the fact that the traditional Chinese writing system, especially as expressed in calligraphy, is itself part of Chinese culture and therefore more than a mere conveyor, have been attacked by opponents of Pinyin who support systems based on Chinese characters (Lyuu 1983:22). Nevertheless it is clear that reformers envisage a continuing role for characters in the transmission of the traditional culture. Essentially their view of writing restricts the indispensability notion to preserving the characters for those who want to study them while adding an independent Pinyin orthography for general use as an aid in China's modernization. Some reformers see a precedent for China in Viet Nam, where the shift from a character-based script to an alphabet-based script enabled more people to read literary classics in Quoc Ngu rendition than were ever able to read them in the Nom original (DeFrancis 1977). In general, Chinese language reformers look to the indefinitely long coexistence of two systems of writing as a means of transmitting Chinese culture to a more broadly literate people.

At best progress along these lines is likely to be painful and long drawn out. Somewhere along the line, however, the indispensability myth will finally reveal itself as such both to the believers in the myth in its crudest form and to more thoughtful opponents of alphabetic writing whose fears can only be laid to rest by the success of reformers in preserving China's heritage in the traditional script while extending access to it through the medium of Pinyin.

13.

The Successfulness Myth

Success, like beauty, is in the eye of the beholder. No other aspect of Chinese characters is so much a matter of subjective judgment. I focus on such modern concerns as mass literacy and see failure. Others, concentrating on other aspects, see great success.

From some perspectives, Chinese characters have unquestionably been a great success. "We all agree," said Premier Zhou Enlai (1965:7), "that as a written record they have made immortal contributions to history." They have indeed made immortal contributions to a civilization deserving of superlative tributes that would extend Edgar Allen Poe's "the glory that was Greece and the grandeur that was Rome" to include also "the splendor that was China."

Given this esteem for the past role of Chinese characters, it seems almost sacrilegious to suggest that because of their difficulty they have failed, and will continue to fail, in meeting some of the major needs felt by modern society. Nevertheless, in the case of one such need, that for mass literacy, I believe that success via characters must be characterized as a myth.

LITERACY THROUGH DEFINITION

In a book that presents a wealth of detail, Rawski (1979:140) contradicts low estimates of literacy in concluding that "information from the mid- and late nineteenth century suggests that 30 to 45 percent of the men and from 2 to 10 percent of the women knew how to read and write." Estimates of literacy in imperial China that appear to be somewhat lower than Rawski's are presented in another carefully researched study by Mote that attacks unsupported guesses of 1 to 2 percent literacy. He considers that 10 percent may be too high a figure for "highly literate persons" but that even in the backward province of Yunnan "basic" literacy was probably somewhere between 7 and 30 percent (1972:110–112).

Rawski's impressive figures lose a great deal of their force when in the next sentence she qualifies them by adding that "this group included the fully literate members of the elite and, on the opposite pole, those knowing only a few hundred characters." If "knowing only a few hundred characters" qualifies a person as knowing "how to read and write," then it is possible that literacy in China has now grown to something like 95 percent—perhaps even 99 percent if we note Barbara Tuchman's observation (1972:31) about encountering some Chinese women who "had learned to read, to the extent of recognizing 100 characters." This generous guess is discounted by some language reformers who think that half the population cannot recognize even this minimum number of characters and that only 10 percent are literate enough to read newspapers (Zhou Youguang: personal communication).

If literacy sights are set low enough it may be possible to claim great success for the characters both in the imperial era and at the present time. Illiteracy can be eliminated by defining it out of existence, which is apparently what the "Gang of Four" did when, according to Zhou Youguang (1980e:21), it proclaimed that China no longer had any illiterates. The picture becomes less rosy, however, if we insist that literacy should be defined as the ability to accomplish such relatively elementary tasks as corresponding about family matters and reading newspapers and instructions in various matters. For this, a knowledge of about four thousand characters is required, and even then Chinese, unlike their poorly educated Western counterparts, will be unable to express in writing everything they can express in speech.

Insistence on such a demanding definition of literacy is not at all meant to belittle the utility of knowing a few hundred or even a few dozen characters. Nor is it meant to suggest that the level of literacy in Western countries was necessarily higher than in China in previous centuries. Even today, and even in a supposedly advanced country like the United States, the incidence of illiteracy is revealed to be shamefully high in such cases as the entry of young men into military service. The fact remains that by any definition of literacy based on the ability to convey thoughts and feelings in writing, which surely should be the aim of any policy based on humanistic considerations, Chinese characters appear to have failed insofar as the Chinese masses are concerned. This was certainly the case in imperial days. It appears to be the case still today.

To be sure, we cannot document the literacy situation in China with hard data. It is therefore possible, as has frequently happened, for visitors to China to be impressed by the number of people they see reading and writing. The sight of many Chinese reading books and newspapers can hardly fail to impress observers unless they take time to note that this may still be only a small percentage of the population. Impressions are all the more likely to be distorted because visitors on quickie junkets mainly centered on cities are unlikely to place in perspective the huge masses of illiterates among the 80 percent of the population comprised by the peasantry.

Such fleeting visitors are particularly susceptible to being gulled by the truly brief briefings they often experience. A case in point is a report on literacy education in China based almost entirely on "one meeting in Chengdu with the head of the adult education unit of the municipal education bureau and his counterpart from the Sichuan provincial bureau." In the fantasyland palmed off on a delegation of American educators by these bureaucrats, children are supposed to learn 2,500 characters in the first two or three years of school, and 86 percent of the total population of 1 billion people is now literate. Despite the disclaimer that "we had no way of judging the efficiency of literacy programs," the visiting delegation concluded that "China's commitment to universal literacy seems unquestionable and its progress toward this goal impressive" (Scribner 1982). More knowledgable visitors, however, might question the commitment and find less impressive the progress achieved—which may well be considerably less than half that claimed in respect to both rate of character learning and extent of literacy.

The rate of character-learning reported to the American delegation appears to echo the claims made by proponents of a get-literate-quick scheme which will be discussed below in the section "Literacy through Common Components." As to the claim of only 14 percent illiteracy reported to the delegation in 1980, the State Statistical Bureau, on the basis of a nationwide census conducted on 1 July 1982 employing face-to-face interviews, reports that of the total population of 1,008,175,288 in mainland China, "illiterates and semi-literates (people 12 years of age and above who cannot read, or can read only a few words) in the 29 provinces, municipalities, and autonomous regions number 235,820,002" (SSBC 1982:20). It is likely that not much credence is to be placed on either the earlier figure of 14 percent illiteracy or the later figure of 23.6 percent, since there is altogether too much imprecision in the details of defining and determining literacy. No doubt, however, since precise figures give the illusion of precision, the new figures of 23.6 percent illiteracy or 76.4 percent literacy will be paraded as gospel truth—or at least as of some use since they are official and none better are available—rather than as the virtually worthless tallies they really are.[1]

In 1978 the Committee on Chinese Language Reform solicited comments from the public on a proposed scheme to simplify another eight hundred or so characters. More than eight thousand letters were received in response to this request. Only eight-tenths of 1 percent came from peasants (Cheng Chin-chuan 1979:49). One wonders to what extent this low rate of response is a more accurate reflection of the low level of literacy among the peasantry.

It should not be necessary to resort to the dubious expedient of speculation and casual observation to answer important questions such as this. Among the many urgent tasks confronting the present Chinese government is that of determining the success of its educational policies by assessing the precise state of literacy among its people. Although a formidable task, it could be accomplished, by the joint effort of language specialists capable of defining levels of literacy and others skilled in statistics and sampling techniques, through a three-tier process involving clusters of geographic areas, stratification based on relevant variables such as rural-urban, education, age structure, occupation, and sex, and then randomization within designated groups. This procedure cannot be a once-only matter but must be followed up by subsequent checks on the rate of relapse into illiteracy, an especially acute problem in the case of Chinese characters. Although error will be involved, such a plan would allow for generalizability and representativeness in a way not even touched by the impressionistic observations.

Until solid information like this becomes available, all we can do is speculate. My own speculations lead me to share the profound skepticism of many Chinese, including Lu Xun, who doubted that the people as a whole could achieve an acceptable level of literacy on the basis of the traditional script, even in its simplified form. Here it must be pointed out clearly that this skepticism has never taken the form of a belief in the absolute impossibility of achieving literacy with a character-based script. The skepticism takes the form, rather, of the belief that the nature of the script and the material conditions of life for the vast majority of people, especially the 80 percent comprising the peasantry, are such that in the not too distant future there is little possibility of their becoming literate in the full sense of the term. This is the only timetable and the only definition of literacy acceptable to many people interested in the ability of the masses to raise their cultural level (DeFrancis 1950).

It is possible, however, that others may count achievements in literacy based on characters a success because they do not accept the emphasis on the importance of mass literacy. They would have much support for this view in some recent trends in thinking about the subject. The conclusion in a book by Scribner and Cole (1981) that literacy does not bring any important psychological development is taken by one reviewer as suggesting that "the extravagant faith in the benefits of universal literacy has very little basis in fact." Moreover, he adds, "conclusions like these are obviously important for the developing nations, where restricted resources often make it necessary to choose between programs aimed at achieving a limited mass literacy and programs aimed at creating a highly literate elite" (Nunberg 1981).

The reviewer may well be right in casting doubt on the claim by Sir Francis Bacon that "Writing maketh an exact man." Nor does it appear that literacy necessarily maketh a better man; some of the most literate nations of the world have engaged in acts of savagery unparalleled in human history. And radio and television may indeed reduce the need for literacy in the areas of mass indoctrination and information. In the light of these considerations, success in an educational system may well be measured, as it is at present in China, less by the ability to solve the problem of mass literacy than by the success in producing a body of technicians and specialists in science and technology.

LITERACY THROUGH MODEST EFFORT

The assertion that the difficulty of the Chinese characters is a prime reason for the lack of success in achieving mass literacy evokes several kinds of responses. One, already noted, is to deny the lack of success. Another is to deny the characters are difficult, which automatically removes one explanation for any failures. Karlgren (1929:40) has expressed the following view:

Even very learned Chinese do not encumber their memory with more than about six thousand characters. Four thousand is, as we have said, a tolerably high figure, and even with three thousand some progress can be made. For a receptive child this is a modest task, and an adult foreigner in the course of a year's study masters without difficulty from two to three thousand characters.

Karlgren's view of mastering large numbers of characters "without difficulty" is not supported by the experience of those involved in teaching reading either to foreigners or to the Chinese themselves. His estimates may be right for someone like himself, who probably had a photographic memory, and for others, especially Chinese intellectuals, whose lifestyle, not to mention livelihood, is characterized by almost full-time involvement in reading and writing, so that they often fail to appreciate the difficulty that ordinary people who spend long hours at hard physical labor encounter in finding the time and the energy to attain *and retain* literacy. As a more observant writer, George Jan (1969:141), has noted:

> Another serious deficiency in mass education in the communes was the tendency for peasants to lapse back into illiteracy because of their failure to practice their newly acquired skill. According to the statistics of Wan-jung County [Wanrong County in Shanxi], of the 34,000 people who had received instruction in reading by October 1958, one-third had again become illiterate, and the other two-thirds were unable even to read newspapers. If this was generally true, the qualitative significance of the illiteracy-elimination program in the communes must be questioned.

LITERACY THROUGH BASIC CHINESE

Another reaction to the difficulty attributed to the traditional script acknowledges that it is indeed difficult but argues that the problem can be overcome. Successive plans have been lauched with much fanfare as providing *the* solution. These have, however, invariably ended in defeat, from which little survives except the Micawber-like hope that something else will turn up.

In the 1930s Y. C. James Yen launched a mass education movement based on his celebrated Thousand Character Lessons (DeFrancis 1950). This sort of "Basic Chinese" approach aroused hopes that proved to be unwarranted and could have been foreseen as such if note had been taken that limitation of characters cannot in itself provide a basis for literacy and cannot be more than a modest pedagogical device to ease the burden of learning the thousands of characters needed for real literacy. The Basic Chinese idea is related to the Basic English concept. The reality of these limited forms of language is often misunderstood. They may serve a useful pedagogical purpose in restricting initial instruction to some basic list of lexical items in order to pave the way more efficiently for the acquisition of the additional items needed to read and to write without any limitation regarding what can be said. But the commonly cited fact that the 1,200 most frequently occurring characters comprise more than 90 percent of the different characters occurring in most texts (Kennedy 1964:7) has only pedagogical significance and cannot solve the contradiction between ease of hearing and speaking and difficulty of reading and writing. A limited number of characters cannot possibly serve (unless they are used as phonetic symbols) as a medium of free expression to convey the thousands of concepts the average Chinese commands in speech.

Yet this idea of literacy through a limited number of characters is widely held and forms the basis for official policy. In 1952 the official definition of "basic literacy" increased Yen's figure of 1,000 characters to 1,500 for peasants and 2,000 for workers (Zhou Youguang 1979:329). Attempts to reach this goal initially placed much emphasis on Mao Zedong's instructions to proceed by searching out in each village the characters locally needed to record work points and to write down names of people, places, implements, and so on. He thought two or three hundred characters would do. Next another few hundred would be learned to handle matters beyond the village. There would be successive additions of characters for a total of 1,500, the mastery of which was considered the test of literacy (Mao 1956: 165; Hu and Seifman 1976). Although 1,500 characters unquestionably have some utility, their mastery can hardly be equated with achieving literacy in the full sense of the term, and even this limited success, as the Wanrong case shows, has tended to be ephemeral.

LITERACY THROUGH PUTONGHUA

Literacy was also supposed to be aided by the promotion of Putonghua—a matter of special importance in the regionalect areas, since literacy is defined as literacy in Putonghua written in characters. As a first step in this direction the Ministry of Education decreed in November 1955 that Putonghua would become the medium of instruction for the Chinese language and literature courses in grades one through six beginning in the autumn of 1956 and that teachers of all subjects were, by 1958, also to conduct their classes in Putonghua (ZGYW 1955:41). To date, more than a quarter of a century later, this objective is so far from being achieved that one can only wonder at the obtuseness displayed in regard to the obvious difficulties involved in attaining such unrealistic goals.

LITERACY THROUGH ALPHABETIC AIDS

The difficulty in mastering characters, which are essential both to learning Putonghua as currently taught and to achieving literacy as currently defined, was supposed to be overcome by various schemes for indicating the pronunciation of individual characters. First the old Zhuyin Zimu, and later Pinyin, were touted as the new panacea. The use of alphabetic transcription to aid the learning of characters was lauded by Lin Feng, a member of the Chinese Communist Party Central Committee, as the key to the success that was claimed for another crash program in Wanrong County subsequent to the failed campaign mentioned above (Fraser 1965:337). The new campaign based on teaching characters with the aid of Pinyin won a citation from the Central Committee for its success in "eliminating illiteracy among young adults in two months" (Zhou Youguang 1979:353). In point of fact, as Zhou Youguang has informed me, the statistics used to bolster the claims of success are most unreliable since people are not willing to make a serious count because "they want to show the success of literacy education."

This desire to claim success is part of a tactic, hardly unique to China, to justify and hence gain support for whatever educational program is being espoused. Obviously, claims of great success need to be received with skepticism, or at least with caution, pending studies conducted with methodological rigor that examine all aspects of the program.

There are indeed some especially interesting aspects of the Wanrong campaign, which unfortunately died a quick death in 1960 following the failure of the Great Leap Forward. The strategy adopted in the campaign was one version of a method that has been employed, with various modifications, in a number of places, first in 1958 in an experimental primary school attached to Peking Normal University, and most recently in several schools in Heilongjiang province.

The unique feature of the method is the use of Pinyin not merely to indicate the pronunciation of individual characters, as is generally (and only minimally) done, but to provide the basis for literacy in the alphabetic script. The Pinyin system is taught for about three weeks and is then used in reading and writing materials in which syllables are joined to form words—a crucial difference from the usual approach. After students have achieved good control of the Pinyin orthography, they are introduced to a gradually increasing number of characters placed under the Pinyin, until the reading matter is entirely in both orthographies. Readers can skip back and forth between the two lines and thus, in theory, acquire many characters by doing a great deal of reading with the aid of at least one script that is thoroughly familiar to them.

Alternatively, characters are interspersed with Pinyin. Texts aimed at teaching children to read provide graduated materials which at first are entirely in Pinyin, next introduce a few characters by substituting them for their Pinyin equivalents, and then gradually increase the number of characters while proportionally decreasing the amount of Pinyin. Writing is taught by requiring that children first write entirely in Pinyin and then gradually replace transcription with characters to the extent that they are able to do so.

There are varying degrees of emphasis on characters and Pinyin in different programs, with characters usually receiving the greater publicity, if not actual attention, because of the need to avoid resistance to Pinyin. Indeed, some programs seek to minimize the teaching of characters and to place primary emphasis on making children and adult learners literate in Pinyin and providing them with a continuous stream of reading materials in that orthography. At its best the method can result in biliteracy. There are, however, other possible outcomes depending on the overall learning process—literacy in Pinyin only, literacy in characters only, or relapse into illiteracy.

The procedure used in this combination of Pinyin and characters has some points of similarity with the prewar use of furigana alongside kanji in Japan and the postwar use of Zhuyin Zimu alongside characters in Taiwan, and with the procedure in both areas of intercalating a limited number of characters among the purely syllabic or alphabetic symbols.[2]

LITERACY THROUGH COMMON COMPONENTS

Another quick-literacy nostrum is the Jízhōng Shízìfǎ ("Concentrated Character-Recognition Method"). The method was initiated in the early 1950s by an army language teacher who was rewarded with a prize in 1952 but soon fell into oblivion as the method showed itself to be too nerve-wrackingly paced for ordinary army recruits. It was later revived in slightly attenuated form.

The method involves teaching groups of characters that have a common component, chief among these being radicals and phonetics. Thus characters containing the phonetic 马 *mǎ* are taught as a group. By this method children are supposedly able to learn some 1,300 characters in the first grade and 2,500 in the second, in contrast to the six years that it ordinarily takes to learn a mere 3,000 characters. Given the official definition of literacy as acquisition of 1,500 to 2,000 characters, this means that children are said to achieve literacy in about one-and-a-half years of schooling.

Apart from the dubious procedure of measuring literacy by number of characters, there is a question as to the utility of the characters that are thus force-fed to students. The list of 1,500 to 2,000 characters that define literacy comprise those of the highest frequency and hence of the greatest utility. The similar number introduced by the Concentrated Method, however, include many characters of low frequency. Thus the character 瑚 *hú*, introduced because the right-hand phonetic 胡 *hú* reflects the pronunciation of the whole character, ranks below the 2,500 level in the Chen Heqin frequency count. It is, moreover, not a productive character, occurring only as a completely bound form in the combination 珊 瑚 *shānhú* ("coral"). It should therefore be learned in combination with the first character representing the syllable *shān*, but this is an even rarer character that ranks below the 4,000 frequency level. (The difference in frequency rank comes from the slightly greater use of *hú* in abbreviated classical writing.) Insofar as both characters are not taught together as forming a morpheme of two syllables, this helps to foster a style of writing that has more in common with classical Chinese than with spoken Putonghua.

A more important fallacy, perhaps, is the notion that preliterates will be greatly helped by the highly imperfect phonetic system of Chinese, the utility of which is actually in proportion to the mastery of characters and skill in the psychological guessing game of reading. The phonetic system is most imperfect in the case of characters of the highest frequency, precisely the ones that one might suppose should form the basis of initial teaching. The limited utility of phonetic elements for novice readers is disguised by the misleading procedure of citing chiefly more or less consistent phonetics like 马 *mǎ* and 胡 *hú* to prove the merits of the Concentrated Character-Recognition Method. There is every reason to suspect that similar misrepresentation and exaggeration are also involved in claims of success for the method.

LITERACY THROUGH SIMPLIFIED CHARACTERS

Simplification of characters was the main strategy adopted to do away with the difficulty of the traditional complex characters. In March 1956, shortly after the government promulgated its list of simplified characters, announcement was made of the "Decision of the Chinese Communist Party Central Committee and State Council Concerning Elimination of Illiteracy." The decision stated that "all places are required to eliminate illiteracy basically in five to seven years in accordance with their conditions" (Hu and Seifman 1976:74).

The failure of literacy efforts to achieve desired results is suggested by a well-publicized episode involving the lower-level cadres or bureaucrats who were supposed to be one of the chief beneficiaries of the policy of character simplification. The *People's Daily* of 10 July 1982 carried a photograph of a Tianjin street lined with electric power poles on which had been painted five characters:

The first two characters are *mǎchē* ("horse cart"), the third does not exist, and the last two are *fèndòu* ("struggle"). An editorial note accompanying the picture remarked that people were baffled by the inscription. Those with a penchant for puzzles wracked their brains and some finally came up with the solution. It appears that the third character is a miswriting of the character 带 (*dài* "carry") and the last two are misspellings for 粪 兜 (*fèndòu* "manure bag"). The inscription is therefore an attempt to exhort cart drivers to carry manure bags so their horses will not litter the streets. "We wonder," the article concludes, "what the publicity effect is of such writing that fails to get its message across."

If this is the level of accomplishment of "literate" cadres, it is not difficult to imagine the results among the population as a whole, especially the peasantry. A detailed study of four anti-illiteracy campaigns between 1952 and 1960 reveals not only repeated lack of success but also continual floundering about and inability to appreciate the difficulties involved (Belde 1980). The lack of realism displayed in the demand that illiteracy be eliminated, even if only "basically," in from five to seven years is on a par with the repeated calls to catch up with the advanced countries of the West before the end of the century.

The true extent to which simplification has eased the burden of learning characters must remain a matter of subjective evaluation until there is firm supporting evidence. Such evidence must take two forms. First is a survey along the lines previously indicated to find out the exact state of literacy among different segments of the population. Second is research to disentangle how much of whatever advance in literacy that has been achieved, and there undoubtedly has been some, is due to simplification itself and how much to other factors, such as improved living conditions and more widespread schooling, especially in urban centers.

My own view is that simplification was a distinctly secondary factor and that high-level decision makers like Mao Zedong, who as members of the educated elite were of course already quite familiar with the simpler characters, through infomal use, were mistaken in thinking that just because they themselves were able to save much time and effort by using the abbreviated forms, therefore illiterates would also find it significantly easier to learn to read and write if the simplifications were officially adopted as part of the writing system. No doubt illiterates thought so too and, according to the official line, clamored for the change. As far as language reformers are concerned, however, many place little stock in extravagant claims of success and reject the ability of simplified characters to contribute to the elimination of illiteracy among the masses. Zhou Youguang (1978a) has expressed the view that the time needed to master characters has not been significantly reduced by simplification. Wang Li (1980:13–15) has dismissed simplified characters as a solution: "Simplified characters are simply a transitional stage. Strictly speaking, they are not even a transitional stage. They are far removed from a basic reform." This comment is in line with the statement attributed earlier to Liu Shaoqi that simplification "will turn out badly in the future" (Wang Boxi 1974:22–23). Although it is by no means certain that Liu actually made this statement, the fact that the criticism was attributed to him suggests that many people have been skeptical of the value of character simplification. Such doubts, which have been echoed directly or indirectly by many advocates of reform, suggest the need for a blunt and harsh conclusion: A whole generation, both of people and of time, has been uselessly sacrificed in a timid, bumbling, and predictably unsuccessful attempt to achieve mass literacy through simplification of characters.

JAPAN AS A MODEL FOR LITERACY

This conclusion is rejected by those who advance a final argument against the idea that the difficulty of the characters, even in simplified form, makes them unsuited for mass literacy. It is argued that although this was true of the old society, the new order initiated in 1949 will eventually make it possible for everyone to learn to read and write. Expression of this view is frequently supported by the contention that Japan with its high rate of literacy in a character-based script provides proof of what China too can accomplish. The superficiality and irrelevance of this argument becomes apparent if we look a little more closely at the true state of literacy in Japan.

Research by a German scholar into prewar Japanese literacy noted that the requirements for graduation after six years of schooling, which was all the education received by most Japanese, included the ability to read and write 1,360 kanji and to recognize another 1,020, a total of 2,380 in all. Tests on military recruits a few years after graduation disclosed that youths with public school education remembered how to write an average of only 500 or 600 characters and still recognized only 1,000 of the 2,380 they had once learned (Scharschmidt 1924:183–187). With such a limited knowledge of characters these youths would have reverted to a state of illiteracy were it not that phonetic furigana symbols were provided alongside the kanji as an aid to reading and phonetic kana symbols were available as a substitute for writing the forgotten kanji.

In postwar Japan the furigana were no longer automatically added alongside characters, but the characters employed in publications were reduced in number to 1,850 (now raised to 1,945) from the 7,000 or so that previously constituted a newspaper font. As before, the kana symbols were interspersed among the characters in such functions as case markers and verb and adjective endings, but they were now given the added function of providing a phonetic replacement for the abandoned characters. This orthographic reform, combined with the unprecedented advance in the standard of living of the whole population, has produced results that are somewhat better than before the war but by no means as great as generally believed. In a summary of the findings of a survey conducted by the Ministry of Education in 1955–1956 among 14–26-year-old subjects in two selected areas—Tokyo and Northeastern Japan—Neutstupñy (1984) notes that those who were considered to "possess no competence in the use of the written language" made up approximately 10 percent of the Tokyo sample and 15 percent of the northeastern sample and that another 50 to 60 percent respectively were also judged to lack sufficient competence and hence could be classified as functionally illiterate.

More recently Sato Hideo, head of the Research Section for Historical Documents, National Institute for Educational Research in the Japanese Ministry of Education, has estimated that public school graduates, who now receive nine years of compulsory schooling, retain a recognition knowledge of the 1,945 kanji but soon forget how to write all but 500 or so (1980:personal communication). As far as this limited kanji orthography is concerned, they may possibly be considered literate in reading it but must surely be considered illiterate in writing it. More precisely, their literacy in reading consists in reading the mixture of partly phonetic kanji and purely phonetic kana, whereas their literacy in writing is largely limited to writing phonetically. Such is the concrete reality of what Neustupñy calls "the myth of 99 percent literacy" in the character-based writing system of Japan.

Moreover, apart from the use of kana by Japanese illiterate in writing kanji, the simple syllabic script is also used, even by those literate in kanji, in many aspects of Japanese life, such as computer technology, and has general application in informal writing because kana is so much quicker and easier to handle than kanji. There are even areas, such as Telex, where rōmaji is the preferred or exclusive medium of communication. Thus the Japanese policy of limiting the number of kanji in the writing system has resulted in consolidating a narrowed use of characters in such obvious activities as schooling while expanding the role of kana and rōmaji in less publicized fields.

The character-based Chinese writing system as presently constituted does not permit the Japanese option of limiting the number of characters in the basic system or of dispensing with them entirely in some areas. It is not clear how much support there would be for the idea of developing a Japanese-like writing system by using a limited number of characters interspersed with alphabetic symbols such as Zhuyin Zimu or Pinyin. Zhou Youguang (1979:337–338) thinks worthy of serious consideration the suggestion made by a fellow language reformer that interspersing Pinyin with characters could serve as a means for effecting a gradual transition to Pinyin. On the other hand, an American delegation to China reported that "when we raised this question, it was glossed over by our Chinese hosts" (CETA 1980:23). This means that the all-character Chinese writing system must be recognized as incomparably more difficult than the mixed writing of Japan. Apart from the greater difficulty in determining what goes with what in a given text, a knowledge of twice the number of characters is essential for an equivalent level of literacy. And all this in turn means that it is superficial in the extreme to view Japan's "success" as providing any sort of model of what China too can accomplish.

TAIWAN AS A MODEL FOR LITERACY

Taiwan has also been advanced as a model for achieving literacy via Chinese characters. There is more relevance to this contention, but not much more, since it needs to be qualified by noting the special conditions that set Taiwan apart from Mainland China. In Taiwan, speakers of Min or Taiwanese and Hakka are intermixed with speakers of Mandarin in a fashion quite different from the situation on the mainland with its huge blocs of regionalect speakers only thinly diluted by speakers of Putonghua. The small size of the island and the ease of communication, both physically and by radio and television, contribute to continual contact among members of different linguistic groups. A relatively efficient educational system, based in part on the fifty-year experience under Japanese occupation, made it easy to shift the medium of instruction from one foreign-imposed language to another form of speech imposed by the dominant group of Mandarin speakers, the majority quite well educated, who took over control of the island in 1945. The latter, in order to survive as an intrusive minority, were forced to promote their own speech among the whole island population with an intensity that is utterly beyond the capacity of the PRC. One result of this situation is that after only a few decades "more than 80 percent of the population is bilingual, speaking both Taiwanese and Mandarin" (Cheng 1978:308). This successful promotion of Mandarin in Taiwan has provided the means to promote literacy in a system of writing based on this standard language. The much higher standard of living in Taiwan, which is unlikely to be matched on the mainland for many years to come, is a major cause of whatever success has been achieved in literacy based on characters. Finally, although the conditions peculiar to Taiwan have undoubtedly aided literacy in characters, a careful assessment of success in more specific terms of level of achievement and particularly of retention of literacy would be desirable before making projections elsewhere, especially in view of the reality behind the myth of 99 percent literacy in Japan.

TWO CRUCIAL FACTORS: TIME AND COST

It is essential to give special consideration to the two crucial factors of time and cost in considering the potential for success in Mainland China. One major cost—the added time necessary for literacy in characters—has been a constant theme in discussion of Chinese writing reform and is receiving new emphasis in connection with China's drive for the Four Modernizations. It is frequently remarked that Chinese children must devote at least two more years than do their Western counterparts to the task of learning to read and write. In an article pointedly entitled "We Can No Longer Waste Time," one writer cites the frequently mentioned calculation that "if we do not change our Chinese characters, with our population of close to a billion people, if each person wastes two years, then in every generation 2 billion [man-] years are lost" (Li Yisan 1979:4). The Declaration of the Chinese Language Reform Association of Institutions of Higher Learning adds to this wastage another three years in each lifetime due to the inefficiency of characters relative to alphabetic writing (Association 1981:284). For a population of a billion literates this would bring the total wastage to 5 billion man-years in each generation, a figure which is probably a gross underestimation.

In introducing considerations of this sort, language reformers are raising questions which are apt to receive subjective responses. How much of its human and other resources can China invest in order to make its population literate? How much—or how little—literacy should be aimed for? How much time should individuals be asked to devote to attaining and retaining literacy? Some of these questions can perhaps be answered by responding to a closely related question. Since, in a sense, literacy can be reduced to a matter of economics, how long will it be before Chinese peasants attain a standard of living, expressed as time available to attain literacy and to retain it, commensurate with that of other societies which have achieved high rates of literacy?

Some people give optimistic answers to these questions. They minimize the difficulties that need to be overcome to achieve success. Literate themselves, and forgetful of the generally favored circumstances which enabled them to become literate, they feel little sense of urgency in pressing for an effective policy that would enable others less favored also to become literate. Wang Li (1981:4–5) is highly critical of such attitudes. He takes to task literates who point to their own command of characters as evidence that these are not difficult, charges them with disregarding the needs of the masses in emphasizing their own need for access to China's literary heritage, and calls on intellectuals to think of the masses by promoting Pinyin. Such views have been expressed repeatedly. The inability of Chinese characters to meet modern needs has been apparent to many Chinese for almost a hundred years. Beginning in the 1890s, and increasingly in recent years, the demand has been growing for what the Chinese call *wénzì gǎigé:* language reform.

Part IV
CHINESE
LANGUAGE REFORM

There are some reformers who are very fond of talking about reform, but when a real reform reaches them it throws them into a panic.

Lu Xun, *The New Writing* (1935)

14.

Speech Reform

"Language reform" is an uncertain though common rendering of the Chinese term *wénzì gǎigé*—literally "writing reform" or, more precisely, "script reform." Use of the term covers a wide range, however. Some writers confine its application to the reform of the symbols used in writing. Others include style of writing, specifically the literary or classical style versus the vernacular, within the scope of the term. Still others extend it to include reform of the spoken language. Because the word "reform" suggests deliberate change it also includes what specialists in the relatively new field of sociolinguistics, the sociology of language, call language planning or language policy. The scope of change is sometimes extended to include not only officially inspired changes but also the more or less spontaneous changes in usage that characterize both speech and writing. The literature dealing with *wénzì gǎigé* in both Chinese and Western languages includes all these aspects but is concerned preponderantly with writing reform as the most complex and perhaps the most important of all the aspects implied by the term "language reform."[1]

Let us confine our attention initially to what linguists would consider the only legitimate application of the term "language reform" —namely, what I have deliberately, if somewhat clumsily, labeled as "speech reform" in order to highlight the need to distinguish it from the better-known subject of writing reform. With regard to speech reform official policy has been most strongly manifested in the attempt to promote a standard form of speech for the country as a whole. With varying degrees of emphasis, this attempt has been in the forefront of official policy from imperial days to the present.

GUANHUA TO GUOYU TO PUTONGHUA

During the period of the empire the government promoted a form of speech called *Guānhuà* ("officials' speech")—the language of officialdom, of the mandarins (whence its English rendering "Mandarin"). As its name implies, this was a form of speech, based largely on that of educated people in the capital city of Peking, which was promoted chiefly as a common means of communication among officials with different dialect backgrounds. Apart from this official usage Mandarin had little application in the narrowly based educational system of imperial times.

The overthrow of the imperial system and the establishment of a republican form of government following the revolution of 1911 initiated a movement to expand the scope of the standard language. In 1913 a Conference on Unification of Pronunciation adopted Mandarin as a standard that was not merely to be used as a means of official communication but also to be taught in all schools from the primary grades up. This standard form of speech, which it was hoped would replace regional forms of speech as the medium of instruction and eventually in ordinary usage as well, was given the new name *Guóyǔ*. This term is generally translated as "National Language," a literal rendering of the two syllables, but it can also be rendered as "State Language" since *guó* can be translated as "state" as well as "nation."

There is a subtle but important distinction in these translations that is reflected in the controversy that developed over the language policy to be adopted in China. At one extreme, some adherents of the Guomindang-dominated government that was established in Nanking in 1927 looked upon Guoyu as a state langauge which was to be the *Biāozhǔnyǔ* ("Standard Language") of a unitary people in China. In this view the various population groups designated by such terms as Chinese, Mongols, and Tibetans were all related by blood to a single *mínzú*, variously translated as "ethnic group," "nationality," "nation" (DeFrancis 1951:146). This *Zhōnghuá Mínzú* ("Chinese Nation") was envisaged as a single people inhabiting a unitary state which had as its ideal a single language spoken by all.

The concept of a China inhabited by a single *mínzú* was rejected by others, especially on the political Left, who contended that China was a multinational state made up of various nationality groups, of which that of the Han Chinese, the largest, was only one (DeFrancis 1951:146–155). Each of these ethnic groups or nationalities, they believed, should be permitted education in its own language. They therefore advanced the concept of *Mínzúyǔ*, which can be rendered as "Ethnic Language" or "Nationality Language," or even as "National Language" in a sense quite different from *Guóyǔ* ("National Language"). The national language defined by the term *Mínzúyǔ* applied to Chinese was also called *Dàzhòngyǔ* ("Mass Language" or "Popular Language"), a term no longer used, and *Pǔtōnghuà* ("Common Speech" or "Common Language"), a term which has become standard in the PRC.

AIMING FOR A SINGLE STANDARD

The language policy embodied in the term Guoyu and pursued by the Nanking regime in the period before its collapse in 1949 sought to achieve a single national language at the expense of the languages spoken by the Tibetans, Mongols, and other ethnic groups and also the regional forms of speech spoken by Chinese in Canton, Shanghai, and other non-Mandarin areas. The sooner all these lesser forms of speech were eliminated the better, some felt, for national unity. In general, this approach reflected the view, which was held to some extent in imperial times but became firmly established with the growth of nationalism, that linguistic diversity was retrograde and linguistic unification represented progress.

During the same period adherents of Putonghua were less concerned with the problem of linguistic unification. The communists in particular were opposed to the linguistic assimilation of the minority peoples. As to the various regional forms of Chinese, they either did not express themselves on this issue, as in the case of Mao Zedong, or gave them urgent consideration, as in the case of Qu Qiubai, an important figure in Chinese language reform. Many Chinese of liberal or leftist persuasion, such as the celebrated writer Lu Xun, shared Qu Qiubai's views on this issue. Insofar as they were concerned at all with the problem of a national language, which some recognized as essential to those involved in interregional communication, they looked upon it as an addition to, rather than a replacement of, other forms of speech. These attitudes stemmed in part from the fact that there was no central authority setting uniform policy in this matter.

The communist bases, for example, were isolated from each other by Japanese occupying forces or hostile Guomindang troops.

With the creation of a strong central government after the establishment of the People's Republic of China in 1949, language policy regarding the regional forms of speech suddenly became fixed in a way unexpected by many on the Left. Language policy involving the ethnic minorities remained much as it had been before; schooling was based primarily on the minority languages, at least in initial schooling, but included education in Chinese, particularly at the higher levels. Policy toward the regionalects, however, became almost identical with that of the ousted Guomindang regime. The official emphasis throughout the country now focused on the promotion of a standard language. Standardization became the main thrust of the extensive language-planning activities carried on at the behest of the government (Barnes 1973). In contrast to the previous support for the regionalects, or at least lack of concern about them, they now came to be denigrated as a barrier to linguistic unification and national unity.

The new uniform language policy found opportune support in an article by Joseph Stalin entitled "Marxism and Linguistics" that was published in the summer of 1950, first in Russian in June and then in Chinese translation in July. This article had nothing to do with China —at least made no mention of the Chinese language problem—but addressed itself to certain problems in Soviet linguistics. In the course of the article Stalin repeated his well-known thesis that a common language is one of the criteria defining a nation or nationality, adding that nations needed a single national language as the superior form to which the dialects, as lower forms, were subordinate.

These ideas were seized upon and widely quoted in China to buttress the new policy. The arguments paralleled the ones employed by anticommunists before 1949 to attack those who stressed the importance of regional forms of speech and opposed the emphasis on an exclusive national language as a requirement for national unity. The promotion of Putonghua as a national standard was now presented as "an important political task," as Zhou Enlai (1958:15), followed by Wu Yuzhang (1978:196) and others, pointedly expressed it. The new attack was mounted in a roundabout fashion by the attempt to define how regional forms of speech should be viewed. In point of fact, virtually all Chinese of all political persuasion have invariably referred to them by using the term *fāngyán*, literally "regional speech" but usually translated as "dialects." Despite this terminological uniformity, what might in overgeneralized fashion be labeled divergent Left–Right approaches were manifested in opposing views as to how these regionalects should be treated. While sharing the common terminology of *fāngyán*, some on the political Left had in effect treated them almost as separate languages.

Instead of attacking this approach directly, which would have required an attack on people like Lu Xun and others who were considered supporters of what was now the dominant political force, an indirect attack was launched by focusing criticism on the foreign use of the word "languages" to refer to what the Chinese preferred to designate as "dialects." At the Technical Conference on the Standardization of Modern Chinese held in Peking in 1955, Wang Li, a prominent Chinese linguist, denounced Leonard Bloomfield as "one of the most reactionary American linguists" for stating that the term "Chinese language" actually refers to a language family made up of a great many varieties of mutually unintelligible languages. To deny that the Chinese have a common language, Wang said, was tantamount to denying that they constituted a common nation. Contending that among the Chinese "dialects" the grammar was basically the same, the lexical differences not great, and the phonology related by rules of correspondence, he asserted that Chinese could not be said to comprise a great many varieties of mutually unintelligible languages (1955:287–290).

In fact neither Bloomfield nor others who followed him, including myself (DeFrancis 1950:192–198), attached any political implications to his statement that "the term *Chinese* denotes a family of mutually unintelligible languages" (1933:44), a designation that Bloomfield obviously arrived at solely on the basis of descriptive linguistic criteria. The denunciation of foreign "bourgeois linguists" and the labeling of emphasis on differences in speech as very dangerous from a political point of view were doubtless motivated not by any analysis of the political thought of linguists like Bloomfield but by considerations of expediency in the political climate of the times.

It was this political climate which forced previous supporters of the regional forms of speech to fall in line. The most that they could do, as did Ni Haishu, a leading historian of the language reform movement, was to express the fears of some speakers that their regionalects would soon be abolished and there might be too narrow a definition of what constituted the national standard (1955:177-179). These twin fears have been a constant refrain in the controversy over a language policy that seeks unity through uniformity.

In the early years of this century, supporters of the ascendency of Mandarin over the regional forms of speech, which are located mainly in the southeast coastal region, advanced the slogan "Force the South to Follow the North." Resistance to this slogan was expressed by the demand that the regionalects be preserved and that some of their features, particularly those related to pronunciation, be taken into account in fixing the national norm. At the 1913 Conference on Unification of Pronunciaton the northerners got their way and adopted a standard pronunciation which initially represented a partial compromise but later gave way to a closer approximation of the Peking dialect. In later years there was an almost incessant struggle involving the degree to which force should be used in promoting the national norm. At one extreme were those who sought to impose Mandarin as the sole medium of instruction in all schools from the first grade on. Others were willing to tolerate the use of local speech forms out of necessity as an initial means of acquiring command of the standard language for further education. Still others sought to preserve the regionalects and to add knowledge of the national language in the case of those who needed it and could manage to acquire it.

As a result of these divergent approaches there were differences of opinion regarding how long it would take to achieve the linguistic goals. In the period when he was in disgrace, Liu Shaoqi was attacked by impatient supporters of linguistic unification for the alleged remark (for which there is no authentication), that it would be all right if the common speech was not popularized for a hundred years (Wang Boxi 1974:22-23). In contrast to the repeated attacks for footdragging on the part of Liu and other "swindlers" and "capitalist-roaders," Mao Zedong was showered with fulsome praise for his repeated urgings to learn the standard language, although in fact his actions, such as writing poetry in the classical style, weakened the attempts to promote a more popular style of speech and writing. Official pronouncements on these matters were more restrained, tending to emphasize linguistic unification as essential to administrative efficiency and national unity. Unofficial rhetoric, however, especially during the period of the Cultural Revolution, was marked by a stridency that inhibited discussion of the issues.

COMPARISON WITH AMERICAN LANGUAGE POLICY

The significance of what may be characterized as a controversy between linguistic integralists and linguistic pluralists can perhaps be made clearer if we view it from the perspective of the somewhat similar controversy over bilingual education in the United States. The traditional Melting Pot approach to non-English-speaking immigrants was to ignore their original languages and provide classes using nothing but English as the medium of instruction, even for the learning of English itself. A new approach began in 1968 with the passage of the Bilingual Act that recognized for the first time in American history that "the use of a child's mother tongue can have a beneficial effect upon his education" (Haugen 1973:50). Further legal rulings led to increased support for the idea of using an individual's native tongue as a medium of instruction for learning English—a procedure which parallels the use of English to supply explanations or translations in foreign-language programs other than those based on the direct approach. Even a dialect of English, namely that of Black English, has been considered sufficiently different to warrant use as a means of learning Standard English (Baratz and Shuy 1969). Non-English languages are also viewed as an alternative means of instruction in other school subjects.

Some supporters of bilingual education are interested only in a sort of transitional bilingualism in which a child's native language is used in the early grades only to the minimal extent needed to aid in the mastery of English. Others espouse a maintainance theory of bilingual education in which children are to be encouraged and helped not only to learn English and acquire knowledge of the usual school subjects but also to maintain knowledge of their native language and their native culture (Fishman 1969). This view is extended to include the idea of preserving the nonstandard varieties of English such as Pidgin English in Hawaii and Black English throughout the United States and supplementing them with a knowledge of Standard English, each form having its own sphere of appropriate usage.

The cultural gap between the Anglo majority and the non-English-speaking minority groups in the United States is much wider than that between the Mandarin-speaking majority and the regionalect-speaking minorities of China. In America the cultural differences are so great that many proponents of bilingualism believe it should be expanded to a bilingual-bicultural approach. The situation in China is quite different. There the problem is centered on the question of language education. As far as the magnitude or difficulty of the learning problem is concerned, there is not much difference between a Cantonese learning Putonghua and a Hispanic learning English— both of whom have much more difficulty than do speakers of Pidgin English or Black English in learning Standard English or speakers of Nanking or Xi'an dialects in learning Putonghua. It is in this sense, and this sense only, that China and the United States can be viewed as having a similar language problem.

The two countries also have in common a passionate disagreement over language policy that might, from a purely linguistic point of view, be labeled as monolingual versus bilingual education in its various forms. In the United States the disagreement is a subject of widespread debate between proponents who stress pedagogical efficiency and cultural humanitarianism and opponents who fear that cultural differences will be exploited to the point of sharpening already existing divisions. In China, although the issue was hotly debated before 1949, it was little discussed thereafter, though in the early fifties there was some discussion, not reflected in actual publication, regarding a one-step versus two-step approach to acquisition of Putonghua —that is, the pedagogical problem of whether or not to resort to children's native speech in teaching them the norm (Hu Tan 1982:personal communication). Although there is still opposition to the emphasis on Putonghua by those who wish to preserve their own forms of speech, such opposition is now expressed orally rather than in writing and is muted by the overwhelming pressure to conform to official policy.

DEFINING AND PROMOTING PUTONGHUA

Within this integralist policy there is still considerable room for disagreement regarding such matters as defining the norm and implementing its acquisition. Earlier definitions of the standard were rejected or modified. Even before 1949 the compromise standard adopted in 1913 that was later modified to the Peking-based National Language was opposed by those who felt it had a bureaucratic taint. Preference was expressed for a *Dàzhòngyǔ* ("Mass Language") or *Pǔtōnghuà* ("Common Speech") that would incorporate features from various regional forms of speech and various social levels. An apparent step in this direction was taken by a supporter of the *Guóyǔ* ("National Language") approach who, refuting the charge that it entailed a kind of authoritarian uniformity, said that it was actually a process of "national language-izing the dialects and dialectizing the national language." The dialects would be gradually absorbed by the national language until they disappeared. The writer made it clear, however, that the dialects would not be permitted to contaminate the national language unduly (He Rong 1932).

In 1955 the name Putonghua was officially fixed as the designation for the national norm. Official commitment to promotion of Putonghua was underscored by including in Article 19 of the revised constitution, adopted in December 1982, a sentence declaring that "the state promotes the nationwide use of Putonghua" (*Daily Reports—China*, 7 December 1982, p. K7; Xu 1982).

Putonghua has been officially defined as the common speech of the Han nationality that takes Northern speech as the basic regionalect, Beijing pronunciation as the phonetic standard, and model modern vernacular works as the grammatical norm. (Zhou Youguang 1979: 98,347). Vocabulary too was envisaged by the 1955 conference on standardization as based on modern Baihua literature (Barnes 1973).

Although this somewhat vaguely defined norm is in practice based to a considerable extent, especially with respect to pronunciation, on the more or less formal speech of educated speakers of the Peking dialect, it has not been so rigidly or narrrowly delimited as previous attempts to define a national standard. Insofar as published materials give any indication of pronunciation, this rarely deviates from the generally accepted representation of the Peking dialect. But as far as actual speech is concerned, individual speakers are permitted considerable latitude in their attempts to master the norm. This leniency is true both of official policy and of popular attitudes. Official insistence on a close approximation to the norm is limited largely to radio and television broadcasting and other nationwide public services. In the educational system the norm is the official medium of instruction, but the dearth of competent teachers in full command of the standard language, plus perhaps the deliberate attempt to preserve the regionalects by using them in the classroom, means that the extent to which Putonghua is used in classroom instruction in regionalect areas and the actual results of such education throughout the country are quite uneven. This situation is indicated by the criticism made by the linguist Wang Li (1980:16) that many students, especially those in teachers' colleges, do not speak Putonghua well and, moreover, that the teaching of Putonghua is so deemphasized after the early grades that students forget how to speak it. Zhou Youguang has noted that teachers of language and literature are required to use Putonghua, though, he adds, "most of them cannot do so well." Teachers of other subjects, such as mathematics, are not required to use Putonghua. Consequently they usually resort to their own native speech to explain the material in the texts, which are, of course, written in characters based on the official standard language but generally read with local pronunciations. In general, middle school students understand Putonghua but are not necessarily able to speak it. In most regions store and sales personnel do not speak Putonghua (Zhou Youguang 1980a:30–32; 1982:personal communication).

Among the public at large, widespread variations from the norm are accepted as the normal state of things; in fact, the speech of many of their leaders is so heavily accented as to be barely comprehensible. Poking fun at the way others talk is a favorite pastime in China, as elsewhere, but it is generally done in a good-natured way. Speakers of Northern Chinese, for example, recite the following doggerel:

Tiān bù pà,	I don't fear Heaven,
Dì bù pà.	I don't fear Earth.
Jiù pà Guǎngdōngrén	I just fear Cantonese
Shuō Guānhuà.	Speaking Mandarin.

If allowance is made for the wide range included in what is considered ability to speak Putonghua, it appears that the spread of the common language has been one of the more successful aspects of language policy in China. To be sure, this success is relative, and caution should be exercised in specifying the degree of success, since estimates usually amount to nothing more than subjective impressions based largely on observations in urban centers rather than on scientific measurements that would include the large peasant population living in isolated villages.

Much of whatever success has been achieved is due to the sheer effort expended for its attainment and to the general recognition of the need for a lingua franca that can be used when necessary among speakers of different regionalects. Apart from the pervasive encouragement and exhortation already noted, the government devotes a great deal of effort to facilitating acquisition of the norm. The radio is widely used to broadcast lessons in the standard language. There has been a great deal of practically motivated linguistic research, including extensive research on the dialects and regionalects, but such work has been of very uneven quality. The quality of materials published for the study of the norm in particular leaves much to be desired.

RECIPROCAL INFLUENCE OF SPEECH AND WRITING

The deficiencies in materials for teaching Putonghua stem largely from the extraordinary degree to which there is reciprocal influence between speech and writing in China. By far the proponderant influence is exerted by writing. The influence of writing is such that most of these teaching materials do not go beyond presenting lessons in Chinese characters with indication in Pinyin of pronunciation for each character. The low quality of the textbooks is indicated by a primary school series in which the first volume has a character-plus-transcription approach that includes such literary morphemes as *zú* and *mù* instead of the spoken forms *jiǎo* and *yǎnjing* for "foot" and "eye" (Ridley, Godwin, and Doolin 1971:13). The characters 足 *(zú)* and 目 *(mù)* were obviously chosen in preference to 脚 *(jiǎo)* and 眼睛 *(yǎnjing)* because of their simplicity, a choice that may be appropriate in teaching to read standard written Chinese but is pedagogically inefficient in teaching to speak standard spoken Chinese. It also results, like the worst of the Dick and Jane series in the United States, in an extremely low content level—far below that contained in Soviet textbooks, in which the reading material is based on a vocabulary of ten thousand words introduced in the first four grades, more than five times as many as in American schools (Trace 1961:11–18). Measured in terms of total amount of material, Chinese textbooks for the first four years have only one-sixth the amount contained in comparable Soviet textbooks. Pointing to the richness of children's spoken vocabulary and the poverty of their textbook fare, Zhou Youguang (1980g:92) calls for greater emphasis on Pinyin in order to solve the contradiction between the two.

The writing approach to teaching spoken Putonghua has also been criticized, but without results, by a prominent linguist, Professor Lyu Shuxiang, who said it is little different from the old-fashioned declaiming of the classics and urged instead the creation of textbooks based not on Chinese characters but on natural speech accurately transcribed in Pinyin by indicating such things as stress, intonation, tempo, and juncture (1960:1–2)—the lat ter be ing es pe cial ly nec es sar y to a void the fre quent prac tice of writ ing all syl la bles sep a rate ly like this, instead of joining them together whenever they comprise parts of words, as in the case of *jiào yuán* versus *jiàoyuán* ("teacher"). Another defect is the widespread practice, especially in frequently seen signs and slogans, of altogether omitting indication of the four tones, in contrast to the care taken by Vietnamese to write their five tone marks (plus two vowel diacritics) in all sorts of circumstances (DeFrancis 1977:251).

The practical solution of the problems that confront regionalect speakers is hardly aided by the tendency to minimize regionalect differences, even (or perhaps especially) on the part of linguists. The contention made by Wang Li, for example, that there are rules of correspondence in pronunciation between the "dialects" has been criticized by one Western student of the subject as of no practical value since application of the rules would require a scholar's knowledge of Chinese historical phonology (Serruys 1962:58, 159).

The effort expended on spreading the norm, though having a mixed success as far as pronunciation is concerned, can perhaps be characterized as having more success in other respects. It has been easier to obtain acceptance for grammatical features of Putonghua because there has long existed a tradition, derived in large part from the written language, to accept the grammatical features of some standard or other. Indeed, this was one of the main thrusts of that aspect of the reform movement known as the Baihua ("vernacular language") movement that started after World War I. This movement called for the replacement of the classical written style by one based on the vernacular.

In the period before the Baihua movement, when the grammatical norm had been that of classical Chinese, Cantonese speakers, for example, accepted that norm but pronounced what they were reading in Cantonese. With the adoption after 1919 of the Baihua style as the grammatical norm of written Chinese, Cantonese speakers, though continuing the habit of reading aloud with a Cantonese pronunciation, accepted this new grammatical norm. The present emphasis on speech reform has therefore encountered no great problem, at least among literate regionalect speakers, in getting Cantonese and others to make the additional step of speaking with the grammatical patterns of Putonghua, especially since these are largely the same as the grammatical patterns of written Baihua. Illiterates from regionalect areas, however, have the additional problem of learning new grammatical patterns as well as new pronunciations.

A somewhat similar situation exists with respect to standardization of lexical items. Here too illiterates encounter more difficulty than do literates in adapting themselves to Putonghua vocabulary that has to a considerable extent already been standardized in written form. The difficulty for illiterates is compounded by the fact that the modern written style has taken over many elements not only from classical Chinese but also from foreign sources. The vocabulary of modern written Chinese is marked by extensive borrowings from abroad. Even the grammar has been influenced as a result of the tremendous amount of translation, some of it quite bad, that ranges over the gamut of literary, political, and scientific works produced in the West.

All these factors taken together compound the problem, especially for illiterates, in learning Standard Chinese. That much more than merely changing one's pronunciation habits is involved is attested by the previously cited statistics indicating that the differences among the regionalects taken as a whole amount to some 20 percent in grammar, 40 percent in vocabulary, and 80 percent in pronunciation (Xu 1982:15).

The influence of writing on speech, a force that is too often minimized by linguists, is particularly strong in the case of Chinese. This is especially true of nonnative speakers of Mandarin since regionalect speakers tend to learn the vocabulary and grammar of Putonghua through writing. The interaction between speech and writing has been reinforced in a situation where a strong central government has in various ways exercised an influence on all aspects of Chinese language. This government is not an abstraction but a body of paper-pushers headed by people who regardless of their subsequent political evolution originated with hardly an exception as members of the educated elite. Mao Zedong, whose traditional education is reflected in his frequent use of literary quotations and his publication beginning in 1957 of poetry in the classical style, was the dominant figure in post-1949 China and has had a particularly strong influence on language developments. Thus it has come about that modern Standard Chinese, more so even than other standard languages, represents an emerging and continuously developing standard with a variety of distinctive features, many of which have been influenced by writing.

One of these features is the politicizing of Chinese speech. The constant bombardment, particularly by radio, of political slogans has created a kind of cliché speaking ("capitalist roaders," "subjectivists," "ultraleftists") that has often been remarked upon by foreign visitors seeking more than a surface indication of what people are thinking. Pithy slogans are frequently created on the basis of the terse literary style. The vituperative expression *Sì Rén Bāng* ("Gang of Four") makes use of both the terseness of classical Chinese (literary *sì rén* instead of spoken *sìge rén*) and the Chinese fondness for numerical expressions. The literary pattern *wèi . . . ér . . .* ("to . . . for . . .") has entered into a number of expressions used in speech, such as *wèi hépíng ér fèndòu* ("to struggle for peace"). A recent study (Li and Thompson 1982:85) "randomly examined selected pages of *Xuéxí, 'Learning,'* a monthly magazine of political propaganda for popular consumption, and found words and phrases taken from classical Chinese, not used in colloquial Mandarin, on every page." Even radio, which in most countries transmits in a style approximating ordinary speech, contributes to the reversal in style in China because a great deal of news broadcasting is done in a style closer to that of formal writing than to that of informal speech (Destenay 1981; Lin Xingren 1983). These examples are all part of a widespread phenomenon that reverses the trend before and briefly after 1949 toward vernacularization of current Chinese. According to Zhou Youguang (1982:personal communication), the reverse trend started with the publication of Mao's poems in the classical style and has continued on even after the Cultural Revolution right down to the present. It is particularly ironic that a supposedly populist government is promoting a form of speech so heavily influenced by writing that it works a special hardship on the 90 percent of the population that in 1952 was classified as illiterate by the then Minister of Education, Ma Xulun (Fraser 1965:131).

The tendency of speech to approach writing is somewhat countered by the absorption of substandard and dialect expressions into the norm. Mao Zedong's penchant for using the vernacular word *gǎo* has helped to fix this word as a general verb of doing. A favorite example frequently cited to illustrate the new egalitarianism in China is the increased currency of a term that used to be frowned upon in polite society. The old terms for "husband" and "wife" are being increasingly replaced by the word *àirén,* which used to have the connotation of "lover" in the sense of an extramarital or illicit affair. The use of *àirén* in the new meaning of "spouse" is by no means universal, however, even in Mainland China, and still less so among Chinese else-where. Foreign students in particular need to be warned not to ask how someone's *àirén* is doing when speaking with Chinese friends in Taiwan and the United States. This and other differences in what Kratochvíl (1973) has aptly called "divided languages" suggests that general admonition "When in Rome, speak as the Romans do."

A BURGEONING VOCABULARY

One aspect of speech in the People's Republic of China has particu-larly struck foreign observers as a product of the new egalitarianism and may even be considered a product of Chinese speech reform in the broad sense of the term. This is the greater verbosity, the more assured command of speech, especially in its politicized form, dis-played by people in all walks of life. This is not to say that the Chi-nese, even the most uneducated, have ever lacked for words. But the new loquacity adds weight to one of the most crucial but also most neglected and misunderstood aspects of human communicaton: the number of words that people know.

Most of the information on this subject is confined to Western lan-guages. The overall significance of the data is not limited to the spe-cific languages involved, however. It applies also to languages in gen-eral and hence to the Chinese language as well. The data have been obtained by various researchers chiefly in two ways. One is to count the number of words actually used by specific individuals, a proce-dure which is possible only in the case of very young children. The other is to estimate vocabulary size by some sort of sampling proce-dure, such as testing individuals on their knowledge of, say, the last entry on every tenth page of a thousand page dictionary with 100,000 entries and then extrapolating from the results obtained from the sample. This approach can be done either orally or in writing and hence can be used to differentiate between spoken and written voca-bularies.

In a summary of early research on vocabulary size, Otto Jespersen, a down-to-earth linguist with a great deal of insight into some of the more practical aspects of language, cites the following figures: 232 words for a seventeen-month-old boy, 489 words for a two-year-old girl and 1,121 for another of the same age, 2,688 for the previously mentioned boy when six years old, 26,000 for Swedish peasants, and about 60,000 for English-speaking college students (1905:212–213).

The last estimate was also reported in a later research project on the vocabulary of American undergraduates (Seashore and Eckerson 1940:36). A study of English undergraduates gives their vocabulary size as close to 75,000 (Oldfield 1963). A study of how many of the 202,000 entries *(cí)* in a Chinese technical and general dictionary were known to Chinese students doing graduate work in various fields in the United States came up with an average figure of 46,000 (Chao, Chao, and Chang 1967).

Estimates of vocabulary size show extremely wide differences. For six-year-olds the range is from the previously quoted 2,688 obtained by actual count to 15,000 obtained by sampling. For undergraduates the range is from 60,000 to more than 200,000. Such extreme variations are taken by Lorge and Chall (1963) to signify serious deficiencies in methodology employed in estimating size of vocabularies. Key problems involve definition of a "word," sampling techniques, and criteria for "knowing." Whether estimates are limited to basic words (such as "quick") or include derivative words (such as "quickly") obviously can make for wide variation. The procedure adopted by some researchers is not always made clear. (Seashore and Eckerson's figure of 60,000 refers to "basic words.") Some of the highest figures were apparently arrived at by including "derivative words."

Although some of Lorge and Chall's criticisms, especially with respect to sampling, seem to be well taken, their objection that "names of persons, geographical names, and word parts" should not be considered words is open to question. Knowing that "Albuquerque" is a city located in the southwestern United States would seem to be on a par with knowing that "carburetor" refers to a thingamajig located under the hood of a car. Lorge and Chall would reduce by 30 percent Seashore and Eckerson's estimate of 60,000 by rejecting as words the categories named above, and they would reduce the figure overall by one-half to three-quarters. This seems excessive. In any case, even if the extremely high estimates that have been advanced by some researchers have to be scaled down considerably, most scholars who have been concerned with this subject conclude that vocabuary size must be recognized as very large—much larger than most people assume it to be.

Although research into Chinese vocabularly size lags far behind that for Western languages, the available data, plus ordinary common sense, suggest that the number of words or expressions, and hence of concepts, known to speakers of Chinese is probably of a similar order of magnitude as in the case or their Western counterparts. In Chinese, as in all languages, the extremely low estimates frequently advanced for vocabulary size must be dismissed, in Jespersen's words, as "the most utter balderdash" (1922:126). That such extremely low estimates continue to be made is due in part to general ignorance of the research done on this subject. Sheer intellectual arrogance is also involved in the common tendency of the better educated to equate book learning with knowledge and to ignore those subjects, such as farming or simply nature itself, where even illiterates excel their scholastic superiors.

If Chinese speech reform has endowed naturally articulate Chinese with an even greater command of verbal expression, their inherently large vocabulary must now be even larger. Whatever the precise size for specific individuals or for types of speakers, it must in all cases, as in all langauges, be of truly astounding proportions, most likely in the range of tens of thousands of words or expressions. This is a fact of the most profound implications for our understanding of language in general and the Chinese language in particular. The most important implications, as I shall bring out in the next chapter, concern Chinese writing reform.

15.

Writing Reform

To many minds the words "writing reform" or "script reform" evoke the concept of "spelling reform" in English. There is some validity in this comparison, but it can also be quite misleading, especially when English orthographic reform is viewed in narrow perspective as a bit of trivia of interest only to cranks. Such a comparison completely misses the significance of writing reform in China. In broad perspective Chinese writing reform is not merely a minor matter of tinkering with the symbols used in writing. It is a major change amounting to nothing less than the most far-reaching cultural revolution in all Chinese history.[1]

The historical context of Chinese writing reform is stressed by the Chinese themselves. In the course of evolutionary change the original pictographs of Shang developed into the formalized symbols of Zhou, and these in turn were replaced by standardized characters as China evolved from disunited tribalism and feudalism to a unified monarchy that was initiated by the Qin dynasty (221–206 B.C.) and lasted until the downfall of the Qing dynasty in 1911 (Tong 1937:61–70). Subsequent reform of the script, said another writer, should be based on upholding "capitalist unity" (Zhang Difei 1937). After 1949 the needs of a new socialist society were widely evoked in support of arguments for reform of the script. The recent stress on modernizing the writing system in order to speed the Four Modernizations is only the latest in a long series of expositions relating changes in script to changes in society.

BEFORE 1950

In the three millennia and more from Shang to Qing the changes in writing were largely limited to changes in the form of Chinese characters without affecting the basic nature of the writing system itself. A fundamental change was deliberated toward the end of the nineteenth century, however, under the dual influence of activities carried on by Western missionaries and events that called into question the very existence of China as a nation. The obvious disintegration of Chinese society and the inability to cope with foreign aggressors led some reformers in contact with missionaries to conceive of carrying out a reform of the writing as part of a general educational reform that would help revitalize the country and save it from extinction.

MISSIONARY INFLUENCE

Missionary concern with Chinese writing had widened in scope following the forced opening of China to Protestant activity as the aftermath of China's defeat in the Opium War of 1839–1842. The earlier Jesuits, who had been active in China since the sixteenth century, had created alphabetic systems for transcribing Mandarin but used them solely as an aid in studying the language. They based their proselytizing strategy on adapting themselves to the cultural outlook of the educated elite centered on Peking rather than attempting to reach out directly to the illiterate masses. But the Protestant missionaries, confined initially to the southeastern coastal provinces with their illiterate millions of non-Mandarin speakers, created separate systems of romanization for these regional forms of speech with the specific aim of educating new literates who could read religious materials published in the new romanizations. Their extensive activities resulted in the publication of literally millions of religious tracts and other materials.

FIRST CHINESE REFORMERS

In the 1890s some Chinese who had worked with Protestant missionaries led the way to creating new phonetic schemes, mostly based on Latin letters, as a simpler means of achieving universal literacy. Almost from the first these attempts to create simple phonetic systems of writing engendered controversy centered on several key issues. One of these issues was the form that the symbols should take. The Latin alphabet was the basis for several schemes of romanization. The Japanese kana signs inspired the creation of symbols based on indigenous Chinese characters rather than on foreign letters. There were other sources of inspiration for schemes that were in some cases rather bizarre in appearance.

A second issue was whether the phonetic symbols should function as an independent system of writing or should be used solely as an adjunct to the traditional characters. Those reformers who argued that the traditional script was too difficult for ordinary people to master wanted a complete break with the characters and the establishment of simple phonetic writing as a system in its own right. Those who pinned their hopes for literacy solely on the characters sought to restrict the use of the phonetic symbols to facilitating mastery of the characters by providing a simple means of indicating their pronunciation.

Perhaps the central issue was just what kind of Chinese speech should be represented by the new alphabets. One group wanted to confine their use to representing Mandarin. Another group argued that literacy even in alphabetic Mandarin was too difficult for some of the illiterate masses and insisted on creating separate phonetic schemes for the various regionalects and relegating use of the Mandarin-based script to situations in which a national orthography was essential.

ZHUYIN ZIMU

Official resolution of these issues was effected by the decisions reached by the Conference on Unification of Pronunciation that was held under government auspices in 1913. Overriding opposition from representatives from the coastal areas, the majority members of the conference reached the decision to adopt a set of thirty-nine phonetic symbols derived from Chinese characters, to use them as an adjunct to the characters, and to confine their scope to representing the Mandarin pronunciation as the national standard. The symbols were initially called *Zhùyīn Zìmǔ* ("Phonetic Alphabet"); later they were also called *Guóyīn Zìmǔ* ("National Phonetic Alphabet"). The fear that they might be considered an alphabetic system of writing independent of characters led in 1930 to their being renamed *Zhùyīn Fúhào* ("Phonetic Symbols").

These symbols have had their primary application in representing the standard pronunciation of Chinese characters in dictionaries and other reference works. They have also been used to indicate the pronunciation of characters in children's books and other printed matter aimed at those who cannot handle the characters without this aid. They have had an extremely limited use as an independent system of alphabetic writing in a few publications. The PRC has made sporadic use of the signs, especially in the 1950s, but not as extensively as Taiwan, where they form the basis of all first-grade instruction and are widely used in character annotation. Overall the symbols have had little impact and have contributed little to Chinese writing reform.

THE BAIHUA MOVEMENT

A more important contribution was that of the Literary Renaissance or Literary Revolution that began in 1917, with antecedents in late Ching, and gained impetus from 1919 on when it merged with the May Fourth movement, a massive upsurge of Chinese national feeling sparked by further humiliations at the hands of foreign powers that evolved into a new search for national salvation. The Literary Renaissance was so named to evoke the renaissance that marked the transition from medieval to modern Europe. It had as its chief premise the idea that the archaic classical style of writing should be replaced by a vernacular style called Baihua ("plain language" or "vernacular language") as a necessary preliminary to any possible reform of the script itself. In China, however, the classical style was replaced by a *single* vernacular based largely on the Peking dialect, whereas in Europe Latin was replaced by *several* written vernaculars such as Italian, Spanish, and French.

Two figures stand out as initiators of the Baihua movement: Chen Duxiu, editor of the leading organ of young Chinese intellectuals who later became one of the founders of the Chinese Communist Party, and Hu Shi, a scholar of quite different political persuasion who served as the Nanking government's ambassador to the United States during World War II. Among their views were those appended to an article published in 1918 by the philologist Qian Xuantong in which he expressed the despairing view held by some scholars that Chinese speech and writing were so unsuited to modern times that they should be replaced by Esperanto or some other foreign language (1935:141–146).

In his appended comments Chen Duxiu rejected this solution as impossible. Instead Chinese speech should be retained, he said, and it should be used as the basis for a new literary style to be written in roman letters rather than in the traditional Chinese characters. A less radical proposal that would involve retention of the characters was presented in the appended comments of Hu Shi:

> I think China will have to have an alphabetic writing in the future. But there are too many monosyllables in the literary language and it would be impossible to change over to an alphabetic script. So it is first necessary to replace the literary writing with Baihua writing, and after that to change from Baihua writing to alphabetic writing.

The idea of a reform in the style of writing was taken up by a wide segment of the literate population but was opposed by others who looked down upon the vernacular style as a vulgar form of writing unsuited to elevated expression of thought. The difference in attitude has some parallels with that involved in the European transition from writing exclusively in the dead Latin language to using living speech such as Italian, French, and English as the basis for a new literary medium. In modern terms it evokes the differences of opinion regarding style or tone considered acceptable in academic and other kinds of writing. In China the classical tradition because of its longer history was even more firmly rooted. Nevertheless, the extreme form of opposition was gradually overpowered by the growing support for the vernacular style.

A greater problem, never completely resolved, was what exactly should constitute the Baihua style. The term Baihua has come to represent a variety of substyles that can be defined by the degree to which they have incorporated elements from classical Chinese on the one hand and everyday speech on the other. Old habits die hard. Apart from some continuation of writing in the purely classical style, as in Mao Zedong's poetry, there is often considerable incorporation of classical elements—stereotyped phrases, truncated terms, even classical constructions—into what is ostensibly a vernacular piece of writing. At the other extreme are works such as those of the popular writer Lao She, well known for depicting the lower depths of society and evoking their manner of speech.

This matter of style is important because it has a direct bearing on the view that vernacular literature based on characters would pave the way to a reform of the script along alphabetic lines. There is a flaw in the reasoning expressed by Hu Shi. It was valid only to the extent that the vernacular written style truly approached the spoken style. Hu Shi in his own writing provided one of the better models in this respect. But insofar as Baihua continued to be influenced by the classical style, which is quite incapable of being transcribed into an alphabetic orthography, it remained incapable of being transcribed in this way. In point of fact, much of what passed for Baihua writing was denounced by Qu Qiubai as a "new classical" style, a "false Baihua" incapable of replacing Chinese characters because it was not sufficiently thoroughgoing. Qu called for a new Baihua style based on what he referred to as Putonghua, an amalgam of various dialects that he said the "proletariat's language" had already evolved into from the concentration in major cities of people from all over China. "Only a real spoken Baihua," he said, "and a real literature written on the basis of such a Baihua, will make it possible to adopt a simple *pīnyīn* [alphabetic] system" (1932:705; Pichowicz 1977). In the same vein, the celebrated writer Lu Xun (1974:50) wrote that despite the well-worn cliché that Baihua should be "clear as speech," there was much Baihua literature that failed to meet this objective, which could be attained only if it were based on actual speech and did away with partially understood characters.

GUOYEU ROMATZYH

Although Chen Duxiu stressed the idea that spoken Chinese should be taken as the basis for the literary style, he failed to pursue his own idea that the symbols used in writing should be changed from the traditional characters. This issue was taken up by a group of outstanding linguists headed by Y. R. Chao who in 1926 created a system of alphabetic writing which they called G.R., short for *Guoyeu Romatzyh* ("National Language Romanization"). As the name indicates, the system was intended to represent only the national language, essentially the speech of educated speakers of the Peking dialect. The scheme is distinguished chiefly in its indication of tones by a system called "tonal spelling." Instead of using superscripts written above a vowel, as in the case of *fēn, fén, fěn, fèn*, the four tones are indicated by variations in spelling: *fen, fern, feen, fenn*. Although G.R. won endorsement from the Ministry of Education in Nanking, being officially adopted in 1928, it had limited appeal. It has been used in a number of dictionaries to give the pronunciation of characters, in several brief translations from English, and in a few attempts at literacy education. Perhaps the use best known to Western students of Chinese is in the compilation of some textbooks by Y. R. Chao that are outstanding for their presentation of everyday speech.

LATINIZED NEW WRITING

In contrast to the limited influence of Guoyeu Romatzyh, another system of alphabetic writing had a much greater impact on the controversy over Chinese writing reform. The new system was created in the early thirties by the joint effort of Chinese communists and Russian linguists for the 100,000 or so Chinese immigrants in the Soviet Union. Initially called Latinxua ("Latinization"), the scheme was also given the name Sin Wenz ("New Writing") or Latinxua Sin Wenz ("Latinized New Writing"). Unlike most other Mandarin schemes, Latinxua was not based directly on the speech of educated people in Peking but rather on a vague version of Northern Chinese influenced by the speech of the Shandong workers and peasants who constituted the majority of Chinese in the Soviet Union. Another distinctive feature was the lack of tone representation. This feature was in sharp contrast to the fixed tonal spelling of the G.R. system, whose four syllables *fen, fern, feen, fenn,* for example, were all represented by undifferentiated *fen* in the New Writing. Apart from its use to liquidate illiteracy among the Chinese immigrants in the Soviet Union, the New Writing was also used in several scores of publications that included textbooks on various subjects, journals, literary works by former illiterates, and translations of poems by Pushkin, a short story of Tolstoi, and the Soviet Constitution.

From the Soviet Union the New Writing soon spread into China, aided by the return of Qu Qiubai, Wu Yuzhang, and others who had been engaged in Latinization work along with their Russian colleagues. In the course of its expansion into China the New Writing acquired an important new feature. This was its adaptation in creating separate Latinization schemes for the various regional forms of speech. Apart from its use to represent Northern Chinese, it was now modified to represent such diverse forms of speech as Cantonese, Hakka, Shanghai, Min, and others. In this respect the New Writing reverted to the principle espoused by the earliest Chinese reformers of the 1890s and stood in opposition to unitary phonetic schemes such as Guoyeu Romatzyh.

Even more than nonindication of tones, a feature that was criticized by supporters of G.R. as leading to unsupportable ambiguity, the New Writing was bitterly attacked because of its use in the creation of separate alphabetic scripts for the various regional forms of speech. Opposition to this feature is well summarized by the statement of one critic that the "dialect romanization" movement was "a cultural movement of traitors" because it denied that China was a single nation, went counter to the need for capitalist unity, and by dividing the country into a large number of separate linguistic units was opening the way to imperialist division of the country into separate autonomous regions each having its own independent script (Zhang Difei 1937).

Despite the opposition to Latinization on both linguistic and political grounds, the New Writing attracted wide interest and support from diverse segments of society. Among the many people expressing support were Mao Zedong, who headed the communists located in the Yan'an area in Shaanxi province; Liu Shaoqi, who was secretary of the Party Central China Bureau in the New Fourth Army area in northern Jiangsu; Lu Xun, the most prominent writer in China; Mao Dun, another writer of note; Guo Moruo, a well-known scholar with wide-ranging interests; Dr. Chen Heqin, a prominent Christian educator trained at Teacher's College in New York; Sun Fo, the son of the founding father of the Chinese Republic, Sun Yatsen; and Cai Yuanpei, the first minister of education after the republican Revolution of 1911. Some of these figures expressed their support merely by adding their signatures to statements urging the promotion of the New Writing. Others played a more active role. The most directly involved in the actual production of Latinized materials was Chen Heqin, who as commissioner of education in the foreign-controlled International Settlement in Shanghai adopted the system, which he viewed as easier and more practical than any other system of writing, for anti-illiteracy work among refugee children in the settlement. He used it to write biographies of a number of noted Westerners and engaged in a variety of other activities aimed at promoting the New Writing.

TOP-LEVEL COMMUNIST SUPPORT

Mao Zedong when interviewed by Edgar Snow in Yan'an in 1936 told the American journalist:

> We believe Latinization is a good instrument with which to overcome illiteracy. Chinese characters are so difficult to learn that even the best system of rudimentary characters, or simplified teaching, does not

equip the people with a really efficient and rich vocabulary. *Sooner or later, we believe, we will have to abandon characters altogether if we are to create a new social culture in which the masses fully participate.* [1968:446 Snow's emphasis]

Mao together with most of the communist leaders lent their signatures to a call issued in 1940 for the establishment of a New Writing Society in Yan'an. The call stated that the masses remained centuries behind the small group of progressives influenced by the May Fourth movement; that China's political and cultural backwardness were partly responsible for this situation; but that the difficulty of the characters was also to blame. Mao became a member of the honorary presidium of the Border Region Sin Wenz Society at its inaugural meeting in November 1940, which was attended by more than a thousand people (DeFrancis 1950:129–130). He and Zhu De, head of the communist military forces, both gave inscriptions for the *New Writing Journal* that started in mimeographed form in 1940 and soon converted to lead type (Tao 1980:114–115).

Although Mao Zedong's early support of Latinization can be documented by contemporary publications, Liu Shaoqi's has come to light only since his political rehabilitation following the downfall of the Gang of Four. A political worker who early in 1941 headed a "Northern Jiangsu Latinization Dissemination Team" in communist-controlled territory behind the Japanese lines tells of receiving a letter in Liu Shaoqi's own handwriting under the date 12 January 1941 lauding the Latinization movement in this area under his jurisdiction, noting its necessity and feasibility, and hoping that it would be earnestly pursued with due care to overcoming problems that might be encountered. In subsequent months propaganda work and compilation of textbooks and other materials were carried on (Zhang Yan 1980). The Latinization work in this area soon came to a halt, however, following a Japanese mopping-up operation in July that resulted in the fall of the communist base to the occupying forces (Zhang Yan 1981:personal communication).

LU XUN AND LATINIZATION

A crucial role in the promotion of Latinization was played by Lu Xun because of his preeminent position in the Chinese literary scene as author of a number of widely acclaimed masterpieces, chief among them his "Story of Ah Q." This master of the character-based script, which he manipulated with consummate skill in his powerful writing, turned against the characters and became an ardent advocate of Chinese writing reform as expressed in the Latinization movement. He wrote in Chinese characters to readers of Chinese characters to appeal for support of a writing system more accessible to the masses as a whole. This case is reminiscent of the situation in turn-of-the-century Viet Nam where nationalist leaders wrote in classical Chinese to readers of classical Chinese in support of the Quoc Ngu alphabetic system (DeFrancis 1977:67).

Lu Xun had shown interest in the problem of writing reform as early as 1913 by participating in the Conference on Unification of Pronunciation that had resulted in the adoption of the Phonetic Alphabet as a means of representing the pronunciation of Standard Chinese. When he encountered Latinized New Writing he became a convert to this system. From August 1934 to December 1935 he wrote a number of articles, subsequently gathered into a small booklet, expounding his views on Chinese writing reform and defending Latinization against its detractors (Lu Xun 1974).

The primary basis of Lu Xun's support for the new system was its simplicity compared to other ways of writing Chinese. He was particularly harsh in his criticism of Chinese characters. These he felt to be too difficult for acquisition by the masses. Only the gentry, he said, had the leisure to master them, and the gentry deliberately kept the writing system difficult, fearing that if writing became easy the masses would no longer venerate it and would also no longer hold the gentry in respect. Characters were a fatal disease; China's very life depended on getting rid of them. Nor would simplified characters (such as those introduced by the Nanking regime in 1935, only to be rescinded the following year) be an acceptable substitute for the more complex characters. They were simply the conventional characters in another form, not a basic solution.

Although Lu Xun supported the general idea of alphabetic writing, he was opposed to Guoyeu Romatzyh as too character-based and too complex for ordinary people. For one thing, he said, its indication of tones made matters needlessly difficult. For another, its excessive emphasis on a standard based on the Peking dialect placed a particular hardship on those who did not know that form of speech and would be forced to learn it in order to read and write. For a poor person from Shanghai or Fuzhou or Canton to have to learn Standard Chinese was almost as difficult as learning a foreign language.

This last point reflected Lu Xun's adamant stand on the question of standard language versus other forms of speech. In the interest of making things easy, he said, it was imperative that separate Latinizations be devised for distinct forms of speech which he variously characterized as *fāngyán* ("regional speech") and *tǔhuà* ("local speech or local dialect"). Although acknowledging that *Běifāng-huà* ("Northern dialect"), which he said was not simply *Běijīng-huà* ("Peking dialect"), had the greatest number of speakers and would doubtless play a pivotal role if a *Dàzhòngyǔ* ("Mass Language") spoken everywhere should really come into being, he placed greater emphasis on reiterating the need for various Latinizations in order to get close to the speech of the people. "From the lips of living people," he said, "take words and phrases that are full of life and transfer them to paper. . . . What can be said can be written." Such a popular style of writing could not be based on characters. Neither could it be based on a single form of speech. In each region people should first learn to read and write in their own local form of speech. In the future, however, it will be the fate of Chinese to have to be familiar with several forms of Chinese. This, he said, can be accomplished through education and communication.

The views of Lu Xun that have been summarized in the preceding paragraphs covered all the main points raised in the extensive discussion that developed regarding the New Writing. His views were sharply attacked by supporters of the National Language Romanization and by those opposed to any sort of alphabetic writing in place of the traditional characters. But they were shared in whole or in part by many advocates of writing reform in general and Latinization in particular. The importance attached to his support of the New Writing is indicated by a pair of eulogistic scrolls submitted by Guo Moruo at the time of Lu Xun's death in October 1936:

> The greatest masterpiece in the world is his *Story of Ah Q*
> But even greater in his life was his activity for Latinization

Some of Lu Xun's views received greater elaboration in the extensive discussions advanced by other supporters of Latinization. His defense of nonindication of tones was extended by the argument that the ambiguity imputed to this procedure would be removed by context in most cases and could be handled whenever really necessary by the limited use of special spellings. His idea that only the gentry had the leisure to master characters received sharper treatment at the hands of Qu Qiubai and others who, viewing characters as a system of writing that was monopolized by the privileged few, discounted their role as a unifying force, asserting that not characters, but class interests, held people together. They particularly stressed the view that the key to Chinese unity was to be found not in a single unified script, whether in characters or in G.R., but in a number of simple Latinized systems that would facilitate achievement of literacy by the masses. This meant literacy first in a writing system based on one's own speech and later, if possible, in a more general system based on a vaguely defined common speech that could be used for national or interregional communication. Literacy in characters was relegated to a still later stage after the New Writing had been studied until it could be used for reading and writing.

YAN'AN ADAPTATION OF LATINIZATION

Against the criticism that the policy of Latinizing the regional forms of speech would lead to political fragmentation might be added another argument that has only recently come to light. In an article that, like many publications since the downfall of the Gang of Four, has revealed information not previously available, the author notes how the problem was handled of teaching what might be called Standard Putonghua Latinization to speakers with nonstandard pronunciations. In this case the local form of speech was not a major regionalect like Cantonese or Hakka but merely a subdialect of northern Putonghua—namely that of the Yan'an area in northern Shaanxi. In this dialect the contrasting final sounds represented by the spellings *n* and *ng* are merged into the single phoneme *n*. In the first two volumes of material prepared to teach the Latinized New Writing to speakers of the northern Shaanxi dialect, the *n-ng* distinction was ignored and only the final *n* was taught. After this had been mastered, a relatively simple matter since it conformed exactly to the local pronunciation, the *n-ng* distinction was introduced in the third volume (Tao 1980:116).

This seemingly minor detail of literacy education in Latinized writing has important implications for handling the problem of local varieties of speech. Essentially it involves the principle of teaching students the phonetic representation of their own form of speech and then having them use their acquired knowledge to learn the standard phonetic writing based on another form of speech. This is precisely akin to the principle espoused by exponents of bilingual education in the United States as expressed at one extreme by the use of the Black English dialect to teach reading in Standard English. In the case of the Yan'an approach, it is even more precisely akin to the principle of transitional bilingualism or transitional biliteracy, since the intention was to use literacy in the local dialect solely as a transitional pedagogical tool for expediting literacy in the standard language.

One of the criticisms frequently leveled against the New Writing approach was that it would result in the complete fragmentation of China since separate Latinizations would be required not only for the eight major regionalects but also for the huge number of dialects and patois that could be considered sufficiently different from each other to require separate treatment. As far as the dialects of Putonghua are concerned, however, the Yan'an handling of the matter because of its transitional nature constituted a refutation of the contention that Latinization would break up the country into scores of autonomous entities each with its own independent system of writing.

DIVERGENT APPROACHES TO LATINIZATION

How general was this approach? It may be that some Latinizers envisaged the application of a similar technique of a sort of transitional literacy in the major regionalects as well. On the other hand, it is apparent that others, such as Lu Xun, held to the idea of a maintenance theory of literacy in the regionalects plus perhaps literacy in the standard system of Latinization.

This is not at all to say that supporters of Latinization thought of these matters in terms of the principles described here. The impression one gets in reading the literature of the thirties and forties is that apart from the general idea of using a Latinized script, there was a sort of ad hoc approach to actually implementing this idea. There certainly was no central authority laying down rules specifying what to do and how to do it. As a result, there were differences in implementation that may simply have represented practical adaptations to diverse regional conditions or may possibly have reflected differences of opinion regarding what should be done. These differences, if they existed, cannot be documented in the currently available literature of the time.

In the southeastern coastal area, the main emphasis in Latinization work appears to have been on the creation of separate alphabetic systems for the various regionalects. Latinization societies were set up throughout the area, separate Latinization schemes were developed for the major forms of speech, and some materials, limited in amount either deliberately or by the exigencies of the situation, were developed to teach the systems and provide reading matter in them. This approach seems to have been initiated by Qu Qiubai, a participant in the creation of Latinization in the Soviet Union who became commissar of education in the Jiangxi Soviet before his capture and execution by Guomindang forces in 1935. It was warmly supported by Lu Xun. Guo Moruo added his approval in an article entitled "The Great Importance of Regional Latinizations" (Ni Haishu 1979:no. 254). Many others also expressed their support by producing Latinized materials in various regionalects.

There were some supporters of the New Writing, however, who did not agree with the separate Latinization approach. This was true even of some working in the regionalect areas. In Shanghai, for example, Chen Heqin preferred to work exclusively in Beila ("Northern Latinization"). Popular attitudes appear to have been divided on the subject.

In most of China, where Putonghua held sway, the primary emphasis was on the promotion of New Writing based on this form of speech. Here almost all the leading communists, including Mao Zedong, lent their support to the promotion of Latinization. But just what aspects of Latinization they espoused is not at all clear. It does not appear, for example, that Mao Zedong, who both then and later had nothing but the highest praise for Lu Xun as a writer devoted to the interests of the masses, expressed himself on the issue of separate Latinizations that had figured so prominently in the thinking of this illustrious writer. Nor is he recorded as having reacted to the statement made by Wu Yuzhang (1978:18) at a widely attended Latinization meeting in Yan'an in December 1941 that the New Writing movement, in contrast to the G.R. approach, advocated separate Latinizations. That he may at this time have supported the idea of separate Latinizations is suggested by his earlier call for "self-determination" of the various regional divisions of China, a request which he extended to the even more startling thought that these regions were "best divided into twenty-seven countries" (McDonald 1976: 769–771), though one scholar (Scalapino 1982:47) believes that his eventual goal was always a "federated" China.

APEX AND NADIR

The lack of an overall policy embraced by all supporters of Latinization does not appear to have impeded promotion of the system and may indeed have aided it. In any event the actual results as measured by the amount of publication in various forms of the New Writing were substantial—especially when contrasted with the meager publications in other systems, except possibly for the systems promoted by Western missionaries in the previous century. Publications included over thirty journals, numerous translations of foreign works, biographies of prominent foreigners (Lincoln, Franklin, Edison, Ford, Chaplin, and others), several stories and sketches by Lu Xun (including his "Story of Ah Q" and "Diary of a Madman"), textbooks on diverse subjects, and a considerable variety of other materials.

Among the latter were many of the laws promulgated by the Border Region government, including the Administrative Program of the region and the Outline of the Land Law. The publication of these laws in a Latinized version was due to a government decree of 25 December 1940 which provided that Latinized New Writing should have the same legal status as Chinese characters. This decree is worth quoting in full because better than anything else it shows the extent to which the New Writing received official support from the Yan'an government:

> 1. As of 1 January 1941, Sin Wenz will have the same legal status as Chinese characters. All official documents, commercial accounts, and other documents written in Sin Wenz will have equal validity as those written in Chinese characters.
> 2. As of 1 January 1941, all announcements and laws of the government will be written in both characters and Sin Wenz.
> 3. As of 1 January 1941, all official documents sent to the Border Region government in Sin Wenz will be valid. [Tao 1980:111–112]

The extensive publication of materials in Latinization does not necessarily mean that the system itself was entirely satisfactory. The lack of tone indication was severely criticized at the time, and while it appears that publication in the New Writing entailed no insurmountable problem of ambiguity, this may have been due more to the redundancy inherent in all systems of writing than to the quality of the system itself. As in the case of writing in general, and as shown specifically in the case of Viet Nam (DeFrancis 1977), the success of an orthographic scheme is a function less of its quality than of the extent to which it is promoted.

Latinization was promoted with unprecedented zeal by its liberal and leftist supporters until their work was disrupted by wartime developments following the expansion of Japanese-controlled areas in 1941 and 1942 and the tightened blockade of communist-controlled areas by Guomindang forces. When foreign newspaper reporters penetrated the blockade in 1944, they found that New Writing activities had come to a halt. Xu Teli, however, the commissioner of education in Yan'an, told the American correspondent Gunther Stein that the communists hoped to reintroduce the New Writing in a unified, democratic China (DeFrancis 1950:134).

SIGNS OF REVIVAL

With the defeat first of Japan in 1945 and then of the Guomindang in the ensuing civil war, the Latinization movement showed signs of revival. Writing early in 1949, when it was already apparent that the communists were winning the civil war, Ni Haishu (1949:570) predicted a great future marked not by a superficial change in the written symbols but by the liberation of the whole Chinese language from the shackles of the Chinese characters. According to information that has recently come to light, on 25 August of the same year, less than two months before the formal establishment of the People's Republic of China, Wu Yuzhang wrote a letter to Chairman Mao asking for instructions on how to go about promoting Chinese language reform. The same day Chairman Mao wrote a letter in his own hand to Guo Moruo and Mao Dun, both leading supporters of Latinization, and Ma Xulun, who was shortly to be appointed minister of education, transmitting Wu's letter and asking them to deliberate on it. The summary of the reply (dated 29 August, only four days later) that they submitted to Mao states: "They recommended using the Latin alphabet to formulate a *Zhōngguó Pīnyīn Wénzì* ["Chinese

Phonetic Orthography"] and promoting Guoyu based on Northern Speech (now called Putonghua). They also recommended establishing an organization for Chinese language reform work" (Anonymous 1979:2; Zhang and Fei 1980:251).

If this is a correct paraphrase of the reply, which may well be the case since it conforms to the general tenor of the remarks, there is a special significance in the use of the term *pīnyīn wénzì*. This expression stands in contrast to *pīnyīn fāng'àn*. The latter has been used to designate a scheme or plan *(fāng'àn)* for spelling out sounds *(pīnyīn)*. The term *pīnyīn wénzì* does not refer to a mere scheme or plan akin to say, the *Zhùyīn Fúhaò* ("Phonetic Symbols") used to indicate the pronunciation of Chinese characters; it has the specific meaning of a full-fledged orthography or writing *(wénzì)* that would be independent of characters and that could be used, like Latinization, as a new system of writing the Chinese language.

After the rehabilitation of Liu Shaoqi in February 1980, Ye Laishi, currently an associate director of the Committee on Chinese Language Reform, published the facsimile of a hitherto unrevealed letter written by Liu on 1 February 1950 to Lu Dingyi and Hu Qiaomu, both active in language reform work, which read as follows:

> As yet, no plan has been decided on for reform of Chinese writing. But now our neighbors, Mongolia, Korea, and Viet Nam, have already been successful in their writing reform. From a certain point of view, their writing reform is more advanced than ours. But originally they learned and used our writing. The Korean alphabet already has a history of many years. According to the Korean ambassador, Yi Kugwŏn, if words of various kinds are transcribed using only the Korean alphabet, there is no difficulty. This is something that we should pay attention to. I think our research workers should look into their experience in alphabets and writing reform. For this purpose, we should send students or researchers to those countries to learn, so that we can make plans for reform of our writing.[2] Greetings! [Ye Laishi 1980a:1]

These early indications of renewed interest in writing reform along alphabetic lines are only a few of the widespread manifestations of such interest. Latinization societies that had been shattered by the vicissitudes of war sprang up again. In Peking itself an unofficial Association for Chinese Language Reform was established under the leadership of Wu Yuzhang on 10 October 1949. Throughout the country journals were resumed and new publications appeared in both the Putonghua and regionalect areas. Official support was clearly expected for this resumption of language reform activities along lines similar to those of earlier years.

AFTER 1950

MAO'S GREAT LEAP BACKWARD

These expectations received a shattering blow when Mao Zedong dropped a bombshell by laying down new guidelines and priorities for language reform. The change in policy was signaled by Wu Yuzhang's convocation of the cadres of the Association for Chinese Language Reform on 10 July 1950 to transmit to them instructions he had received from Mao the month before. In these instructions Mao Zedong, presumably reflecting a collective decision of the government, ignored the recommendations made by Guo Moruo, Mao Dun, and Ma Xulun and ordered that reform of the writing system should start with simplification of characters, that writing reform "should not be divorced from reality or make a break with the past," and that the effort to create a new alphabetic system should abandon the previous use of Latin letters and concentrate instead on devising a "national-in-form" set of symbols based on Chinese characters (Wu Yuzhang 1952:1; Zhang and Fei 1980:254).

It thus appears that some time within the half-year period between February, when Liu Shaoqi wrote that "as yet no plan has been decided on for reform of Chinese writing," and June, when Mao Zedong's directive laying out a specific program was transmitted to Wu, a decision was reached to abandon a radical change from characters to alphabet and adopt instead a more conservative policy based on simplifying the traditional characters, which would be aided, as may have been obvious at the time but was not reported until later, by a "national-in-form" set of phonetic symbols to be used primarily for character annotation but not as an independent orthography.

The detailed background of the change in policy is unclear. There appears to have been no public discussion of the issues, particularly by those with power to make decisions—a matter of more than usual opaqueness in China. Although some behind-the-scenes discussion doubtless took place, this remains buried in archives that it is hoped will one day be opened for study. Our present state of knowledge enables us to do no more than guess that while the final decision may

have been made some time in the first half of 1950, it was perhaps
building up well before that, perhaps even as early as the suspension
of Latinization work in Yan'an in 1944 or shortly before. How much
of the decision is due to Mao personally, as is suggested by the literature quoting him almost exclusively on the subject, is another of the
tantalizing uncertainties whose resolution awaits further information.

The major unanswered question is exactly what motivated the
turnabout in policy. It is easy to speculate on the reasons for the reversal. Nationalistic feeling was clearly an all-pervasive factor. It may be
that in the euphoria of coming to power after a decades-long struggle
that was partly a civil war and partly a war of national liberation
against Japanese invaders and American supporters of the Guomindang regime, the new leaders of China were confident that they
could also succeed in turning the indigenous system of writing into a
truly mass medium of communication rather than the insurmountable barrier it had earlier appeared to be. A major reason for the
reversal was undoubtedly the opposition of many people, particularly
those already literate, to any fundamental change in the traditional
system of writing, especially one based on the alien concept of alphabetic writing.

Zhou Enlai subsequently told a former French minister of education:

> In the 1950s, we tried to romanize the writing. But all those who had
> received an education, and whose services we absolutely needed to
> expand education, were firmly attached to the ideograms. They were
> already so numerous, and we had so many things to upset, that we
> have put off the reform until later. [Peyrfitte 1973:153]

These remarks are misleading since there is no evidence that the government actually "tried to romanize the writing" in the 1950s as it
had tried to do in the thirties and forties under even less favorable
conditions. They suggest, however, that the revolutionary leaders
who could lead China along new economic and political paths considered the matter but drew back from adding this controversial issue to
the already extensive list of problems confronting the new government, problems which may have included the need to consolidate the
home front in face of the uncertain international situation created by
the outbreak of the Korean War in June 1950. Better to restrain the
eager reformers who were still of Lu Xun's way of thinking, to under-

take a moderate reform that would not engender too much opposition, and to put off a decision on a basic change to some time in the indefinite future.

Mao Zedong's directive that was revealed to cadres on 10 July received wider publicity in the inaugural issue of a new journal, *Zhonguo Yuwen ("Chinese Language"),* that was published in June 1952. The journal was the organ of a new and this time official Committee for Research on Chinese Language Reform that was set up following a Ministry of Education initiative in this direction in July 1950. Ma Xulun, the minister of education and chairman of the new committee, and Wu Yuzhang, the vice-chairman, both reported on the talks they had had, apparently about the same time, with Mao Zedong in which he specified the new direction that writing reform was to take. Wu Yuzhang added little new, but Ma Xulun expanded on Mao's directive by quoting him as saying: "The writing system must be reformed; it should take the phonetic direction common to the languages of the world; it should be national in form; the alphabet and system should be elaborated on the basis of the existing Chinese characters" (Ma 1952:4–5; DeFrancis 1979:139–142). This statement became a kind of holy writ that was cited over and over again in the years immediately following in discussions of Chinese writing reform.

As official policy gradually unfolded it revealed itself as centering on the following points:

1. Placing primary emphasis on simplified characters
2. Developing a phonetic system based on Chinese characters for use primarily in character annotation and indefinitely deferring consideration of its use as an independent orthography
3. Promoting Putonghua as an exclusive standard at the expense of other forms of speech

SIMPLIFICATION OF CHARACTERS

According to one perceptive student of Chinese language reform, the emphasis on simplification of characters was motivated in part by the urgent need to develop a corps of literate cadres as lower-level bureaucrats, a need that it was thought could most expeditiously be met by such a moderate reform (Tao Jianqin 1982:personal communication). It is apparent, however, from many subsequent official and unofficial pronouncements, that simplification was also widely viewed as a means of achieving universal literacy. This was certainly the view of the people as a whole, who conceived of literacy solely as literacy in characters.

In June 1950, even before Mao's directives were transmitted, the Ministry of Education had begun work on simplification of characters (Zhang and Fei 1980:254). Despite some opposition and considerable coolness to this emphasis (Milsky 1974; DeFrancis 1967a), after nationwide discussion concerned mainly with secondary aspects the government proceeded to implement character simplification along two lines: reduction in total number of characters and reduction in the number of strokes in individual characters.

Reduction in number of characters was achieved mainly through the publication in 1955 of a list of 1,050 variant characters that were to be eliminated. Further reduction was impeded by a request put forward by Mao Zedong that character simplification should make greater use of the cursive form of characters, a procedure which is helpful in reducing the number of strokes in characters but not in eliminating characters. The latter can best be achieved by replacing complex characters with simpler characters of the same sound, but this procedure was little used. As a result, there has been little reduction in number of characters—of the ten thousand characters in the Chinese Telegraphic Code, a reduction of only 7 percent has been achieved, of which 4 percent comprised variants and a mere 3 percent nonvariants (Chang 1976; DeFrancis 1979:148–150).

Reduction in the number of strokes in complex characters has been more extensively carried out. In 1956 the government promulgated a plan calling for the simplification of 515 characters plus an indeterminate number containing one of 54 character components that were also simplified, such as 讠 for the radical 言. In 1964 further simplification increased the number to 2,238 out of the approximately 7,000 characters in general use (Hsia 1956; Cheng 1979). This progress has resulted in a reduction of 12.5 percent in the average number of strokes in the 2,000 most frequently used characters (11.2 before simplification, 9.8 after). A count of a quarter of a million characters of running text showed that simplification had resulted in a reduction from 9.15 to 7.67, or 16.1 percent, in the average number of strokes per character (Zhou Youguang 1979:341–342).

The procedure adopted in most cases involved giving official recognition to forms which were generally known to those already literate and were used by them as abbreviations in informal writing, such as the cursive forms 乐 for 樂 (*lè* "happy") and 马 for 馬 (*mǎ* "horse"). Current publications appear with the simplified characters. These are what children learn to read and write from the first grade on. The complex characters are used in older materials and must also be learned by anyone interested in reading anything published before 1956 or in communicating with Chinese in Taiwan, Hong Kong, and other areas that continue to use the old forms.

A further list of simplified characters was drafted during the turmoil of the Cultural Revolution. It was prepared by some members of the working staff of the Committee on Chinese Language Reform without consultation with and of course without the approval of the official members of the committee. The draft was sent directly to the State Council for approval and was published in 1977 on a trial basis. The new simplifications, unlike the earlier batch, were not simply familiar abbreviations. They therefore encountered strong opposition, so much so that the government quietly withdrew them from use in 1978. Since then the official line has been that further simplifications will be undertaken after the problem has been given more thorough consideration. The task of restudying the abandoned draft plan of 1977 was submitted to a special committee headed by Wang Li.

The work of this committee is greatly complicated by the fact that there are widely divergent views about the goals and methods of simplification. Further simplification, it has been objected, may make characters easier to write but more difficult to discriminate in reading as they approach each other in appearance. There is disagreement whether further simplification should be based, as before, on forms already in informal use, on more systematic simplification of components, on greater use of the phonetic principle by regularizing the phonetic elements or by replacing whole characters with simpler forms of the same sound but different meaning, or on still other considerations. Even more widespread is the opposition to any further changes at all in the characters. It appears, therefore, that any further simplification will be very difficult to carry out.

This is perhaps for the best. The constraints placed on the work of competent scholars by a policy that touts a so-called mass line, which really means a line of least resistance to the indiscriminate demands of a populace left ignorant of the intricacies of writing reform, appear to rule out any really thorough and systematic overhaul of the character system. Previous intervention may have worsened an already capricious system. At least now it may be kept from becoming still more of a mess.

CREATION OF A NEW ALPHABET

The second major effort, that of developing a new alphabetic system, was taken up by the public at large as well as by specialists in the field of writing reform. Between 1950 and 1958 something like 1,700 schemes of various kinds or adaptations of earlier proposals were submitted for consideration (Zhou Youguang 1980g:62–63). The task of developing a new alphabetic system encountered difficulty because of Mao Zedong's request that it be a "national-in-form" scheme based on Chinese characters. For several years those engaged in writing reform attempted to meet Mao's specifications. A scheme submitted to him in 1953 was rejected as not sufficiently simple and convenient. The Soviet linguist G. P. Serdyuchenko, who was in China from 1954 to 1957 as a consultant to the Institute of Linguistics, tried repeatedly to persuade leading language reformers like Wu Yuzhang and Ye Laishi to adopt the Cyrillic alphabet, but his urgings were rejected (Ye 1981:61). After intensive deliberation, the Committee on Chinese Language Reform submitted for consideration six alternative alphabetic schemes. Four were based on Chinese characters, one on the Cyrillic alphabet, and one on the Latin alphabet. The following year the committee, with the approval of higher authorities, decided in principle to use the Latin alphabet in devising a draft alphabetic scheme. Thus the attempt to devise a "national-in-form" scheme was quietly shelved in favor of one based on the Latin alphabet (Zhou Youguang 1980g:64; Wu 1978:151–152; DeFrancis 1979).

Mao's reaction to this failure to carry out his directive does not appear to have been publicly expressed. In a speech delivered on 24 January 1956 at a meeting of the Communist Party Central Committee on "The Problem of the Intellectuals," however, he made some informal remarks that were disseminated clandestinely during the Cultural Revolution (DeFrancis 1979:146–147), were reported in fragmentary form starting in 1978 (Wang Zongbai 1978:250; ZY 1979:3), but were only presented in full in a "cleaned up" or edited version in 1980 in a speech made by Ye Laishi, an associate director of the Committee for Chinese Language Reform. What Mao said is worth quoting in full:

I strongly approve of the remarks made at the meeting by Comrade Wu Yuzhang advocating language reform. Do you approve or not adopting the Latin alphabet in the future? As I see it, there is no great problem among the broad masses; there are some problems among the intellectuals. How can China adopt a foreign alphabet? However, on examination, it is better after all to adopt such a foreign alphabet. Comrade Wu Yuzhang's comments on this point are well taken. Because such letters are few in number, only twenty-odd, and are written in one direction, they are simple and clear. Our Chinese characters certainly cannot compare with them in this respect. If they can't compare, well then they can't compare, and one mustn't think that Chinese characters are so good. Several professors have said to me that Chinese characters are the best writing system in "all the countries in the world" and cannot be reformed (laughter). If the Latin alphabet had been invented by Chinese, probably there would not be any problem. The problem stems from the fact that the foreigners did the inventing and the Chinese did the copying. However, the phenomenon of foreigners inventing and Chinese copying manifested itself long ago. For example, haven't we long made use of Arabic numerals? The Latin alphabet made its appearance in Rome; it is in common use in the vast majority of countries in the world. If we make use of it, will we then be strongly suspected of selling out the country? I think it is not necessarily a betrayal (laughter). All good things from abroad, things that are useful to us, we should study and take over entirely, digesting them and transforming them into our things. In the history of our country, the Han dynasty acted like this, and so did the Tang dynasty. The Han and Tang dynasties were both famous, powerful, and flourishing dynasties in our history. They were not afraid to absorb foreign things; if there was something good, they welcomed it. As long as the attitude and the method are correct, imitating good things from abroad is very beneficial to oneself.[3] [Ye Laishi 1981:60–61; see also Zheng Linxi 1981:5]

A formal defense of the decision to base the new phonetic system on Latin letters was presented by Zhou Enlai in a speech delivered in January 1958 at the time of the formal promulgation of Pinyin. His speech followed a Communist Party decision which stated: "The Central Committee recognizes that it is more suitable to use the Latin alphabet in the Scheme for a Chinese Phonetic Alphabet." Premier Zhou was given the task of outlining government policy on this matter. Addressing himself to the question "Will the adoption of the Latin alphabet in the scheme for a Chinese phonetic alphabet be

inconsistent with the feeling of patriotism of the Chinese people?",
he noted the unsuccessful attempt to create an indigenous alphabet
and defended the adoption of Latin letters by citing their widespread
use by other countries in which they had become "the alphabet of
each nation's own alphabet." He concluded: "The adoption of the
Latin alphabet will, therefore, not harm the patriotism of our people" (Zhou Enlai 1958:26–27).

From Mao's own remarks it appears that sensitivity to adopting
non-Chinese symbols of writing was greater among the intellectuals
than among the masses as a whole. In any case in approving the use of
Latin letters he noted that there would be no great problem with
regard to the masses and singled out professors as a source of opposition to the use of the foreign script. That such important observations
were not openly presented in China, but remained buried until officially revealed more than two decades later, suggests how much more
information may be buried in the archives and how little the public
at large is informed about important issues involved in Chinese
language reform (see page 295 for another Mao pronouncement
released in 1984). Even the fact that Mao originally requested a
"national-in-form" alphabet has become uncommon knowledge as
the second half of his directive presented to Ma Xulun was discreetly
expurgated after 1958 in the ubiquitous citations of his thoughts on
the subject.

As far as the actual devising of the alphabetic scheme is concerned,
the story ends rather happily—thanks in part to the expertise that
outstanding linguists like Lo Changpei and Li Jinxi, who earlier supported G.R., brought to bear by their participation in the task. In
addition to the use of Latin letters to create the generally excellent
Pinyin system, an important improvement over the old Latinization
was the use of four marks (as in *mā, má, mǎ, mà*) to indicate the
tones of Standard Chinese. This change was probably due to the
insistence of G.R. supporters that tones be taken into account in
devising the alphabetic system. Their preference for "tonal spelling,"
however, gave way to a compromise scheme of marks that, as Zhou
Youguang points out (1980g:177–178), has the added advantage of
being flexible—that is, being used or not according to need or preference, a matter that made it possible to attain broader support for
Pinyin.

Officially promulgated in January 1958 as the *Hànyǔ Pīnyīn
Fāng'àn* ("Chinese Phonetic Scheme" or "Chinese Phonetic Plan"),

it is learned in the first grade, forgotten in the second, and used only in certain places. Language reformers, as part of their effort to expand the use of Pinyin, eagerly point out the areas that Pinyin has so far succeeded in penetrating. These include some dictionaries and textbooks requiring character annotation; some library catalogues and other situations involving alphabetic sequence; special education for the blind; transmission of international news by the New China News Agency; labeling of industrial and commercial products; names of streets, post offices, and railway stations; flag signaling between ships; and transcription of Chinese terms in United Nations usage (Wang and Zhou 1983:3). Pinyin is now the official way of transcribing Chinese personal and place names, thereby providing a means, for those who accept this official usage, to end the former chaos in the way Chinese names have been written by accepting, for example, "Zhou Enlai" for "Chou Enlai" in English usage and "Tchou Enlai" in French usage.

In general, the chief functions of Pinyin have been to indicate the standard pronunciation of Chinese and to aid acquisition of Putonghua via annotated characters. In contrast to the large-scale production of materials entirely in the Latinized New Writing, very little has been produced entirely in Pinyin. Also in contrast to the Latinization approach, the use of Pinyin is not extended beyond Putonghua to include the regionalects. Official policy stresses use of Putonghua as the medium of instruction, simplified characters as the official writing in place of the obsolete complex graphs, and Pinyin as an adjunct to characters in the promotion of Putonghua and literacy.

CLASSLESSNESS OF CHARACTERS

The emphasis on Putonghua over other forms of speech was greatly aided, as noted in the previous chapter, by the use made of Stalin's "Marxism and Linguistics." Its publication in Chinese in July 1950 shortly after Wu Yuzhang's disclosure of Mao Zedong's directive was also used to support the new policy of relegating alphabetic writing to a position secondary to that of Chinese characters. One of Stalin's main concerns was to refute the thesis expounded by N. Y. Marr, long a dominant figure in Soviet linguistics, that (1) language has a class nature in that it is part of the superstructure (the political, legal, and other areas of society and the political, legal, and other institutions corresponding to them) which is erected on the base (the economic structure of society at a given stage of development) and that (2) language changes when the economic base undergoes change as a new class comes to power, as in the transition from feudalism to capitalism to socialism. On the contrary, said Stalin (1951), language does not form part of the superstructure, does not change when a new class comes to power, does not serve one class to the exclusion of other classes, and hence does not have a class nature.

Stalin's views on language in general were applied in China to the Chinese language in particular. In the process the concept of language came to include writing as well. In the case of Russian, which Stalin used to illustrate his point, it happens that the Cyrillic writing system represents fairly well and fairly easily the spoken form of the language. Although Stalin did not discuss writing and therefore did not separate it from spoken language, his remarks relating to speech could also be applied without undue strain to Russian in its written form. These fine distinctions were lost when Stalin's thesis was applied to the "Chinese language." Qu Qiubai, Lu Xun, Wu Yuzhang, and other supporters of Latinization had argued that *Chinese writing*—that is, Chinese characters—had a class nature. In what is perhaps the most pernicious instance of the confusion of speech and writing, Wu Yuzhang, referring to Stalin's comments about *language,* made a self-criticism and said that he had been in error in thinking that Chinese *writing* had a class nature (Wu 1952:5; DeFrancis 1979:142–143). Others followed Wu in permitting themselves to be routed by the use made of Stalin's essay without attempting to point out the distinction between spoken language and written language and to suggest that Chinese characters might indeed have a class nature since the privileged classes of society were so largely favored in achieving literacy based on such a difficult system of writing. Within a given community of speakers, they might have argued, communication by speech is more or less equally accessible to all, whereas communication by writing certainly is not.

It is of course unreasonable to think that such an approach requiring an exegesis of Stalin's work could be adopted in the political climate of the time. The official Chinese interpretation of his views was not directly challenged, though some writers, such as Zheng Linxi (1952), managed to note certain class aspects of characters while seeming to support the official line. The official position was later reinforced in 1957 when Mao Zedong stated:

The big-character posters do not have a class nature, just as *yŭyán* ["spoken language"] does not. Baihua does not have a class nature. In lecturing we speak Baihua, Chiang Kaishek also speaks Baihua. . . . The proletariat speaks Baihua, the bourgeoisie also speaks Baihua. [ZY 1979:1]

The thesis that the Chinese written language lacks a class nature required some explanation as to why so much emphasis was placed on reforming it. The standard explanation was expressed by Wen Hua (1973:12):

Written language is a system of symbols recording speech. It does not bear any class nature itself, but the work of reforming it has a clear-cut class nature. Subordinated to the political line of a particular class, reform of written language serves the interest of that class. The language reform which we are now carrying out is part and parcel of our socialist revolution and construction and serves to consolidate the dictatorship of the proletariat.

At the time no one appears to have come forth to question this convoluted reasoning. Recently, however, the explanation was dismissed in a refreshingly striking fashion by Zhou Youguang, a prolific and insightful scholar who is one of the leading members of the Committee on Chinese Language Reform. Asked whether he agreed with the statement that writing had no class nature but writing reform did, Zhou mockingly replied, *"Ng? Ng?"*, and he answered several other related questions with variations on this interjection: *"Ng? Ng!"*, *"Ng! Ng?"*, *"Ng! Ng!"*, *"Ng . . . ng"* (1980c:283). The interjection *ng* basically acknowledges only that one is listening, somewhat like *uh-huh* in English, but as rendered by Zhou the sound is clearly intended to represent various intonations expressing derisive disagreement.

The thesis propounded by Mao Zedong that characters lacked a class nature seriously weakened the position of those interested in fundamental reform. In blurring the distinction between speech and writing and ignoring completely the difference between Putonghua and other forms of speech, Mao lent authority to those who wished to place primary emphasis on acquisition of the Common Speech by all Chinese and literacy in simplified characters as the written form of Putonghua. These steps, he said in 1951, were required for the transition to alphabetic writing: "Before carrying out Pinyinization, it is necessary to simplify Chinese characters as an aid in its current application, and at the same time to carry out various kinds of preparation" (ZY 1979:3).

FROM NEGLECT TO REPRESSION OF PINYIN

Mao's views about preparing for an eventual transition to Pinyin writing were phrased in such general and ambiguous terms that they have been subjected to various interpretations regarding what should be done and when. The failure to provide clear support and encouragement for "various kinds of preparation" looking toward eventual "Pinyinization" led to a general neglect of activities aimed at developing rules of writing Pinyin and gradually extending its use as an independent orthography and to indifference if not outright hostility to such activities as were attempted. When Zhou Youguang took up the problem in 1961 of how to apply Pinyin to library catalogues, he was criticized on the grounds that it was "too early" to raise the issue (DeFrancis 1967a:150). When Mao Dun in the following year urged a policy of consolidating children's acquisition of Pinyin, his plea fell on deaf ears. His failure is of particular significance because what he was seeking was relatively easy to achieve and yet could be a major contribution to the preparatory work mentioned by Mao Zedong.

Mao Dun had noted that his granddaughter on finishing first grade had mastered Pinyin so well that she was able to correspond with her mother when the latter went to work in the countryside. In the second grade, however, she was given so little practice in Pinyin that she lost the skill, without, of course, achieving literacy in characters. Incensed at an educational policy which permitted literate first graders to relapse into a state of illiteracy, he called on teachers to help children retain mastery of Pinyin while seeking to add command of the characters. He called this a policy of "walking on two legs" (DeFrancis 1967a:146–147).

Mao Dun's suggestion may also be considered a sort of "literacy insurance" which guarantees that children—or adults—are at least literate in Pinyin should they be unable to go on and achieve literacy in characters. On a broad theoretical level, the policy of "walking on two legs" might be called one of "digraphia" (DeFrancis 1984). This term is intended to suggest a parallel in writing to Ferguson's well-known concept of "diglossia" in speech: the use of two related but quite different forms of speech, High and Low, in different situations. A case in point is the sharp contrast between formal lectures and informal speech in languages like Arabic; both levels are commanded by some speakers, but only one, the Low, by others (Ferguson 1959). Mao Dun's suggestion, if followed through, might have led to a situation of Chinese digraphia in which writing in characters would doubtless be considered the High form and writing in Pinyin the Low. Here too some individuals might command both forms, others only one.

The alternative approaches to literacy described in these terms were the subject of lively discussion before 1949. Subsequently there was little discussion of these alternatives and some, such as the possibility of separate regionalect Pinyin systems, appear to have been deliberately suppressed. The initial post-Liberation flurry of activity along these lines gradually died down and apparently flickered out completely in 1953 (Milsky 1974:261). Lu Xun's views on this subject, apart from being included in a 1956–1958 reprint of his complete works, were ignored until 1974, when a separate pamphlet was published by the Committee on Chinese Language Reform in which all his articles were brought together without comment (Lu Xun 1974). This publication was followed the next year by another pamphlet, also published by the committee, reprinting several articles by various writers that had appeared from 1973 to 1975. One of the articles, none of which does justice to Lu Xun's views, is a blatantly dishonest piece that attacks Liu Shaoqi by quoting him, without giving the context, or a citation that would make it possible to establish its authenticity, as saying that "it won't cause anyone's death if Common Speech is not promoted for a hundred years." To buttress his attack the author cites Lu Xun's isolated comment about the central role of the Northern dialect in the eventual emergence of Mass Language while omitting any reference to his repeated and emphatic advocacy of separate Latinizations (Xia 1975).

In view of the fact that separate alphabetic treatment for the regionalects has been a virtually tabooed subject since 1949, it comes as a surprise that among the revelations following the downfall of the Gang of Four is an account by Prof. Huang Diancheng of Amoy University of the adaptation of Pinyin to the Southern Min speech of Amoy and its use in the production of anti-illiteracy textbooks and other activities.[4] Huang reports that during the Cultural Revolution people possessing materials in Min alphabetic writing were denounced as "foreign lackeys" and were forced to take the materials out to the street, kneel down alongside them, set them afire, and reduce them to ashes (Huang 1980). Elsewhere repression of Pinyin in any form was undertaken by xenophobic Red Guards, themselves staunch supporters of character simplification, who tore down street signs written in Pinyin as evidence of subservience to foreigners.

The Nazi-like book-burning episode and other acts against the use of Pinyin are fitting testimony of the repression exercised against activities concerned with fundamental issues in Chinese writing reform. In these actions the positive idea that China should stand on its own feet without demeaning reliance on foreign aid was expressed in its most xenophobic form as a sort of anti-intellectual blood-and-soil nativism that constitutes a danger, still present, of a Chinese-style fascism. The young student storm troopers who sought to humble the old-time intellectuals, far from following Lu Xun in embracing the one system of writing that would have done most to equalize things between illiterates and *all* those who had received an education, supported instead the lesser reform of character simplification that might enhance their own position relative to the older generation.

AFTER THE CULTURAL REVOLUTION

The bitter legacy of conflict and repression engendered by the Cultural Revolution and by the two previous decades of official hostility even to discussion of certain aspects of writing reform has by no means been completely dissipated by the changes that have taken place since the downfall of the Gang of Four. Nevertheless the considerably freer atmosphere of recent years has led to a significant increase in activities of various kinds, including publication. Apart from some items already cited, perhaps the chief publication of interest is a new journal started in 1980 that is published at irregular intervals. Called *Yuwen Xiandaihua,* it carries the English title *Modernizing Our Language,* an obvious and widely emphasized tie with the current emphasis on the Four Modernizations. The journal is the organ of a new organization, the Language Reform Association of Chinese Institutions of Higher Learning, that appears to have been set up to bypass or at least supplement the conflict-ridden Committee on Chinese Language Reform by undertaking activities which the committee as an official government agency is unable to carry out. The association, for example, is expected to carry forward the type of separate Pinyin-only publications that the committee, at Ni Haishu's initiative, undertook through the publication in 1981–1982 of *ABC*, an excellent series of elementary readers that was terminated, according to the notice in the sixth and final volume, "at the request of the leadership."

The chief aim of the association is to gain support for the promotion of Pinyin and other language reform activities by establishing branches in many educational institutions (130 of which had joined the association by the summer of 1982) and enlisting the aid of a broad spectrum of the educational establishment for the many tasks that need to be undertaken. Its establishment in 1981 capped several years of preparatory work that was warmly supported by Ni Haishu and Zhou Youguang, both prominent members of the committee whose views as originally expressed were in conflict with the main post-1949 language reform trends, as well as by many of the leading linguists, including Wang Li, Lyu Shuxiang, and Zhu Dexi. A significant reinforcement for the older supporters of alphabetic writing is represented by the adherence of a number of young computer specialists who stress the need for a script that can be readily adapted to the new technology basic to the current modernization drive. One older scholar, though not himself a computer specialist, echoed this view and chastised those who, "too lazy" to learn Pinyin, "still twaddle about the Four Modernizations" (Luo 1980:28).

The extensive discussions that accompanied the establishment of the new organization and the new journal contained many expressions of hope for the future but also concern about the difficulties that lie ahead. One of the main points made in the journal and elsewhere is the need to make a transition from a mere *Pīnyīn Fāng'àn* ("Pinyin Plan") to a full-fledged *Pīnyīn Wénzì* ("Pinyin Orthography") independent of characters. Wang Li and Lyu Shuxiang in their separate comments criticized the prevailing idea that the promotion of Pinyin writing independent of characters had to wait until Putonghua had been generalized throughout the country. Wang Li said it was impossible to wait until the speech of the whole country was unified. Such a requirement would make it impossible to change over to Pinyin writing in a hundred or even a thousand years. "In the present stage," he said, "if we concentrate the intelligence and strength of 900 million people, it is entirely possible to effect a comparatively satisfactory Pinyin orthography" (1980:13–15). Wang also reversed the argument that it was first necesary to generalize Putonghua by contending that the immediate promotion of Pinyin would accelerate expansion of Common Speech (1981:5), a view expressed also by Lyu Shuxiang (1981:109) and many others.

Another point that was strongly emphasized by a number of people was the need to produce a great deal of material written in Pinyin. Ye Laishi, one of the associate directors of the Committee on Chinese Language Reform, called for extensive use of Pinyin to write poetry, essays, and fiction, and to translate into Pinyin from materials published in characters and in foreign languages, so that people would have something to read in Pinyin and would therefore not forget it (1980b:16–17). Zhou Youguang presented similar views, adding that in order for Pinyin writing to be consolidated it must become a commonplace of written communication and in addition must receive legal recognition on a par with characters (1980a, 1980b, 1980g)—something which, he might have noted, the communists had already accorded to Latinization four decades earlier.

Although language reformers have not succeeded in getting the enormous boost that would result from such legal recognition, they profess to be greatly heartened by the fact that promotion of Putonghua has for the first time been written into law, in the revised constitution of 1982, for they contend that promotion of the standard language implies the use of Pinyin and hence consolidates its position, such support being specifically intended by the inclusion of the new clause (Zhou Youguang 1982:personal communication). In any case, reconciling themselves to the lack of official equality for Pinyin, reformers have taken the position that they must do the best they can to push the use of Pinyin as a preliminary to its official acceptance as an independent orthography. "Better to have the fact without the name," said Zhou Youguang (1979:360), "than to have the name without the fact." In line with this approach, reformers are seeking to expand the use of Pinyin into various fields, such as computer technology, and to consolidate its acquisition and use by schoolchildren.

Another prominent theme in discussions in the journal and elsewhere was the idea that two systems of writing, namely Pinyin and characters, would coexist and have their own sphere of use. This is generally referred to as "walking on two legs" or a "two-track system," and, as we have suggested, might also be called a policy of digraphia. How long the period of transition to a full-fledged Pinyin orthography would be depended on the effort expended for its attainment. In any case the situation envisaged by Wu Yuzhang and others of characters being studied as a special subject only from the middle schools on was a long way off, and there was no question whatsover of getting rid of characters (Wu 1978:125–126; Wang Li 1980; Ni 1980).

CONTINUED OPPOSITION TO PINYIN

Although the earlier exaggerated rhetoric about getting rid of Chinese characters is no longer expressed—Lu Xun's remarks were specifically repudiated as the views of one individual and not as official policy (Wang and Zhou 1983:4)—the fear of such an eventuality is recognized as one of the main reasons for opposition to Pinyin writing. Where does the opposition come from? Wang Li stated: "I think it comes primarily from intellectuals, especially from high-level intellectuals." He added that the worker and peasant masses strongly support the reform (1980:14). Zhou Youguang and Ni Haishu, however, expressed a more pessimistic view. Zhou felt that the intellectuals are split on the subject and that the greatest obstacle is the indifference if not hostility of the peasant masses, who feel no urgency for literacy education (1982:personal communications). Ni Haishu contended that the lack of familiarity with Pinyin, in contrast to the long-established characters, was a problem involving the people as a whole, and that the general attachment to characters was such that it would be impossible to overcome without overwhelming effort along different lines. He stressed that "one-sided statements that characters are bad will not convince people, nor will one-sided statements that Pinyin writing is good. Chinese characters have their good points, and Pinyin writing has its bad points." Spouting empty principles would not do. Hard work and much time were required. "Habit is a very irrational thing," he said. "The force of habit of a billion people is a force to be feared" (1980:35–38).

This force of habit applies to all segments of the population, even the illiterate, who, according to Prof. Huang Diancheng, have been so brainwashed into revering characters that they would not dream of using printed matter for toilet paper (1982:personal communication). The general feeling that only literacy in characters is real literacy has led parents to object to their children learning Pinyin. According to Zhang Zhigong, however, people have been won over to Pinyin once the whole subject is thoroughly explained to them (1982:personal communication). The views expressed by Mao Zedong, Wang Li, and others also suggest that the masses can be won over and that they are therefore not the main problem.

A more serious problem is the quite different atmosphere, as compared to the thirties and forties and part of the succeeding decades, that appears to permeate Chinese society today as the aftermath of the turmoil of the Cultural Revolution and the twists and turns of policy since 1949. Before and during the war a mood of self-sacrificing patriotism roused many Chinese, especially the young, to throw themselves into a broad movement of national salvation that included the promotion of Latinization as one means of aiding the masses and bringing them into a united effort. In contrast, the prevailing mood appears to be one of widespread cynicism, battle fatigue, and me-firstism that has diminished the interest of many who are already literate in supporting language reform activities along the lines of earlier years.

A perhaps even more serious problem is the opposition of those in position to impede change now as they have in the past. As a result of this opposition, said Ni Haishu (1980:35), many people have lost heart; the damage wrought by the Gang of Four is considerable. Apart from the poisoned atmosphere which still lingers on, one aspect of this damage is the fact that *Wénzì Găigé (Language Reform)*, the official organ of the Committee on Chinese Language Reform, only resumed publication in August 1982 after a hiatus of sixteen years. The prolific reformer Zhou Youguang, whose bibliography contains eighty-three articles and books published between 1950 and 1964, was unable to publish anything more for fourteen years (*Hanzi Gaige* 1981:8–11). These lost years included, of course, the period of the Cultural Revolution, when members of the committee abandoned language reform for enforced thought reform along with many of the older intellectuals. When such large chunks of time are subtracted from the years since 1958, when Pinyin was adopted, the duration of more or less active promotion of Pinyin shrinks to very little.

There is clear evidence of opposition to Pinyin even within circles that one might think would be favorably disposed toward it. Zhou Youguang (1980d) recounts that in one of his articles published in *Zhongguo Yuwen*, now the organ of the Institute of Linguistics in the Chinese Academy of Social Sciences, the editors showed their antipathy to adopting Western usages by even going so far as to change his arabic numerals to Chinese characters, as follows:

"78" changed to "七 分词连写： Linkage
"11%" changed to "

Another case invol
together, to hyphenat(
solve in a consistent
tions, such as already (
ones are found. In ans
as to how long it wou
Zhou replied: "Twent
cation). The linkage p
be overcome before Pi
obviously reflects his
that has resulted in such meager progress in Chinese writing reform.

Zhou Youguang and others have also recently revealed that when the Pinyin system was created, it was submitted for discussion under the name *Hànyǔ Pīnyīn Wénzì Fāng'àn* ("Chinese Phonetic Writing Plan"), but that before its official promulgation by the National People's Congress in 1958 the word *Wénzì* ("Writing") was deleted. (Zhou 1980a:36). Before the Great Leap Forward of 1958 it was intended to develop Hanyu Pinyin into a Hanyu Pinyin Wenzi in an informal draft program for ten years. But with the coming of the Great Leap this intention was abandoned, and the Committee on Chinese Language Reform was subjected to a sharp reduction. It appears that the euphoric expectations of progress by uniquely Chinese means embraced the area of writing as well.

Opposition to the recent revival of the term Hanyu Pinyin Wenzi as a step in promoting a separate orthography has again been expressed. In a letter to the editor of *People's Daily*, a certain Li Tao objected to "some specialists" designating *Hànyǔ Pīnyīn Fāng'àn* as *Hànyǔ Pīnyīn Wénzì Fāng'àn* and referring to it as "the current direction of writing reform." He felt this to be a usurpation of government authority and contrary to the decision made by the National People's Congress. "There must be a uniform centralized leadership," he said. "Everyone cannot go his own way." Li Tao's letter was published just above another by a certain Xu Dejiang entitled "Writing Must Conform to the Situation in the Country" that extolled the superiority of characters relative to "Latinization" and "phonemicization" (*People's Daily*, 29 December 1981).

The government newspaper in publishing Li Tao's letter identified him as affiliated with the Committee on Chinese Language Reform. According to Zhang Zhigong (1982:personal communication), a member of the committee, of whom there are twenty-two appointed by the State Council, Li Tao was not an actual member of the Committee but merely one of its staff workers, and the official prominence given to his views aroused considerable resentment among language reformers.

Further light on the Li and Xu letters that reveals their broad ramifications is supplied by Zhou Youguang (1982:personal communications). It appears that both Li and Xu are followers of Yuan Xiaoyuan, a wealthy Chinese expatriate who returned to China from the United States in the seventies to found the Society for Research on the Modernization of Chinese Characters as a means of promoting a writing system of her own creation. Her system consists of 108 characterlike symbols used in various combinations to indicate consonants, vowels, and tones, with 58 out of the 108 also being used as radicals to distinguish homonyms—all these elements for a particular syllable being written in a square, like the original character they were suppose to invoke. It was support for this "character alphabet" and opposition to Pinyin that prompted *People's Daily* to publish the two letters by Li and Xu. Yuan was so successful in getting publicity and acquiring adherents that she was able to put the Committee on Chinese Language Reform on the defensive for failing to support her scheme, which she was even able to promote in the classroom—a move which prompted a prominent Pinyin supporter (Luo 1981:109) to the irate comment that "it is most unfitting that foreigners should be permitted to come and conduct experiments on the soil of the People's Republic of China."

Another comment on this episode was made by Hu Qiaomu, a high official who currently holds the important post of secretary of the Communist Party Central Committee Secretariat, headed the Chinese Academy of Social Sciences until 1982, and has been a member of the official Committee on Chinese Language Reform since its inception in 1951. In an important speech to an audience that included prominent language reformers, linguists, and representatives of the press, including the *People's Daily,* Hu pointedly remarked that no official support of any kind could be given to a privately created scheme for Chinese writing, of which over 1,600 new schemes or adaptations of old proposals had been submitted to the committee between 1958 and 1980. The legally established Hanyu

Pinyin Fang'an, he said, is "absolutely unshakable." He considerably weakened his support, however, by adding that while Hanyu Pinyin *Fang'an* was inviolable, the question of a Hanyu Pinyin *Wenzi* was open to discussion in all its aspects.

Although actually devoting most of his attention to the problem of further simplification of characters, Hu (1982) expressed himself in favor of some sort of alphabetic writing, which he too thought would coexist for a long time with the character script, each being used where it was best suited. He might, however, have greatly strengthened the position of Pinyin had he stated that it was still an open question whether China would adopt a Pinyin Wenzi—that is, an alphabetic orthography independent of characters—but if it did the orthography selected would be based on the present Pinyin. A decisive official stand in this matter is needed to end the wasteful concern with half-baked alternative schemes, trumpeted by a swarm of faddists, of which that of Yuan Xiaoyuan and another advocating a two-symbol representation of syllables (Martin 1982:288–298; Lyuu 1983) have had the most diversionary effect.

LACK OF TOP-LEVEL SUPPORT

The byzantine maneuverings just described point to what appears to be the major weakness of the new stage of writing reform—namely, the lack of clear and unequivocal support from the highest levels of government, such as that provided for Latinization in the thirties and early forties. Without such support it is likely that even with the assistance of prestigious linguists like Wang Li and Lyu Shuxiang those seeking a thoroughgoing reform of the Chinese writing system may not be able to overcome the apathy of the masses and the opposition of the entrenched scholarly, educational, and government establishment.

The overthrow of the Gang of Four has not been accompanied by a top-level repudiation of their stand on language reform. Nor have the views held by those currently in the highest positions of power been made clear. Perhaps they simply do not give the matter much thought if they remain unaware of the connection, stressed in the title of the new journal devoted to language reform, between the Four Modernizations and "modernizing our language." It may also be that the recent upsurge of activity, if not due solely to the initiative of the reformers themselves, reflects a decision to permit more discussion than in the past to see what the public reaction might be. Only one high official, Hu Qiaomu, has publicly, though somewhat equivocally, expressed support for Pinyin, which he envisages as coexisting as an independent orthography along with that in characters over a long period of time, each serving the functions for which it is best suited (Hu 1982:3–11). Another high official, Vice-Premier Bo Yibo, has also expressed support for Pinyin writing, but only to a visiting delegation of German social scientists, who were refused the minutes of the meeting (Helmut Martin 1981:personal communication). Where Deng Xiaoping, currently the most powerful figure in China, stands in the matter is not at all clear. In 1974, in an interview with Saionji Kinkazu, a specialist on China, and other members of a visiting Japanese delegation that expressed regrets for the harm done by Japan to China, he is quoted as having said: "Even though China suffered damage from the invasion of Japanese militarists, this was only a matter of a few decades. On the other hand, historically China has been causing difficulties for Japan in two respects. One is Chinese characters; the other is the philosophy of Confucius and Mencius. Confucian philosophy has influenced the traditional Japanese way of thinking for over 1,700 years, and for this I feel very sorry" (*Asahi Shimbun*, 6 June 1974, morning edition). These remarks seem to suggest a negative attitude toward Chinese characters, but they hardly provide the kind of unequivocal support needed by Chinese language reformers, especially since the remarks do not appear to have been publicized in China.[5]

It is difficult to know just what to make of this repeated pattern of pronouncements being made to foreigners but kept from the Chinese populace. Perhaps it reflects general support for something that high officials do not consider of high priority and are too busy to think about in detail; they cannot do more than toss off a remark that will not be heard by their constituents and hence will not further roil the domestic situation. Another explanation, by no means excluding the one just suggested, is that dissemination of the views of maximum leaders is a policy decision that is made only as a result of infighting over control of information. Mao's important comments made in January 1956 supporting the Latin alphabet as the basis for Pinyin were withheld until 1981—a specific example of the shifting balance of forces in regard to dissemination of information bearing on the promotion of Pinyin. In recent years language reformers have repeatedly, but for the most part unsuccessfully, pleaded for top-level support, and they deplore the fact that since the death of Wu Yuzhang in 1966 there is no longer an advocate for their cause sufficiently high placed to have the ear of the top leadership (Luo 1980:27; Yang 1980:19).

LU XUN AND THE DECENTRALIZATION ISSUE

However desirable it might be to have the ear of China's top leaders, the support of a wider public would also seem crucial, but this seems hardly obtainable unless there is full and free discussion of all the possible alternatives that have been advanced for Chinese writing reform. The context in which this discussion might take place is an issue—centralization versus decentralization—that has been a key aspect of the internal struggles both before and after 1949. There has been extensive discussion in recent years concerning decentralization, especially in the economic sphere. The issue of linguistic decentralization along the lines advocated by Lu Xun, however, is still tabooed. It is absent from the six-page-long list of "Items Projected for Scientific Research in Language Reform" that was drawn up by the Language Reform Association of Chinese Institutions of Higher Learning and published in the fifth number of *Yuwen Xiandaihua* in 1981.

The failure to revive this issue undoubtedly reflects official as well as public indifference and indeed opposition to the whole idea. After a generation in which the idea has been denounced, in terms almost identical to those used by anticommunists before 1949, as unpatriotic and subversive of Chinese unity, it is perhaps even more difficult to reopen the matter now. For one thing, it would be necessary to face up to the fact that the officially revered Lu Xun himself supported this approach. Since 1949 this fact has largely been swept under the carpet. Not only this specific aspect of Lu Xun's views, but even his general support for alphabetic writing, have been largely ignored. In contrast to Guo Moruo's eulogy at the time of Lu Xun's death in 1936, in which his activity in support of Latinization was lauded as of even greater importance than his literary contribution, in 1981, the centenary of his birth, the journal *Yuwen Xuexi* [Study of language and literature] devoted large portions of two issues to various aspects of his life and work, including even such detail as an analysis of his punctuation, without any reference to his interest in writing reform. The extensive display in the Lu Xun Museum in Peking of material related to his life and work contains not a single reference to his interest in such reform, an omission which is clearly a matter of deliberate policy.[6]

Since neither Lu Xun's patriotism nor his concern for Chinese unity are open to question, in any resurrection of his views his advocacy of separate Latinizations would either have to be proved wrong, which of course needs to be considered a possibility, or acknowledged to be right, which would involve an uncomfortable shift in position. In any case this would have the effect, doubtless opposed by some, of helping to dissipate the smoke screen that alphabetic writing is a foreign gadget accepted only by domestic lackeys.

The failure to discuss the issue of separate Latinizations for the various regionalects is by no means due to the lack of support for such a procedure.[7] It reflects the quite realistic decision not to impair the promotion of Pinyin by adding at this time a complication that is bound to deepen opposition to its use—already beleaguered by mass indifference if not hostility, by the renewed emphasis on characters and a return to the classics, and by attempts to promote "character alphabets" or some other phonetic scheme in place of Pinyin. The immediate need is to accustom people to Pinyin and to learn more about the difficulties involved in Pinyinization. Perhaps such activity will engender acceptance of Pinyin to write Putonghua and this in turn may lead to demands for its use to write the various regionalects.

It would appear, therefore, that a return to the approach advanced by Lu Xun is not in the offing. Yet it is not impossible in the future. This may eventually come about if the present integralist policy regarding literacy fails to produce the expected results and if awareness grows that Lu Xun's approach is after all the most efficient means of achieving universal literacy, the only one that can avoid the main contradictions that account for the failure to date to make any significant progress toward reaching that goal. One contradiction is the incongruity between the difficulty of the characters and the limited ability of the masses to acquire the requisite mastery. Another contradiction, discussed in the preceding chapter, is the incongruity inherent in using characters to achieve a style of writing close to speech. Still another is that involved in the policy that replaces characters by a single Putonghua Pinyin orthography and places on regionalect speakers the extra burden of setting aside their own speech and learning Putonghua for purposes of literacy. In all these cases an enormous burden is placed on the segment of the population that is least able to afford the time and effort needed to attain and retain mastery of the writing system.

Lu Xun's approach solves all these contradictions. A phonetic orthography based on the way people actually speak, he pointed out, enables them to write anything they can say. And as we have seen in the discussion of vocabulary size, people can say a great deal. We must assume that average Chinese, even of the peasant class, have a spoken vocabulary of at least ten thousand expressions, perhaps scores of thousands. They can learn to write all these expressions without undue difficulty if Pinyin is used to represent their own speech (or a form of speech close enough to their own to be readily intelligible to them). It would require far more time and effort for Chinese as a whole to achieve the same results in characters or for regionalect speakers to do so in Putonghua Pinyin.

LITERACY IN ENGLISH AND CHINESE

These crucial aspects of the literacy problem in China can be further illuminated if we look at some related aspects of reading and writing in English. In the West at a very early age children acquire the idea of alphabetic representation of speech and often invent their own spelling. The efforts of one such five-year-old inventor are reported and analyzed in fascinating detail in a book by his observant mother entitled *GNYS AT WRK* (Bissex 1980). The title comes from a sign her child had posted over his workbench-desk: DO NAT DSTRB GNYS AT WRK. The genius at work is a capacity for phonetic expression that manifests itself among adults as well as children who readily continue to invent their own spellings if they have not been able to achieve full mastery of standard orthography. Using the alphabetic system that forms the basis of English orthography, a minimally educated wife might leave her husband a note like the following:

Bill:
I gotta go see a sik frend an aint got time to go by grossereez we need lettus sellery kukumber buckweet sirrup woodja pleez git im

Mary

It must be observed that Mary is 100 percent literate in writing. She can write, in her spelling, all sorts of words, even those of relatively low frequency, such as carbrater, dieper, roadadendrin, makril, Albakirky. Both she and Bill are 100 percent literate in reading the kind of writing of which the letter is an example. That they misspell words and use substandard vocabulary and grammar is wholly irrelevant to their having accomplished one of the main tasks involved in literacy: the ability to communicate in writing without any restriction in using the thousands or tens of thousands of words they command in speech. To be sure, this major achievement is limited by their inability to cope, especially in reading, with standard orthography, vocabulary, and grammar. This shortcoming can be remedied either by further education or by modifying standards of writing to approach their needs. The former is the only likely approach. The literacy already achieved provides an excellent basis for further educational advances. And if this is not possible Bill and Mary are at least already insured against illiteracy.

In the case of Chinese, the level of literacy attained by Bill and Mary is much harder to achieve in characters. To take the Chinese equivalent of two items in Mary's shopping list, the character 芹 *(qín)* in 芹菜 (*qíncài* "celery") does not occur within the two thousand most frequent characters, and the character 荞 *(qiáo)* in 荞麦 (*qiáomài* "buckwheat") does not occur within the five thousand range (Sino 1980). These two characters might, to be sure, be replaced by familiar characters that constitute misspellings, the so-called *biézì* ("other characters")—as for example by writing 琴菜 and 桥麦, which are able to represent the required sounds *qíncài* and *qiáomài* with characters of higher frequency and are not likely to be taken in their literal meanings of "lute vegetable" and "bridge wheat."

Bill and Mary are able to write their thousands or tens of thousands of words with only twenty-six letters (fifty-two if capital letters are counted separately). Their Chinese counterparts have the considerably harder task of learning either 398 or 1,277 characters—depending on whether or not tones are taken into consideration—that would be needed to be able to do the same. And the acquisition of these characters is now impossible since the Chinese orthographic system has not singled out these minimum numbers of characters needed to write Chinese in the syllabic equivalent of our alphabet. The nearest approach to this sort of solution is the suggestion made by Zhou Youguang (1980a:29–30) to limit the number of characters in current publications to a standard three thousand or so by using certain fixed *biézì* as phonetic substitutes for the additional three thousand in current use that lie outside this standard list.

As noted earlier, a different approach to literacy in characters was proposed by Mao Zedong (1956:165). The paltry capacity for expression in characters on the part of peasants using Mao's approach contrasts with the full literacy, on the level of Bill and Mary, of Chinese children using Pinyin. A study made on 19 November 1962 of diaries written by first graders in Harbin revealed the ability of even the weakest pupils to give touching expression to their thoughts and feelings after a mere ten weeks of schooling. The researcher noted that the first diary entries were entirely in Pinyin, that the first characters, five in number, appeared on 18 October intermixed with Pinyin and that thereafter there was a gradual increase in the number of characters. A particularly touching item is the following diary entry, with the original errors left in, made by a pupil near the bottom of the class:

11 月 19 日 míng 天 yòu kǎo shì 了 我 要 zhēng quě dǎ yì bǎn fēn 老 师 zhǒng 説 我 写 的 字 不 hǎo 我 yí dìng yào huéi dào 家 lǐng liàn hǎo 字 wán.

11 month 19 day tomorrow having another test I must trie to get a hunderd the teacher allways says the characters I write are no good I have to go back hom and practice the characters until I have learned them the end.[8]

Thanks to the superiority of Pinyin orthography over English orthography, these Harbin first graders were far in advance of their American counterparts in being able to express themselves so fully at such an early stage in their studies. As Mao Dun noted in the case of his granddaughter, this ability is lost in the second grade owing to the policy of almost exclusive emphasis on the study of characters, not enough of which could be learned at this stage to achieve literacy in the traditional script. From these episodes it is apparent that Mao Dun's complaint about the handling of his grandaughter's education amounts to a searing indictment of Chinese educational policy as one of unparalleled incompetence and narrow-mindedness in that it actually creates illiterates out of children already literate, albeit literate "merely" in Pinyin.

Understanding the contrast in literacy levels of peasants using characters and first graders using Pinyin may help us to comprehend the sense of urgency, the almost desperate plea, of language reformers like Mao Dun, Wang Li, Zhou Youguang, and a host of others for a policy of digraphia, "walking on two legs," instead of the present single-minded obsession with Chinese characters. It also underscores the need to resurrect Lu Xun's passionately expressed views about language reform so that *all* the alternatives that might be available can be given the thorough consideration that is needed for a rational attempt to reform the Chinese system of writing.

At present the only alternative that has received any measure of official approval and is openly supported by many reformers is a policy of what might be called monoglossia and digraphia—that is, exclusive emphasis on Putonghua as the medium of instruction, even in the regionalect areas, and literacy only in Putonghua, first in Pinyin and then in characters. The alternative advanced by Lu Xun, although never spelled out in detail and officially tabooed since 1949, amounts essentially to a thoroughgoing policy of diglossia and possibly digraphia as well. His emphasis on literacy in what might now be called Regionalect Pinyin is equivalent to the use of the native regionalect in both its spoken and Pinyin forms as the initial medium of instruction, to be followed later by the learning of the standard language, again in both its spoken and Pinyin forms. Learning the character version of the standard language was not among the views advanced by Lu Xun, who indeed called for destroying Chinese characters, but this rhetoric no doubt simply meant an optional digraphia with the study of characters relegated to a still later stage, ultimately only by those who, like himself, were intensely interested in the rich literary heritage of the past.

LANGUAGE REFORM IN BROAD PERSPECTIVE

For a full understanding of language reform in either of the alternatives summarized above, it is necessary to place the whole subject in proper perspective. Chinese language reform has frequently been compared with language reform in other countries, particularly Turkey, Viet Nam, and the Arab countries, all of which, like China, have taken up the problem of language reform as part of modernization efforts initiated within the past century. Such broad comparisons need to be supplemented by more attention to differences as well as similarities.

In the Arabic-writing world, as in China, there is a great tradition of a classical literary language that continues to influence the written style of what Meynet (1971) calls *"la caste des lettrés."* There is also an aesthetic appreciation of calligraphy as an art, a rationale of the unique fit between features of the script and features of the language, a belief in the unifying force of the script in the face of disparities in speech, a fear of losing contact with the culture of the past. These parallels between the Chinese and Arab worlds combine to create another parallel: limited progress in the direction of fundamental reform.

Yet there are important differences between the two areas. Written Arabic represents a language whose speakers, according to Meynet (1971:96–103), consider it to be "above all the language of the Koran, of religion." China lacks this religious impediment to change. China is also aided by the fact that its political unity makes decision-making easier than in the fragmented Arab world. It is also favored by a body of reformers with extensive practical experience in language reform. These factors suggest that there may be more possibility for change in China.

The prospects, however, do not warrant a comparison with the successful reforms already carried out in Turkey and Viet Nam. The reform in Turkey involved replacing the Arabic alphabet with the Latin alphabet—a relatively simple change that, thanks in part to the secular and anti-Arabic aspects of Turkish nationalism, could be carried out in a few months, though the accompanying drive to replace Arabic terms with those based on Turkish roots proved to be more difficult and took longer to carry out (Heyd 1954). The Vietnamese reform involved replacing alien writing systems, Chinese and French, with a Latin script for the indigenous language—a more complex change which the anticolonial modernization movement was able to carry out in a matter of decades (DeFrancis 1977). The Chinese reform is more complex than either of these cases. The course that Chinese language reform is likely to take suggests that the most valid comparison may turn out to be not with either of these countries but with Europe in its shift from writing in Latin to writing in the vernaculars. This process, which involved, of course, not a change in script but a change in the language of writing, took centuries to bring about.

Writing in Italian hardly existed before the twelfth century and only became extensive in the thirteenth and fourteenth centuries, thanks in large part to the influence of Dante (1265–1321). For many years it was confined largely to literature. The first scientific work in Italian was not published until 1537, and Italian only became established as the language of science after 1612, when Galileo shifted from Latin to Italian by publishing his first work in the latter language (Devoto 1978:190–250). In the rest of Europe, Latin survived as a medium of written communication well into the seventeenth century and, in a more attenuated form, even into later years. In sum, Latin and the vernaculars coexisted for centuries with a gradually shifting balance toward the latter until Latin became a dead language studied in schools and used only by specialists.

The process of Chinese language reform, even if it receives top-level support and is promoted with the utmost vigor, is likely to be more or less equally protracted because of the myriad practical difficulties presented by an impoverished nation of a billion people—and even more because of attachment to characters that have been used for a much longer period of time than was Latin, boast a much vaster body of literature, and have far more users today than Latin ever had at any one time and perhaps even in all time. A system so deeply embedded in Chinese society is naturally far more resistant to change, even to merely sharing its role with another system through a policy of digraphia.

There is therefore no assurance that a policy of digraphia will in fact be adopted or that it can nevertheless be carried out, as some reformers hope, in a piecemeal fashion on a more or less informal basis. It is even less possible to predict the precise form that a policy of "walking on two legs," if it comes about, will take, since there are many possible combinations of monoglossia, diglossia, monographia, and digraphia that might emerge in China taken as a whole and among the various classes and divisions of Chinese society.

What is certain is that the whole subject will continue to provoke in the future a sharper and broader controversy than was the case in Europe, much less in Turkey and Viet Nam. The subject of language reform, it is apparent, is an extremely sensitive issue. It arouses deep passions. Attachment to the traditional writing system is doubtless pervasive among all segments of society, from the galaxy of Chinese scholars to the masses of illiterate peasants.

The issue has some parallels with the policy recently instituted in China of limiting family size to a single child. This policy is by no means universally accepted, but it appears to be essential, for the policy of unrestricted reproduction endangers success in economic and other areas. Writing reform may be even more unpopular, though not necessarily so if presented in the context of digraphia, and it appears to be almost equally essential. China's modernization, to say the least, is impeded by sole reliance on a script that has shown itself unsuccessful in producing mass literacy and meeting other needs of a modern society.

To be sure, it is quite possible to maintain indefinitely an unevenly developing society polarized into a small minority in full command of the traditional script and a huge mass of people "literate" to the extent of knowing the few hundred characters needed for minimal record-keeping in their personal activities. This two-class literacy can even, except for the silenced few, be quite acceptable to all concerned —the minority, because it has the satisfaction of having attained a hard-to-reach goal, and the majority, because it has been conditioned to be satisfied with its meager "literacy" and has not been provided with a simpler means not only to meet *all* their practical needs but also to achieve a richer life of the mind and the spirit. In this situation it is perhaps quixotic to call for change involving a system of writing so strongly entrenched in the thoughts and feelings of the Chinese people.

Yet to an ever-increasing extent the Chinese themselves are beginning to question the successfulness of official policy on speech and writing. If this trend that began after the downfall of the Gang of Four is not again stifled but is able to press forward to a thorough and judicious consideration of divergent views, it is possible that a citizenry fully informed of all the options available to it will for the first time be able to participate in the fateful decisions that must be made regarding Chinese language reform.

A hard choice confronts the Chinese. If they maintain the quintessentially Chinese system of characters as the exclusive means of writing, it seems certain that many if not most of the people will be doomed to perpetual illiteracy and that China's modernization will be seriously impeded. If they adopt a policy of digraphia by making Pinyin a full-fledged orthography in order to meet the needs of a modern society, they risk a divisive struggle over how to preserve their cultural heritage and maintain their unity as a people.

Should the decision be made to press toward a sweeping reform, and should this decision result in the worst of all possible outcomes, posterity will never forgive the cultural and political breakup of China. But should these fears prove to be ungrounded, a fully literate people risen to new heights of greatness will have cause to look back on Chinese language reform not as a cruel sham but as a genuine Great Proletarian Cultural Revolution.

Notes

The Mao quote on the dedication page is from Lyell 1976; I have changed his spelling of Lu Hsün to Lu Xun. The Guo Moruo quote is from Ni 1941.

Introduction

1. I am grateful to the American Council of Learned Societies and the Social Science Research Council for grants which made it possible for me to initiate this research during my sabbatical year 1973–1974. The Vietnamese phase of the research resulted in a book: *Colonialism and Language Policy in Viet Nam* (1977).

2. See the Glossary for definitions of this and other technical terms.

3. Most writers who have noted Leibniz's interest in a universal script have exaggerated his role in promoting what has been called "the project of a universal character." They also err in their estimation of Leibniz's interest in Chinese. The project of a universal character aroused great interest during the Enlightenment and, according to one student of the subject, "seems in fact to have been an intellectual commonplace in seventeenth-century Europe" (Cohen 1954:49 ff). Another writer notes that "Chinese, however, failed to meet Leibniz's rigid requirements in the quest for a universal language" and further quotes him as making the following disillusioned comment: "If you know Chinese characters, I believe that you will find a little more precision in them than in the Egyptian hieroglyphics, but basically they are far removed from that analysis of thought which comprises the essence of my plan . . ." (Lach 1941:93–94).

4. I have seen only the 1957 edition of this work, in which the appendix occupies pages 254–272. All my citations refer to this edition.

5. Support for Chinese characters as the universal writing system has been promoted in the postwar period by a well-known French literary scholar, Etiemble, who refers to the characters as *"la langue internationale par excellence."* Etiemble (1960:136) further states: "For someone like me, who tries to see the world as it is, I wouldn't be at all upset if a great civilization such as the Chinese, which has so often proven itself, were to give to those poor people who are prisoners of their alphabetic languages a universal instrument which would uncontestibly facilitate that communication of intellectual lights which Leibniz wished for."

6. The spellings *seti* and *satu* are in the official Japanese romanization. Their equivalents in the perhaps more familiar Hepburn system are *sechi* and *satsu*.

7. Strange as this way of writing English may appear at first glance, an intriguing assessment is the comment by Reischauer that hangul "is perhaps the most scientific system of writing in general use in any country" because "the advantages of an alphabetic script and a syllabary (in which each symbol represents a whole syllable) are combined by bunching the individual letters into syllabic groups" (Reischauer and Fairbank 1960:435–436).

8. In fact, the postwar period has seen a change in the Japanese writing system that involves a reduction in the number of officially permitted characters to a little under two thousand and a reform in the People's Republic of China that involves simplification of complex characters, as in the case of the character for *ràng* ("to cause"), which was simplified from a twenty-four stroke form to a five-stroke form as follows:

讓　让

In North Korea the Chinese characters have been abandoned in favor of an orthography based on hangul. The changes instituted in China and Japan represent a setback for movements in both countries toward eventual replacement of Chinese characters by a system based on the Latin alphabet, a reform which has been instituted only in Viet Nam (DeFrancis 1947, 1967a, 1977).

Chapter 2

1. The figure of 1,277 tonal syllables is from Chao (1976:107), that of 398 "segmental syllables" is from EC (1971:8–9), and that of 418 such syllables is from Zhou Youguang (1979:336). These figures apply to Standard Chinese. Other forms of Chinese are phonologically more complex. Southern Min spoken in Fujian and Taiwan, for example, has 773 syllables not counting tones (Cheng and Cheng 1977). Cantonese has 664 not counting tones, 1,813 with tones (Zhang Liyan 1983:28).

2. Chinese aversion to phonetic loans was noted by Mao Zedong in a conversation with Nikita Khrushchev that the latter reports (1970:474) as follows:

There is, however, one thing I know for sure about Mao. He's a nationalist . . . [H]e started to discourse on the distinctiveness of China. As an example he mentioned that there are no foreign words in the Chinese language. "All the rest of the world uses the word 'electricity,' " he boasted. "They've borrowed the word from English. But we Chinese have our own word for it." His chauvanism and arrogance sent a shiver up my spine.

3. Including my own, on which much of the present sketch of spoken Chinese is based. My basic textbook, *Beginning Chinese* (DeFrancis 1976), is the first of a dozen volumes, all published by Yale, for teaching spoken and written Chinese.

Chapter 3

1. According to Xu Shirong (1983:personal communication), these figures are based on Prof. Zhan Bohai's article of 14 February 1979 in *Guangming Ribao* and on his book *Xiandai Hanyu Fangyan* [Modern Chinese regionalects] (1981).

Chapter 5

1. For different interpretations of this character see Creel (1938:277–278) and Boodberg (1937:344–345; 1940:270–274).

2. There are still many undeciphered Shang characters. The total number of

deciphered and undeciphered characters has been estimated at 4,500 (Yu 1981:44). Cheng Te-k'un assigns another 129 characters to the category that we have called the phonetic loan principle, making a total of 1,106 deciphered characters. These 129 characters represent 12 percent of the total number of deciphered characters, indicating that the phonetic loan principle was fairly important at the early stage of Chinese writing. It became quite negligible later as the semantic-phonetic principle took over, amounting to only about 1 percent in the Xu Shen dictionary (Cheng 1980:35). On the basis of their original meaning and function, the phonetic loan characters should, properly speaking, be assigned to one of the four principles dealing with the composition of characters.

3. The term "morphosyllabic" has also been used by M. A. French (1976:126) in his thoughtful study of the Chinese writing system that was kindly brought to my attention by Paul Kratochvíl. However, his single mention of the term does not appear to carry the precise application indicated in my discussion here and in the following pages.

Chapter 6

1. YJ (1978); Li Min (1979); Hu Tan (1983:personal communication). In explanation of the fact that although Yi has four tones there are only three symbols per tone (see Figure 6), Prof. Hu Tan notes that the first-line characters represent the first tone, the third-line characters represent the fourth tone, and the second-line characters represent two tones, the third if unmarked and the second if marked with the symbol ^ on or above the character. He adds that there is also a transcription system for Yi (see Figure 6) which makes use of tone letters (-*t* for the first tone, -*x* for the second, zero or no mark for the third, and -*p* for the fourth), that in this system the letter combinations *ie* and *uo* are not diphthongs, and that final *r* represents the feature of stricture.

2. At this point in his reading of the manuscript, Prof. Hsieh Hsin-i penciled in the margin the following delightful comment: "You ask a very interesting question from a Western point of view; from a Chinese point of view the answer is quite simple: A scribe who can memorize all the characters becomes a master scribe, and once he becomes established, he can invent or eliminate characters. Like everything in good old China, nothing is done in the Westerner's methodical way."

3. *Changyong gouci zidian* [Dictionary of common word-formation] (Beijing, 1982), edited by Fu Xingling and Chen Zhanghuan, uses 186 radicals. *A Chinese-English Dictionary* (Beijing, 1981), compiled by the Beijing Foreign Languages Institute, uses 226 radicals and places 11 miscellaneous characters in an "extra category" numbered 227. *The Sino Chinese-English Dictionary,* an abbreviated version of the preceding work published in Hong Kong, omits its radical 207 and renumbers 208–226 as 207–225 with 226 as the "extra category." Two articles published in *Wenzi Gaige* 8 (1983) on the need to unify the radical classification mention that the revised edition of the well-known dictionary *Cihai* uses 250 radicals and that two other dictionaries, *Xinhua Zidian* and *Xiandai Hanyu Cidian,* use 189. (The 1962 edition of *Xinhua Zidian* used 191.) According to a report in the same issue, the Committee on Chinese Language Reform (which was not responsible for this chaotic mess since it has never been given sufficient authority or resources to make and carry out the kind of coherent language reform of which the leading scholars of the Committee are

capable), convened a conference in June 1983, to consider the problem of classifying characters by radicals.

4. Soothill (1942) has the numeration 1–888, but he skipped over six numbers and added thirteen unnumbered characters (Fenn 1960:xiv). I have retained Soothill's original numeration to facilitate reference to his work. The radical numbers for his characters refer, of course, to the 214 radicals of the Kang Xi system, not to any scheme used in the PRC since the simplification of characters.

5. I do not understand the dropping off in percentage after the 2,001–2,100 high. I would have thought that the rarer the character, the more likely it is to be a phonetic compound and to have escaped the attrition of higher-frequency characters, thereby preserving a useful phonetic. Further study is needed of low-frequency characters, including those not in Chen's list.

6. These figures include ten characters (two in the 2,001–2,100 group, one in the 3,001–3,100 group, and seven in the 4,001–4,100 group) which do not actually include one of Soothill's 895 phonetics but are composed, apart from the radical, of one other element which is obviously being used as a phonetic, as in the case of *xià* "descend" used as the phonetic in *xià* "frighten":

> 下 *xià* "descend"
> 吓 *xià* "frighten"

7. These three sets of figures are provided so that those who may not agree with my criteria for usefulness can determine where to draw their own line.

8. Of this 47 percent, the fifty-two independent phonetics account for 23.6 percent and the forty-eight phonetic compounds for 23.4 percent.

9. Estimated from the number of independent phonetics in the five samples of one hundred characters (that is 52–22–7–7–3).

10. Based on Karlgren's estimate.

11. Lu Xun (1963:1–2). This edition of Lu Xun's work is in simplified characters, which I have converted back into the complex forms for present purposes.

12. I originally put this expression in quotation marks, but then it occurred to me that there is no reason why the concept of spelling should be monopolized by alphabetic scripts. In this connection, note Boodberg's extended use of the term "phoneme" (1937:331): "When referring to Chinese, the term *phoneme* is used by the writer to designate a *syllabic phoneme.*"

Chapter 7

1. The passage cited, together with a fairly literal translation, is:

今天晚上,很好的月光.我不見他,已是三十多年.

"Today, evening, very nice moonlight. I have not seen it already for over thirty years."

2. The following examples illustrate the four subcategories of semantic relationship between radical and compound or composite character: (1) There is identity in meaning between the radical 頁 *yè* "head" and the compound character 頭 *tóu* "head." (2) There is a clear but imprecise or unspecific relationship between the broad semantic area of the radical 艹 *cǎo* "vegetation" and the specific meaning of

the composite character 芹 *qín* "celery." (3) There is a less clear and even less precise relationship between the meaning of the radical 玉 *yù* "jade" and the meaning of the compound character 玻 *bō* "glass." (4) There is a relationship so obscure as to be for the average reader effectively nonexistent between the meaning of the same radical and the meaning of the composite character 理 *lǐ* "principal; manage." As these examples show, the four subcategories of semantic relationship, although roughly parallel to the four subcategories of phonetic relationship, are not really equivalent to them since, in general, semantics lacks the precision of phonology. These matters are discussed in detail in my article entitled "Phonetic versus Semantic Predictability in Chinese Characters" to be published in the *Journal of the Chinese Language Teachers Association*. In a thoughtful reaction to reading the manuscript of this article, Yin Binyong of the Committee on Chinese Language Reform estimates that radicals are less than half as useful as phonetic elements in predicting the meaning of Chinese characters (1984:personal communication).

Chapter 8

1. L. J. Gallagher, in his translation into English of Nicola Trigault's Latin version of Matteo Ricci's original Italian work, uses the terms "ideographs" and "ideographic" (1942:42–48; 1953:26–30). These renderings are anachronistic and without foundation. The terms actually used by Trigault (1615:25–29) are various declined variations of the Latin words *littera* and *character* to translate Ricci's Italian *lettera* and *carattere* (1942:36–40). See also Chapter 11, note 1.

2. Pronounced like the English word "lug." The sound has evolved into modern Chinese *lái*.

Chapter 10

1. For a trenchant deflating of the Imagist approach to Chinese characters see Kennedy (1964:443–462).

2. As reported in subsequent publications (for example, Gleitman and Rozin 1973, 1977), Rozin has joined with Gleitman in carrying out research along somewhat similar lines as that by Woodcock and his associates. He and Gleitman have also modified the earlier exclusive emphasis on Chinese orthography as a system that maps directly onto meaning by noting, albeit in a muddled fashion, that the writing system contains "phonetic complements" that give a clue to the pronunciation of characters. Finally, they also correct the misleading impression suggested by the title of the earlier article by stressing the phonetic aspect in the process of reading English. To date, however, the misconceptions fostered by the more widely publicized initial article have not been appreciably affected by the subsequent publications with their added batch of inaccuracies about Chinese.

Chapter 11

1. In DeFrancis (1950:15–16 n. 5), following Gallagher (1942:43–47), I attributed this and several other remarks to Nicola Trigault (1615). Gallagher (1953:26–30), based on his reading of Ricci (1942), corrects the attribution to Matteo Ricci. Gallagher's works should be used with caution since it turns out that they are a liberal English version of Trigault's liberal Latin version of Ricci's original Italian manuscript, now available in Ricci (1942). See also Chapter 8, note 1.

2. The figures are a composite of two samples of one hundred characters each that produced similar results. Characters classified in the dictionary as both F and B have been counted half in each category. Characters in the L category perhaps should not be counted at all but have been included with the F category.

3. This meaning is attached to the character, whose basic meaning is "black jade" and whose pronunciation is *jiǔ*, because of the identity in sound. The more complex character is used in place of the simpler one on bank notes, checks, and so on to avoid fraud.

Chapter 13

1. This rejection applies only to the literacy data, not necessarily to the population figures, the evaluation of which must be left to demographers. Merely counting heads is difficult enough in itself. Determining what is in those heads, which is what determining literacy involves, is an infinitely more difficult task, the handling of which often leaves something to be desired even in countries with the professional resources to cope with the myriad technical details of the task.

2. As this book went to press, information belatedly became available about the most recent adaptation of the method just described. Experiments carried out in several schools in Heilongjiang Province in 1982–1983 are reported at some length in various articles and comments in *Quan-Guo Yuan-Xiao Wenzi Gaige Xuehui Tong-xun* 3 (1983) and *Wenzi Gaige* 10, 12 (1983). The work has been promoted there under the slogan *Zhùyīn shízì, tíqián dúxiě,* "Achieve literacy through representing sounds, move up reading and writing." Several writers refer to the great success of the program, success so astounding as to be "hard to believe." Zhou Youguang adds a note of caution by calling for rigorous scientific tests to determine the precise factor or factors that account for what was accomplished. Amen.

Chapter 14

1. The present discussion is based largely on DeFrancis (1950, 1967a, 1979), in which extensive references to Chinese and Western-language materials will be found. In the present discussion sources are cited only for new bits of information and in certain special cases.

Chapter 15

1. This discussion is based largely on DeFrancis (1950, 1967a, 1979).

2. Delegations were in fact sent to North Korea and Viet Nam. They reported very favorably on advances in literacy in both countries, which they attributed to the use of simple alphabetic scripts, and recommended that China adopt a similar approach to its literacy problem (Waiguo 1957; Zhou Youguang 1982:personal communication). Of the three countries mentioned by Liu Shaoqi, only these two have made use of Chinese characters in their writing systems. The phrasing in his letter appears to suggest that this was also true of Mongolia, but its writing system is not based on Chinese characters.

3. The earlier version, which was presented in DeFrancis (1979), has only "Comrade XXX" where the present version identifies him as "Comrade Wu Yuzhang." The earlier version contains the statements, missing here, that "literacy will be very

easy" if Chinese is written in a roman script and that "we should take everything good from abroad and transform them into our things in order to catch up with the international level in one or two decades." There are other discrepancies of lesser importance.

It may be useful to note that besides publishing in 1981 this edited version of Mao's remarks made in 1956—the delay doubtless being the result of internal debate regarding if and when to release information—Ye Laishi has also just presented (1983:7) a summary of the policy recommendations made to Mao by Guo Moruo, Mao Dun, and Ma Xulun on 29 August 1949 that appears to be at variance with the brief, earlier version presented by an anonymous author that was quoted on pp. 255-256. The earlier version seems to point to a primary emphasis on promoting an independent Pinyin orthography, whereas Ye's summary of the recommendations is more in line with Mao's new guidelines of June 1950 that were transmitted by Wu Yuzhang in the following month.

The practice of editing if not actually doctoring materials relating to leading figures, rather than quoting them verbatim, of course complicates the task of assessing their precise significance, a task that necessarily involves close attention to nuances of phraseology.

A further note on this subject is called for by the last-minute arrival, as this book neared the end of the final page-proofs stage, of the first issue for 1984 of *Wenzi Gaige,̄* the official organ of the Committee on Chinese Language Reform. This issue prominently displays the facsimile of a letter (see frontispiece) written by Mao Zedong in 1955 to Jiang Zhuru, an old schoolmate from normal school days, expressing support of Pinyin Wenzi, that is, a "Pinyin writing" or "Pinyin orthography" independent of characters, as a basic reform which must be eventually carried out. The facsimile was reproduced in the journal from *Mao Zedong Shuxin Xuanji* [Selected correspondence of Mao Zedong], compiled by the Documentary Research Office of the Chinese Communist Party Central Committee and published in December 1983 by the People's Publishing House. The letter reads as follows:

Dear Zhuru:

I have received and read your esteemed letter of last February. Many thanks! Your study of spoken and written language presents distinct views, and although I cannot agree with them, nevertheless debate is bound to be useful. I have already passed on your letter to the Committee on Chinese Language Reform for study. Pinyin writing is a form of writing that is relatively convenient. Chinese characters are too complicated and difficult. At present we are only engaged in reform along the lines of simplification, but some day in the future we must inevitably carry out a basic reform.

Together with this reply I send best regards.

Mao Zedong
May 1, 1955

4. In commenting on this passage and on my puzzled reference (1967:149) to draft phoneticization plans drawn up in 1960 for four Guangdong varieties of Chinese (Cantonese, Hakka, Chaozhou, Hainan), Zhou Youguang (1983:personal communication) notes that the schemes were drawn up by a group of linguists in

Guangdong and were officially adopted by the Guangdong Provincial Government. The schemes were based on Pinyin, created no new letters, and made use of tone marks. They were published in Peking by the Committee on Chinese Language Reform in a booklet entitled *Wenzi Gaige Shouce* [Language reform handbook]. Intended for limited purposes, the schemes were actually not used at all.

5. Deng's remarks were quoted again in the 20 July 1977 morning edition of *Asahi Shimbun*. Miller (1982:186) cites this later source for an extension of Deng's remarks that includes a direct quotation stating that "we in China . . . are on our way to getting rid of" the Chinese writing system. The extended remarks do not appear in the morning edition of 20 July that is available in the University of Hawaii library. Mr. Saionji Kinkazu, when contacted by phone on 22 February 1983, said he had not heard Deng make the remark attributed to him about getting rid of Chinese characters.

6. An international "Conference on Lu Xun and His Legacy" held in the United States in August 1981 also made no mention of this subject.

7. I raised the issue of Lu Xun's views in my paper "Some Contradictions in Chinese Language Reform—An American Perspective," which was delivered at the 15th International Conference on Sino-Tibetan Languages and Linguistics in Peking in August 1982. Several Chinese scholars went out of their way to tell me that they personally agreed with Lu Xun's approach. I was asked to present the identical paper at a meeting held at the headquarters of the Committee on Chinese Language Reform. The paper was subsequently published in the committee's official journal (DeFrancis 1982). It is also worthy of note that Prof. Huang Diancheng of Amoy University submitted a paper to the Conference on Linguistic Modernization and Language Planning in Chinese-Speaking Communities held in Hawaii 7–13 September 1983 in which he expressed the view that the Southern Min variety of Chinese should be provided with a writing system based on the Latin alphabet.

8. The errors made by the young diarist are the following: *zhēng què* should be *zhēngqǔ; yì bǎn* should be *yībǎi; zhǒng* should be *zōng; huéi dào* should be *huí dào;* and *líng* should be *lí*. It is worth remarking that there are no errors in the tones, but only in the segmental phonemes, and that the errors are not serious enough to impair intelligibility (DeFrancis 1967a:146–147).

Glossary

The following nontechnical explanations are given for some of the main terms used in this book that may be unfamiliar to some readers.

Agglutinative. Adjective used to describe languages, such as Japanese, Korean, and Turkish in the Altaic family of languages, which are characterized by the piling up of suffixes on base words. Example: Japanese *ikitakunai* ("not like to go") consists of a base *iki* ("go"), the verb suffix *taku* ("like to"), and the negative suffix *nai* ("not").

Alphabet, alphabetic. Terms referring to writing systems in which letters such as those used in English, or symbols equivalent to such letters, are used to represent the basic sounds of a language. The terms stand in contrast to "ideographic" and "syllabic."

Aspirated. Marked by release of a puff of air; usually applied to consonants. Example: English *p* is aspirated in *pie,* unaspirated in *spy.*

Bound form. Two kinds of syllables, semibound and completely bound. A syllable is semibound if it has meaning but must be joined with another syllable. Example: English *er* in *teacher,* Chinese *yuán* in *jiàoyuán* ("teacher"). A syllable is completely bound if it has no meaning and must combine with another syllable. Example: English *cor* in *coral,* Chinese *shān* in *shānhú* ("coral").

Dialects. Mutually intelligible varieties of a single language.

Furigana. Phonetic kana signs placed alongside kanji (characters of Chinese origin used in Japan) to give their pronunciation. Example: 國⸮ The two small symbols on the right spell the two syllables *koku.*

Grapheme. A basic unit of writing analagous to the phoneme or syllable in speech. Example: The English letters *p, a,* and *t* in *pat,* the Chinese character 丁 representing the syllable *dīng.*

Guoyeu Romatzyh ("National Language Romanization"). Alphabetic scheme created in the 1920s and distinguished by "tonal spelling."

Guoyu ("National Language"). One of the terms used, especially before 1949, to designate Standard Chinese based approximately on the Peking dialect. It is still used in Taiwan.

Hangul. Korean alphabet created in the fifteenth century. Example: ㄱ (k), ㅁ (m).

Hiragana. Cursive form of kana; roughly equivalent to English running hand.

Ideograph, ideographic. Terms referring to writing systems in which the graphic symbols are defined as representing a thing or idea and not a particular word or phrase. The terms are also used by those who do not necessarily accept the foregoing definition but continue to use the terms in relation to Chinese characters merely because they are in general use.

Idiolect. The distinctive speech of a single member of a speech community.

Isogloss. A boundary line between places or regions that differ in a linguistic feature.

Isolating. Adjective used to describe languages such as Chinese, Vietnamese, and Tibetan in which every unit of meaning, usually called a word, has an immutable form unchanged by affixes, inflections, and the like as in English "pats" versus "pat" or "come" versus "came."

Juncture. The link between successive spoken syllables. Example: English *nitrate* versus *night rate,* Chinese *piao* versus *pi'ao.* (The apostrophe is a juncture mark in Chinese.)

Kana. Japanese syllabic signs based originally on Chinese characters. There are two varieties, hiragana and katakana. (See Figure 7.)

Kanji. Japanese term meaning "Chinese characters."

Katakana. Angular form of kana; roughly equivalent to English block letters.

Latinxua ("Latinization"). Alphabetic scheme for Chinese based on Latin letters; created by Chinese and Russian scholars in the Soviet Union in the early thirties.

Logograph, logographic. Terms (from Greek *logos:* "word") referring to a system of graphic symbols that represent words.

Morpheme, morphemic. Terms referring to the smallest meaningful units of speech. Example: English "teachers" consists of the three morphemes *teach, er,* and *s.* Chinese *jiàoyuán* consists of the two morphemes *jiào* ("teach") and *yuán* ("one who does something").

Morphophonemic. Term referring to the way in which the morphemes of a language are represented by its phonemes. Morphophonemic notation stands in contrast to phonemic notation, as in the case of final *s* in "pots" and "pods." Here the spelling is morphophonemic since the plural morpheme is represented by the same symbol *s* instead of being differentiated according to the actual pronunciation by rendering the words phonemically as "pots" and "podz."

Orthography. A conventional writing system used by a specific language community.

Phoneme, phonemic. Terms used in reference to the smallest features of speech by which one thing is differentiated from another. Example: English "pit" and "bit," "pat" and "pad," "pit" and "pat," Chinese *bā* and *pā.*

Phonetic. Term dealing with sounds that is used in two different senses. On the one hand, it is used in contrastive situations such as "phonetic writing" versus "ideographic writing," the former referring to a system that represents sounds, the latter to a system that supposedly represents ideas. On the other hand it is used in the contrast of "phonetic" versus "phonemic." The former refers to notations that use [p'] and [p], for example, to differentiate between aspirated *p* in "pot" and unaspirated *p* in "spot." The latter refers to notations such as the spelling of "pot" and "spot," which lumps the two different phonetic realizations of *p* together since the distinction does not make for a difference in meaning in English (though it does in Chinese).

Phonetic Alphabet. An alphabet created in 1913; in appearance it is like simple Chinese characters. Example: ㄈ (f), ㄢ (an).

Pinyin (literally "spell sounds"). General term for alphabetic spelling; also specific name given to the alphabet based on Latin letters that was adopted in 1958 by the PRC.

Putonghua ("Common Speech"). Term officially adopted in the PRC to replace Guoyu ("National Language"); loosely based on the Peking dialect.

Quoc Ngu. Vietnamese orthography based on Latin letters. (See Figure 9.)

Regionalect. Mutually unintelligible forms of *fāngyán* ("regional speech") such as Cantonese, Hakka, and Putonghua.

Segmental phonemes. Vowel and consonant (but not tone) phonemes in Chinese.

Syllabic, syllabary. Terms used in connection with systems of writing in which graphic symbols represent not individual phonemes but whole syllables.

Tempo. The speed of utterances.

Tone. The pitch of utterances. In English, differences in pitch express differences in attitude. Example: "Yes!" (emphatic agreement), "Yes?" (inquiry). In Chinese, differences in pitch reflect differences in meaning of words. Example: *mǎ* with pitch similar to "Yes?" means "hemp," *mà* with pitch similar to "Yes!" means "revile."

Voiced. Characterized by vibrating vocal chords, as in producing all vowels and some consonants. Example: voiced *b* in *"bat"* contrasts with unvoiced or voiceless *p* in *"pat."*

Zhuyin Zimu. See Phonetic Alphabet.

Suggested Reading

The following list is offered for nonspecialists who would like to go further into some of the matters taken up in this book. Full names and bibliographic details are provided in the References.

Baratz and Shuy. 1969. *Teaching Black Children to Read.* Apart from dealing with the narrowly linguistic aspects of Black English, this collection of articles also takes up broad sociolinguistic aspects of the teaching of reading that are relevant to other situations.

Bolinger. 1946. "Visual Morphemes." A useful reminder that while writing is related to speech there are meaningful elements in writing that have independent existence.

DeFrancis. 1950. *Nationalism and Language Reform in China.* An extensive study of the linguistic, social, and political aspects of the pre-1949 controversy over the problem of characters versus an alphabetic system of writing.

————. 1977. *Colonialism and Language Policy in Viet Nam.* Historical survey of language and writing in Viet Nam with emphasis on sociolinguistic and sociopolitical aspects as the decisive elements.

DuPonceau. 1838. *A Dissertation on the Nature and Character of the Chinese System of Writing.* A book filled with common-sense observations about Chinese writing that is composed in a charming, old-fashioned style. Because the author slipped up on several points, this work should be read in conjunction with Chao (1940).

Fishman. 1969. *Bilingual Education: An International Sociological Perspective.* The case for bilingual education presented from a broad perspective and with much feeling. Useful especially as a theoretical framework from which to view related problems in China.

Garvin. 1954. "Literacy as a Problem in Language and Culture." A good case study, on a small scale, of the cultural restraints on creating a linguistically ideal orthography.

Gelb. 1963. *A Study of Writing.* The best general work dealing with systems of writing and their classification.

Goodman. 1976. "Reading: A Psycholinguistic Guessing Game." Emphasizes reading as a multifaceted task in which redundancy and guesswork are major elements.

Kavanagh and Mattingly. 1972. *Language by Ear and by Eye: The Relationships Between Speech and Reading.* Collection of articles, many of them quite technical, that range broadly over many aspects of the subject.

Kennedy. 1964. "The Monosyllabic Myth." A witty and highly readable presentation of the case against calling Chinese monosyllabic.

———. 1964. "The Butterfly Case." An expanded and somewhat more technical, but still quite readable, presentation of the case against the monosyllabic idea.

Kōno. 1969. "The Chinese Writing and Its Influences on the Scripts of the Neighboring Peoples . . ." Rather technical, but valuable for its discussion of the Chinese influence on the scripts of other peoples besides the Koreans, Japanese, and Vietnamese.

Kratochvíl. 1968. *The Chinese Language Today.* An excellent general description, though somewhat technical, of Chinese language and writing.

Liu. 1969. *Chinese Characters and Their Impact on Other Languages of East Asia.* A book filled with much miscellaneous interesting information about Chinese characters used in several countries.

Martin. 1972. "Nonalphabetic Writing Systems: Some Observations." Stimulating, succinct account of Chinese characters from a broad Asian perspective.

Newnham. 1971. *About Chinese.* As simple and nontechnical an introduction to the Chinese language and its writing system as one can get without undue sacrifice of accuracy.

Palmer. 1931. *The Principles of Romanization.* An important work which should be read by anyone interested in writing systems based on Chinese characters and the linguistic problems attending their reform, particularly the problem of homonyms. The chief emphasis is on Japanese, but the principles are universally valid.

Voegelin and Voegelin. 1964. *Languages of the World: Sino-Tibetan.* Stimulating discussion of Chinese language and writing.

References

ABC. 1981–1982. (This is a series of six little Pinyin booklets published in Peking by the Committee on Chinese Language Reform as supplements to its journal *Pinyin Bao.*)

Allen, P. David and Dorothy J. Watson, eds. 1976. *Findings of Research in Miscue Analysis: Classroom Implications.* Urbana, Ill.

Alloco, Vincent Anello. 1972. "Phonetic Orthographic Method of Organizing Chinese Characters Used in the Republic of Korea: New Alternative to Rote Memorization." Ph.D. dissertation, United States International University.

Anonymous. 1822. "Review of Lettre à M. Dacier . . . , by Champollion." *Quarterly Review* 28:188–196.

———. 1979. "Guo Moruo Tongzhi rexin wenzi gaige er san shi" [Some enthusiasms of Comrade Guo Moruo concerning writing reform]. *Hanyu Pinyin Xiaobao* 191:2.

Arlotto, Anthony T. 1968. "On Defining 'Monosyllabism.'" *Journal of the American Oriental Society* 88:521–522.

Association. 1981. "Quanguo gaodeng yuan-xiao wenzi gaige xuehui chengli xuanyan" [Declaration at the establishment of the Language Reform Association of Chinese Institutions of Higher Learning]. *Yuwen Xiandaihua* 5:284–287.

Aylmer, Charles. 1981. *Origins of the Chinese Script.* Cambridge.

Aymonier, Etienne. 1890. *La langue française et l'enseignement en Indochine.* Paris.

Baratz, Joan and Roger W. Shuy. 1969. *Teaching Black Children to Read.* Washington, D.C.

Barnard, Noel. 1978. "The Nature of the Ch'in 'Reform of the Script' as Reflected in Archaeological Documents Excavated under Conditions of Control." In David T. Roy and Tsuen-hsuin Tsien, eds., *Ancient China: Studies in Early Civilization.* Hong Kong.

Barnes, Dayle. 1973. "Language Planning in Mainland China: Standardization." In Joan Rubin and R. Shuy, eds., *Language Planning: Current Issues and Research.* Washington, D.C. Reprinted in Joshua A. Fishman, ed., *Advances in Language Planning,* The Hague, 1974.

———. 1977. "To er or not to er." *Journal of Chinese Linguistics* 5 (2): 211–236.

Barrett, David Dean. 1934. *A Primer in the Writing of Chinese.* Shanghai.

Bartolli, Daniello. 1663. *Dell'historia della compagnia di Giesu. La Cina. Terza parte dell'Asia.* Rome.

Belde, Klaus. 1980. "Saomang: Kommunistische Alphabetisierungsarbeit im ländichen China vom Jiangxi-Sowjet bis zum Ende des Grossen Sprungs nach vorn." Ph.D. dissertation, University of Bonn.

Bernard, Henri. 1933. *Aux portes de la Chine: Les missionaires du seizième siècle, 1514-1588.* Tientsin.

Bissex, Glenda L. 1980. *GNYS AT WRK: A Child Learns to Write and Read.* Cambridge, Mass.

Bloomfield, Leonard. 1933. *Language.* New York.

Bodman, Nicolas Cleaveland. 1967. "Historical Linguistics." In Thomas A. Sebeok, ed., *Current Trends in Linguistics,* vol. 2, pp. 3–58. The Hague.

Bolinger, Dwight L. 1946. "Visual Morphemes." *Language* 22:333–350.

Boodberg, Peter A. 1937. "Some Proleptical Remarks on the Evolution of Archaic Chinese." *Harvard Journal of Asiatic Studies* 2:329–372.

———. 1940. " 'Ideography' or Iconolatry?" *T'oung Pao* 35:266–288.

———. 1957. "The Chinese Script: An Essay on Nomenclature (the First Hecaton)." *Bulletin of the Institute of History and Philology, Academia Sinica* 39:113–120.

Boxer, C. R. 1953. *South China in the Sixteenth Century.* London.

Brunner, Hellmut. 1974. "Hieroglyphic Writing." *Encyclopedia Brittanica* 8:853–857.

Budge, E. A. Wallis. 1967. *The Book of the Dead.* New York.

Bunakov, I. V. 1940. "Kitaiskaya pis'mennost' " [The Chinese written language]. In B. M. Alexeiev, L. I. Duman, and A. A. Petrov, eds., *Kitai* [China]. Moscow–Leningrad.

Callery, J. M. 1841. *Systema phoneticum scripturae sinicae.* 2 vols. Macao.

Carroll, John B. 1972. "The Case for Ideographic Writing." In James F. Kavanagh and Ignatius G. Mattingly, eds., *Language by Ear and by Eye: The Relationships Between Speech and Reading.* Cambridge, Mass.

CETA. 1980. *Computers, Language Reform, and Lexicography in China: A Report by the CETA (Chinese-English Translation Assistance) Delegation.* Jim Mathias and Thomas L. Kennedy, eds. Pullman, Wash.

Chadwick, John. 1967. *The Decipherment of Linear B.* London.

Chailley, Joseph. 1887. *Paul Bert au Tonkin.* Paris.

Champollion, Jean François. 1822. *Lettre à M. Dacier relative à l'alphabet des hiéroglyphes phonétiques.* Paris. Reprinted Aalen, 1962.

Chang, Su-chen. 1979. "Reduction in Number of Chinese Characters." *Journal of the Chinese Language Teachers Association* 11:187–191.

Chao, Chih-ch'ao, Chao Tze-yi, and Frank F. K. Chang. 1967. "How Many Words Do Chinese Know?" *Journal of the Chinese Language Teachers Association* 2 (2): 44–58.

Chao, Yuen Ren. 1940. "A Note on an Early Logographic Theory of Chinese Writing." *Harvard Journal of Asiatic Studies* 5:189–191.

———. 1948. *Mandarin Primer.* Cambridge, Mass.

———. 1968a. *A Grammar of Spoken Chinese.* Berkeley and Los Angeles.

———. 1968b. *Language and Symbolic Systems.* Cambridge.

———. 1976. *Aspects of Chinese Sociolinguistics.* Stanford.

Chao, Yuen Ren and Yang Lien Sheng. 1962. *Concise Dictionary of Spoken Chinese.* Cambridge, Mass.

Chen, Heqin. 1928. *Yutiwen yingyong zihui* [Characters used in vernacular literature]. Shanghai.

Chen, Liyi and Chen Zhenqun, eds., 1981. *Jimei Aoyuan tike tanben* [Rubbings of inscriptions in Ao Garden in Jimei]. Fuzhou.

Chen, Mengjia. 1956. *Yinxu buci zongshu* [Comprehensive survey of divination texts from the wastes of Yin]. Peking.

Chen, Minguan. 1982. "Jisuanji chuli Hanzi de liangzhong yunsuan he xingshi wenfa" [Two operations and formal grammar of Chinese character processing by computer]. *Yuyan Yanjiu* 1:52–59.

Cheng, Chin-chuan. 1979. "Language Reform in China in the Seventies." *Word* 30 (1–2): 45–57.

Cheng, Robert L. 1978. "Taiwanese Morphemes in Search of Chinese Characters." *Journal of Chinese Linguistics* 6 (2): 306–313.

———. 1981. "Borrowing and Internal Development—Comparison of Taiwanese Words and Their Mandarin Equivalents." Paper presented at the 14th International Conference on Sino-Tibetan Languages and Linguistics, Gainesville, Florida.

Cheng, Robert and Susie Cheng. 1977. *Taiwan Fujianhua de Yuyin Jiegou ji Biaoyin Fa* [Phonological structure and romanization of Taiwanese Hokkien]. Taipei.

Cheng, Te-k'un. 1980. *The World of the Chinese—A Struggle for Human Unity.* Hong Kong.

Cheung, Kwong-yue. 1983. "Recent Archaeological Evidence Relating to the Origin of Chinese Characters." In David N. Keightley, ed., *The Origins of Chinese Civilization.* Berkeley.

Chiera, Edward. 1938. *They Wrote on Clay.* Chicago.

Chmielewski, Janusz. 1958. "The Problem of Early Loan-Words in Chinese as Illustrated by the Word 'p'u-t'ao.' " *Rocsnik Orientalistczny* 22 (2): 7–45.

Civil, Miguel. 1973. "The Sumerian Writing System: Some Problems." *Orientalia* 42:21–34.

Cohen, Jonathan. 1954. "On the Project of a Universal Character." *Mind* 63:49–63.

Cohen, Marcel. 1958. *La grande invention de l'écriture et son évolution.* Paris.

Conrad, R. 1972. "Speech and Reading." In James F. Kavanagh and Ignatius G. Mattingly, eds., *Language by Ear and by Eye: The Relationships Between Speech and Reading.* Cambridge, Mass.

Cook, Albert. 1980. Myth and Language. Bloomington.

Creel, Herrlee Glessner. 1936. "On the Nature of Chinese Ideography." *T'oung Pao* 32:85–161.

———. 1937. *The Birth of China.* New York.

———. 1938. "On the Ideographic Element in Ancient Chinese." *T'oung Pao* 34:265–294.

———. 1938–1952. *Literary Chinese by the Inductive Method.* 3 vols. Chicago.

DeFrancis, John. 1947. "Japanese Language Reform: Politics and Phonetics." *Far Eastern Survey* 16 (19): 217–220.

———. 1950. *Nationalism and Language Reform in China.* Princeton. Reprinted New York, 1972.

———. 1951. "National and Minority Policies." *Annals of the American Academy of Political and Social Science* 277:146–155.

——. 1967a. "Language and Script Reform." In Thomas A. Sebeok, ed., *Current Trends in Linguistics,* vol. 2. The Hague. Reprinted in Joshua A. Fishman, ed., *Advances in the Creation and Revision of Writing Systems.* The Hague, 1977.

——. 1967b. "Syntactic Permutability in Chinese." In William A. Austin, ed., *Papers in Linguistics in Honor of Leon Dostert.* The Hague.

——. 1976. *Beginning Chinese.* Second rev. ed. New Haven.

——. 1977. *Colonialism and Language Policy in Viet Nam.* The Hague.

——. 1979. "Mao Tse-tung and Writing Reform." In Joshua A. Fogel and William T. Rowe, eds., *Essays in Honor of Professor C. Martin Wilbur on the Occasion of His Retirement.* Denver.

——. 1982. "Zhongguo wenzi gaige zhong de yixie maodun—yige Meiguorende kanfa" [Some contradicitons in Chinese language reform—an American perspective]. *Wenzi Gaige* 3:7–9, 14.

——. 1984. "Digraphia." *Word* 35(1):59–66.

Destenay, Patrick. 1981. *Chinese Radio Broadcasts: A Course in Aural Comprehension Based on News Bulletins.* Aix-en-Provence.

Devoto, Giacomo. 1978. *The Languages of Italy.* Translated by B. Louise Katainen. Chicago.

Driver, Godfrey Rolles. 1976. *Semitic Writing: From Pictographs to Alphabet.* Oxford.

DuPonceau, Peter S. 1838. *A Dissertation on the Nature and Character of the Chinese System of Writing.* Philadelphia.

EC. 1971. *Elementary Chinese.* Peking.

Edgerton, William F. 1940. "Egyptian Phonetic Writing, from Its Invention to the Close of the Nineteenth Dynasty." *Journal of the American Oriental Society* 60:473–506.

——. 1941. "Ideograms in English Writing." *Language* 17:148–150.

Egerod, Søren. 1967. "Dialectology." In Thomas A. Sebeok, ed., *Current Trends in Linguistics,* vol. 2. The Hague.

Elman, Benjamin. 1982. "From Value to Fact: The Emergence of Phonology as a Precise Discipline in Late Imperial China." *Journal of the American Oriental Society* 102 (3): 493–500.

Etiemble. 1960. "L'écriture." In *Le régime et les institutions de la République Populaire Chinoise: Journées d'études 12–16 Octobre 1959.* Brussels.

Fenn, Courtenay H. 1960. *The Five Thousand Dictionary.* Eighth printing. Cambridge, Mass.

Ferguson, Charles. 1959. "Diglossia." *Word* 15:325–340.

Fishman, Joshua A. 1969. *Bilingual Education: An International Sociological Perspective.* Rowley, Mass.

Forrest, R.A.D. 1948. *The Chinese Language.* London.

Fraser, Stewart. 1965. *Chinese Communist Education: Records of the First Decade.* Nashville, Tenn.

French, M. A. 1976. "Observations on the Chinese Script and the Classification of Writing-Systems." In W. Haas, ed., *Writing Without Letters.* Manchester.

Gabelentz, Georg von der. 1881. *Chinesische Grammatik.* Leipzig.

Gallagher, Louis J. 1942. *The China That Was: China as Discovered by the Jesuits at the Close of the Sixteenth Century.* Milwaukee. (This is a translation of Book I of Trigault 1615.)

———. 1953. *China in the Sixteenth Century: The Journals of Matthew Ricci.* New York. (This is a translation of Books I–V of Trigault 1615.)

Garvin, Paul. 1954. "Literacy as a Problem in Language and Culture." *Georgetown University Monographs in Languages and Linguistics* 7:117–129.

Geertz, Clifford. 1963. "The Integrative Revolution: Primordial Sentiments and Civil Politics." In Clifford Geertz, ed., *Old Societies and New States: The Quest for Modernity in Asia and Africa.* New York.

Gelb, I. J. 1963. *A Study of Writing.* 2nd ed. Chicago.

———. 1973. "Writing." *Encyclopedia Brittanica* 23:817–819.

———. 1979. "Forms of Writing." *The New Enclyclopedia Brittanica, Macropedia* 19:1033–1045.

Geogheghn, Sheila et al. 1979. *Language Files.* Reynoldsburg, Ohio.

Gernet, Jacques. 1963. "La Chine. Aspects et fonctions de l'écriture." In *L'écriture et le Psychologie des Peuples.* Paris.

Gleitman, Lila A. and Paul Rozin. 1973. "Teaching Reading by Use of a Syllabary." *Reading Research Quarterly* 8 (4): 447–483.

———. 1977. "Structure and Acquisition of Reading I: Relations between Orthographies and the Structure of Language." In Arthur S. Reber and Don L. Scarborough, eds., *Toward a Psychology of Reading.* Proceedings of the CUNY Conferences. Hillsdale, N.J.

Goodman, Kenneth S. 1976. *Reading: A Psycholinguistic Guessing Game.* In Henry Singer and Robert B. Ruddell, eds., *Theoretical Models and Processes of Reading.* Newark, Del. Reprinted from *Journal of the Reading Specialist,* May 1967.

Gordon, Cyrus H. 1968. *Forgotten Scripts.* London.

Gough, Philip B. 1972. "One Second of Reading." In James F. Kavanagh and Ignatius G. Mattingly, eds., *Language by Ear and by Eye: The Relationships Between Speech and Reading.* Cambridge, Mass.

Grootaers, Willem A. 1946. "Dialectes chinois et alphabétisation. A propos de la Romanisation Interdialectique." *Bulletin de l'Université l'Aurore,* Series III, 8:207–235.

Halle, Morris. 1969. "Some Thoughts on Spelling." In Kenneth S. Goodman and J. T. Fleming, eds., *Psycholinguistics and the Teaching of Reading.* Newark, Del.

Hanzi Gaige. 1981. "Zhou Youguang yuwen zhuzuo mulu" [List of works on language by Zhou Youguang]. *Hanzi Gaige* 3:8–11.

Haugen, Einar. 1966. "Dialect, Language and Nation." *American Anthropologist* 68 (4): 922–935.

———. 1973. "The Curse of Babel." *Daedalus* 102 (3):47–57.

He, Rong. 1932. "Guoyu tongyi he fangyan" [Regionalects and the unification of the national language]. *Guoyeu Joukan* 52, September.

Heyd, Uriel. 1954. *Language Reform in Modern Turkey.* Jerusalem.

Hsia, Tao-tai. 1956. *China's Language Reforms.* New Haven.

Hu, Qiaomu. 1982. "Ba wenzi gaige de huoyan ranliaoxiaqu—xuexi Hu Qiaomu tongzhi 1982 nian l yue 23 ri guanyu wenzi gaige wenti de jianghua" [Rekindle the flame of language reform—study the speech given by Comrade Hu Qiaomu on 23 January 1982 on the problem of language reform]. *Wenzi Gaige* 1:3–11. (This is an edited version of Hu Qiaomu's speech.)

Hu, Shi Ming and Eli Seifman. 1976. *A Documentary History of Education in the People's Republic of China, 1949–1976*. New York.

Huang, Diancheng. 1980. "Min Nan fangyan pinyinhua de chuantong he jingyan" [Tradition and experience in Pinyinization of the Southern Min regionalect]. *Yuwen Xiandaihua* 1:116–128.

Humboldt, Wilhelm von. 1827. *Lettre à M. Abel-Rémusat, sur la nature des formes grammaticales en général, et sur le génie de la langue en particulier*. Paris.

Jan, George P. 1969. "Mass Education in the Communes." In Stewart E. Fraser, ed., *Education and Communism in China*. Hong Kong.

Jespersen, Otto. 1905. *Growth and Structure of the English Language*. Leipzig.

———. 1922. *Language*. London.

———. 1928. *Monosyllabism in English*. London.

Jorden, Eleanor. 1963. *Beginning Japanese*. New Haven.

Karlgren, Bernhard. 1923. *Analytic Dictionary of Chinese and Sino-Japanese*. Paris.

———. 1926. *Philology and Ancient China*. Oslo.

———. 1929. *Sound and Symbol in Chinese*. London.

———. 1936. "On the Script of the Chou Dynasty." *Bulletin of the Museum of Far Eastern Antiquities* 8:157–258.

———. 1940. *Grammata Serica: Script and Phonetics in Sino-Japanese*. Stockholm. Reprinted from *Bulletin of the Museum of Far Eastern Antiquities* 12.

———. 1949. *The Chinese Language*. New York.

Kavanagh, James P. and Ignatius G. Mattingly, eds. 1972. *Language by Ear and by Eye: The Relationships Between Speech and Reading*. Cambridge, Mass.

Kennedy, George A. 1964. *Selected Works of George A. Kennedy*. Edited by Tien-yi Li. Pp. 1–9: "A Minimum Vocabulary in Modern Chinese" (reprinted from *Modern Language Journal* 21 [8][1937]: 587–592); pp. 104–118: "The Monosyllabic Myth (reprinted from *Journal of the American Oriental Society* 71 [3] [1951]: 161–166); pp. 238–241: "The Fate of Chinese Pictographs"; pp. 274–322: "The Butterfly Case" (reprinted from *Wennti* 8, March 1955); pp. 443–462: "Fenellosa, Pound, and the Chinese Character" (reprinted from *Yale Literary Magazine* 126 [5][1958]: 24–36).

Khrushchev, Nikita. 1970. *Khrushchev Remembers*. Translated by Strobe Talbot. New York.

Kindaichi, Haruhiko. 1978. *The Japanese Language*. Translated by Hirano Umeyo. Rutland, Vt.

Knowlson, James. 1975. *Universal Language Schemes in England and France 1600–1800*. Toronto.

Kolers, Paul A. 1969. "Some Formal Characteristics of Pictograms." *American Scientist* 57 (3): 348–363.

———. 1970. "Three Stages in Reading." In Henry Levin and Joanna P. Williams, eds., *Basic Studies in Reading*. New York.

Kōno, Rokurō. 1969. "The Chinese Writing and Its Influences on the Scripts of the Neighboring Peoples with Special Reference to Korea and Japan." *Memoirs of the Research Department of the Tōyō Bunko* 27:84–140.

Kramer, Samuel Noah. 1961. *Sumerian Mythology.* Revised edition. New York.

Kratochvíl, Paul. 1968. *The Chinese Language Today.* London.

———. 1973. "The Norm and Divided Chinese." *Journal of the Chinese Language Teachers Association* 8 (2): 62–69.

———. 1977. "Tradition in Chinese Linguistics: Fact or Fiction." *Cahiers de Linguistique: Asie Orientale* 1:17–30.

Kroll, J. 1966. "A Tentative Classification and Description of the Structure of Peking Common Sayings (Hsieh-hou-yü)." *Journal of the American Oriental Society* 86 (3): 267–273.

Krykov, M. V. 1980. *The Language of Yin Inscriptions.* Moscow.

Lach, Donald Frederick. 1941. "Contribution of Chinese to German Civilization, 1648–1740." Ph.D. dissertation, University of Chicago.

Lamasse, H. and Ernest Jasmin. 1931. "L'écriture alphabétique du chinois." *Collectanea Commissionis Synodalis* 4:639–657, 755–793, 1061–1073.

Leong, Che Kan. 1973. "Hong Kong." In John Downing, ed., *Comparative Reading: Cross-National Studies of Behavior and Processes in Reading and Writing.* New York.

Li, Charles and Sandra A. Thompson. 1982. "The Gulf Between Spoken and Written Language: A Case Study in Chinese." In Deborah Tannes, ed., *Spoken and Written Language: Exploring Orality and Literacy.* Norwood, N.J.

Li, Fang-kuei. 1973. "Languages and Dialects of China." *Journal of Chinese Linguistics* 1 (1): 1–13.

Li, Min. 1979. "Yi wen" [Yi writing]. *Minzu Yuwen* 4:304–306.

Li, Tao. 1981. "Wenzi gaige lingyu yao jianchi baijia zhengming" [The sphere of writing reform should stick to the policy of letting a hundred schools of thought contend]. *People's Daily,* 29 December.

Li, Yisan. 1979. "Buneng zai langfei shijian le" [We can no longer waste time]. *Hanyu Pinyin Bao* 195:4.

Lin, Xingren. 1983. "Mantan guangbo de yuyan tedian" [Informal comments on the linguistic peculiarities of broadcast scripts]. *Yuwen Xuexi* 1:54–56.

Liu, Shi-hung. 1969. *Chinese Characters and Their Impact on Other Languages of East Asia.* Taipei.

Lorge, Irving and Jeanne Chall. 1963. "Estimating the Size of Vocabularies of Children and Adults: An Analysis of Methodological Issues." *Journal of Experimental Education* 32 (2): 147–157.

Lu, Xun. 1963. "Kuangren riji" [Diary of a madman]. In *Lu Xun Xuanji, shang* [Selected works of Lu Xun, vol. 1]. Peking.

———. 1974. *Lu Xun lun wenzi gaige* [Lu Xun on language reform]. Peking.

Luo, Zhufeng. 1980. [Comments made at the language reform conference held in Shanghai in May 1979]. *Yuwen Xiandaihua* 1:26–30.

———. 1981. "Wenzi gaige de renwu yingdang tidao geng gao de zhanlüe jiaodu lai kaolü" [The tasks of language reform should be considered from a higher strategic angle]. *Yuwen Xiandaihua* 5:106–110.

Lyell, William A. 1976. *Lu Hsun's Vision of Reality.* Berkeley.

Lyu, Shuxiang. 1960. "Zai lun pinyin zimu he yuyan jiaoxue" [More on the phonetic alphabet and language teaching]. *Wenzi Gaige* 10:1–2.

———. 1981. *Yuwen Changtan* [Chats on language]. Peking.

Lyuu, Tzuohshin. 1983. "Jungguor pinyin werntzyh taaulun'de jiaandan jieh-shauh" [A brief introduction to the discussion concerning a Chinese alphabetic orthography]. *Shin Tarng* 3:17–25.

Ma, Xueliang and Dai Qingxia. 1982. "Yi yuzhi yuyin bijiao yanjiu" [Comparative study of the phonology of the Yi language branch]. In *Minzu Yuwen Yanjiu Wenji* [Collected research studies on nationality languages]. Peking.

Ma, Xulun. 1952. "Zhongguo wenzi gaige yanjiu weiyuanhui chengli hui kaihui ci" [Opening remarks at the inaugural meeting of the Committee for Research on Chinese Language Reform]. *Zhonguo Yuwen* 1:4.

Mallery, Garrick. 1866. *Pictographs of the North American Indians.* Fourth Annual Report of the Bureau of Ethnology, Smithsonian Institution, pp. 1–256. Washington, D.C.

Mao, Dun. 1962. "Guanyu xiaoxuesheng xuehui pinyin zimu huisheng wenti" [Concerning the problem of elementary school children losing their mastery of the phonetic alphabet]. *Wenzi Gaige* 6:2.

Mao, Zedong. 1956. *Zhongguo nongcun de shehui zhuyi de gaochao* [Socialist upsurge in the Chinese countryside]. Vol. 1. No place, no date (1956 is date of speech cited).

———. 1969. *Mao Zedong Sixiang Wansui* [Long live Mao Zedong thought]. No place.

Margouliès, Georges. 1957. *La langue et l'écriture chinoises.* Paris.

Marshman, Joshua. 1814. *Clavis Sinica: Elements of Chinese Grammar.* Serampore.

Martin, Helmut. 1982. *Chinesische Sprachplanung.* Bochum, Germany.

Martin, Samuel E. 1972. "Nonalphabetic Writing Systems: Some Observations." In James F. Kavanagh and Ignatius G. Mattingly, eds., *Language by Ear and by Eye: The Relationships Between Speech and Reading.* Cambridge, Mass.

Mathews, R. H. 1945. *A Chinese-English Dictionary.* American edition. Cambridge, Mass.

McDonald, Angus W., Jr. 1976. "Mao Tse-tung and the Hunan Self-Government Movement, 1920: An Introduction and Five Translations." *China Quarterly* 68 (December): 751–777.

McGraw-Hill. 1963. *Modern Chinese-English Technical and General Dictionary.* New York.

Mead, Margaret and Rudolph Modley. 1968. "Communication Among All People, Everywhere." *Natural History* 77 (7): 55–63.

Mémoires. 1776. *Mémoires concernant l'histoire, les sciences, les arts, les moeurs, les usages &c des Chinois, par les missionaires de Pekin.* Vol. 1. Paris.

Meynet, Roland. 1971. *L'écriture arabe en question.* Beirut.

Miller, Roy Andrew. 1967. *The Japanese Language.* Chicago.

———. 1982. *Japan's Modern Myth: The Language and Beyond.* New York and Tokyo.

Milsky, Constantin. 1974. *Préparation de la réforme de l'écriture en République Populaire de Chine.* Paris.

Morohashi, Tetsuji. 1960. *Dai Kan-Wa Jiten* [Great Chinese–Japanese dictionary]. 13 vols. Tokyo.

Mote, F. W. 1972. "China's Past in the Study of China Today: Some Comments on the Recent Work of Richard Solomon." *Journal of Asian Studies* 32 (1): 107–120.

Neustupñy, J. R. 1984. "Literacy and Minorities: Divergent Perceptions." In F. Coulmas, ed., *Linguistic Minorities and Literacy*. The Hague.

Newnham, Richard. 1971. *About Chinese*. Harmondsworth.

Ng, Sally M. 1976. "The Phonetic Aspect of Character Simplification." *Journal of the Chinese Language Teachers Association* 11 (3): 179–186.

Ni, Haishu. 1941. *Zhongguo zi Ladinghua yundong nianbiao* [Chronology of the movement for the Latinization of Chinese writing]. No place.

———. 1949. *Zhongguo yuwen de xinsheng* [Rebirth of the Chinese Language]. Shanghai.

———. 1955. "Yonghu Hanyu guifanhua gongzuo" [Support Chinese standardization work]. In *Xiandai Hanyu guifanhua wenti shuxue huiyi wenjian huibian*, 177–179. Peking.

———. 1979. *Ladinghua Xin Wenzi Yundong Biannian Jishi* [Year-by-year chronicle of the Latinized New Writing movement]. 2 vols. Peking.

———. 1980. [Comments made at the language reform conference held in Shanghai in May 1979.] *Yuwen Xiandaihua* 1:35–39.

Nunberg, Geoffrey. 1981. [Review of Scribner and Cole 1981.] *New York Times Book Review*, 13 December.

Ober, J. Hambleton. 1965. *Writing: Man's Great Invention*. Baltimore.

Oldfield, R. C. 1963. "Individual Vocabulary and Semantic Currency: A Preliminary Study." *British Journal of Social and Clinical Psychology* 2:122–130.

Palmer, Harold E. 1931. *The Principles of Romanization*. Tokyo.

Pei, Mario. 1952. *The Story of English*. Philadelphia and New York.

Pelliot, Paul. 1936. "Brèves remarques sur le phonétisme dans l'écriture chinoise." *T'oung Pao* 32:162–166.

Peyrfitte, Alain. 1973. *Quand la Chine s'éveillera . . . le monde tremblera*. Paris.

Pichowicz, Paul G. 1977. "Ch'ü Ch'iu-pai and the Chinese Marxist Conception of Revolutionary Popular Literature and Art." *China Quarterly* 70:296–314.

Potter, Simeon. 1966. *Our Language*. Baltimore.

Price, R. F. 1980. *Education in Modern China*. London.

Qian, Xuantong. 1935. "Zhongguo jin-hou zhi wenzi wenti" [The problem of the present and future script]. In Zhao Jiabi, ed., *Zhongguo Xin Wenxue Daxi*, vol. 1, pp. 141–146. [Shanghai?]. Reprinted Hong Kong, 1962, vol. 1, pp. 169–174.

Qu, Qiubai. 1932. "Xin Zhongguo wen cao'an" [Draft of a new Chinese script]. *Qu Qiubai Wenji* 2:705–851. Peking, 1953.

Rawski, Evelyn Sakakida. 1979. *Education and Popular Literacy in Ch'ing China*. Ann Arbor.

Reischauer, Edwin O. and John King Fairbank. 1960. *East Asia: The Great Tradition*. Boston.

Ricci, Matteo. 1942. *Fonti Ricciani*. Vol. 1. Edited by Pasquale M. D'Elia. Rome.

Ridley, Charles Price, Paul H. B. Godwin, and Dennis J. Doolin. 1971. *The Making of a Model Citizen in Communist China*. Stanford.

Robert, Paul. 1977. *Le petit Robert: Dictionaire alphabétique et analogique de la langue française*. Paris.

Rogers, Lawrence. 1979. "Rags and Tatters: The Uzuragoromo of Yokoi Yayū." *Monumenta Nipponica* 34 (3): 279–310.

Rozin, Paul, Susan Poritsky, and Raina Sotsky. 1971. "American Children with

Reading Problems Can Easily Learn to Read English Represented by Chinese Characters." *Science* 171:1264–1267, 173:190–191.

Sansom, George. 1928. *Historical Grammar of Japanese.* Oxford.

Scalapino, Robert A. 1982. "The Evolution of a Young Revolutionary—Mao Zedong in 1919–1921." *Journal of Asian Studies* 42 (1): 29–61.

Scharschmidt, Clemens. 1924. "Schriftreform in Japan: Ein Kulturproblem." *Mitteilungen des Seminars für Orientalischen Sprachen* 26–27 (1): 163–212.

Schmandt-Besserat, Denise. 1978. "The Earliest Precursor of Writing." *Scientific American* 238 (6): 50–59.

Scribner, Sylvia. 1982. "Observations on Literacy Education in China." *Linguistic Reporter* 25 (3): 1–4.

Scribner, Sylvia and Michael Cole. 1981. *The Psychology of Literacy.* Cambridge, Mass.

Seashore, Robert H. and Lois D. Eckerson. 1940. "The Measurement of Individual Differences in General English Vocabularies." *Journal of Educational Psychology* 31:14–38.

Serruys, Paul L-M. 1960. "Note on Archaic Chinese Dialectology." *Orbis* 9 (1): 42–57.

———. 1962. *Survey of the Chinese Language Reform and the Anti-Illiteracy Movement in Communist China.* Berkeley.

Seybolt, Peter and Gregory Kuei-ke Chang. 1978. *Language Reform in China: Documents and Commentary.* White Plains, New York.

Sino. 1980. *The Sino Chinese-English Dictionary.* Hong Kong and New York.

Slaughter, Mary. 1982. *Universal Languages and Scientific Taxonomy in the 17th Century.* Cambridge.

Smith, Frank. 1973. *Psycholinguistics and Reading.* New York.

———. 1979. *Reading Without Nonsense.* New York.

Snow, Edgar. 1968. *Red Star Over China.* First revised and enlarged edition. New York.

Soothill, W. E. 1942. *The Student's Four Thousand Character and General Pocket Dictionary.* (Preface dated 1889.) 16th ed. London.

SSBC. 1982. State Statistical Bureau of China. "The 1982 Census Results." *Beijing Review* 25 (45): 20–21.

Stalin, Joseph. 1951. *Marxism and Linguistics.* New York.

Stubbs, Michael. 1980. *Language and Literacy: The Sociolinguistics of Reading.* London, Boston, and Henley.

Suh, Cheong-soo. 1974. "Some Characteristics of Korean Language." In Suh Cheong-soo and Pak Chun-kun, eds., *Aspects of Korean Culture.* Seoul.

Swift, Jonathan. 1977. *Gulliver's Travels.* (Preface dated 1727.) New York.

Tao, Jianqin. 1980. "Yan'an shidai de Xin Wenzi yundong" [The New Writing movement in the Yan'an period]. *Yuyan Wenzi Yanjiu,* pp. 108–118. Peking.

Tong, Zhenhua. 1937. *Zhongguo wenzi de yanbian* [The evolution of Chinese writing]. Shanghai.

Trace, Arthur E., Jr. 1961. *What Ivan Knows That Johnny Doesn't.* New York.

Trager, George L. 1974. "Writing and Writing Systems." In Thomas A. Sebeok, ed., *Current Trends in Linguistics* 12 (1): 373–496. The Hague.

Treiman, Rebecca A., Jonathan Baron, and Kenneth Luk. 1981. "Speech Recoding in Silent Reading: A Comparison of Chinese and English." *Journal of Chinese Linguistics* 9:116–125.

Trigault, Nicola. 1615. *Christiana expeditione apud Sinas . . . Augsburg.* (This is a liberal rendering into Latin of Matteo Ricci's Italian manuscript subsequently published in Ricci 1942.)

Tsien, Tsuen-hsuin. 1962. *Written on Bamboo and Silk.* Chicago.

T'sou, B.K.Y. 1981. "A Sociolinguistic Analysis of the Logographic Writing System of Chinese." *Journal of Chinese Linguistics* 9(1): 1–19.

Tuchman, Barbara. 1972. *Notes from China.* New York.

Tzeng, Ovid J. L. and William S-Y. Wang. 1983. "The first two R's." *American Scientist* 71:238–243.

Tzeng, Ovid and Daisy Hung. 1980. "Reading in a Nonalphabetic Writing System: Some Experimental Studies." In James E. Kavanagh and Richard L. Venezky, eds., *Orthography, Reading, and Dyslexia.* Baltimore.

Tzeng, Ovid, Daisy L. Hung, and Linda Garro. 1978. "Reading the Chinese Characters: An Information Processing View." *Journal of Chinese Linguistics* 6 (2): 287–305.

Tzeng, Ovid et al. 1977. "Speech Recoding in Reading Chinese Characters." *Journal of Experimental Psychology: Human Learning and Memory* 3:621–630.

Voegelin, C. F. and F. M. Voegelin. 1964. *Languages of the World: Sino-Tibetan.* Bloomfield.

Waiguo. 1957. *Waiguo Wenzi Gaige Jingyan Jieshao* [Introduction to the experience of foreign countries in language reform]. Peking.

Wang, Boxi. 1974. "Kong lao-er shi fandui Hanzi geming de zu shiye" [Old man Confucius is the granddaddy of opposition to the revolution in Chinese characters]. *Shenru pi-Lin pi-Kong cujin wenzi gaige.* Peking.

Wang, Li. 1955. "Lun Hanyu guifanhua" [On standardization of Chinese]. *Xiandai Hanyu guifanhua wenti shuxue huiyi wenjian huibian.* Peking.

———. 1980. [Comments made at the language reform conference held in Shanghai in May 1979.] *Yuwen Xiandaihua* 1:13–15.

———. 1981. "Hanzi he Hanzi gaige" [Chinese characters and Chinese character reform]. *Pinyin Bao,* 15 July, pp. 4–5.

Wang, Li and Zhou Youguang. 1983. "Jinyibu fahui 'Hanyu Pinyin Fang'an' de zuoyong" [Further promote the functions of the Chinese phonetic scheme]. *Wenzi Gaige* 2:3–4.

Wang, William S-Y. 1980. Review of *Language and Linguistics in the People's Republic of China.* Winfred P. Lehman, ed. *Language* 56 (1): 197–202.

Wang, Zongbai. 1978. "Wu Yuzhang tongzhi dui Zhongguo wenzi gaige de gongxian" [Comrade Wu Yuzhang's contributions to Chinese language reform]. In Wu Yuzhang, *Wenzi Gaige Wenji* [Collected works on language reform]. Peking.

Wen, Hua. 1973. "On reforming written Chinese." *Peking Review* 32:11–13.

Wieger, Leon. 1965. *Chinese Characters.* New York. Reprint of 1915 edition.

Woodcock, Richard W. 1968. "Rebus as a Medium in Beginning Reading Instruction." *IMRID Papers and Reports,* vol. 4, no. 4. Nashville, Tenn.

Woodcock, Richard W., Charlotte R. Clark, and Cornelia Oakes Davies. 1967–1969. *The Peabody Rebus Reading Program.* 7 vols. Circle Pines, Minn.

Wu, Yuzhang, 1952. "Zai Zhongguo wenzi gaige yanjiu weiyuanhui chengli hui shang de jianghua" [Speech at the inaugural meeting of the Committee for Research on Chinese Writing Reform]. *Zhongguo Yuwen* 1:5.

———. 1978. *Wenzi Gaige Wenji* [Collected works on language reform]. Peking.

Xi, Boxian. 1979. "Cong ling yi fangmian kan shengpang de biaoyin gongneng" [Another view of the effectiveness of phonetics in representing sounds]. *Zhongguo Yuwen* 5:388–392.

Xia, Yubing. 1975. "Xuexi Lu Xun: Gaige Hanzi" [Learn from Lu Xun: reform Chinese characters]. *Xuexi Lu Xun: Gaige Hanzi*. Peking. Reprinted from *People's Daily*, 4 November 1974.

Xu, Shirong. 1982. " 'Guojia tuixing quanguo tongyong de Putonghua'—du 'Xianfa xiugai cao'an' di ershi tiao" ["The state promotes Putonghua which is universally used throughout China"—On reading Article 20 of the "Draft of the Revised Constitution"]. *Wenzi Gaige* 2:15–16.

Yang, Chunlin. 1980. [Comments made at the language reform conference held in Shanghai in May 1979.] *Yuwen Xiandaihua* 2:18–21.

Yang, Lien Sheng. 1949. "The Concept of 'Free' and 'Bound' in Spoken Chinese." *Harvard Journal of Asiatic Studies* 12:462–469.

Yau, Shun-chiu. 1983. "Temporal Order in the Composition of Archaic Chinese Ideograms." *Journal of Chinese Linguistics* 11 (2): 186–213.

Ye, Laishi. 1980a. "Shaoqi Tongzhi dui wenzi gaige gongzuo de guanhuai" [Comrade (Liu) Shaoqi's solicitude concerning language reform work]. *Hanyu Pinyin* 34:1.

———. 1980b. [Comments made at the language reform conference held in Shanghai in May 1979.] *Yuwen Xiandaihua* 1:15–17.

———. 1981. "Guanyu wenzi gaige de jige wenti" [Some questions regarding language reform]. *Yuwen Xiandaihua* 5:59–67.

———. 1983. "Wu Yuzhang tongzhi dui wenzi gaige de zhuoyue gongxian [Comrade Wu Yuzhang's outstanding contributions to language reform.] *Wenzi Gaige* 12:6–9.

YJ. 1978. *Yiwen jianzifa* [Classification schemes for Yi writing]. Chengdu.

Yu, Zi. 1981. "Hanzi jiujing you duoshao?" [How many Chinese characters are there after all?]. *Yuyan Jiaoxue yu Yanjiu* 1:44.

Zachrisson, R. E. 1931. "Four Hundred Years of English Spelling Reform." *Studia Neophilologica* 4:1–68.

ZGYW. 1955. "Jiaoyubu fabu tuixing jianhua Hanzi de tongzhi he tuiguang Putonghua de zhishi" [The Ministry of Education releases circular on promoting simplified characters and instructions on popularizing Putonghua]. *Zhongguo Yuwen* 12:41.

Zhan, Bohai. 1981. *Xiandai Hanyu Fangyan* [Modern Chinese regionalects].

Zhang, Difei. 1937. "Zhongguo tongyi yu Zhongguo hua Ladinghua" [The unity of China and the Latinization of Chinese]. *Wenhua Jianshe* 3 (5): 39–48.

Zhang, Liyan. 1983. "Guangzhouhua you yin wu zi yinjie zongji" [The total number of Cantonese syllables without corresponding characters]. *Yuwen Zazhi* 10:28–35.

Zhang, Peng and Fei Jinchang. 1980. "Wenzi gaige 30 nian jishi" [Thirty-year chronicle of language reform]. *Yuwen Xiandaihua* 4:250–257.

Zhang, Yan. 1980. "Liu Shaoqi Tongzhi he Subei Ladinghua bozhong-dui" [Comrade Liu Shaoqi and the Latinization Dissemination Team in Northern Jiangsu]. *Yuwen Xiandaihua* 4:228–234.

Zheng, Linxi. 1952. "Zhongguo wenzi you meiyou jiejixing, ke bu keyi gaige?" [Do Chinese characters have a class nature, can they be reformed?]. In Zheng Linxi et al., eds., *Zhongguo Wenzi Gaige Wenti* [The problem of Chinese writing reform]. Shanghai.

————. 1981. "Weishenme 'minzu xingshi' 'Pinyin xingsheng zi' xingbutong?" [Why won't "national in form" and "Pinyin phonetic plus radical characters" work?]. *Hanzi Gaige* 5:2–5.

Zheng, Qiao. ca. 1150. "Liu shu lüe" [Monograph on the six classes of characters]. *Tong Zhi* [Encyclopedic annals]. Commercial Press ed., 1:487–522.

Zhou, Enlai. 1958. "Current Tasks of Reforming the Written Language." In *Reform of the Chinese Written Language*. Peking.

Zhou, Youguang. 1978a. "Hanzi jianhua wenti de zai renshi" [Problems of Chinese character simplification revisited]. *Guangming Daily*, 16 June.

————. 1978b. "Xiandai Hanzi-zhong shengpang de biaoyin wenti" [To what degree are the "phonetics" of present-day Chinese still phonetic?]. *Zhongguo Yuwen* 3:172–177.

————. 1979. *Hanzi Gaige Gailun* [Survey of Chinese character reform]. Third edition. Peking.

————. 1980a. "Dangqian wenzi gaige de jige wenti" [Some questions concerning current writing reform]. *Yuyan Jiaoxue yu Yanjiu* 4:28–37.

————. 1980b. [Interview published in the Hong Kong newspaper]. *Wen Hui Bao*, 28 November.

————. 1980c. "Wengai gongzuo you jiejixing ma?" [Does writing reform work have a class nature?]. *Yuwen Xiandaihua* 2:283.

————. 1980d. "Alabai shuzi jinji" [Arabic numerals tabooed]. *Yuwen Xiandaihua* 2:281–282.

————. 1980e. [Comments made at the language reform conference held in Shanghai in May 1979.] *Yuwen Xiandaihua* 1:21–26.

————. 1980f. *Hanzi Shengpang duyin Biancha* [A handy guide to the pronunciation of phonetics in Chinese characters]. Kirin.

————. 1980g. *Pinyinhua Wenti* [Problems of Pinyinization]. Peking.

————. 1981. "Hanzi Pinyin Zhengcifa Yaodian" [Basic points of Pinyin orthography]. *Yuwen Xiandaihua* 1:91–101.

ZY. 1979. "Jiaqiang dui Mao Zhuxi de yuyan lilun he yuyan shiji de yanjiu—jinian Mao Zhuxi bashi-wu zhounian danchen" [Strengthen study of Chairman Mao's linguistic theory and linguistic practice—in commemoration of Chairman Mao's 85th birthday anniversary]. *Zhongguo Yuwen* 1:1–3.

Index

About the Author

John DeFrancis, emeritus professor of Chinese at the University of Hawaii, began his career in Chinese immediately after graduating from Yale in 1933 by spending three years studying and traveling in China. Apart from academic study, his learning experience included grass-roots contact with the language and the people in the course of a 4,000 mile trip in Northwest China and Mongolia that involved trekking 1,000 miles across the Gobi Desert by camel and floating 1,200 miles down the Yellow River on an inflated sheepskin raft. He returned to the United States for graduate work leading to the M.A. and Ph.D. degrees from Columbia University and embarked on a teaching career at several institutions. He is the author of scores of articles and two dozen books, including the widely used 12-volume set of materials for teaching spoken and written Chinese and works on Asian sociolinguistics such as *Nationalism and Language Reform in China* and *Colonialism and Language Policy in Viet Nam.* His miscellaneous works include a translation, *Chinese Agent in Mongolia; Chinese Social History,* with E-tu Zen Sun; *Chinese-English Glossary of the Mathematical Sciences;* and *Things Japanese in Hawaii.*

Production Notes

This book was designed by Roger Eggers. The in-text calligraphy was done by Kathy Takamoto. Composition and paging were done on the Quadex Composing System and typesetting on the Compugraphic 8400 by the design and production staff of University of Hawaii Press.

The text and display typeface is Garamond.

Offset presswork and binding were done by Vail-Ballou Press, Inc. Text paper is Writers RR Offset, basis 50.